The Politics of Indonesia–Malaysia Relations

This book provides a comprehensive overview of the relationship between Indonesia and Malaysia, focusing especially on how the relationship has developed in the past fifty years. It argues that the political relationship between the two countries has been largely defined by rivalry, despite the fact that the processes of national self-determination began by emphasizing Indo-Malay fraternity. It shows how the two countries have different, contested interpretations of Indo-Malay history, and how the continuing suspicion of Javanese hegemony which defined much of the history of the Indo-Malay world is also a key factor in the relationship.

Joseph Chinyong Liow is an Assistant Professor at the S. Rajaratnam School of International Relations, Nanyang Technological University, Singapore.

Routledge Contemporary Southeast Asia Series

The Politics of Indonesia–Malaysia Relations

One kin, two nations

Joseph Chinyong Liow

Routledge
Taylor & Francis Group

LONDON AND NEW YORK

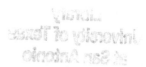

First published 2005
Asia Pacific paperback edition first published 2008
by Routledge
2 Park Square, Milton Park, Abingdon, Oxon OX14 4RN

Simultaneously published in the USA and Canada
by Routledge
270 Madison Ave, New York, NY 10016

Routledge is an imprint of the Taylor & Francis Group, an informa business

© 2005, 2008 Joseph Chinyong Liow

Typeset in Times by Wearset Ltd, Boldon, Tyne and Wear
Printed and bound in Singapore by Markono Print Media Pte Ltd

British Library Cataloguing in Publication Data
A catalogue record for this book is available from the British Library

Library of Congress Cataloging in Publication Data
A catalog record for this book has been requested

ISBN10: 0-415-34132-9 (hbk)
ISBN10: 0-415-47025-0 (Taylor & Francis Asia Pacific paperback edition)
ISBN10: 0-203-47932-7 (ebk)

ISBN13: 978-0-415-34132-5 (hbk)
ISBN13: 978-0-415-47025-4 (Taylor & Francis Asia Pacific paperback edition)
ISBN13: 978-0-203-47932-2 (ebk)

For Ai Vee and Euan

He who kills me, who will it be but my kinsman;
He who succours me, who will it be but my kinsman.
(Lozi proverb)

Contents

Preface

'To what extent is the factor of kinship a viable organizing principle for relations between two sovereign nation-states whose histories have intersected intimately, and whose populations continue to share socio-cultural affinities across territorial borders?' This question frames the present study of the evolution of political relations between Indonesia and Malaysia. Despite repeated claims by leaders of Indonesia and Malaysia that the people of their two countries are 'blood brothers' and of the same '*rumpun*' (racial stock), bilateral relations between these two major states in the Indo-Malay world have regularly experienced rivalry and discord beneath such espousals of fraternity. This state of affairs, however, has not deterred many, including people in political leadership, from continuing to look to kinship for greater meaning and intelligibility in the bilateral relationship between Indonesia and Malaysia. This book attempts to unravel the conundrums and contradictions in Indonesia-Malaysia relations generated by this tension between the historically intimate ties that link the peoples, cultures, and societies of these two states, and the need for the respective leaderships to look beyond sentimentality and romanticism in their conduct of political relations.

In the course of conceptualizing this book, the question arose on several occasions, not least in my own mind, how, in an international political arena broadly understood to be dominated by the pursuit of material interests, the concept of kinship can be deemed relevant as a framework for exploring Indonesia–Malaysia relations. At first glance, the rationale was obvious, and has already been stated above. Both states share a common history, and the legacy of this proximity, not just in territorial form but social and cultural as well, continues to broadly inform thinking on and the language of Indonesia–Malaysia relations (broadly, in the sense that this history informs our understanding not just of political relations, but of cultural, social, economic, religious relations etc.). Moreover, while it is easy for us in this era of the modern nation-state to dismiss 'primordial' motivations such as kinship (as expressed for example by the proponents of pan-Malayism), we must also recognize that such views represent what many people, including those in positions of leadership, once believed, and in certain instances continue to believe. They therefore assume a certain pertinence, for, however erroneous they may seem, they played an integral part in shaping Indo-Malay identity and politics in terms of their influence on how political leaders in colonial and post-colonial Indonesia and Malaysia viewed each other and interpreted the terms of their 'special relationship'. In so doing, the kinship factor has surely played its part to condition the course of Indo-Malay history. There are, however, two caveats to be kept in mind: first, kinship should not and cannot be automatically equated with harmony; and second, the kinship factor is not, and has never been, as unwavering and incontrovertible a source of influence on relations as its champions and proponents would like to believe. This book, then, is an account of how kinship has both shaped and been shaped by the range of forces that drive Indonesia–Malaysia relations.

This project has entailed research into a wide and disparate range of sources. Beyond available secondary material, the book has closely studied local historical texts and folklore in order to understand more deeply pre-colonial sources of socio-cultural affinity that continue to inform certain perspectives of bilateral relations. The study has also perused an array of archival records from British, Australian, American, and Malaysian sources, many of them hitherto unpublished, in order to trace the contours and permutations of Indo-Malay perceptions and understandings of the relevance of their shared social-cultural histories to their contemporary political relationship. While attempts were made to gain access to indigenous sources in Kuala Lumpur and Jakarta, the 'sensitivity' of the topic and absence of a 30-year rule governing the release of classified government material meant that access to Malaysian and Indonesian archives was limited. Even so, relying on foreign material does have its benefits, not least among which is the fact that foreigners are likely to be more impartial and objective in their reporting of events and negotiations that took place between the leaders of Indonesia and Malaysia. By using primary resources and indigenous historical texts, this study hopes to respond to criticisms regularly levelled by historians and area studies specialists that scholars of the international relations of Southeast Asia are empirically weak and often overly reliant on secondary sources. Historians will see that much of the primary material used here, with the possible exception of the material on Confrontation (*Konfrontasi*), has not been previously published. Similarly, area studies specialists will see that the chapters in Part I of the book introduce a new dimension to indigenous historiography of the Indo-Malay world by comparing local renditions of Indonesian and Malay histories in order to explore their intersections and points of departure, as well as relevance for the contemporary era. Finally, there is also a substantial amount of anecdotal evidence, accrued through interviews with retired policy-makers and journalists, that highlights the intricate details of statecraft and diplomacy between the leaders of the two states. Given the unavailability of archival material for that period, these interviews assume greater importance in Chapter 6 (which is admittedly thin in terms of primary material) as a primary resource.

While I recognize that the study could have been integrated into broader regional developments in order to generate a wider perspective, I have avoided doing so explicitly for four reasons. First, I suggest that certain socio-political impulses, such as the kinship factor under scrutiny here, generate primarily bilateral dynamics. Second, expanding the scope of the study would necessitate sacrificing depth for width; this would almost certainly dilute its main objective of fostering a deeper understanding of Indonesia–Malaysia relations. Third, extant studies on *Konfrontasi* and others on the broader topic of Southeast Asian security to a large extent already locate Indonesia–Malaysia relations in wider regional and international developments. In contrast, there is a paucity of studies that focus predominantly on the bilateral dynamics in this relationship. Finally, students and scholars of the international politics of Southeast Asia will realize that it has always been the bilateral edifice that lies at the heart of questions of regional security.

Acknowledgements

I have incurred numerous debts to individuals and organizations in the course of conceptualizing, writing, and completing this book. What follows is as much their work as it is mine, though I alone am responsible for errors that appear.

This book had its genesis in a doctoral dissertation at the London School of Economics and Political Science. It was the late doyen of the International Relations of Southeast Asia, Michael Leifer, who first encouraged me to research and write on the difficult topic of kinship in Indonesia–Malaysia political relations, and who provided first-rate supervision in my early years as a postgraduate student in London. Professor Leifer's death has been a great loss to students and scholars in the field, and I can only hope that this book does some credit to his memory. I would also like to express my gratitude to Chris Hughes and Ulrich Kratz, who played an important part in the writing of the dissertation on which this book is based by assuming supervisory duties upon Professor Leifer's passing.

It was an Institute of Defence and Strategic Studies (IDSS), Singapore, scholarship that enabled me to pursue my doctoral studies and conduct fieldwork research in the United Kingdom, Australia, Malaysia, and Indonesia. My own brief intellectual journey that led to the completion of this book owes a great debt to three senior ex-colleagues at IDSS who have always been generous with their time, advice, and encouragement, and to whom I wish to express my heartfelt thanks and appreciation. S.R. Nathan, Khong Yuen Foong, and Ang Cheng Guan. Barry Desker, Mushahid Ali, K. Kesavapany, Edward Lee, Wong Chow Ming, and Clara Juwono arranged and facilitated meetings and interviews with Malaysian and Indonesian officials. Kwa Chong Guan, Tan See Seng, and Khong Yuen Foong read various chapters and provided careful and critical comments and suggestions. Mushahid Ali brushed through the entire manuscript with a fine editorial comb, verifying the accuracy of my reconstruction of historical events along the way. I am also grateful to the staff of the Public Record Office (London), the National Archives of Australia (Canberra), Arkib Negara (Kuala Lumpur), as well as in the libraries of the Institute of Southeast Asian Studies (Singapore), the School of Oriental and African Studies (London), and the London School of Economics (London) for their assistance rendered in the course of research. The staff at RoutledgeCurzon, and in particular Peter Sowden and Dorothea Schafter, were highly efficient and professional during the publication of this book. I would also like to record my gratitude to IP Publishing for permission to use material from my article ' "Visions of Serumpun": Tun Abdul Razak and the golden years of Indo-Malay blood brotherhood, 1967–75', published in *Southeast Asia Research*, vol. 11, no. 3 (November 2003), and to the journal *Contemporary Southeast Asia* for permission to cite from my article 'Malaysia's Illegal Indonesian Migrant Worker Problem: In Search of Solutions', published in April 2003.

The argument in this book benefited greatly from the critical comments and suggestions from Stephen Hopgood, Jürgen Haacke, James Cotton, the late Ralph Smith, Tony Stockwell, Matthew Jones, Peter Carey, Tim Huxley, Vladimir Braginsky, Michael Yahuda, Tim Harper, J.M. Gullick, Jack Snyder, Cheah Boon Kheng, Khoo Kay Kim, Ariffin Omar, Sharon Siddique, Dewi Fortuna Anwar, and Alfitra Salaam. Johnny Parry at the LSE anthropology department graciously gave me a one-hour lecture surveying the literature on kinship. Indonesian and Malaysian policy practitioners both past and present, in particular, Ghazali Shafie, Ali Alatas, Zainal Sulong, Abdullah Ahmad, Mochtar Kusumaatmadja, and Des Alwi kindly shared their time and experience. Other foreign and defence officials from Indonesia and Malaysia who have been equally helpful have been requested to remain anonymous.

At IDSS, Kumar Ramakrishna, Leonard Sebastian, Tan See Seng, Ang Cheng Guan, Joey Long, Sinderpal Singh, Bhubhindar Singh, Ralf Emmers, Helen Nesadurai, Mely Anthony, Evelyn Goh, and Bernard Loo created the perfect intellectual and social environment – you people are truly the best colleagues one could hope for. Mom, Dad, and Sis, thanks for your constant support. To my wife, Ai Vee, and son, Euan, who was born in the final stages of the preparation of this book, you have been a constant source of motivation and inspiration; your contributions to this work are beyond measure. Finally, this book could only have been completed by the grace of my Lord Jesus, which has kept me steadfast and sustained me in times of trial and doubt. I am merely his imperfect instrument – to Him be the glory.

Abbreviations

AAPSO	Afro-Asian People's Solidarity Organization
ABIM	*Angkatan Belia Islam Malaysia* (Muslim Youth Movement of Malaysia)
AFTA	ASEAN Free Trade Agreement
AMDA	Anglo-Malayan Defence Agreement
ANZAM	Australia, New Zealand, and Malaya
APEC	Asia Pacific Economic Cooperation
API	*Angatan Pemuda Insaf* (Cohort of Conscious Youths)
ASA	Association of Southeast Asia
ASEAN	Association of Southeast Asian Nations
BPKI	*Badan Penjelidik Usaha Persiapan Kemerdekaan Indonesia* (Committee for the Investigation of Preparatory Efforts for Indonesian Independence)
CEPT	Common Effective Preferential Tariffs
EAEC	East Asian Economic Caucus
EAEG	East Asian Economic Grouping
EEC	European Economic Community
EEZ	exclusive economic zone
FBIS	Foreign Broadcast Intelligence Service
FPDA	Five-Power Defence Arrangement
GAM	*Gerakan Aceh Merdeka* (Aceh Independence Movement)
GATT	General Agreement on Tariffs and Trade
GBC	General Border Committee
ICJ	International Court of Justice
ICMI	*Ikatan Cendikiawan Muslim Indonesia* (Indonesian Muslim Intellectuals' Association)
IKD	*Institut Kajian Dasar* (Institute of Policy Studies)
JCM	Joint Committee Meeting
JI	*Jemaah Islamiyah* (Islamic Organization)
KMM	*Kesatuan Melayu Muda* (Young Malays Union) *Kumpulan Mujahidin Malaysia* (Mujahidin Movement of Malaysia)

KNI	*Komite Nasional Indonesia* (Indonesian National Committee)
KOGAM	*Komando Ganjung Malaysia* (Crush Malaysia Command)
KRIS	*Kesatuan Rakyat Indonesia Semenanjung* (Union of the People of Peninsular Indonesia)
LEPIR	*Lembaga Pendidikan Rakyat* (People's Education Board)
MABBIM	*Majlis Bahasa Brunei, Indonesia, dan Malaysia* (Brunei–Indonesia–Malaysia Language Board)
MATA	*Majlis Agama Tertinggi Malaysia* (Malayan Supreme Religious Council)
MNP	Malayan Nationalist Party
MPSF	Malayan People's Socialist Front
MSS	Malay Security Service
NAA	National Archives of Australia
PAS	*Partai Islam Se-Malaysia* (Islamic Party of Malaysia)
Pemesta	*Piagam Perjuangan Semesta Alam* (Universal Struggle Charter)
PIJ	*Political Intelligence Journal*
PKI	*Partai Komunis Indonesia* (Indonesian Communist Party)
PKKM	*Partai Kebangsaan Melayu Malaya*
PMIP	Pan-Malayan Islamic Party
PNI	*Partai Nasional Indonesia* (Indonesian Nationalist Party)
PP	*Persatuan Perjuangan* (Struggle Union)
PRO	Public Record Office
PRRI	*Pemerintah Revolusioner Republik Indonesia* (Revolutionary Government of the Republic of Indonesia)
PSI	*Partai Sosialis Indonesia* (Indonesian Socialist Party)
SEAFET	South-East Asian Friendship and Economic Treaty
SEANWFZ	South-East Asian Nuclear Weapons Free Zone
SEATO	South-East Asia Treaty Organization
SITC	Sultan Idris Training College
SWB	*Summary of World Broadcasts*
TAC	Treaty of Amity and Cooperation
UMNO	United Malays National Organization#
UNCLOS	United Nations Conference on the Law of the Sea
ZOPFAN	Zone of Peace, Freedom, and Neutrality

Introduction

The relationship between Indonesia and Malaysia has often been acknowledged along the corridors of power in ASEAN as the cornerstone of the organization. Some have even suggested that, together with Singapore, Indonesia and Malaysia form the 'security core' of Southeast Asia.[1] Given the centrality of the Indonesia–Malaysia relationship to regional security and order in Southeast Asia, it is unfortunate that it has yet to be subjected to detailed scholarly investigation. Except for the period 1963–1966, when Indonesia launched its policy of Confrontation (*Konfrontasi*) in response to the formation of Malaysia, no attempt has been made in the fields of either international relations or Southeast Asian studies to explore the dynamics that frame harmony and discord in this bilateral relationship.[2] This study hopes to address this lacuna in the literature, employing the concepts of kinship and nationalism to understand the historical basis to Indonesia–Malaysia relations, the importance of conceptions of affinity and difference in how political leaders understood the premises of bilateral relations over the years, and why and how bilateral ties have taken the shape that they have. The point of entry to this study will be the construction of Indo-Malay racial, cultural, and ethnic affinity and fraternity, which has long fascinated area studies scholars and has been liberally evoked by political leaders.

The historical and cultural premises of Indonesia–Malaysia relations have sparked much interest among area studies scholars. Historians have uncovered the world of the *Hikayat* (tales), which provide insight into the interconnectedness of the pre-colonial Indo-Malay world, where a regional system of trade, intermarriage and politics was already thriving before the arrival of colonial powers. Anthropologists and linguists have also subjected Indo-Malay culture to extensive investigation, and have flagged cultural commonalities and differences that define the identity of an Indo-Malay world independent of the influence of Western colonialism. Essentially, it was geographical proximity that facilitated this socio-cultural exchange. Although the Indo-Malay Archipelago was not closed to the outside world, communications, trade, and intermarriage were largely contained within the region, to the extent that avenues of congruence took shape alongside the evolving history of the Indo-Malay world; a common language was increasingly shared among the peoples of the archipelago, as were religion and certain practices of culture and statecraft. Many of these pre-colonial conceptualizations remain, and continue to inform the socio-cultural continuity of the archipelago. It is on the back of these intimate historical ties between the peoples and cultures of present-day Indonesia and Malaysia that both states can be considered 'kin states'. Be that as it may, this sense of affinity and kinship also had its ambiguities, and the relationship was in no way a perfect representation of harmonious kinship. One such ambiguity revolved around the identity of the region. The characterization of the Indo-Malay Archipelago as the 'Malay world', for instance, could be interpreted as a categorical error of historiography in the sense that the nature of Malay ethnicity and the geographical extent of Malay identity, which underpin this notion, are themselves contentious. Likewise, despite the kinship network and continuity of the region, regional politics was equally profoundly defined by rivalry and discord. In particular, a feature of this socio-political landscape was an enduring concern for the assertion of Javanese dominance and hegemony among the populations and principalities of the Indo-Malay world. Such contradictions meant that while Java could at times be considered an integral part of the Indo-Malay civilization, and indeed arguably even its definitive source, on other occasions and under other circumstances it could be perceived as a threat to Indo-Malay identity, not so much in the sense that it lay 'outside' the Indo-Malay world, rather that it sought to dominate it from within.

Such ambiguities take on a further dimension when one considers how these socio-cultural considerations have been politicized in the form of pan-nationalist motivations to statehood premised on this historical proximity, and subsequently in the enunciation of a 'special relationship' between Indonesia and Malaysia. In tandem with current trends in the field of international relations that are moving away from purely materialist explanations of international political phenomena, this study looks specifically to explore the influence of kinship and nationalism on the evolution and shape of Indonesia–Malaysia relations, and questions the extent to which they help explain harmony and discord in post-colonial Indonesia–Malaysia political relations.

The notion of kinship has been a prominent feature in the diplomatic discourse of bilateral relations, encapsulated in the idea of 'blood brotherhood' or '*serumpun*' (similar stock or race), which is often evoked as a rhetorical premise for Indonesia–Malaysia relations. The basis of this 'blood brotherhood' can be traced to particularistic readings of Indo-Malay history by nationalist ideologues and local historians that attempt to highlight commonalities of race, ethnicity, and culture from a historical vantage point. From a conceptual perspective, such social-cultural renditions of history are reconcilable with, and can be constructed as, the idea of kinship in accordance with the social-anthropological literature on 'fictive' and 'pseudo' kinship. In terms of the politicization of kinship, one ultimately finds that kin fraternity is indelibly expressed in the process and experience of national self-determination, which, in accordance with the theories of nationalism propounded by scholars such as Anthony Smith imply the politicization of such ties of affinity and fraternity as those refer- red to in the Indo-Malay language as 'blood brotherhood'. The impor- tance of nationalism and the experience of national self-determination in dictating the shape of relations between kin states is clear when one con- siders how congruent nationalisms can foster harmony and commonality of objectives such as pan-nationalism, while divergent nationalisms can generate different and contending outlooks towards, and perspectives of, one another.

Nationalism and the experience of national self-determination take on further relevance in the context of relations between Indonesia and Malaysia; these experiences, framed in terms of historical proximity and a common anti-colonial struggle, generate expectations and obligations. Here, it was the contrasting processes of national self-determination as experienced by Indonesia and Malaysia, where the politicization of kinship in the form of nationalism took on different and contending paths, that ultimately led each to different understandings of the expectations and obligations of their 'special relationship', resulting in a contest for primacy and recurring bilateral acrimony and rivalry in the era of post-colonial relations.

In essence, this study will argue that despite the fact that there is a basis upon which to define Indonesia and Malaysia as kin states, their 'special relationship' has been characterized predominantly by tension. This state of affairs has been a consequence of the perceived failure of these kin states to fulfil the expectations and obligations of kinship. This, in turn, has been born of fundamental differences in their respective historical experi- ences and the forging of their national identities, which contravened the loyalties deriving from the kinship factor.

In focusing exclusively on the bilateral relationship between Indonesia and Malaysia, this study recognizes that some benefit could have accrued from a broader approach that located Indonesia–Malaysia relations in the wider context of regional and international developments. Even so, the scope of this study remains deliberately limited to the dynamics of Indone- sia–Malaysia relations, for it is the contention of this study that, in so far as the study of Southeast Asian politics is concerned, research on regional security issues should necessarily begin and end with the bilateral edifice, given that bilateral tensions and suspicions have often been identified as the primary obstacle to greater cooperation within Southeast Asia.[3]

Methodology and modes of inquiry

This study treats the exploration of international politics from a historical perspective, choosing to focus on evolutionary processes and historical sociology in international relations that permit one to delve to a greater extent into the historical contexts that frame Indonesia–Malaysia relations. In tandem with the English School tradition of international relations scholarship that deals with the evolution of contemporary international society across history, the emphasis here will be the context against, and process through, which historical kinship links between Indonesia and Malaysia have intersected with the emerging identities and politics of the Indo-Malay world. Because political phenomena never take place in a political or historical vacuum, in the context of its attempt to understand the role and impact of kinship and nationalism in Indonesia–Malaysia relations this project delves into history 'not as a bank of information which might falsify a theory, but as a narrative which permits a greater appreciation of the origins, evolution, and consequences of an event'.[4]

A historical approach would be especially pertinent to the present study because it essentially involves two new 'Third World' nation-states consisting of much older societies with their own sense of identity and history reaching back into the pre-colonial era.[5] This intersection between old and new dispensations creates conceptual and practical problems, for it leads to contradictions surrounding non-Western nation-states' desires to associate themselves with what is clearly a predominantly Western international society through the declaration of independence and the establishment of political and territorial boundaries, while still maintaining what their nationalists have identified as pre-colonial identities – thus drawing attention to the importance of nationalism and the process and experience of national self-determination in our understanding of Indonesia–Malaysia relations.

Another facet of the methodological approach taken here is the emphasis on statecraft, which introduces the normative role of perceptions and interpretations of the kinship factor among policy practitioners.[6] Perception and interpretation are vital considerations for scholars of international politics because they

> interleave the logic of more materially driven theories of the international system ... with the view that sentience makes a difference, and that social systems cannot be understood in the same way as physical ones. When units are sentient, how they perceive each other is a major determinant of how they interact.[7]

Consequently, it is not power and interest *per se* that dictate the course of international politics, but the employment of instruments of power in pursuit of the values of security and survival as perceived and interpreted by statesmen. Two reasons lie behind the decision taken here to focus explicitly on the role of practitioners of statecraft. First, it is a fact that as agents of the state, personalities such as Tunku Abdul Rahman, Sukarno, Suharto, Abdul Razak, Ghazali Shafie, Adam Malik, Mahathir Mohamad and Subandrio dictated the course of Indonesia–Malaysia relations through their domination of policy processes. It is through the perceptions of these statesmen, as well as their interpretations of the terms of kinship relations, that the politicization of kinship has been conceptualized. Further to that, many of these practitioners actually share personal kindred relations, and these ties have informed their perception of the terms of inter-state relations and conduct of foreign policy. Ghazali Shafie and Adam Malik, for instance, were distant cousins, and not surprisingly their domination of foreign policy in their respective governments coincided with the 'golden years' of bilateral relations. Likewise, Abdul Rahman's close relations with the Sultanate of Langkat in Sumatra certainly played a role in his interpretation of Malaysia's ties with Indonesia in relation to Sumatra, and Abdul Razak's Buginese descent may well have influenced his archipelagic outlook during his office.

Structure

The book is essentially divided into two parts. The first consists of three chapters that deal with the theoretical and conceptual framework as well as how kinship was conceptualized and politicized in the context of anti-colonialism in the Indo-Malay world. Chapter 1 will present a working definition of kinship and draws its associations with nationalism, drawing primarily from Carsten's work on kinship identities and Anthony Smith's on nationalism. In a reflection of ongoing debates in the field of social anthropology, it will suggest that kinship cannot be defined only on genealogical and biological premises; it can also exist as a socially and culturally constructed relationship that is built on expectations and obligations. The chapter will relate this understanding of kinship to the phenomenon of nationalism, and argue that nationalism (as defined by Anthony Smith) is an expression of the politicization of kinship. Subsequently, the relationship between politicized kinship, nationalism, and international relations is made. It is because the process by which a state comes into being has an integral part to play in how that state views its political surroundings and formulates policies in response to it that notions such as kinship and nationalism, which the study suggests have played an integral role in the formation and realization of the Indonesian and Malaysian sovereign states, take on prominence.

Because the discourse of kinship in Indonesia–Malaysia relations is always initiated with a reference to the past, it is necessary to revisit this past in all its complexities in order to verify the basis on which Indonesia and Malaysia can indeed be considered kin states. Chapter 2 will search for precedents in the construction of kin identity among the respective political elite and ideologues in the Indo-Malay world, looking at how the phenomenon of trade and migration led to the spinning of a genealogical web across the Indo-Malay world, and exploring social-cultural avenues of kinship construction such as language, religion, and concepts of statehood and community. More importantly, the issue of colonial intervention and its introduction not only of terrestrial borders (which were non-existent in the pre-colonial Indo-Malay world), but also of ideas such as race, ethnicity, identity, and nationalism which eventually inspired the mobilization of kinship for political purposes in the form of pan-Malay identity that echoed the romanticism of Western nationalism of the late nineteenth and early twentieth centuries, is explored in detail. Consequently, the chapter will look at how this search for precedents yielded different understandings of the past, resulting in contested versions of the basis of Indo-Malay kinship.

The construction of kin identity and the mobilization and politicization of kinship by pan-Malay nationalists in the anti-colonial movement will be the focus of Chapter 3. This chapter will investigate the rise and demise of the pan-national concepts of *Indonesia Raya* and *Melayu Raya* within the framework of contested prescriptions for nationhood not only within, but also between, the Dutch East Indies and British Malaya. Here it plots the different paths to nationhood – civic and republican nationalism on the part of Indonesia and ethno-nationalism on the part of Malaysia – and how these choices laid the grounds for subsequent perceptions and interpretations of kinship in the post-colonial era. In essence, Chapters 1, 2, and 3 lay the conceptual and historical foundations of the central argument that in so far as the kinship factor is concerned, it was its translation into a political phenomenon, in this case nationalism, that resulted in contending interpretations among Indonesian and Malaysian political leaders as to its meanings and reference points for bilateral relations.

The second part of the book consists of a further three chronologically organized chapters that trace the diplomatic history of Indonesia–Malaysia relations from Malayan independence to approximately the turn of the twentieth century. These chapters serve to look specifically at the functional aspect of relatedness in so far as political relations between the kin states of Indonesia and Malaysia were concerned. Chapter 4 will explore the tensions that arose as Indonesian and Malayan political leaders sought to premise relations on their respective interpretations and perceptions of their shared historical legacy, culminating in the events of *Konfrontasi*.

Chapter 5 will cover the period from 1967 to 1980, when a significant improvement in relations, brought about by the euphoria of the termination of *Konfrontasi* as well as the advent of the Tun Abdul Razak administration in Malaysia, was evident. It will outline the contours of an Indonesian and Malaysian foreign policy that drew its coherence and uniformity from an apparent change in mindsets and outlook in Kuala Lumpur decision-making circles towards Jakarta.

Chapter 6 will carry the study into the 1990s. This chapter will look at what are essentially bilateral relations during the 'Mahathir era' of Malaysian foreign policy, after Mahathir Mohamad had succeeded Tun Hussein Onn in 1981. Again, it is not just policies *per se* that are of interest, but more so how they have exposed the widening gulf in perceptions and outlooks of political leaders as both Indonesia and Malaysia pursued activist foreign policies in what shaped up to be a contest for primacy in the Indo-Malay Archipelago, resulting in a prestige dilemma that bore some semblance to earlier epochs in bilateral relations when a 'clash of nationalisms' underscored bilateral differences and discord.

The conclusion describes how, despite the regular use by political leaders of the language of blood brotherhood to inject meaning and intelligibility into relations, the construction of Indo-Malay fraternity has always been riddled with unresolved ambiguities. Though both sides agree that they share a 'special relationship', their understandings and interpretations of the terms of this relationship remain contested. The ethno-racial terms of reference have never been resolved, and have been accentuated by the historical tension between Javanese and Malays that has informed (and continues to inform) political decision-making. Beyond that, the conclusion also looks at how the politicization of kinship has in fact engendered discord. What began as pan-Malayism in fact resulted in the formation of separate territorial states whose respective experiences of national self-determination have been highly influential in fostering negative views and perceptions of each other. The association between kinship and nationalism, then, has been an integral part of the understanding not only of how political leaders continue to present kinship as a means for greater meaning and intelligibility to bilateral relations, but, more importantly, of why relations between Indonesia and Malaysia have largely been prickly.

Part I
Theoretical and conceptual framework

1 Kinship and nationalism in international relations

According to mainstream paradigms of international relations, the arena of international politics is populated by sovereign states all pursuing their own 'self-interest'.[1] While this may be to a large extent true, one particular category of inter-state relations stands out, in which the pursuit of material interest may only be half the story to be told. This pertains to what is referred to in the terminology of international politics as 'special relationships'.

The concept of 'special relationships' describes relations between states whose populations share historical and sentimental bonds, and whose leaders impute meaning into their relations on the back of these bonds. Such relationships warrant an almost immutable belief (on the part of their leaders and populations) that they, at least in theory, are meant to share a relationship driven by more than purely material factors.[2] One can observe such dynamics, for example, in Australian involvement in the First World War and the Boer War, and the historical record of ties between Russia and Serbia; it has also found expression in pan-Africanism and pan-Arabism, Anglo-American relations, and a host of other bilateral and multilateral relationships. Yet often too, one notices a discrepancy between the persistent use of the discourse of 'special relationships' and the regular collapse of such relationships into animosity. It is precisely this dichotomy that interests this study. While realists might not find the collapse of 'special relationships' puzzling, given their belief that international relations are fundamentally competitive, it is suggested here that since social anthropological logic lies at the heart of these relationships, such approaches might offer equally persuasive modes of understanding as to the matter of cooperation and rivalry between states that share 'special relationships'.[3] The point of entry of this study is the suggestion that kinship and nationalism, the latter expressed in the process of national self-determination that in the Indo-Malay world gave political justification to historical conceptions of kinship, have played a profound historical role in shaping the political relationship between Indonesia and Malaysia, and hence set in place the historical context for the understanding of bilateral relations.

Locating kinship and nationalism in the international relations research agenda

Few would disagree that the lexicon of Southeast Asia's international relations remains predominantly realist.[4] Several reasons account for this. The path to independence for many states in Southeast Asia has mostly been defined by domestic and international struggle and conflict. This legacy remains to inform policy choices today, and politics continues to be viewed through realist eyes, where the state continues to dictate the policy process in the name of national interest and where power, security, and threat remain key preoccupations in so far as international affairs are concerned. Added to that, the mainstay of classical realism, the vital role played by statesmen and women in orchestrating international affairs, remains relevant in the political context of Southeast Asia. Hence despite the paucity of work in the international relations field that deals explicitly with political relations between Indonesia and Malaysia, it can be plausibly argued that any study of Indonesia–Malaysia relations should begin in the realist camp.[5]

International relations, so the realist mantra goes, are premised on power, be it an end in itself or a means to survival.[6] The importance of power and perceptions of power in the international politics in Southeast Asia has come across starkly in the writings of many scholars.[7] Extrapolating from this, neo-realism will suggest that Indonesia's larger size and bountiful resources make it a preponderant power in Southeast Asia, and the Malaysian response should be a policy of balancing. Realists are also likely to suggest that Indonesia–Malaysia relations are conducted on the basis of 'states acting as states', where both pursue their respective interests based on material calculations, what Morgenthau termed the 'guiding star' of decisions. Bilateral differences, then, reflect a 'clash' between these interests, and enmity between Malaysia and Indonesia is to be expected owing to the size, power, and capability differentials in this bilateral relationship. Indeed, given the track record of contentious relations between these two key players in the Indo-Malay world, realism appears vindicated.

While realist observations on the conflictual end result of international politics may be accurate, realism's means of arriving at these conclusions demand scrutiny.[8] It is suggested here that the foci and objectivity of realist international relations theory, and in particular its behaviouralist strains, essentially lend themselves to an over-simplification of international politics. The ambiguity of power, for example, has been well documented.[9] How does the positivist realist measure or 'operationalize' it? Are material yardsticks its only measurements?[10] How does one reconcile, for example, Geertz's argument, made in specific relation to the Indo-Malay world, that power could in fact be culturally manufactured?[11]

Vagaries arising from privileging the state as the primary unit of analysis, without considering the process through which it comes into being, lead further to the problem of defining the concept of 'interest' so often evoked by policy-makers and realist scholars as an explanation for state policy. 'Interest' is ultimately a normative concept, and without further conceptual clarification its applicability in academic study will be diluted.[12] One scholar has intimated that the elusiveness and ambiguity of the concept of 'interest' is such that 'political objectives remain so frequently hidden behind the verbal flannel of political argument that some political scientists are tempted to dismiss the concept [of interest] altogether'.[13] Indeed, what precisely is the 'national interest' involved for Malaysia and Indonesia, and what is its source? As this study shows, the ambiguities surrounding these concepts are problematic when applied to cases such as those under scrutiny here – of sovereign states that experience, particularly in the immediate post-colonial years, tension between the pursuit of national interests as the elite see it, and enduring communal loyalties, which inevitably influence policy choices for reasons of, *inter alia*, political expediency.

Realism's conceptual shortcomings have led students of international relations to search elsewhere for equally, if not more, persuasive explanations for international political phenomenon. The gradual shift from material to cognitive and sociological contents and perspectives that one witnesses in the field in recent times is indicative of this trend.[14] Consider, for example, the resurgence of interest in ethnic conflict, where scholars have located underlying explanations in non-material factors.[15] Consequently, this move to conceive the international political environment as a social rather than a natural phenomenon has spawned a literature that has introduced concepts such as culture and identity into the international relations lexicon.[16] Culture and ideology, for example, have been pinpointed as alternative lenses through which issues of conflict, war, and policy formulation can be viewed.[17] The material yardsticks for measuring power, the cornerstone of realism's objectivity, have been challenged by scholars who have identified 'soft power' as equally important to understanding influence in international politics.[18] Likewise, security, another mainstay of realist theory, has been considered an issue of identity as much as interest. Wendt notes, for instance, that 'the distribution of power may always affect states' calculations, but how it does so depends on the intersubjective understandings and expectations, on the "distribution of knowledge", that constitute their conceptions of self and other.'[19] Accordingly, it has been suggested by proponents of identity that questions of how states relate to their environment necessarily begin with the perception of 'self'.[20] These trends that attempt social-communicative understandings of international relations indicate that, while concerns of realist international relations theory are well taken, it is likely that the dynamics of international politics are varied and dictated by a combination of factors, and likewise that any attempt to understand these dynamics might well benefit from greater theoretical flexibility.

Unfortunately, such conceptual and paradigmatic 'compromise' is sometimes rejected in certain circles of international relations. In particular, this epistemological problem is associated with the empiricism of the American social-scientific tradition, which focuses on explanation via the construction of covering-law models. Intra- and inter-paradigmatic restructuring remains markedly difficult within this tradition because of the need to maintain theoretical 'parsimony' and 'determinism' in preserving the all-important core premises of 'first-order theories'. Any attempt to engage in such an exercise within the American tradition is quickly demonized as the 'degenerative' compromising of intellectual beliefs.[21] Consequently, scholars are epistemologically straitjacketed. As Gunther Hellman rightly observes:

> The thrust of their [American social science positivists'] argument is the equivalent of an unfriendly takeover in the business world: The liberal/epistemicist bid involves defining and delimiting the 'proper' borders of the territory that realists can rightly claim, thereby expanding the jurisdiction of liberal and epistemic rule. Paradigmatic battles such as these, however, tend to occur in an anarchic realm of science, where the knowledge dilemma assumes the role of the security dilemma in international relations: If realists could rightly claim more knowledge territory, paradigmatic liberals, epistemicists, institutionalists, and idealists are likely to perceive that there is less knowledge for them to claim. As a result, each side charges its opponents with lacking 'coherence', 'distinctiveness', and other sorts of epistemological ammunition.[22]

From an academic perspective this is an unfortunate state of affairs, and as Barry Buzan has implied in his attempts to nuance traditional realism, there certainly should be room to 'broaden the perceptions of those within realist orthodoxy, and build bridges to those who ... are unnecessarily outside it'.[23] It is with this as an epistemological point of entry that the study explores kinship and nationalism and its influence on Indonesia–Malaysia relations. The meanings of these terms are, however, contested in the fields of anthropology and sociology, and it may be helpful to identify the sense in which this study applies them.

Kinship, race, and culture

Within the social sciences, kinship describes a principle of association originating from the field of anthropology.[24] Understood from a biological perspective, kinship refers to the characteristic of blood ties that define relations within a family structure. This manner of relation is determined by both patrilineal and matrilineal ties and essentially narrows the scope of kinship studies to smaller structures of human interaction. Within the anthropological literature, the superlative statement in support of genealogical-biological interpretations of kinship has been that of Meyer Fortes, who in studying kinship made reference to 'the irreducible genealogical connections, the given relations of actual connectedness, which are universally utilized in building up kinship relations and categories'.[25] Fortes then proceeds to contend that kinship 'arises from the generally recognized fact that the relations they [the genealogical connections] designate have their origin in a distinct sphere of social life, the sphere which, for both observers and actors, is demarcated by reference to the base line of genealogical connection'.[26] While bloodlines and descent are clearly important dimensions to the understanding of kinship, anthropologists since Fortes have begun questioning whether kinship is indeed an ontological given. In this regard, quite apart from direct blood ties, descent or biological characteristics, it has been claimed that the concept of kinship can carry other meanings as well.

In a critique of Fortes's narrow interpretations, David Schneider argued that the idea of kinship carries a plurality of meanings, and does not merely adhere to the 'natural' facts of procreation or genealogy.[27] Central to Schneider's concern is the fact that kinship is not so much a biological as a social phenomenon, whose meanings and interpretation are subject to social and cultural influences. Schneider's conclusions have since been corroborated by Schweitzer, who observes that

> [K]inship comes in a variety of packages and with a multitude of meanings attached.... Instead of insisting on universal characteristics as a precondition for the analytical validity of kinship, variation is viewed as a practical necessity resulting from detailed fieldwork and observation of social reality that does not *a priori* privilege certain aspects of social relatedness over others.[28]

Further emphasizing that kinship is not only biologically prescribed, Nuttall has concluded that

> The boundaries of kindred and descent-based groups are shifting constantly, as are the interpersonal relationships that are defined in terms of kinship. ... Kinship may appear to have distinct biological roots, but in practice it is flexible and integrates non-biological social relationships that are considered to be as 'real' as any biological relationship.... Kinship relationships are not always permanent states (as a strict biological interpretation would suggest) ... it is a system that is inherently flexible and allows extensive improvisation in that people can choose their kin.[29]

Indeed, convictions of kinship and myths of common ancestry need not, and often do not, accord with biological descent. Cultural symbols are often used as markers of biological affinity, and the basis for an existential sense of community.[30] Implicit in these observations is the argument that kinship can also be said to exist when social interactions within cultural frames of reference allow genealogical logic to be transcribed onto non-biological relationships. In the main, such approaches extend the meaning of kinship beyond the immediate family structure and suggest that kin relations can be based on the assumption of ethnic similarity and shared cultural identity as well – untraceable yet sociologically 'real' kinship.[31] Social anthropologists refer to this as 'quasi', 'pseudo' or 'fictive' kinship, indicating an imagined or constructed idea, where 'kinship ... is not necessarily a correlate of biogenetic or agnatic ties, but rather a culturally defined domain'.[32]

The fact that meanings of kinship may be extended outside the genealogical grid is illustrated, for example, in the work of Clifford Geertz, who applies kinship in this manner when he relates the metaphorical concept 'blood brother' to the interaction of what he calls 'primordial attachments', a common historical and cultural relation that underpins the relationship between two groups.[33] Here the idea of 'blood', commonly used in the study of genealogy, is applied in a broader sense to denote a close relationship grounded on familial-like affiliation, suggesting 'a relation of alliance or consocation by which individuals not related by kinship acquire ties of pseudo-kinship, the rights and duties that compose the relationship being modelled on those of brotherhood'.[34] Kinship in this sense hence implies more than just familial relations. It has not merely ethno-genealogical dimensions, but social and cultural ones as well. Mark Nuttall notes: '[K]inship is a cultural reservoir from which individuals draw items they can use to define and construct everyday social interaction.'[35] In other words, when ascribed to a particular relationship the kinship factor may be equally understood as a social-cultural construction as well as the 'reality' of blood ties.

Recent anthropological literature has taken this re-conceptualization of kinship further. Carsten proposes to adopt 'a broad and imaginative view of what might be included under the rubric "kinship"' and to describe 'the ethnographic particularities of being related in a specific cultural context'.[36] This is accomplished by introducing the concept of 'related-ness', which she maintains allows her to 'suspend the assumptions behind the biological and social faces of kinship' and to circumvent the analytical dichotomy between the biological and the social.[37] In using the concept of relatedness one could conceivably explore a particular relationship via the implicit paradigm of kinship without having to rely on an arbitrary distinction between biological-genealogical and social-cultural, and without pre-supposing what constitutes kinship. In turn, this permits one to see the unity as opposed to the separation of the biological and the social.[38] Other scholars, however, have not shied away from explicit attempts at merging the two interpretations. Strathern, for example, contends elsewhere that quite apart from conceptual distance, kinship is a 'meeting place between nature and culture'.[39]

The implications of these findings are critical to the understanding of kin affinities. No longer is kinship confined to biological affinity; it also refers to identities constructed along social and cultural lines where congruities of language, religion, custom, and history all have an ineffable cohesiveness in and of themselves, working to bind one to one's kinsman or kinswoman or fellow-believer not merely out of necessity or interest, but also by virtue of some absolute import attributed to the very tie itself. In sum, social and cultural ingredients impute into relationships a corporate sentiment of oneness that makes those who are charged with it feel as if they are kith and kin. An important corollary to the social-cultural construction of kinship is the fact that it is action that gives intelligibility and meaning to relationships characterized as relationships between kin. Again, this has been reflected in recent trends in the field, where anthropologists have argued for a shift in attention from what 'kinship is' to what 'kinship does', or, as Carsten puts it, 'the hard work of making and maintaining relations'.[40]

There is a further dimension to this construction of affiliation: it inspires action. Such a functional notion of kinship, then, as David Schneider has described, 'is more one of *doing* than of *being*. It is based largely on the interaction, the doing, of exchange and less on the state of being, of having some substance, quality, or attribute'.[41] It should be evident that because it often exists as a social and cultural construction, the presence and operation of the kinship factor are also based largely on perception and interpretation, particularly of those who evoke and appropriate it for political causes. The matter of the perception, interpretation, and appropriation of kinship metaphors for political purposes hence is fundamental to any attempt to understand the discourse and function of the kinship factor between people, communities, or states. Put differently, the kinship factor entails obligations and expectations.

Expectation and obligation are largely accepted as givens in the context of biological kinship, but take on equal importance for kinship defined as socially and culturally constructed relatedness. In other words, expectations and obligations are the norms of kinship that distinguish it from other, less intimate forms of relationships; the stronger the relationship, the greater is the obligation to both give and receive help, with dependence and trust both a function of and reinforced by these expectations and obligations. Likewise, as a functional and dynamic concept the kinship factor also dictates that concern be given to how these norms work out in the behaviour and action of peoples and groups identified as 'kin'. Again, the importance of interaction among, and expectations of, kin can be found in the anthropology literature. Roy Wagner, for example, surmised that 'exchange defines; consanguinity relates'.[42] Elsewhere, Rita Astuti has concluded that notions of identity and relatedness are established through performance rather than substance.[43] Similarly, Charles Stafford's work emphasizes the importance of obligation and reciprocity in the construction of related-ness.[44] Likewise, Barbara Bodenhorn contends that it is the work process more than birth or blood that creates 'immutable rights' associated with kinship.[45] Indeed, extending Schneider's critique of Fortes, it can be suggested as an extreme that without consideration for the functional aspects of relatedness, the 'state' of being kin may well be rendered meaningless.

Focusing on the functional and dynamic dimension of kinship performs three important tasks. First, it gives further clarity to the argument that kinship can be a social-cultural construction by providing the terms upon which such kin identities take shape. Second, it opens analytical avenues for the detailed study of the impact of relatedness on social-political action between people, communities, or even modern nation-states. Finally, it provides a framework for the conceptual separation of kinship from inter-related notions of identity such as ethnicity. Presenting what remains a widely accepted definition, Max Weber contended that the basis of ethnicity essentially revolves around characteristics such as customs, the belief in and partaking of common history and ancestry, shared language, and religion.[46] Common ethnicity, then, implies two communities or groups that share some of or all these traits. At first glance, the difference between ethnicity and social-cultural interpretations of kinship appears merely a matter of semantics, for it has been argued that even ethnicity is not a given, but chosen and contextual.[47] Yet there is a subtle but crucial difference between ethnicity and kinship in so far as analytical consequence is concerned. While kinship shares the same core assumptions or bases of ethnicity, its major conceptual point of departure lies in the more self-conscious and assertive nature inherent in its meaning. That is, one could say that the concept of 'relatedness' carried in the meaning of kinship takes on a more dynamic and functional form than in ethnicity. This is because although ethnicity denotes likeness, kinship connotes action in the name of or resulting from it. In point of illustration, people may share common histories or historical myths (as with common ethnicity), but it is how they perceive and interpret these commonalities that determines whether they form the basis or impetus for social-political mobilization. This distinction carries important implications, for the factor of kinship involves not only the sharing of common ethnicity, but also *the translation of such relatedness into socio-political action*. In the political sense, this entails its utility as a 'value' through which policy-makers view their world.[48] In that manner, kinship provides the reference point for relations between states that are perceived to share historical commonalities. Drawing attention to this distinction between kinship and ethnicity, it has been noted that

> [E]thnicity is an aspect of social relationship between agents who consider themselves as being culturally distinctive from members of other

groups with whom they have a minimum of regular interaction. It can thus also be defined as a social identity (based on a contrast vis-à-vis others) characterized by metaphoric or 'fictive kinship'.[49]

However, formulated and presented thus, the symbols of ethnic identity must be appropriated and internalized before they can serve as a basis for orchestrating social-political action. It is suggested here that it is the sense of kinship that invests these bonds with a potential for action and mobilization.

The kinship factor can therefore be understood as ethnicity appropriated, internalized, and politicized, where common ethnicity, history, and social-cultural relatedness such as similar religion and cultural practices are constructed to create a strong psychological sentiment between two groups of people not necessarily directly linked by bloodline, which in turn encourages political action on behalf of the other. In the study of a social or political relationship, the kinship factor refers to how this socially and culturally constructed relatedness between two groups or populations results in co-identification, which is often expressed in terms of bonds of kinship despite the paucity of direct consanguineal or affinal relations. It is suggested here that such politicization of kinship takes on one of its most trenchant forms in the phenomenon of nationalism.

Kinship and nationalism

Given that kinship can be defined not only on genealogical but also on sociological premises, it follows that there is a close association between the idea of kinship and the logic of nationalism, with permutations of the former playing a crucial role in shaping the latter. This comes across clearly in the theory of nationalism championed by Anthony Smith.

In his investigations into the origins of nationalism, Anthony Smith argues that the basis of the modern nation can be found in the *Ethnie*, which he defines as 'clusters of population with similar perceptions and sentiments generated by, and encoded in, specific beliefs, values and practices'.[50] Smith later refines it to 'named units of population with common ancestry myths and historical memories, elements of shared culture, some link with a historic territory and some measure of solidarity, at least among their elites'.[51] One should note that the idea of *Ethnie* differs from that of the nation, which Smith presents as 'a named human population which shares myths and memories, a mass public culture, a designated homeland, economic unity and equal rights and duties for all members'.[52] Hence, while Smith would concede that nationalism is a modern doctrine, to him it is based on pre-modern premises.[53] By suggesting that this dimension of identity comprises 'historical clusters of myth, memory, values and symbols', Smith in fact evokes Geertz's notion of the 'primordial attachments' of kinship.[54] To Smith's mind, the sense of shared destiny that underscores the birth of nationalist ethos is based primarily on the construction of relatedness on the back of perceived commonalities, not least of which is a particular interpretation of its own history; in other words, it is premised on the social-cultural construction of what anthropologists discussed earlier identify as 'fictive' and 'pseudo' kinship. It is interesting too that Smith emphasizes the importance of 'historical clusters, or heritages, of myths, memories, values and symbols for cultural community formation' over the state of ethnic ties, emphasizing that the *Ethnie* is in fact more than common ethnicity.[55] Thus, in Smith's view there is a very distinct political dimension to the co-affiliation dynamics generated within the *Ethnie*, and this lies in the process through which the *Ethnie* becomes a modern nation.

The pertinence of Smith's conclusions for this study can be distilled at two levels. First, he has clearly illuminated how the kinship factor can function through the politicization of relatedness in the context of *Ethnies* for the objectives of national self-determination. David Brown has suggested, for example, that the nation is also a 'mythical kinship community'.[56] In other words, it can be argued that it is the kinship factor that drives people to sacrifice and die for 'their people' in the name of national liberation. This point was further elaborated on by Brown when he described the 'invention' of the ideology of nationalism as 'individuals [who] sought imagined communities which could *mimic* the kinship group in offering a sense of identity, security, and authority'.[57] Similarly, while Anderson would suggest that the co-affiliation of Smith's *Ethnies* in and of themselves are insufficient in scope to shape a population into a nation-state with territorial boundaries, he does agree that 'primordial forces' such as kinship are important in the 'imagination' of the nation-state:[58] just as the nation-state is imagined on this basis, so too kinship can be constructed.

It is easy to deduce from Smith's study of nationalism how the idea of kinship can be constructed for purposes of political mobilization. His definition of *Ethnie* reflects the kinship factor at work at forging a national identity, for he identifies the manner by which ethnic bonds are mobilized towards the formation of a nation-state. The mobilization of kinship in this manner has been cited as a particularly appropriate description of the process of national self-determination in Asia, where 'the absence of democratic traditions led the nation to be imagined as a community of blood ties, in other words in exclusive and narrowly ethnic terms'.[59] Indeed, the relevance of Smith's version of nationhood for this study will come to the fore later when the study considers how kinship discourse was framed by nationalists either side of the Melaka Straits (Straits of Malacca) precisely in terms of a shared interpretation of a common history (what Smith terms the 'myth–symbol complex'), for it was through this lens of history that kin-type affinity was constructed and mobilized during the pre-war and immediate post-war anti-colonial struggles in British Malaya and the Dutch East Indies, where attempts had to be made to reconcile conceptions of nation with communal loyalties. This was illustrated most poignantly in the agitation for pan-Malay unity.[60]

Nationalism and the international

Nationalism is one of the most salient phenomena in the contemporary world, although the full depth of its impact on international politics has yet to be adequately grasped. The international society that we live in and the international relations that we study do, after all, concern sovereign nation-states, many of which came into being through the process of national self-determination. The most obvious impact of nationalism on international society is its influence as a creator and destroyer of states. This influence has been subjected to extensive study through topics such as the international dimensions to ethnic conflict, secession and self-determination among minority groups, the securitization of migration, as well as the politics of global diasporas.[61] Not surprisingly, this interest in the international dimension of nationalism peaked with the end of the Cold War and the collapse of communist regimes throughout Eastern Europe and the former Soviet Union.

Returning to the implications of Anthony Smith's studies on nationalism, one should not, of course, assume *ipso facto* that the transition from *Ethnie* to the modern nation is necessarily unilineal. Even assuming that the 'nation' would ultimately find territorial expression, many of its 'members' could also conceivably be left outside its borders. Forces such as colonialism, migration, and war, for example, can conceivably separate an *Ethnie*, leading eventually to the creation of *separate* nation-states from the same *Ethnie*. The question to be posed here in this event, and one that has eluded studies of nationalism in international relations, is to what extent the kin ties that bind people within an *Ethnie* continue to define, organize, and influence relations between nations and nation-states constituted into different territorial entities, but originating from the same *Ethnie*. Put differently, what happens to kinship when *Ethnies*, or nations (which for Smith are the successors to the *Ethnie*) for that matter, evolve into separate states, and how does one reconcile the similarities that kinship has with nationalism, stopping short of a claim of one state for one *Ethnie*? This would certainly pose a conceptual problem if the modernist principles of nationalism include the acceptance of Mayall's 'national idea' that the nation is the proper basis for the sovereign state.[62] Most, if not all, Third World states arise out of older communal bonds and identities, many of which pre-date the 'modernity' of Westphalian statehood by centuries, but were nevertheless thrown together into a singular political entity, often via plotting of colonial political boundaries. Often they consist of distinctly different, sometimes even antagonistic, sub-national identities that had modern statehood thrust upon them without any outlet for historical antipathies. The question of how a state's worldviews, outlooks, and policies arise out of these historical complexities should be a matter of more than passing interest for scholars whose empirical expertise lies in the study of Third World states.

In this respect, this study pays particular attention to history and historical context in the study of Indonesia–Malaysia relations, accepting the epistemological premise that 'the key actors on the international stage are themselves historically constituted subjects who understand their mutual relationships in historical terms'.[63] While the study does not contest 'statist' perspectives that the formation of the sovereign nation-state and the acceptance of 'the standard of civilization' of international society mark the watershed in 'national' histories, one should also note that structures of pre-colonial political orders were not abandoned wholesale and overnight in order to embrace the concept of 'sovereignty of the nation-state';[64] nor did the European model of international society go unchallenged.[65] On the contrary, what is of interest in a study on kinship and nationalism such as this is the process by which the territorial and ideational boundaries of the state come about, and the impact that this process has on a state's perception of its place in the international arena, particularly in relation to other sovereign states that conceivably arise from a similar *Ethnie*. Given that Mandaville contends that anthropological perspectives to international politics demand consideration as 'political dimensions of various transnational social forms, some of which seem to challenge the limits of the political as defined by the modern state.... Because transnationalism creates forms of political identity which do not fit the taxonomies of political modernity', the question to pose is to what extent the residues of kinship that were mobilized for anti-colonial struggle continue to be a viable factor for the organization of relations between 'kin states' in the post-colonial era.[66] It is in this sense that the study argues that how territorial and ideational borders come about has an impact on international politics because such experiences inform the perception among state elites of their position in the world.

As the previous discussion highlighted, nationalism is also a necessary consideration in the study of international politics, not only in the manner in which it represents the politicization of the kinship felt among peoples and communities that underpin the national cause, but also in how experiences of nation-building and state formation frame the worldviews and outlooks particularly of Third World states looking to enter into an international order dictated by Western (often former colonial) states. Put differently, is the spirit and meaning of self-determination confined to dislodging alien rule, or does it remain a popular principle for the purposes of the political mobilization of the population? This second issue is trenchant for the study of international relations, for it considers that nationalism is sustained in the post-colonial era to define and direct a post-colonial state's relations with its geopolitical environment. Consider, for example, how the progenitors of the Non-Aligned Movement, which sought to distinguish the Third World from the communist and capitalist blocs, were states that were motivated by a sense of consequence born out of revolutionary struggle against Western colonial powers.[67] Explaining how and why nationalism might be sustained by post-colonial states, James Mayall further elaborates:

> The European powers did not cease to exist; they simply withdrew to their own homelands, from where they continued to exercise consider- able economic, military and political influence. This meant that they were almost inevitably used as models for nation- and state-building; it also meant that they were available as targets, that the quest for national self-determination could be continued after independence and by other means.[68]

To that effect, an observation of nationalism that this study suggests is the fact that the nationalist imperative is often sustained after the formation of the sovereign territorial state; it becomes a 'value' through which outlooks and worldviews are organized, and a motivation for policy. States born of revolution and bloody anti-colonial struggle hence often uphold, if not nourish, their nationalist ideals in opposition to colonialism and the pre- vailing international order dictated and managed by Western hegemony.

Kinship, nationalism, and Indonesia–Malaysia relations

Interest in the role played by kinship and nationalism in Indonesia– Malaysia relations begins with an observation that discourses of 'brother- hood' have been employed regularly and liberally between these two 'kin states'. The idea of politicized kinship first took on prominence in anti- colonial discourse. Early nationalist movements in both Indonesia and Malaysia were not averse to the contemplation of a unified ethno-religious and historically based identity defined as *Indonesia Raya* (Greater Indone- sia) or *Melayu Raya* (the Greater Malay kingdom). This was certainly the case at least until the end of the Pacific War in August 1945, although pockets of activists continued to agitate for unification in the 1950s. Through the ideas of prominent Indonesian and Malay thinkers such as Muhammad Yamin, Ibrahim Yaacob, Burhanuddin Al-Helmy, Ahmad Boestamam, Ishak Mohamad, Mokhtaruddin Lasso, and Sukarno, attempts were made at conceptualizing an independent political entity predicated on the premise that a Malay world existed and thrived in the pre-colonial era, one that could be revived in the context of post-colonial territorial boundaries with this historical legacy and bonds built across time as a chain of reference.

Though the political discourse of pan-unity eventually subsided as a result of the consolidation of Indonesia and Malaysia into sovereign polit- ical entities in their own right, it remained a residual phenomenon linking pockets of the Indonesian and Malaysian populations. One need only consider the extent of social-cultural interaction that continues across the Melaka Straits. The recent resurgence in collaborative civil society activities across the Melaka Straits draws further attention to this relationship. More interestingly, revelations of the depths of collaboration between Islamic groups in Indonesia and Malaysia, where evidence has emerged that not only have links between moderate Islamic movements such as *Muhammadiyah* (Indonesia) and ABIM (*Angkatan Belia Islam Malaysia*, the Islamic Youth Movement of Malaysia) strengthened over recent years, but links with more extremist movements such as the *Jemaah Islamiyah* as well, highlight the potential of Islam as a factor that might foster further cohesion between the two societies in a manner that again might either enhance, as with Islamic civil society movements, or challenge, as with the radical and militant Islamic networks, prevailing international order.[69] While such relations are not taken as representative of Indonesia–Malaysia state or societal relations as a whole, the persistence of such ties against the historical background of bilateral relations certainly commands interest.

Such is the apparent resilience of common identity in the diplomatic language between Indonesia and Malaysia that it regularly informs academic study as well, specifically work in the area studies tradition.[70] Particularly evocative, if historically flawed, intellectual thinking on the kinship factor has derived from the ideologies and writings of prominent Indonesian and Malay nationalists who championed the pan conceptions of *Indonesia Raya* and *Melayu Raya*.[71] These academic and ideological traditions illustrate how many scholars have tried to understand aspects of Indonesia–Malaysia relations from the perspective of kinship. The popularity of indigenous scholarship on shared Indo-Malay historical, ethnic, and cultural consciousness indicates that although the political unity of the region in the post-colonial era has so far been elusive, the sense of co-identity remains a sufficiently significant issue to be pondered. Many of these themes have also been discussed in numerous Indonesia–Malaysia public forums, including the Meeting of the Malay World Conference, the Malindo (Malaysia–Indonesia) Youth Forum, and the Indonesia–Malaysia Conference.

Be that as it may, it is the political and decision-making elite that is the central focus of this study, for in the context of Indonesia and Malaysia it is through them that perceptions and interpretations are given expression in policy. Leaders of Indonesia and Malaysia, as this study will go on to show, have persistently looked to kinship for meaning and intelligibility as they grappled with issues in relations. This has been most pronounced in the regular assertion of *pribumi* (indigenous) identity against Chinese minorities, which illuminates the exclusivity of kin-based relations. These concerns seemed to be implicitly written into former Indonesian President Abdurrahman Wahid's diatribe against Chinese-dominated Singapore for the latter's apparently insolent attitude towards the 'Malay' community.[72] While Wahid's evocation of ethnic solidarity between Indonesia and Malaysia may be tenuous from an anthropological point of view (as Chapter 2 will show), what remains valid is the sub-text of his statement, which clearly implicates Chinese communities (in this case Singapore) as a viable 'other' against which Indonesia–Malaysia brotherhood can be reinforced. Some time later, the rhetorical device of kinship was evoked again when an Indonesian minister called on Malaysian authorities to take in greater numbers of Indonesian labourers by impressing upon them that 'after all, Indonesia and Malaysia are part of the Malay Archipelago and are one big family'.[73] The sense that Indonesia–Malaysia relations have an immutable base in the form of blood brotherhood can be summarized in the following comment by former Malaysian deputy Prime Minister and Foreign Minister Ghazali Shafie made at the Third Indonesia–Malaysia Colloquium held in Bali in December 1992:

> What I am driving at is that the relationship between the peoples of Indonesia and Malaysia goes back to the age of *Rumpun Melayu*. It was colonialism of the West which divided the Malay world and now perforce we are discussing in Bali about the relationship between two peoples, the people of which belong to the same cluster like bamboos with each tree growing on its own or '*Hidup Berkampung*' that is in togetherness.[74]

Alluding to the special nature of Indonesia–Malaysia relations, the Malaysian Foreign Minister, Abdullah Badawi, contended at the Second Malaysia–Indonesia Conference, held in 1990, that

> The five principles of peaceful co-existence which order relations between the family of nations alone *should not be* what relations between two countries such as Malaysia and Indonesia are founded upon. If relations between Malaysia and Indonesia are pegged at mere peaceful co-existence, then we pitch our relationship *on the lowest possible note in the relations between two nations*. Our ties would be no better, no worse than our ties with our most distant friends. *What we strive for and what we already have to a considerable degree, is relations at the fullest, relations suffused with maximum understanding, mutual empathy and reciprocal concern.*[75]

Implicit in Abdullah's statement is his invocation of what John Baylis describes as the 'Evangelical' approach to international relations, where the Indonesia–Malaysia relationship is again portrayed as a fraternal association of peoples whose common culture, language, and religion 'set them apart from "normal" relations between states in the international system'.[76] This implies the hope that kinship affinity can still take on greater prominence in relations even after decades (or even centuries, if one considers pre-colonial relations) of bilateral rivalry. Equally striking was the suggestion by Yang Razali Kassim, a prominent commentator on Indo-Malaysian affairs, that 'the Malaysian respect for Indonesia as the Big Brother, whatever the Big Brother's shortcomings may be, continues unabated. On the other hand, Indonesia's concern for Malaysia's well being continues to underpin ties with Kuala Lumpur.'[77] As will become evident by the end of this study, such intimations were modelled along a tradition of political discourse rendered on the basis of 'blood brotherhood', embodied in the local concept of *rumpun* (racial stock) and repetitively employed by leaders to romanticize the foundation of the 'special relationship' between these two states in kinship terms.

Notwithstanding the regular references made by political leaders both sides of the Melaka Straits to conceptions of *serumpun* or 'blood brotherhood' as a source for harmony and cohesion, the problem posed for students of the international politics of the Indo-Malay world is to what extent conceptions of kinship premised on race, culture, and common history translate into organizing principles for bilateral relations. Indeed, how far can the analogy be pushed, given that it is quite obvious that the track record of Indonesia–Malaysia ties reflect less harmonious relations than considerations of 'blood brotherhood' might suggest? It is against this background that the study suggests two considerations that need to be taken into account in the study of this phenomenon.

First, before assessing its political impact, the notion of Indo-Malay kinship has to be studied closely from a historical and anthropological perspective. A careful study into the terms of reference adopted by Indonesian and Malaysian champions of kinship is necessary in order to understand the strengths and limitations of the concept as a tool for political mobilization. For example, there will be a need to draw distinctions between the concepts of race and ethnicity, and to examine how these ideas, introduced via European colonialism, are understood and appropriated by the chief nationalist ideologues and local historians in the Indo-Malay Archipelago. Of particular importance is the need to study the historical contexts that frame Indo-Malay understandings of these concepts and categories. How, for example, does one reconcile the logic of inclusivity proposed by ideologues such as Burhanuddin Al-Helmy and Muhammad Yamin, two of the chief proponents of Indo-Malay ethnic fraternity, with the historical tensions between the Javanese, the dominant ethnic group in the Indonesian archipelago, and their neighbours, in particular the Malays and Minangkabau, who form the bulk of the Malay population in Malaysia today? While some might suggest that such ethno-cultural considerations are peripheral, it is argued here that they are in fact integral to the study of politics in the Indo-Malay world, and must most certainly be taken into account in Indonesia–Malaysia relations.[78]

Indeed, as the study will later show, much of this historical tension continues to play itself out in contemporary relations.

Second, the influence of the kinship factor must also be understood in the context through which it derives its political relevance – that is, nationalism in the Indo-Malay world. Indeed, as the above analysis has already highlighted, kinship and nationalism cannot be divorced in the study of the international politics of the Indo-Malay world. Nationalism comes to the fore in Indonesia–Malaysia relations because it is precisely through the experience of national self-determination that Indonesia and Malaysia shared initial motivations and objectives, and hence fostered fraternal association. It is also the case that as nationalism progressed, the two countries subsequently embarked on differing paths to nationhood precisely as a result of contested interpretations of race, ethnicity, and history that defined how the political leadership in the two states viewed their counterparts in terms of the norms of expectations and obligations they developed as kin states in the post-colonial era; and these norms of expectations and obligations have been tied intimately to notions of sovereignty, primacy, and deference.

Seeing that a strong kinship bond was fostered around the shared anti-colonial struggle of two peoples whose respective nationalist histories attempted to paint the Indo-Malay world (accurately or otherwise) as a contiguous social-cultural unit, one of the key obligations that defined this relationship, especially in the immediate post-colonial era, was, logically, unyielding support from each for the other's sovereignty and territorial integrity. Likewise, given that Indonesia and Malaysia fell into the category of Third World states whose independence was often contested from within as well as outside the territorial state in the early years of independence, expectations that both would reaffirm the sovereignty of the other in times of crisis was a definitive term to their relations. Summarizing the importance of expectations and obligations as the definitive marker and expression of Indo-Malaysian fraternity, a former Malaysian Ambassador to Indonesia, Abdullah Zawawi, observed that the dilemma for bilateral relations was precisely that 'much is expected from it – each harbouring hopes that the other could be sympathetic because of the common heritage – more than we expect from others, including our immediate neighbours and friends'.[79]

Dovetailing into this framework lay the matter of deference and primacy. Scholars of Indonesian politics have identified Jakarta's 'proprietary attitude' of 'regional entitlement', born of the Indonesian experience of national self-determination, as a fundamental encapsulation of Indonesian views of its position in the region.[80] This sense of entitlement has derived largely from a Javanese worldview, one that can be traced to the pre-colonial era, when Java sought to dominate the international system of archipelagic Southeast Asia.[81] While the fact that Indonesia is *primus inter pares* in Southeast Asia in generally accepted in the field, there is a case to be made that this sense of primacy was particularly pronounced in relation to Malaysia. Indeed, the special attention paid by Jakarta to Malaysian acknowledgement of, and response to, its political primacy in the Indo-Malay world has become a definitive feature of bilateral relations. For example, as Chapters 3 and 4 will illustrate, Indonesia took an active interest in Malay nationalism, and this interest in Malayan affairs continued into the post-colonial period as it sought to influence the direction of Malayan foreign policy. Likewise, Malaya was constantly singled out in Indonesian quarters as a state that required 'revolutionizing', while Malayan independence, gained in cooperation with the British, was seen in Jakarta circles as 'counterfeit'.[82] Even in more recent times, anecdotal evidence suggests that former Indonesian President Suharto was particularly incensed that it was Malaysia, a state formed without national struggle, that was attempting to usurp Indonesia's rightful role as the manager of regional order and leader of the Third World. These observations will be elaborated upon later. Suffice it to say that such an attitude betrayed the sense of primacy that Indonesian, and particularly Javanese, leaders felt towards their Malaysian counterparts. Given the historical ties between the two countries, this primacy clearly translated into expectations of deference on the part of Jakarta, particularly so in the formative post-colonial years. Likewise, bilateral harmony during these early periods depended on whether Malaya acknowledged Indonesian primacy. Once again, it is not surprising here that in terms of relations with Indonesia, the thinking of many leaders in Kuala Lumpur has been framed in response to the preponderance of Javanese influence in Jakarta circles. Equally important, however, was how Indonesia responded to Malaysian expectations of respect for its sovereignty, or the extent to which Jakarta desired to influence decision-making in Kuala Lumpur. To that effect, events such as *Konfrontasi* would have had a severe impact on Malaysian perceptions of the terms of kin affiliation with Indonesia. In the same vein, Kuala Lumpur's attempts to assume a position of political consequence during the administration of the Malaysian nationalist Mahathir Mohamad threatened Indonesia's long-standing belief, born of its revolutionary experience and process of national self-determination, which continues to inform Jakarta's view of its relations with the surrounding geopolitical environment, in its political primacy in the Indo-Malay world, if not the entire region of Southeast Asia.

The politicization of kinship in Indonesia–Malaysia relations, then, appears to be riddled with ambiguities in terms of its expression. Theoretically speaking, 'pseudo' and 'fictive' notions of kinship appear to bind the two in a kin-state relationship. Be that as it may, the proximity of their ties has also generated much tension. The premises of this kin rivalry, this study suggests, can first be traced to the historically contested interpretations and perceptions of the frames of references for Indo-Malay kinship.

2 Kinship and Indo-Malay historiography

Kinship in Indonesia–Malaysia relations tends to be located, accurately or otherwise, in the notion of Malay-Muslim blood brotherhood often espoused by political leaders and emphasized to a certain extent in scholarship on the Indo-Malay Archipelago. Conceptualizing affinity between Indonesia and Malaysia, however, is a rather more delicate task than at first appears, and academic discussions arguably give rise to more controversies than unanimity of opinion. While there is little doubt that ethnocultural considerations have an impact on the conduct of politics, the interface between the two will nevertheless have to be carefully drawn out from a complex conceptual maze. This is especially so with regard to the subject matter at hand, for the cultural and ethnic correspondence that some would suggest defines Indo-Malay identity obtains alongside very diverse and complex social-political phenomena that temper not only the contiguous identity of the Indo-Malay world, but the very existence of Indonesia and Malaysia as unitary nation-states in their own right. Certainly, scholars are well aware that the 'national' identities upon which these modern states are built are in fact agglomerations of diverse ethnic, religious, and linguistic groupings, each with its own particularistic character and history.[1] It is bearing these considerations in mind that this chapter sets forth to explore the historiography of kinship in the Indo-Malay world. This chapter sets out the premises not only for the grounds upon which the kinship factor between Indonesia and Malaysia can be and has been built by its proponents, but also for the conceptual and practical problems one encounters in the process of defining the kinship factor in Indo-Malay history.

Kinship and the pre-colonial regional system

Much of the thinking about kinship systems in Indo-Malay historiography arises from the historical record of interaction and intermarriage that has defined the identity of this region, and that has been transcribed in historical texts such as *Tuhfat al-Nafis* or *Sejarah Melayu dan Bugis* (History of the Malays and Bugis), where the main theme is the relationship between the Malay rulers of Riau, Johor, and Trengganu with the Siak (in Sumatra) and Bugis.[2] The writers of the text also focused on the matter of ethnic origin and relations in light of a vast network of intermarriages linking Riau-Johor, Kedah, Perak, Selangor, Pahang, and Terengganu on the peninsula, and the east and west coasts of Sumatra and Kalimantan respectively.[3] Similar tales of co-identification resulting from intermarriages, such as that between Sultan Mansur Shah of Srivijaya and the Princess Radin Galah Chandra Kirana of Majapahit, can be found in the *Sejarah Melayu* (Malay Annals).[4] Intermarriages paved the way for genealogical tracing of the most rudimentary sources of kinship: common ancestry. Indeed, right up until the eve of the Pacific War, intermarriages between Malay and Sumatran royal families remained a principal feature of the socio-political landscape in the Indo-Malay world, leading to close alliances between the ruling elites of British Malaya and Sumatra respectively.

Intermarriage and migration also brought into being large trading states and kingdoms that at their peak of power encompassed within their spheres of influence territories of present-day Malaysia and Indonesia, and where power and influence over the Indo-Malay world ebbed and flowed through pre-colonial history. Among the more prominent of these kingdoms was the Srivijaya Empire, which lasted approximately from the seventh to the thirteenth century. With its capital settled in Palembang in Sumatra, the influence of the Srivijayan Empire is suspected to have spread throughout Sumatra and the west coast of the Malay Peninsula up towards the Isthmus of Kra.[5] At times, its influence appeared to extend to the island of Java as well.[6]

The existence of Srivijaya in the history of archipelagic Southeast Asia intersected with the land-based Javanese kingdom of Majapahit (*c.*1293–1520).[7] At the height of its power, the physical boundaries of the Majapahit Kingdom may have been roughly coterminous with much, though not all, of modern Indonesia. Certain historical records suggest that at some time or other, Majapahit also exerted a measure of influence over principalities on the Malay Peninsula, though in truth the extent of its influence remains an issue of scholarly debate.[8]

The decline of Majapahit coincided with the emergence of another centre of power in the Indo-Malay world, located in Melaka.[9] The Melaka Sultanate was centred along the southwestern coast of the Malay Peninsula. While there remains disagreement among historians as to the extent to which Melaka can be considered a direct successor to the Srivijayan Empire, what is certain is its strong Sumatran roots.[10] The similarities in political and economic organization, as well as security outlook, of the kingdoms have been illuminated by Rosemary Brissenden:

> We know that the political and defence tasks, as well as the need to
> cope with a large international and itinerant sector of the population

which formed the basis of its economy had been much the same in Srivijaya as they were in Malacca [Melaka]. Thus it does not seem entirely outrageous to take the organization of political and economic life in Malacca as a reflection in some senses at least of the structure of trading kingdoms in Indonesia.[11]

With the advent of Portuguese colonialism, the Melaka Sultanate declined in the early sixteenth century, and the indigenous centre of power shifted to the kingdoms of Aceh, Johor, and Riau. Some scholars have gone so far as to suggest that the Malay Peninsula and Sumatra enjoyed a degree of interaction and integration within the spheres of these early kingdoms to the extent that Srivijaya's traditions continued in an almost unbroken line to Melaka, Johor, and Riau.[12]

These kingdoms and empires formed the pivot to a pre-colonial international system that was premised on trade, war, migration, and marriage. It was such interaction that provided a historical basis to the perception that many of inhabitants of the contemporary Indo-Malay world in fact come from the same ancestry, thus justifying the term *rumpun* that is used in local discourse to refer to the fraternal peoples of Indonesia and Malaysia.[13]

Concepts of community and statehood

While differences obviously existed across the social-political structures of these kingdoms, one thread of similarity can be found in shared understandings of statecraft and concepts of community.[14] As but one example, conceptions of the role and status of the aristocracy in traditional Malay and Indonesian societies up to the end of the Second World War were by and large similar.[15] The concept of *kerajaan* (kingdom) stood as the main political institution throughout much of the history of Sumatra and the peninsula, while in the Javanese inland agrarian kingdoms (*kraton*), the *Negara* (State) took on similar precedence.[16] Within this structure, 'the pre-eminent figure ... was the Sultan, whose right to the throne was primarily based on his unbroken descent from a glorious ancestor'.[17] So too, one finds in traditional forms of authority and dogma, village structures and decision-making procedures many similarities that resulted from centuries of interchange and integration.[18] An indication of this can be found in the shared ascription to the concepts of *musyawarah* and *muafakat* (consultation and consensus) that underpinned decision-making in the traditional social-political structure of the village.[19] Even the *adat* (customary law) inherited from pre-Islamic Hindu cultural reference was to a great degree shared by Malay and certain Indonesian communities, to the extent that some have suggested that what is called Malay *adat* is essentially Indonesian in origin.[20] In the same way, shared village culture carried with it a sense of obligation, where 'in Malay villages, it is often difficult in practice to separate the principles of kinship and neighbourhood for the two may coincide. . . . Neighbours should be the first to render assistance in times of need.'[21]

It is important to register here that concepts of statehood that defined the character of these pre-colonial kingdoms differed substantially from the terrestrial state in Western scholarship. Traditional states in the Indo-Malay world did not have clearly defined boundaries. They were amorphous in character and based on loyalty to the person of the ruler (known in indigenous terms as *Raja* or *Sultan*);[22] while the size and influence of kingdoms were determined by the number of people owing allegiance to a ruler at any given time as well as the amount of trade that passed through the kingdom.[23] Jan Christie notes in her study of the Melaka Sultanate, for example, that Malay rulers 'conceived of their states more in terms of populace and patron–client relationships than in terms of bounded territory'.[24] To this can be added Wolters's observation that 'the territorial scale of a political system is certainly not the correct measurement for describing and defining it. Instead, we should think of sets of socially-definable loyalties that could be mobilized for common enterprises.'[25] It was primarily trade, not land, that provided the resources by which the elites in the Indo-Malay world increased their following and expanded the realm. Accordingly, trade-centred rivalry was an important feature of pre-modern politics in the region. Marriage also played an important role in determining the power and influence of these trading kingdoms. Typically, the elites of a particular port would, upon subduing its rival, marry into the ruling families there. In this manner the kingdoms in the Indo-Malay world came to be linked to each other through genealogical lines and marriage ties as well, bringing into existence kingdoms in Kedah, Malacca, Palembang, Brunei, Sulu, Aceh, and Sulawesi from the tenth to the fifteenth century.[26]

The role of these kingdoms in political myth-making in contemporary Indonesia and Malaysia is worthy of note, as is the sense of affiliation among the Indonesian and Malay peoples deriving from popular histories. This was registered by Mackie, who observed that 'pride in the greatness of ancient Malay–Indonesian kingdoms is taught in the classrooms of both nations without much concern about the boundaries created by the colonial powers'.[27] Yet while their legacy has been a welcome tool for political mobilization, it is precisely the amorphous character of these kingdoms that renders their memory impractical for modern state-building. In no way are modern Indonesia and Malaysia coterminous with the kingdoms of the pre-colonial era. This, as the present study will endeavour to show, was a problem pan-Malay nationalists paid little attention to in their enthusiasm to conjure up a glorious history to justify their anti-colonial project, and one that consequently resulted in greater problems in their attempt to frame their relations in terms of kinship.

Common identity was also reinforced in the course of interaction with external forces. The pre-colonial Indo-Malay world was not a hermetically sealed one, pried open only with the advent of colonialism. It has already been noted that relations had long been established between the various islands within the Indo-Malay Archipelago, laying the grounds for inter-action and exchange. Beyond that, external influences also came in the form of Indian, Chinese, Arabic, and Japanese trading activity. Historical records indicate the existence of early trading networks that not only linked the peninsular and archipelagic worlds together, but also linked them to more complex international networks stretching to Africa, India, and China. Such international trading links and interaction with other cultures and peoples also played an important role in reinforcing the sense of kinship and shared identity among the people of the Indo-Malay Archipelago by augmenting affinity in relation to foreign cultures, identities, and language.

Constructing relatedness: language and religion

Two common threads established during this pre-colonial era that had the potential to act as agents for the construction of kin affinity and identity were language and religion.[28]

Malay was originally spoken as a mother tongue only in parts of Sumatra, Riau, the Malay Peninsula, and perhaps parts of the Philippines. However, it received a stimulus when Melaka became the centre for trade in archipelagic Southeast Asia in the late fifteenth century. Subsequently, many of the various ethnic groups in the Indo-Malay Archipelago adopted one essential lingua franca to facilitate their integration into the regional network built around Melaka, giving rise to the spread of the Malayo-Polynesian language and its cognate derivatives from the Austronesian language family throughout the peninsula and archipelago with trade.[29] Language, then, became the first channel that gave the Indo-Malay world a semblance of unity.[30] Be that as it may, there is a need also to recognize that this semblance of unity derived from linguistic congruence was itself a product of the creation of a linguistically consistent form of Malay from Malayo-Polynesian and its cognate derivatives by the Dutch and British on the basis of their reading of indigenous texts such as *Sejarah Melayu*, and their understanding of the spoken language in Riau and Johor, which they viewed as the centre of the 'Malay world'. In the words of Henk Maier:

> This newly created form of Malay, primarily laid down in the written form of grammars and textbooks, was then provided with the notion of 'good' Malay and then with the notion of 'real Malay'. Thus, a novel form was turned into a norm. It was Malay that was meant to serve as an effective communication as well as a careful description of the world.[31]

Contested though the historiography of the unity of the Malay language may be, it was not without political import. It is significant that Malay emerged as the national language of both Malaysia, as *Bahasa Melayu*, and Indonesia, in the form of *Bahasa Indonesia*. The importance of the Malay language as a bonding agent for Indonesia and Malaysia was given greater impetus when it was adopted as the language of the nationalist movement at the 1928 Second Indonesian Youth Congress in Indonesia (known as the Bandung Declaration). No doubt the decision to choose Malay over Javanese as the national language of Indonesia was a tactical one, the underlying objective of which was to quell suspicions of Javanese dominance.[32] After all, compared to the feudalistic roots of Javanese, the Malay language was viewed as a 'democratic language'.[33] Consequently, the Malay language provided a channel through which the sense of kinship affinity could be better communicated throughout the Malay-speaking Indo-Malay world.[34]

After independence, the issue of orchestrating a shared spelling system between Malay and Indonesian gained prominence in cultural relations when efforts were made to bridge differences resulting from different transliterations of the Malay script under colonialism. The persistence of language as an avenue of affiliation today is exemplified in the work of MABBIM (*Majlis Bahasa Brunei, Indonesia dan Malaysia*, the Brunei–Indonesia–Malaysia Language Council). Established in 1972 as part of the resurgence of cultural exchange resulting from the termination of *Konfrontasi*, MABBIM has continued to pursue the unity of the two languages in order to foster a closer understanding of the historical and cultural similarities that bind their societies.[35] At another level, the influential role that the Malay language played in the building of identity in the Indo-Malay world was further attested to by its position as a literary and philosophical language of Islam.[36]

As with language, religion, in this case Islam, forms a pillar for the social-cultural construction of relatedness.[37] One justification for this logic lies in the fact that those who claim to adhere to Islam are considered part of the *Ummah* or brotherhood. More specific to the Indo-Malay Archipelago, however, was the fact that Islam provided a cultural avenue through which affiliation could be built, whereby the Indo-Malay Archipelago can be broadly viewed as a single religious entity.[38]

Islam is generally acknowledged to have been introduced into the region by Muslim traders from India around the thirteenth century, though Muslim traders from the Middle East had by then already begun converting pockets of local communities. It was with the aid of the Malay language that Islam spread throughout this region, and in so doing consolidated the Muslim worldview through the medium of Islamic philosophical literature published in the Malay language. In that sense, the fact that an archipelago-wide lingua franca already existed facilitated the spread of Islam throughout the Indo-Malay world.

There have been some distinctive characteristics about the Islamization of the Indo-Malay Archipelago that distinguished it from that of other regions such as the Middle East and South Asia. One such distinction was the nature of Islam's arrival in the region: Islam came not by force, but through trade. Historical records suggest that trading communities along the coastal areas of the Indo-Malay Archipelago were the sites of the first conversions, with Aceh in North Sumatra and Melaka along the south-western coast of the Malay Peninsula seen as the closest geographical points of Southeast Asia to the original locale of Islamic penetration. Because it was not a conquering force, Islamic theology was brought mainly by religious teachers and advisers; and because it was a movement spread through trade and not war, the introduction of Islam in effect created an indigenous Muslim network across the archipelago.

While the introduction of Islam into the region has been attributed to Indian Muslim traders, Malay scholars have traced the spread of the religion to the Melaka Sultanate.[39] The expansion of Melaka's sphere of influence, they suggest, occurred simultaneously with the court's conversion to Islam.[40] This led simultaneously to the Islamization of vassal states of the Sultanate. While the extent of Melaka's role in transmitting this new religion throughout the archipelago remains debatable, there is a consensus that trade was a key channel through which Islam was spread.[41] In time, Islamic schools were established throughout the Indo-Malay world, and the instruction of Islamic theology became an activity that invited cross-strait interaction and exchanges between Muslim scholars and teachers, particularly between Sumatra, Java, and the peninsula. Needless to say, these channels remain active today.[42] The period between the 1920s and 1950s, notable for the emergence of modernist and political Islam in the region, witnessed the bulk of Malay religious students being sent to Indonesian (mostly Sumatran but Javanese as well) *pesantren* and *madrasah*,[43] these being respectively Javanese Islamic institutions and modernist Islamic schools.

Notwithstanding the general impact that Islam has had on the social and political environment in the Indo-Malay Archipelago, its influence was neither uniform in its acceptance nor adaptation. To be sure, there was great variety in the way Islam was integrated into everyday political and social life in different parts of the Indo-Malay world.[44] Much of this variation has its roots in the porous and shifting local cultures of the region, which adapted Islamic philosophy to traditional practices. Differences emerged as to the precise status and practice of Islam in these societies. In Java, Western anthropologists have noted two distinct streams of Islam based on the adherence to Islamic strictures and the practice of Muslim lifestyles: the more nominal *Abangan*, which incorporated elements of Buddhism, Hinduism, and animism, and the orthodox *Santri* (primarily Javanese).[45] No such dichotomy has been identified in Malaysia, though some would suggest that Islam is generally more strictly adhered to in the northern Malay states. The difference in interpretation and acceptance of Islam in Indonesia was explained by Geertz as being a result of Islam's movement into what he called 'one of Asia's greatest political, aesthetic, religious and social creations, the Hindu–Buddhist Javanese state'.[46] Koentjaraningrat makes the further distinction between *Agama Jawi* (Javanese religion) and *Agama Islam Santri* (Islam of the religious people), as if Java possessed a religious identity of its own.[47] There are other scholars, however, who argue that the *Abangan–Santri* divide has become a rather tenuous characterization of Islam on Java. These scholars in fact have noticed a shift towards greater Islamic consciousness among the Indonesian population in general.[48] Further to that, differences in how Islam was administered by the British in Malaya, who refrained from direct involvement in religious matters, and the Dutch in the East Indies, who deliberately sought to influence the development of Islam, contributed to the convolutions beneath the façade of religious unity.[49]

Historically, strong precedence for the conception of kinship along religious lines can be found in indigenous historical texts such as the *Hikayat Merong Mahawangsa*, where the relationship between Kedah in the peninsula and Aceh in Northern Sumatra is discussed from the perspective of Islam (and in opposition to Siam). More recently too, as later chapters will illuminate, the Islamic factor provided a pivotal link for the nationalisms of Malaysia and Indonesia, even as both subsequently emerged as secular nation-states.[50] Yet while it can certainly be said that at an abstract level, Islam can prove a viable channel of kinship for the Indo-Malay Archipelago by virtue of its broad appeal and acceptance in the region, taking the above observations into consideration one must also be sensitive to the nuanced differences in the practice of Islam throughout the Indo-Malay Archipelago before making conclusions as to its effectiveness as a bonding agent towards common identity.

Rivalry and discord in the Indo-Malay world

Avenues of affinity did not eliminate schisms in the pre-colonial Indo-Malay Archipelago. Indeed, the theme of rivalry left as indelible a mark on the politics of the region as did perceptions of affinity.

That rivalry was a distinct feature of the pre-colonial kinship-based regional system stems from the fact that the history of the region was not a unilineal progression from kingdom to kingdom, empire to empire. Kingdoms and empires coexisted at various points, and each possessed different impressions of the contiguity of the Indo-Malay Archipelago that they sought to control.[51] As a noted scholar of Indonesia ventured:

> These continuities were so widely accepted that when Malay–Indonesian kingdoms went to war or made peace, they did it with their fellows within this vast archipelagic community. The Sultans of what is

now Malaysia rarely battled the rulers of Siam or Burma. Rather, their alliances and conflicts were with peoples from Aceh to east Indonesia. The Bugis and Makasarese of Sulawesi traded widely in Southeast Asia, but their political and trade heartland was the Malay–Indonesian archipelago. When a Javanese king had grand imperial pretensions, it was to other states in the archipelago that he turned for tokens of obeisance – which they, under most circumstances, refused to give.[52]

From this, one could certainly argue that a source of this historical tension seemed to stem from the impetus of geopolitics. The crossing of paths of the Srivijaya and Majapahit kingdoms, two historical centres of power in maritime Southeast Asia, appears to have resulted in the sort of power struggle that has defined international relations through the centuries. A scholar has described the struggle as follows:

> Their [Malay coastal states] activities in guarding the sea in pursuit of their economic interests and their military activities to safeguard these interests led to conflicts between the Javanese, based in Java, and Malays based in Srivijaya. Struggles for rights of passage at sea frequently occurred, which in turn led to political and cultural rivalry.[53]

After the demise of the Melaka entrepôt, fragmented rivalries emerged as Aceh, Johor, Riau, and the Bugis wrestled for prominence in the Indo-Malay world. Thus, considerations of kinship in the Indo-Malay world also need to take into account centuries of rivalry and wars between the various kingdoms and principalities within it.

A recurring theme that has imposed itself on the historiography of the Indo-Malay Archipelago has been conflict born of the apprehension of peoples in the region concerning Javanese domination.[54] This was best exemplified by the struggles of the Srivijaya and Melaka kingdoms against their Java-based nemeses.[55] These struggles were of such severity that the downfall of Srivijaya has been traced to the invasion of Majapahit under the Javanese king Kertanegara in 1275.[56] Indeed, the sub-topic of wars between Java and Sumatra has been one of interest to a handful of historians of the region.[57] This apprehension felt outside Java towards Javanese domination has been documented in Malay records such as *Hikayat Hang Tuah*, *Hikayat Raja Pasai*, and *Sejarah Melayu*, where the central theme has been the relationship between the Minangkabau and Malays, often portrayed as underdogs against the hegemonic tendencies of the Javanese.[58] For example, in the *Hikayat Hang Tuah*, a great part of the text revolved around fierce rivalry between the courts of Melaka and Majapahit, expressed through the exploits of the Malay hero, Hang Tuah, against the Javanese.[59] It has also been recorded how the Javanese were often portrayed as a self-aggrandizing people proud of their 'refined' culture, whereas the Malay language was depicted as the crude and crass language of Java (compared to the more 'cultured' Javanese language).[60] The presence of Javanese passages and reference to Javanese that can be found in the *Sejarah Melayu* further suggests Javanese cultural influence.[61]

Many other instances can be found to illustrate how the Majapahit court in Java sought to exercise influence over the Malay principalities. As but one example, it has been recorded how in 1378, the ruler of Majapahit, in response to a move by the Jambi local rulers (in Sumatra) to establish independent relations with the Ming court, waylaid and murdered the Chinese envoys sent to the archipelago.[62] There is also the famous story of the Javanese–Minangkabau bullfight found in the *Hikayat Raja Pasai*, where through their characteristic wit the Minangkabau managed to successfully repel a Javanese attempt to conquer their land. While the case can be made that many of the stories and events are Malay folklore, what stands out is the acute concern for excessive Javanese influence within the Indo-Malay world. Describing in later years this recurrent sentiment in the context of pan-Malay nationalism and the revival of past kingdoms, Kwa observed:

> To the Javanese with his strong ethnocentric perspective of history ... Majapahit is the first historic 'Indonesian unitary state', a symbol of Indonesian political grandeur and cultural renaissance. But to other Indonesians all this stinks of a political and cultural imperialism, of a Javanese domination of the Nusantara ... [which] in old Javanese proper, refers to the outer islands, foreign countries, as viewed from Java.[63]

Extrapolating from this, it will be demonstrated in the following chapter how these historical misgivings haunted the pan-nationalist movements that agitated for *Indonesia Raya* and *Melayu Raya*.

Colonialism

The preceding discussion has contextualized the basis of the kinship factor as a function of historical intersection and the emergence of language and religion as bonding agents. These factors took on greater significance with the imposition of imperialist intent, and it was under the shadow of colonialism, and its large-scale introduction of alien (most notably Chinese) communities as a consequence of the expansion of the colonial economic enterprise, that the search for common identity began in earnest in the Indo-Malay world. Ironically, this search for common identity would be motivated by an alien colonial ideology: nationalism.

Colonialism was to have a paradoxical impact on the search for common identity. At one level the imposition of colonial administration divided the Indo-Malay Archipelago and brought into being the terrestrial entities of Indonesia and Malaysia. Yet it was also colonialism that generated abstract notions of Indo-Malay identity. Indeed, the most striking, if accidental, contribution of colonialism was the introduction of the erstwhile foreign concept of nationalism, and with it notions of race and ethnicity.

To certain degrees, Indonesia and Malaysia exist today as independent states whose territorial configurations resulted from the imperialist exercise of cartography and diplomacy.[64] However convincing the sense of pre-colonial relatedness was as a result of the influences and interactions discussed earlier, the advent of colonialism cemented the formerly fluid terrestrial boundaries of the Indo-Malay Archipelago. While the process of colonialism is too complicated to be dealt with at any length here, the Anglo-Dutch Treaty cannot pass unmentioned. Signed in London in 1824, the treaty was both a reflection of European politics and a culmination of colonial politics and competition over spheres of influence in the Indo-Malay Archipelago between Britain and the Netherlands. By the beginning of the nineteenth century, the Dutch had more or less established control over Java, and were expanding their influence throughout the vast Indonesian Archipelago. Britain, on the other hand, had only just arrived in the region.[65] This meant that the Netherlands was the preponderant power in so far as Western influence over, and control of, archipelagic Southeast Asia were concerned. That notwithstanding, Britain's increasing trade and economic activity in Southeast Asia, coupled with a concern for the possibility of French expansion into the archipelago, compelled London to re-assess its interests in the region. This eventually led to the founding of a free port in Singapore, which lay at the foot of the Malay Peninsula, in 1819. The founding of Singapore upset the delicate commercial balance that existed between the British and the Dutch. The presence of this British-controlled free port meant that trade flow from the Indian Ocean and South China Sea was gradually being diverted away from the Dutch port of Batavia in Java to Singapore, and this caused the Dutch much anxiety.

The result of this was the signing of the Anglo-Dutch Treaty in 1824, which arbitrarily demarcated British and Dutch spheres of influence. Yet the treaty did not merely lay the basis for the contemporary boundaries of Indonesia and Malaysia. By artificially fracturing the Indo-Malay Archipelago, it transformed the course of history.[66] The terms of the Anglo-Dutch Treaty saw Melaka and other bases ceded by the Dutch to the British, thus consolidating British control over the peninsula and the Melaka Straits. In return, Britain surrendered control of its East Indies possession at Bencoolen to the Dutch, and in so doing cemented Dutch influence over the entire East Indies Archipelago. Remarkably, then, through this act of colonial diplomacy the territorial forms of modern Malaysia and Indonesia came into being. The legacy of this 'accidental intervention' has been summarized as such:

At the most obvious level, the division of the Malay world down the Melaka Straits laid the basis for the contemporary boundary between Indonesia and Malaysia. But there were other even more far-reaching ramifications, as centuries of history were set aside without a qualm.... Ties between individuals and communities remained close but the division into 'Dutch' and 'British' spheres meant that the easy movement of Melayu leadership back and forth between the Peninsula and the east coast of Sumatra was now a thing of the past. What were effectively political divisions also affected academic scholarship as a new generation of British 'orientalists' concentrated on collecting and compiling Malay texts associated with the peninsula, leaving the study of Malay culture in Sumatra and southwest and southeast Borneo to their Dutch counterparts. But the latter, with some notable exceptions, were not drawn to the study of coastal Malays. In Sumatra their descriptions of 'Minangkabau' or 'Aceh' tended to accentuate differences rather than similarities with Melayu traditions.[67]

Semenanjung Melayu: the bridging of identities

From an anthropological perspective, the strongest case for this perception that colonialism fragmented a contiguous entity and identity stems from the link between the island of Sumatra and the Malay Peninsula, which in effect sets the context for this idea of Indo-Malay kinship.[68] Indeed, Sumatra had long been considered an integral part of *Semenanjung Melayu* (the Malay Peninsula), conceived as a cultural, not political, entity.

Genealogy has long influenced ties between the peninsula and Sumatra, and the great majority of the Malays in the peninsula are ethnographically almost indistinguishable from those of northeastern Sumatra, because most Malays are descendants of Minangkabau and Acehnese migrants. These ties have roots traceable to the early coastal kingdoms that ruled the archipelagic waters of the region.[69] Consequently, ties of blood obtained alongside strong ethnic and cultural links to define the belt that ran across the Melaka Straits and that emphasized kinship as an organizing principle for relations between the polities along the west coast of the Malay Peninsula and the eastern principalities of Sumatra. These ties were strengthened by the extensive religious and trading links that were established across the archipelago, and augmented by the centripetal forces of large kingdoms such as Srivijaya and Melaka. This far-flung Malay political culture was reinforced by the profession of Islam, a widely circulating Malay-language literature, subscription to a similar *adat*, loyalty to the *kerajaan*, and frequent intermarriage across the seas.[70] In parts of the peninsula (particularly in Negri Sembilan), Malays are still proud of their origins in the Sumatran district of Minangkabau, which is regarded locally as 'the cradle of the Malay race'.[71] In key Malay historical classics the description 'Malay' is closely linked to Sumatra.[72] And, of course, a fundamental feature of peninsula–Sumatra kinship was built around a shared aversion for Javanese dominance. This was particularly so during the pre-Islamic era, but has also carried on into more contemporary times.

Until the advent of the Indonesian revolution of 1945–1949, relations between the sultanates of the peninsula and those of Sumatra were extremely close. Such was the early Indonesian central government's concern for the proximity between Malays in the peninsula and their cousins in Sumatra that former Vice-President Mohammad Hatta once intimated to Tunku Abdul Rahman that Indonesians 'were becoming very afraid of the gravitational attraction of the Federation of Malaya upon Sumatran Malays. The Sumatrans even now were beginning to dislike being called Indonesians.'[73] These concerns were aggravated by comments such as these made by the Sultan of Deli after the regional rebellion of 1957–1958: 'We Sumatrans would do better to leave the Republic altogether and join Malaya. Most of the Sultans are relatives of mine, and one really has so much more in common [than with the Javanese]).'[74] It is not surprising, hence, that during the early stages of relations Jakarta was careful not to have Sumatrans in its Kuala Lumpur embassy.[75]

Yet it is also the case that relations between Sumatra and peninsular Malaya in part set the context for the consideration of kinship affiliation between the broader entities of Indonesia and Malaysia. No doubt enthusiasm for the portrayal of kinship between Indonesia and Malaysia should not lose sight of the fact that from an ethnic perspective, the links are really between Malays and Sumatrans. But as we shall see shortly, it was precisely around this link that the inhabitants of the Indo-Malay world constructed a sense of common identity. Even the Javanese, who loathe being classified as ethnic Malay, stop short of denying kinship links with Malays owing to other factors such as myths of descent, historical memories, and elements of common culture. On that note, one finds even in the *Hikayat Hang Tuah*, well known for its anti-Java undertone, concessions that Malays of the proud kingdom Melaka were considered 'bastardised Malays, mixed with Javanese from Majapahit'.[76] Furthermore, the fact that Sumatrans had of their free choice been an integral part of the Republic of Indonesia since 1945, and Sumatran nationalists crucial to the independence struggle, lends further justification to the link between the Malay Peninsula and Indonesia. Beyond that lies the fact that, quite obviously, immigrants who originated from Indonesia did not come only from Sumatra. Broadly speaking, a substantial percentage of the Malay population, particularly in the western states of Perak, Selangor, Johor, and Negri Sembilan, are descended from Indonesians who had migrated from other parts of the archipelago. For example, beyond the link between some west-coast states such as Negri Sembilan to central Sumatra, there have been similarly close kin relations based on ethnicity and descent between the Malays in Pahang and Johor and the Bugis and Boyanese from the Celebes and the Riau islands of Indonesia. Also, Javanese people migrated in large numbers to the various states of the Malay Peninsula as a result of British colonial policy, and in so doing took on 'Malay' identities in so far as colonial census was concerned. Indeed, it was estimated by British colonial sources in 1960 that a third of the Malay population in Malaya was of Indonesian descent.[77]

Again, it was this complex web of migration that spun the kin-based network linking the population of the peninsula with their places and cultures of origin across the Indonesian Archipelago and facilitated the perception and interpretation of kinship based not merely on bloodlines and descent, but on the social and cultural constructions of relatedness set in motion by this historical process of trade and migration, as well as the adhesive influence of language and religion. Does that mean, however, that Indonesians are racial and ethnic kin of Malays? Indeed, this question occupied much early Indonesian and Malay nationalist discourse; and it takes on greater significance when one considers the emergence and impact of pan-Malay nationalism on Indo-Malay political history. The key to understanding this important question of identity and its relation to politicized kinship can be found, once again, in the colonial legacy.

Kinship as colonial sociological enterprise

While colonialism brought into being the terrestrial entities of Indonesia and Malaya, its influence at the intellectual level was equally profound.[78] One feature of European scholarship during the colonial era was that it effected a fundamental change in the discursive domain of politics by insisting upon the identification of community in an innumerable sense. Whereas colonial administration demarcated this Indo-Malay world by drawing borders, colonial historiography did the same by categorizing its inhabitants.[79] It was colonial scholarship that established a template for the history of the Indo-Malay world. The assumptions underlying this template postulated a region that possessed a fixed territorial and ethnographic character, rather than the amorphous intermix of kingdoms and principalities that greeted it upon its arrival. Summarizing this phenomenon, Farish Noor observed:

> As the process of colonization progressed, the Malay world was opened up, studied, categorized and finally quarantined within the colonizer's order of knowledge. Raffles, Brooke, Hugronje, Swettenham, Clifford and other colonial administrators took to the task of regulating and compartmentalizing the Malay world within their own ethnocentric worldview which necessarily placed the native as well as his culture, beliefs and symbols on an inferior, subjugated register.[80]

Hence, it was colonial scholar-administrators who identified the expansive archipelago as the 'Malay Archipelago' or 'Malay world'. Pre-war Western historians suggested that the Dutch East Indies comprised 'the major part of the Malay Archipelago', which to them included the peninsula;[81] others wrote of the Dutch East Indies being part of the 'Malay world'.[82]

In so doing, colonial anthropologists and ethnographers fashioned conceptual instruments that exaggerated affinity and subsequently created dilemmas for nationalist leaders, who later appropriated their ideas in the name of pan-nationalism.[83] Colonialism was a black-and-white affair, and colonial scholars, imbued with a belief in the Enlightenment tradition of scientific classification and romanticized visions of racial and language-based nations, presented the case that the inhabitants of the 'Malay world', in so far as they shared the same basic 'proto' and 'deutero' Malay traits and features, were all essentially Malay-speaking families of the Malay–Polynesian race.[84] One such scholar argued: 'both race and Archipelago are singular in their kind'.[85] A prominent historian of Indonesia further took the view that 'in racial terms Indonesia's population is basically of Malay stock'.[86] British historians wrote of how the Dutch East Indies and the Malay Peninsula were, for all intents and purposes, both part of the 'Malay Archipelago' as well.[87] This was exemplified in the work of the prominent British colonial scholar R.O. Winstedt, who wrote of the Malay identity:

> [O]f recent years the Malay is sometimes called an Indonesian.... Less confusing is the connotation of the term Malay, which denotes more particularly the civilized Malays of Sumatra and the Malay Peninsula and in a broader sense almost all the inhabitants of the Malay Archipelago.[88]

Raffles himself intimated that 'I cannot but consider the Malayu nation as one people, speaking one language, though spread over a wide space, and preserving their character and customs, in all the maritime states lying between the Sulu Seas and Southern Oceans'.[89] Not surprisingly, indigenous works soon echoed these categorizations. Milner has observed, for instance, how in indigenous Malay writings the Javanese were described as a 'branch of the Malay race'.[90] Illustrating this strong imprint of colonial scholarship on indigenous perceptions of self in Malaya, Milner further noted that Malay renditions of history necessarily placed 'the entire investigation in the context of the expansion of Europe. The truth of its empirical context seems ultimately to be endorsed by the power of a confident imperialism.'[91] This interest given to race reflected intellectual trends in Europe, where racial interpretations of all aspects of human behaviour were expanding in popularity and racial myths became standard explanation for the establishment of nations, where 'the nation was or should be ... really a family held together by ties of blood'.[92] Hence alongside language and religion, race emerged as a category in colonial intellectual discourse to classify the inhabitants of the Indo-Malay world.

In certain respects, this use of racial yardsticks did gain credence with an indigenous audience already familiar with the fact that many among them came from the same 'stock', for reasons explicated earlier.[93] Yet one should also consider that prior to the advent of colonialism, Malays did not see a need to explicitly identify themselves as a single people or a distinctive 'race'. Such categorization was clearly of European inspiration, and it was with these impressions of the contiguity of the 'Malay Archipelago' that orientalist apologists portrayed colonialism as essentially an alien influence that dismembered two identities whose fates were indelibly intertwined:

> Drifted, perhaps, is not quite the word – were forced apart, rather, for the peninsular and Indonesian areas, each caught up in an earlier extensive Far Eastern version of the *Drang nach Osten* of the Western powers, inevitably followed the lead and consequently the divergence of their colonial patrons, the British and the Dutch.
>
> Thus, two areas which formed an ethnic and cultural whole were artificially separated more or less by historical accident, for if the British or Dutch had never come to the East they might never have been divided; or if either of the two Western powers had held influence over both areas, these might well have grown together in strength and unity in the process of forming the inevitable opposition to colonial rule and in the pursuit of ultimate independence.[94]

Others have noted further that

> The countries that go to make up Malaysia are, in fact, only part of a larger Malayo-Indonesian world, which was partitioned in very recent times ... by the forces of colonialism. The only claims that Malaysia has to being any kind of distinctive historical entity is that her territories were subject, to varying degrees, to British and not to Dutch or Spanish colonial control. It is British colonial rule during the nineteenth and twentieth centuries that constitutes the one unique element that divides the existing Malaysian territories from the remainder of the Malayo-Indonesia world.[95]

For the first time in their history, then, the territories of modern Indonesia and Malaysia were given a specific geopolitical and anthropological identity. The terrestrial area was called the 'Malay Archipelago'; and it was largely inhabited by people who were known as 'Malay'. The anthropological and historiographical basis to these Western claims remains a hotly debated topic in Southeast Asian studies, but stands beyond the scope of this study. What matters more for purposes here is the manner in which these Western perceptions in effect provided frames of reference for the construction of pan-Malay identity by local thinkers schooled in Western thought.[96] It was eventually the ideas of these indigenous architects of pan-Malay identity and those of their detractors, revolving around the notion of 'Malayness', that set the stage for the politicization of kinship in Indo-Malay history.

Constructing pan-Malay identity

The manner in which colonial ideas were internalized by indigenous historians, scholars, and nationalists was manifested in their renditions of history.[97] Robert Young has described this influence of colonial thought in the following manner: '[A]nti-colonialism was a diasporic production, a revolutionary mixture of the indigenous and the cosmopolitan, a complex constellation of situated local knowledges combined with racial, universal political principles.'[98] This dynamic characterized much of early indigenous political thought.

In Indonesian political parlance, for example, the sense of an unbroken territorial entity that existed to encompass all the various other factors of affiliation such as race, religion, and language, and that encompassed modern-day Indonesia and Malaysia, emerged in the form of the concept *Nusantara* (the Malay Archipelago), and has been expressed most poignantly in early Indonesian nationalist writings by Muhammad Yamin, Ruslan Abdulgani, and A.H. Nasution.[99] Correspondingly, Yamin and Nasution interpreted anti-colonialism as a movement towards the realization of *Indonesia Raya*, which to them was a modern territorial expression of the *Nusantara*.[100] Yamin drew precedence for *Indonesia Raya* from the Javanese kingdom of Majapahit, and it was the *Negarakertagama*, court transcripts of Majapahit, that played an important role in influencing his rendition of geopolitics.[101] According to the document, discovered by Dutch archaeologists in 1919, the influence of the Majapahit Empire had encompassed a land so vast that it included not only the entire East Indies Archipelago, but also the Malay Peninsula and Borneo.[102] The utility of such historical visions, however mythological, was not lost on nationalists such as Yamin and Sukarno, the latter applying them liberally in his political orations aimed at transforming the ancient *Nusantara* into the modern state of Indonesia.[103] While the exact expanse of Majapahit continues to be debated today, for Yamin the notion of a timeless territorial entity covering the peninsula and archipelago would certainly appear corroborated by trends in colonial scholarship on the terrestrial boundaries of the 'Malay Archipelago' at the turn of the century discussed earlier.

The centrifugal tendencies of *Nusantara* also had a secondary racial logic, however flawed, behind it. Within its boundaries, *Nusantara* was populated by peoples with similar 'Malay' and 'proto-Malay' racial traits.[104] The racial characteristic defined within this territory was emphasized by Nasution, who referred to the idea of '*Naluri Rumpun Melayu*' (Malay family or stock instinct) in explaining this affiliation between the peoples of *Nusantara*.[105] Clearly, for Yamin and Nasution, Indonesians and Malays were of the same 'racial stock'.[106]

While pan-Malayism originated from Indonesia, it had its proponents among peninsular Malays as well. Chief among them was Ibrahim Yaacob. Yaacob drew analogies between *Nusantara* and his own conception of *Dunia Melayu* (Malay world). Historically, *Dunia Melayu* has been associated with a wide range of expressions and meaning. This concept, found in traditional indigenous literary works dating to the nineteenth century, has been popularized by historians of Malaysia studying the pre-modern era of the history of the Indo-Malay Archipelago.[107] In essence, proponents of the *Dunia Melayu* concept desired to articulate a Malay world based on language and religion, populated by 'Malays' defined as an ethnic group that loosely incorporated the vast majority of Indonesians as well. What is of interest from this train of thought is how these Malay ideologues sought to include Indonesians in the ethnic category of 'Malay'.

In response to colonial attempts to create indigenous identity, Peninsular Malay writers conceptualized 'Malayness' and Malay community in a manner that has various meanings: racial, linguistic, religious, and political.[108] Without getting into the nuances of definitions of the terms 'race' and 'ethnicity', it can be established that from a racial perspective, 'Malayness' contains the same essential meanings as that which Indonesian writers have envisaged, namely, that most of the indigenous people of the peninsula share similar physical traits with their counterparts throughout the archipelago.[109] As an ethnic concept, however, 'Malayness' in Malay socio-political discourse carries much deeper connotations that did not necessarily correspond with those of their Indonesian counterparts. As Ibrahim Yaacob, a champion of pan-Malayism from the peninsula, expressed it:

> There is no other *Bangsa* in this world which has extended culture on a vast scale for the whole race at the same time and pace as the *Bangsa Melayu*. The *Bangsa Melayu* has absorbed three cultures one after another, which has fulfilled the character and soul in the descent of the *Bangsa Melayu*, that is, Hindu culture for thousands of years and for a thousand years the soul and blood of the *Bangsa Melayu* flowed with Buddhist culture. From the eleventh century A.D., Islamic culture has replaced these two cultures and flourished in splendour and glory with the light of God that is pure in the soul of the *Bangsa Melayu* as a whole.[110]

Bangsa Melayu, then, refers to the notion of 'Malay' as a culturally constructed concept.[111] This led Milner to contend that 'the problematic character of *Bangsa* (Malay identity) is its impermanence'.[112] This impermanence is embodied in the discourse on Malay identity, and exemplified in the concept *Masuk Melayu* (to become a Malay). The prominent

Malay cultural activist Zainal Abidin Ahmad has argued that to be considered a Malay, a person had essentially to originate from the Indo-Malay Archipelago, adhere to Malay *adat*, speak the Malay language, and profess Islam as their religion.[113] Among these traits, it has often been emphasized that Malay identity is most closely associated to Islam; to be Malay is, for all intents and purposes, to be Muslim.[114]

Given this variety in definitions, it is clear that the ethno-cultural boundaries of 'Malayness' are elastic.[115] Demonstrating this, one scholar has noted that 'despite the persistence of enmity among the Bugis, Malays and Minangkabaus, the distinction between their ruling classes became increasingly blurred. Migrant groups gradually adopted Malay, and Malay titles were used rather than Bugis and Minangkabau honorifics.'[116] Defined in this manner, the Malay *Bangsa* can conceivably consist of Javanese or Boyanese, Minangkabau, Bugis or Rawa. More than anything, it is this that allows the conceptualization of affinity among the people within an abstract 'Malay world', permitting the conceptual extension of the Malay identity to encompass other ethnic groups that broadly share similar histories and cultures with the Malays, including the inhabitants of present-day Indonesia.[117] Correspondingly, it was on the basis of such a definition of *Bangsa Melayu* that Ibrahim Yaacob proceeded to include 2½ million people in Malaya and 65 million in Indonesia as Malay and residents of the *Dunia Melayu*.[118] Another scholar has articulated the nuance in the following manner:

> On close examination, it will be found that the modern Malays are made up of peoples of diverse racial origins among which cultural, social and economic distinctions are becoming more evident, to such an extent, indeed, as to invalidate the statement that they belong to a community that is culturally homogeneous. This is even more apparent if by the term Malay one has to include not only the Malays in Malaya, but also those of Malaysia and Indonesia.[119]

The fluidity and ephemerality of Malay identity, which continues to this day to be a subject of great debate, is itself represented in historical folklore such as *Hikayat Hang Tuah*, where in response to suggestions by his hosts at Indrapura that he was '*Melayu Sungguh*' (authentic Malay), Hang Tuah retorted: 'I may not be as pure as you think I am; I am the servant of a hybrid community and am living in a mixed context.'[120] Reflecting on this, Maier has observed:

> Reading *Hikayat Hang Tuah* is like being constantly given the suggestion that this is what Malayness is all about: it is the desire to create a feeling of communality and kinship between concrete human beings instead of the blind obedience to a set of abstract conventions, considerations of geography, or the belief in a stable personal identity.

Flexibility and the willingness to play, in other words, is what counts in being a Malay, in acting out Malayness.[121]

It appears that in Malay sociological parlance, then, the definition of 'Malayness' is fluid, and if anything relies primarily on socio-cultural construction.[122] 'Malayness' has various overlapping spheres: it defines a linguistic group, is an ethnographic term, a cultural concept, and, returning to what was established earlier, a loose territorial entity in the form of the 'Malay Archipelago'. It is this train of thought that permits the proponents of the *Dunia Melayu* to believe that by virtue of their language and religion, most (if not all) of the people of the Indo-Malay Archipelago are, in essence, 'Malay'.[123] In this sense, it is not difficult to see how the cultural definition of 'Malayness' allows many Indonesians to slip through the definitional net. Indeed, while the post-colonial leaders of Malaya may have opposed the ideology of Ibrahim Yaacob and harboured their own reservations towards Indonesians, it is nevertheless a fact that ethno-cultural links behind pan-Malay identity were elusive enough for them to have encouraged Indonesians to migrate to Malaysia in the 1960s and 1970s to maintain 'Malay' political primacy over the Chinese and Indian populations.[124]

An important, if unwritten, dimension to this broad definition of 'Malayness' in Indonesian and Malay nationalist discourse is its functional and exclusive expression. In this domain where kin identity is created, activated, and sustained, one finds functionality in two forms. First, it is already evident that the drive to establish a pan-Malay political entity, *Indonesia Raya* or *Melayu Raya*, was viewed by the pan-nationalists as the logical extension of pan-Malay identity. Second, however, was the fact that identities were by then also coalescing among the inhabitants of the Indo-Malay world against alien Europeans and Chinese who were flooding into the archipelago to sustain various commercial ventures, giving greater resonance to Indo-Malay kinship. 'Malayness' hence was also defined against particularly the alien Chinese communities in both the Dutch East Indies and British Malaya.

The perceptual gap

While it no doubt had proponents on either side of the Melaka Straits, conceptions of pan-identity suffered from fundamental definitional problems. Several points need to be appreciated to that effect. First, it is important to note that the proponents of pan-Malayism among Indonesian thinkers, notably Muhammad Yamin and Abdul Haris Nasution, were not Javanese; they were Sumatran, and of Minangkabau descent. Hence the fact that they had no difficulty reconciling Malay and Indonesian identities should not be taken as representative of the political proclivities of their non-Sumatran colleagues.

Moreover, while Robert Curtis's observation that 'most of the important ethnic groups in the area, the Malays, Atjehnese [Acehnese], Javanese, Sundanese, Minangkabao, Buginese and Makassarese belong to the so-called Deutero-Malay racial group and have obvious physiological and cultural traits in common'[125] is generally correct, equally pertinent are the differences and sense of distinction that existed across the vast ethno-cultural web of Indonesia. Here, it should be emphasized that notwith-standing the exertions of Yamin and Nasution, there was a clear distinction in Indonesian anthropological thought between '*Rumpun Melayu*' (the same Malay racial stock) and '*Suku Melayu*' (Malay as a lineage group associated with a particular territory). Put differently, the distinction is one between race and ethnicity. To Indonesian minds, identity measured in terms of ethnicity is an issue of locality: Malays as an ethnic group resided around the Melaka Straits and Riau, and made up only a small percentage of the overall Indonesian population. Hence suggesting that a modern state could be born out of pan-Malay identity the way Yamin and Nasution did arguably implied a distinctly ethnic basis to Indo-Malay solidarity, though they themselves did not explicitly champion that interpretation. Given the ethno-cultural differences in colonial Indonesia, this betrayed a lack of sophistication born of a fundamental misinterpretation of history.

This tension between race and ethnicity in Indonesian nationalism was reflected in the intellectual contest between ethno 'pan-Malayism', as Yamin's '*Nusantara* nationalism' implied, and a civic nationalism that circumvented the complexities surrounding explicit compartmentalization of the inhabitants of the Dutch East Indies into racial and ethnic groups. In that regard, the 1928 Bandung Declaration requires mention. It was at Bandung that the decision was made to build nationalism on a civic and republican logic premised not on racial and ethnic identity, but on the staunch anti-Dutch sentiment shared by the people throughout the archipelago. This in turn was registered in the Bandung mantra 'One Language, One Flag, One Nation'. Cognizant of these tensions, the respected nationalist Mohammad Hatta, himself of Minangkabau (Sumatran) origin, staunchly opposed attempts by some among his colleagues to conceptualize national identity along ethnic lines. Hatta challenged Yamin's conception of *Indonesia Raya* on the basis of *Tumpah-dara Indonesia*, 'the Indonesian fatherland', which he feared was disturbingly similar to the German nationalist idea of *Kultur und Boden* (culture and soil) propounded by the Nazi Party.[126] To his mind, his fellow Sumatran's attempt at inventing Indonesian authenticity was perilously close to being interpreted as Javanese hegemony premised on the revival of the Majapahit kingdom, and hence was nothing short of a veiled attempt at Javanese imperialism. In retrospect, it seemed that some architects of identity in Indonesia were in fact aware of this problem of defining national identity along racial and ethnic lines, and it was with the Bandung Declaration that they registered a refusal to use the Javanese language and ethnicity as the core of Indonesian language and identity.[127] Hence it is evident from the Bandung Declaration that Yamin and Nasution's attempt to place race and ethnicity at the forefront of nationalism was rejected, as racial or ethnic terms of reference were viewed in Indonesian nationalist circles as anathema to the nationalist cause.

Clearly, from ethnographic perspectives, distinctions existed between Indonesian and Malaysian conceptions of 'Malayness'. As argued earlier, in early-twentieth-century Indonesian thinking Malay was accepted as a racial definition for the large majority of the population of Indonesia. Yet as an ethnic marker 'Malayness' was limited to the inhabitants of the Riau islands, peninsular Malaysia, and portions of northeastern Sumatra.[128] Even the notion of Malay primacy implicit within the concept of the *Dunia Melayu* is debatable owing to the fact that most Malays are purportedly not in the strictest sense *orang asli* (natives) in the peninsula.[129] One scholar for example has highlighted that according to Chinese chronicles, Malay emigrants from Sumatra began to settle on the coast of the peninsula only in the seventh and eighth centuries.[130]

The representation of all Indonesians as ethnic Malays on cultural grounds is particularly objectionable to many Javanese.[131] As discussed earlier, to them their culture, a key component of ethnicity, is very distinct from, if not altogether superior to, that of the ethnic Malay community.[132] Further to that, from an Indonesian perspective a racial definition of Malayness would also permit the possibility of 'Malays' professing a religion other than Islam (this, indeed, is the case with Batak Protestants, Balinese Hindu, and Javanese Buddhists, for example). Yet the thought of this is anathema in peninsular Malay discourse, where Malayness is synonymous with Islam.[133] In essence, then, there is a tension between Indonesia's pride in ethno-cultural diversity, expressed in the Indonesian national motto *Bhinneka Tunggal Ika* (Unity in Diversity), and peninsular Malays' tendency to focus on similarities framed in ethno-cultural terms.[134] Likewise, because many Indonesian political traditions are in fact drawn from the legacy of Majapahit (owing to Javanese political dominance), it should not be surprising that the Javanese outlook and worldview might differ from that of the ethnic Malay, whose claim is to the legacy of Srivijaya. Such distinction, as was alluded to earlier, has resulted in the traditional tension between Java and the ethnic Malay world, echoing the historical contestations between Srivijaya and Majapahit. Not surprisingly, such differences would also have an impact on the terms of affinity between both states as interpreted and understood by their leaders.

Another reason accounted for Indonesia's reluctance to frame national identity in ethnic terms in the way the Malays in the peninsula did. As was suggested earlier, and as Chapter 3 will show in greater detail, the very existence of Indonesia as a unitary and sovereign nation-state was grounded not on ethnographic logic, but on a nationalist tradition that deliberately avoided emphasizing ethnic affiliation. Indonesian identity had no ethnic rationality. Much unlike other justifications of nationhood, Indonesia has never had, or rather has never chosen, an ethnic core. Instead, the Indonesian identity was built upon revolutionary struggle against a common oppressor. It is on these terms that one finds some Indonesians, particularly those who originate from eastern Indonesia, resentful of kinship discourse in bilateral relations framed in ethnic terms in the way peninsular Malays frame it.[135] Peninsular Malays, on the other hand, appear more comfortable with the ethnic logic to nationhood. Contrary to the Indonesian experience, race and ethnicity in Malaysia formed the cornerstone of its nation-building project. 'Malayness' in Malaysia is and has always been a political/constitutional identity where being Malay permits one to lay claim to rights and privileges given to *Bumiputra* (literally, Sons of the Soil).[136] It was on this basis that peninsula proponents of pan-Malayism such as Ibrahim Yaacob and Burhanuddin al-Helmy rationalized the incorporation of Indonesian identity into that of the Malay.

In later years, these fundamental differences between Indonesian and Malay understandings of race and ethnicity would surface in bilateral meetings such as the UNESCO-funded project on Malay culture in 1971 and the Indonesia–Malaysia youth meetings of the early 1990s. Both these projects were undertaken to locate commonalities upon which to build harmonious relations between the two kin states. In both instances, it was precisely the issue of the definition of 'Malayness' that caused them to flounder. As Taufik Abdullah shared with the author, in both instances the point of departure was over 'Malay insistence on the ethno-cultural definition of Malay identity' and 'Indonesian opposition to this definition'.[137] Underlying this was a fundamental difference of opinion between Indonesian discourse on the social anthropology of the Indo-Malay world, which avoided ethno-racial expressions of identity as political reference points, and peninsular Malay thinking, which sought to construct and politicize a brittle veneer of ethno-cultural commonality.[138]

It appears from this exploration of the search for kinship precedents in Indo-Malay historiography that attempts to trace avenues of affinity lead one through a conceptual and historical minefield, where pressures for intellectual coherence and clarity are confronted with the need to reveal the full extent of the depth of complexities, not to mention scholarly divisions and disagreements, that underlie this notion of Indo-Malay kinship. At the heart of this tension lies the concept of Malayness, and the vexing question of how to conceptualize Indo-Malay identity. In peninsular Malay discourse, the 'Malay' identity was a complex maze incorporating dimensions of race, religion, culture, and ethnicity. To Indonesian minds, however, Malay identity was a much simpler concept: though Indonesians may be racially 'Malay' (in so far as racial markers remain relevant), as an ethnic group Malays are a mere minority residing in parts of Sumatra. Anthropological debate over the contested nature of Indo-Malay identity, as this study has shown, throws up complexities and discrepancies that have to be appreciated. The construction and counter-construction of identity discussed here, however, are not merely matters of polemics. They provide crucial cultural and historical backdrop, and would have a definite impact on the conceptual space available for the construction of affinity among political leaders.

Concluding remarks

The objectives set out in this chapter have been to survey the basis to popular conceptions of kinship, and perceptions held among the political elite as to how affinity can be constructed for political goals. With these objectives in mind, it is suggested here that given the fact that kinship can be a socially and culturally constructed phenomenon, there appear to be broad grounds upon which Indonesia and Malaysia can be classified as kin states. Language and religion are critical to this sharing of identity. Trade and migration also figured prominently in the construction of the kinship system that defined the borderless character of the pre-colonial Indo-Malay Archipelago. Indeed, anthropological debate aside, it became increasingly fashionable by the early twentieth century to construct kinship between the inhabitants of the Dutch East Indies and British Malaya precisely along the problematic lines of race and ethnicity. Reflecting the earlier discussion on Smith's theories of nationalism, in order for pan-nationalists to construct a nation that included the inhabitants of the peninsula and archipelago, the language of 'Malay' kinship was used. This notion of kinship and common identity constructed by indigenous thinkers and ideologues stemmed from the appropriation of ideas and categories of race and ethnicity articulated in Western social-political thought. European models and concepts of nation, citizenship, and nationalism, and the captivating romantic ideologies of movements such as Pan-Slavism and Pan-Germanic nationalism that stemmed from them, inspired advocates of pan-Malayism to use these ideas to define how people in the Indo-Malay Archipelago related to their neighbours who spoke Malay, or shared the Islamic faith.[139] The struggle of the peoples of the Dutch East Indies and British Malaya to throw off the yoke of colonialism, then, became the struggle of the 'Malay people'. Such sentiment was implicit in the following comment made by Tun Dr Ismail, former Malaysian Home Minister:

> One of the greatest events in the life of our young nation had been the conclusion of a Treaty of Friendship with Indonesia – the first of its kind entered into by the Federation of Malaya – reflecting our desire to restore those ties of race and culture with Indonesia; ties which were interrupted by the accidents of history.[140]

Framed in anti-colonial terms, the politics of affinity did have resonance with the vast majority of the respective populations. Hence while colonialism drew Indonesia and Malaysia apart territorially, it seemed to have inadvertently brought them together in terms of the anti-colonial ideology that emerged from Western ideas and ideologies, and that challenged conceptually the 1824 partition.

Be that as it may, many of the contradictions in this construction of Indo-Malay fraternity, such as the historical record of tension born of seemingly timeless suspicions of Javanese pretensions and the contestable anthropological basis of ethno-cultural affinity between the populations of Indonesia and Malaysia, remained unresolved. Because of this, problems lingered when pan-nationalists at the forefront of Indo-Malay nationalism looked to the kinship factor for meaning and intelligibility as they plotted their political agenda centred on the creation of a unitary archipelagic state encompassing the peninsula and the archipelago. With this in mind, the study will now venture to consider the ideological and institutional shape of contending discourses that defined the place of pan-Malay ideology in the kinship politics of the Indo-Malay world.

3   A tale of two nationalisms

A striking paradox in the emergence of nationalism in the Indo-Malay world was the fact that it did not begin with the objective of forming sovereign states out of coterminous colonial territories. Rather, anti-colonial consciousness inspired the imagination and construction of a pan-Malay nation centred on the contested concept of 'Malayness' and manifested in the 'imagined' communities of *Indonesia Raya* and *Melayu Raya*. Pan-Malayism emerged as the predominant political ideology in the pre-war anti-colonial movement, where

> the dream of *Melaya-Raya* or *Indonesia-Raya* was not merely a nostalgic return to the past: it recognized the traumatic manner in which the Indo-Malay world had been torn apart by treaties and pacts agreed upon by foreign powers that had descended upon the Malay people and their homeland.[1]

Indeed, the ideologies and events behind the formulation of this pan-identity would become as significant to an understanding of the politicization of kinship in Indonesia–Malaysia relations as the reasons and ramifications behind its demise.

Converging nationalist motivations: the emergence of modernist Islam

The politicization of kinship can be traced to the Malay and Indonesian student movements at Al-Azhar University in Cairo in the early twentieth century.[2] These movements were influenced profoundly by ideas of reformist Islam as a tool for regenerating what they perceived to be a Malay-Muslim identity that had been eroded by Western colonialism. Writing his classic study of Indonesian nationalism, George Kahin noted that in the politics of the Indo-Malay world, 'the Mohammedan religion was not just a common bond; it was indeed, a sort of in-group symbol as against an alien intruder and oppressor of a different religion'.[3] Through journals such as *Seruan Azhar*, *Al-Imam*, and *Al-Manar*, students regularly published the works of Arab scholars glorifying the Islamic reformation, and disseminated them not only to the student community in Cairo, but in Indonesia and Malaya as well.[4]

Beyond serving as mouthpieces for Islamic awakening, these journals also harboured a nationalist agenda. One such publication described its motivation in the following manner: '[It] is for our homeland, because we recognize Indonesia and the Peninsula as one community, one people, with one *Adat*, one way of life, and what is more, virtually one religion.'[5] To underscore camaraderie, students from the Indo-Malayan archipelago formed activist organizations such as *Djama'ah al-Chairiah al-Talabijja al-Azhariah al-Djawiah* (Welfare Association of *Jawa* Students, with *'Jawa'* representing all Muslims indigenous to Southeast Asia).[6] Roff further described how the cover of one such journal, *Seruan Azhar*, was embellished with a drawing of a globe with Southeast Asia in the centre and the territories of Dutch Indonesia and British Malaya shaded in black. Alongside them was printed: 'The united world of our beloved people', and in the introduction:

> All our people ... whether in Java, or in Sumatra, or in Borneo, or the Malay Peninsula, must unite and share a common purpose and agreement to strive for advancement, seek the best ways of doing this, and on no account allow ourselves to split into separate parties.[7]

The awakening wrought by reformist Islam in both Indonesian and Malayan circles generated a social-political discourse plotted along the lines of the *Kaum Tua* (Conservatives)–*Kaum Muda* (Progressives) dispute. What is relevant for our purposes here about this philosophical dispute is the fact that the *Kaum Muda* Young Turks, whose worldview echoed the modernist interpretation of Islam emanating from the Middle East, posed a fundamental challenge to what was viewed as the status quo of the day by presenting Islam as a basis upon which to formulate a full-fledged nationalist agenda. The experience in Cairo at the height of Islamic reformation and Arab nationalism would politicize these Indo-Malay students to the degree that many of them would return to the peninsula and the archipelago to lead nationalist movements.[8] Upon returning to their respective countries, these Indo-Malay nationalists, imbued with modernist Islam, continued to maintain ties with each other through regular correspondence.[9] In the Malay Peninsula, the political platform and rhetoric of *Kaum Muda* elements quickly focused upon the pursuit of independence within the context of a greater Indonesia.[10] In Indonesia as well, returning students from Cairo and Mecca as well as Lahore, Qadian, and Aligarh brought with them the reformist agenda that inspired the transformation of traditional Islam throughout much of the archipelago. As for the response of the general population, it was noted that 'the Muslim community, threatened commercially by Chinese competition and religiously by heightened activities of Christian mission-aries in Central Java in the first decade of the twentieth century, eagerly embraced the new message'.[11] In 1912, reformist Islam was given organi-zational expression with the formation of *Muhammadiyah*, and it soon became 'the dominant force in Indonesian Islam; in fact, it became the largest and most viable Indonesian association, overshadowing other reli-gious as well as political organizations'.[12] Not surprisingly, Dutch alarm at the expansion of reformist Islam led the colonial government to ban reformist publications in Java and Sumatra.[13] In Malaya too, the British administration and Malay sultans expressed concern about the impact of the Cairo experience on Malay students.[14]

Socialist and nationalist interpretations of *Melayu Raya–Indonesia Raya*

It was not only in reformist Islamic philosophy that anti-colonial move-ments in the Indo-Malay world found solidarity; the emergence of socialist ideology also generated ideological propinquity.[15] This socialist-nationalist movement shared a reciprocal relationship with Islamic forces on the basis of anti-colonial agitation. Many of the Malay students returning from the Middle East linked up with Malay-educated and politically conscious students in the peninsula from peasant backgrounds, themselves already being influenced by the teachings of Indonesian reformists, nation-alists, and socialists.[16] The socialists tapped into secular and libertarian ideals of Western concepts of nations and nationalism, and, unlike the modernist Muslim-nationalists, perceived the construction of pan-unity on the basis of a civic and egalitarian anti-colonial nationalism. This was cer-tainly so in the case of the Malay socialists from the peninsula, with most of them originating from the Sultan Idris Training College (SITC), a hotbed of socialist and nationalist ideas in the pre-war years.[17] Notably, the college was particularly susceptible to Indonesian nationalist influence.[18] Many of the students from the SITC had maintained contacts with Indonesian nationalists (including the communists), while several even joined Sukarno's PNI (*Partai Nasional Indonesia*) upon its formation in 1927.[19] Ibrahim Yaacob, one of the prominent socialist leaders of the *Kaum Muda* movement, articulated the movement's aspirations in the following manner:

> The aspiration of the *Bangsa Orang Melayu* [the nation of the Malay people] is to struggle for the independence of the land and the *Bangsa Melayu* [Malay nation] who will unite again in one great country according to the interest and desire of the people as a whole. The aim of *Melayu Raya* is the same as *Indonesia Raya* which is the aspiration of the Malay nationalist movement, that is to revive again the heritage of Srivijaya, which is a common unity of the *Bangsa*.[20]

Shorn of ideological embellishing, the subtext to this position primarily stemmed from a concern with the burgeoning alien Chinese population on the peninsula. To the Malay socialists, it was better to be assimilated into a society broadly allied in race, ethnicity, and religion than to be overwhelmed on their own soil by the Chinese. The objectives of co-identification with Indonesia put forward by Ibrahim Yaacob would subsequently take on greater organizational coherence in the form of the KMM (*Kesatuan Melayu Muda*, The Young Malays' Union).

Formed in 1938, the KMM was the first explicitly political organization in Peninsular Malaya, and it had as its political objective the fostering of a polity based on one race, one language, and one nation with Indonesia. The KMM was a meeting ground for reformist Islamic elements and socialists from the SITC, who were becoming increasingly exposed to Indonesian literary and political works written in the Malay language.[21] Membership also consisted of a fair number of Indonesians as well.[22] Later, with the outbreak of the Indonesian revolution in 1945, many from the KMM would participate actively in the Indonesian revolution, which to them was also a Malay nationalist struggle. Scholars have emphasized how Malay radicals from the peninsula provided arms to freedom fighters in Sumatra and Java, though the extent of support remains difficult to determine.[23] Beyond that, it has also been highlighted that prominent Malay nationalists from the KMM such as Ibrahim Yaacob, Manaf (leader of the *Giyu Gun*, a volunteer army formed by the Japanese), Abdullah Hussain, Othman Abdullah, Baharom Basar, Abdullah Sanggora, Zulkifli Ownie, Karim Rashid, Dahari Ali, and 'hundreds of others' directly participated in the Indonesian revolution on either a military or a political level.[24] Agitation for post-war unification with the Indonesian nation would subsequently take on more institutionalized forms such as KRIS (*Kesatuan Rakyat Indonesia Semenanjung*, Union of Peninsular Indonesians), formed in July 1945, and PKMM (*Partai Kebangsaan Melayu Malaya*, Malay Nationalist Party of Malaya) in October 1945, both successors to the KMM. Many among the Malay leaders also proceeded subsequently to take up membership in Sukarno's PNI. The formation of these political organizations allowed the radical movement to propagandize their political objectives throughout the peninsula in tandem with elements in Indonesia who were sympathetic to the Malay cause of pan-unification.

Although a detailed comparative study of congruence between Indonesian and Malayan anti-colonial nationalisms remains to be undertaken, it is widely accepted that nationalism in Indonesia developed and matured much faster than in Malaya. Nevertheless, those engaging in pre-war Indonesian anti-colonial rhetoric also found in the discourse of kinship a frame of reference to contextualize relations with their enthusiastic but less accomplished Malay cousins. As previously discussed, some framed the Indo-Malay discourse of political kinship in terms of the peninsula's geographical inclusion in the Indonesian nationalist vision to translate the historical polity of Majapahit into a modern nation-state.[25] Sukarno, for example, asserted such a historical basis to Indonesia's ongoing nationalist struggle, and his vision was shared by Malayan counterparts such as Ibrahim Yaacob and Burhanuddin Al-Helmy. Other Indonesian leaders such as A.H. Nasution and Muhammad Yamin, a nationalist ideologue close to Sukarno and of Sumatran origin, were equally enthusiastic in proclaiming a historical basis to the incorporation of the peninsula into the territorial bounds of Indonesia.[26] During the Japanese occupation of 1942–1945, the incorporation of both Sumatra and Malaya into the 25th Army military administration of the Japanese occupation force between 1942 and 1944 lent further credence to thinking about the incorporation of the peninsula into a greater Indonesian territorial state.[27]

Japanese occupation

The dismantling of colonial administration during the Japanese interregnum and Japanese sympathy towards anti-colonial movements opened a window of opportunity for Malay pan-nationalists to ensure that the issue of political union and absorption of the peninsula into an independent Indonesia remained foremost on the minds of their Indonesian counterparts as the latter plotted the political future of the Dutch East Indies. On 28 May 1945 in Jogjakarta, the BPKI (*Badan Penjelidik Usaha Persiapan Kemerdekaan Indonesia*, Committee for the Investigation of Preparatory Efforts for Indonesian Independence) met to deliberate the terms and conditions to be presented to the Japanese military administration for Indonesian independence.[28] Among the items tabled was the absorption of the Malay Peninsula and Borneo into an independent Indonesia. At that historic meeting, representatives voted 39 to 25 in favour of the incorporation of the Malay Peninsula into an independent Indonesia.[29]

Another landmark event worthy of mention was a meeting between Malay and Indonesian nationalist leaders that took place at Taiping, Perak (Malaya), on 12 August 1945 to lay the grounds for the potential incorporation of the peninsula into independent Indonesia.[30] That meeting, and the events that took place immediately after, was a telling prelude to Malayan and Indonesian independence. Quoting from Ibrahim Yaacob's memoirs, Radin Soenarno wrote:

> After lunch the delegation left for the Taiping Airport and it was there, in one of the reception rooms, that Sukarno and Hatta held a brief discussion with Ibrahim and Dr. Burhanuddin who gave them the assurance that Malaya's aim was independence united with Indonesia. Sukarno told them that the Declaration of Independence was to be made the following week. To this Ibrahim answered that he was preparing an Eight-Man Delegation to Jakarta to represent

Malaya in the Declaration Ceremony and also to take part in the forming of the Republic of Indonesia with Malaya as a part. It was in this short conference that Sukarno, flanked by Hatta, shook hands with Ibrahim Yaacob and said, 'Let us form one single Motherland for all the sons of Indonesia.'... This event in Taiping marked the peak of the political success of the left-wing movements of the Malays.[31]

The significance of the Taiping meeting, however (and for that matter the BPKI vote as well), has to be viewed in the broader context of political developments in the region. It was three days after Taiping that Japan surrendered. Two days later, on 17 August, Sukarno and Mohammad Hatta proclaimed the independence of Indonesia. Conspicuously absent from the proclamation was any mention of Malaya. This sudden detour was certainly portentous. At one level, it perhaps demonstrated that any successful political merger between Malaya and Indonesia could only be realized under the umbrella of Japanese occupation, for it was only then that Malaya and Indonesia were ever united under one central authority, colonial or indigenous. On their part, while the Japanese military administration stopped short of actively encouraging political unification, the fact that it supported both the radical Malay nationalists and the Indonesian nationalist movement while at the same time crippling the influence of the Malay traditional elite in the peninsula (whom the Japanese viewed as British sympathizers) did indicate a possible tacit backing of the idea.[32] In any case, the end of the Pacific War and the Japanese surrender severely curtailed chances for unification. Yet the fact that it was highly likely Malaya would have eventually been integrated into *Indonesia Raya* had Japanese occupation lasted a while longer, or if Japan had not capitulated so soon after Taiping, should not be lost when one considers, for example, how in his memoirs Ibrahim Yaacob alluded to the real possibility that Sukarno was preparing to include Malaya in his scheduled independence proclamation.[33]

Notwithstanding the undoubted significance of the Taiping meeting from the Malayan perspective as revealed in Ibrahim Yaacob's memoirs, the importance accorded it by mainstream Indonesian nationalism, characterized by Sukarno's PNI-led republican movement, was conspicuously less apparent. Evidently, all existing published accounts of this groundbreaking Taiping meeting cite Malayan sources. There has been no mention of the Taiping meeting in any of Sukarno or Mohammad Hatta's memoirs or autobiographies.[34] Hatta's memoirs instead recorded a meeting with representatives from the Sumatran Independence Preparatory Committee on 13 August consisting of Teuku Mohammad Hassan, Dr Amir Syarifuddin and a Mr Abas.[35] While the fact that the Taiping meeting did indeed take place is not being challenged here, this omission of any reference to it in Indonesian sources is nevertheless telling both of the accuracy of Ibrahim Yaacob's account of Sukarno's commitment to unification and of the importance his Indonesian counterparts attributed to this meeting and what it represented in the larger context of Indonesian nationalism. What is certain is that it was the pace of events over those few days leading up to 15 August 1945, and not the ideologies of either the Malay radicals or Indonesian nationalists, that shaped the historical trajectory in the Indo-Malay Archipelago. Sukarno's snatch at independence upon Japanese surrender was necessary in order first and foremost to prevent the re-imposition of colonial rule in the Dutch East Indies, and his volte-face on Malaya was hence seen as necessary to dispel suspicions of collaboration and expansionism.[36] Together with opposition from several prominent revolutionaries such as Vice-President Hatta, hopes for *Melayu Raya* or *Indonesia Raya* were diminished with the turning tide of the war.

The pan-Malay cause had also found support from members of the Indonesian communist movement, who considered unification an inseparable objective of Indonesian anti-colonialism. Among them was the Minangkabau communist nationalist Tan Melaka and his followers. In so far as Malaya was concerned, Tan Melaka was of the view that Indonesia had an obligation to maintain an active interest in and influence on Malayan affairs. This attitude was reflected clearly in his writings:

> Just as village people do not allow snakes to run wild in their gardens, so the Indonesian people are not content merely to sit on their hands in the face of the conspiracies and destruction wrought by British imperialism in Malaya. Solidarity between the Indonesian peoples of Malaya and Indonesia is a crucial matter.... Its importance will surpass even what is implied in the statement by Malay–Indonesian political organizations that they join together and stake their life in fighting for independent Indonesia.[37]

These convictions were echoed during the Fourth Congress of PP (*Persatuan Perjuangan*, Struggle Union), an organization established to consolidate the efforts of radical youth movements (popularly known as *Pemuda*, Youth) at Madiun on 16–17 March 1946. Mirroring the BPKI decision, it was at Madiun that PP called for independence to be declared not only over the Dutch East Indies, but including Malaya, North Borneo, Timor, and Papua as well.[38] Unlike the mainstream nationalists, though, whose interest in pan-unification was comparatively passive to begin with, and was subsequently superseded by the Indonesian revolution, Indonesian radicals continued to espouse Indonesia–Malaya kinship against colonialism as part of their revolution, providing ideological support for their Malayan cousins in their struggle against the British colonial government and the traditional Malay elite. Indonesian influence would only ebb as the revolution wore on and contingencies mounted, and as the nationalist politics of Malaya started itself to shift away from pan-unification.

Consolidating the Indonesian nation

The drama of anti-colonial agitation is often defined and perpetuated by a multiplicity of actors. Correspondingly, forces of change come into conflict not only with foreign rule, but also traditional elites who, as beneficiaries of colonial administration, resist socio-political and economic change threatened by anti-colonialism.

The traditional elites in Indonesia and Malaya largely originated from two camps. Most were members of the aristocracy and/or the Western-educated elite, whose loyalties were to the colonial government. In Malaya, conservative forces were uncomfortable with and highly suspicious of the anti-colonial sentiments of modernist Islam as well as socialist and nationalist ideologies, and shared the British colonial administration's concern for the potential challenge of pan-nationalism to the status quo.[39] In Indonesia's case, anti-colonialism was countered by aristocrats and officials who favoured the progress that Dutch education and lifestyles represented, and agitation for change never went beyond minor reforms.[40] While the contest between the conservatives and nationalists hung in the balance during the pre-war period (largely because of the colonial government's harsh policies towards the latter), nationalist politics took a swift and severe turn to the detriment of the conservatives in the form of the onset of the Indonesian revolution in September 1945.

Any study of the Indonesian revolution will necessarily have to distinguish between its political and its social dimensions. As a political phenomenon, the revolution was marked by competing ideologies vying for political and ideological space within the nascent Indonesian republic. Apart from republican nationalism, other ideologies such as political Islam, communism, and federalism sought to exert their influence on the shape of Indonesian politics. Taking place within the broader context of this political struggle, however, was a bloody social revolution that destroyed Indonesia's traditional feudal society. The revolution was without doubt a watershed event in the context of Indonesian history, and, while its origins were clearly domestic, it would have a profound impact on the shaping of the Indonesian worldview. In particular, the experience of revolution would have substantive repercussions for the evolution of Indonesia–Malaysia relations in the post-colonial era in the way it transformed the perception of kinship at a national level in the eyes of the respective political leaderships and set the two post-colonial political identities on a collision course.

Considering the spontaneity and opportunism that characterized the Indonesian revolution, it is clear that its impetus did not come from the political elite. Instead, this agitation for popular sovereignty, characterized by the sweeping aside of the anachronistic old order, was distinctly a mass-based, mostly *Pemuda* phenomenon:

In reality a political, social and economic revolution is in progress. The government supports the revolution which is arising from the people, and this is only proper in terms of democratic beliefs. The government is simply a body which carries out the will of the people, and the government can only exist with the people's support.[41]

The hardship and depravity during the war, coupled with inadvertent support from the Japanese for nationalist forces, gave impetus to mass mobilization on a scale never before experienced in Indonesian history.[42] The role of the *Pemuda* was especially crucial as a driving force behind the social revolution;[43] it was they who led a movement for the destruction of long-established social structures: 'Every old fashioned attitude with a feudal smell must be done away with. Every structure and action which is not in accordance with the people's demands at this time must be changed.'[44] In particular, traditional centres of authority that had been co-opted into both the Dutch and the Japanese colonial administrations and that entertained 'hopes of succour from the returning Dutch' stood out as prime targets of these ideologically diverse reactionaries.[45] This tension between the old order and the emerging spirit of egalitarianism has been succinctly summarized in the following observation on East Sumatra:

The respect and consideration which the Malay rulers formerly enjoyed has gradually declined, and people have come to regard most rulers here as having power in consequence of the political contracts (indeed it is these that give authority, not the love and affection of their people), and as nouveaux-riches, but not as good leaders. . . .

There is criticism now and it is malicious. It is directed not only at the behaviour and values of the *Kerajaan* [royal government], but it goes further and dwells upon history, making comparisons with rajas under the *Korte Verklaring* and with the rulers in Java. Formerly this criticism did not exist, people were satisfied with the aura which used to hang around the sultans.[46]

Economic and political malaise under Dutch colonialism and the grave depredation and suffering caused by Japanese occupation meant that a reactionary mood was already percolating among a large proportion of Indonesians. The sudden departure of the Japanese provided the catalyst that precipitated the inevitable backlash against established centres of power. In the quest to build an egalitarian society and post-colonial identity, traditional forms of authority such as sultans and the aristocratic and administrative elite (*priyayi* and *pangreh praja*) were labelled agents of the repressive old colonial orders, and removed forcibly; in some instances traditional structures were demolished arbitrarily. From the perspective of the reactionaries, the social revolution was also necessary in order to disprove Dutch accusations that the new republic was an illegitimate Japanese creation 'promised' as it were to the traditional ruling elite in return for their allegiance during the occupation years.

On the revolution itself, it is notable that it was in Sumatra, the island closest in ethnic, geographical, and cultural proximity to the Malay Peninsula, that the structural foundations of the old order were most dramatically dismantled. The Sumatran sultans and traditional elite had long been cautious of the nationalists and were at best measured in their support of the objective of independence, most being content with the colonial status quo. Anthony Reid noted, for example, how the Malay sultans of Eastern Sumatra 'gained much from their association with Dutch colonialism, and most of their Malay subjects appeared content to bask in their reflected glory';[47] some within the old *Kerajaan*-based order even viewed Indonesian nationalism as a threat.[48] Not surprisingly, their scepticism called into question their commitment to the republic, and their loyalty to the old order would prove costly. For instance, in Banten the police and local residency were targets of a reactionary nationalist backlash. In Eastern Sumatra, it was the social structure of the Malays, long viewed as the privileged indigenous ethnic group, that fell victim to revolutionary zeal. There, the sultans and rajas, symbols of Malay identity and tradition not only in Sumatra but in Malaya as well, crumbled in the wake of bloody revolutionary violence that began in March 1946.[49] Likewise in North Sumatra there was much ill feeling among the population towards elements that had been incorporated into the old colonial administrative apparatus, resulting in the upheaval of December 1945 and January 1946.[50] As a result of this backlash, the Sultans of Langkat, Serdang, Asahan, and Indragiri were either killed or incarcerated. Several scholars have provided vivid descriptions of this wholesale destruction of the traditional social-political configuration. One noted, for example, that

> early in 1946 a social revolution broke out around Medan among the brutalized Javanese coolie population and radical youth. A number of Medan intellectuals tried to moderate, guide or exploit this jacquerie, but it rapidly moved beyond their control. The sultanate families were decimated. Many were butchered, others tortured.[51]

The social revolution in Indonesia was in fact a manifestation of the long-brewing struggle between the old and new orders (*Kaum Tua* and *Kaum Muda*) that by the end of the war had come to characterize politics within the Indo-Malay world. To that end, it is interesting to register how the militant *Pemuda* movement in Sumatra 'never saw itself as an "anti-government" movement except in relation to the *kerajaan*, because the republican government had no capacity to oppose it as in Java'.[52] Even Sumatran sultans, rajas, and aristocrats who were more receptive to anti-colonial ideology favoured federalists who were more sympathetic towards the *kerajaan*.[53] The moderates in the central government themselves were predisposed to Sumatra's integration into the republic without violence and bloodshed. To achieve this, they established KNI (*Kanite Nasional Indonesia*, Indonesian National Committee) *daerah* (regional Indonesian national committees) in Sumatra to discuss Sumatra's absorption into the Indonesian Republic. The *Pemuda*, however, did not share the republican government's conciliatory spirit, and its leaders 'did not think much beyond abolishing the rajas'.[54] So strong was popular support for the *Pemuda* movement against the old order that the republican movement was unable to curb the slide into violence.[55] The inability of the central government to react was further exacerbated by the fact that, unlike in Java, it lacked a substantial leadership and institutional presence in Sumatra that could harness the full potential of its social-political forces constructively for the nationalist cause. This leadership vacuum led Sumatrans to seek out their own models of revolution, and inspiration was eventually found in the regicidal legacy of the French revolution.[56] It was only when traditional authority was made to yield to the imperatives of popular sovereignty (either by surrender or bloodshed) that the tide of social revolution in Sumatra receded, making way for the post-colonial project brought forth through republican nationalism.[57]

Even though the Indonesian social revolution effectively ended by the late 1940s, its legacy would continue to resonate beyond Indonesia's territorial borders. As Robert Curtis observed, 'a jacquerie of this sort was something new and ominous in South East Asian history. It revealed to the feudal aristocracy the real weakness of their position, without effective outside backing, in the face of a mass-based social upheaval.'[58] The implications of this jacquerie would have greatest resonance for Malaya, where the traditional elite and aristocracy were just beginning to position themselves at the forefront of a Malay nationalist movement. Indeed, the point of departure for what was emerging in Malaya from what had emerged in Indonesia was that for the former, the conservative political structure was to be a rallying point, not victim, of nationalism. While many in Malaya sympathized with the Indonesian national struggle, the widespread violence in general, and hostility targeted at the Malay old order in particular, generated much unease among the traditional leadership classes in Malaya.[59] Sensitivity towards the disruptive nature of the Indonesian example would be further sharpened when radical Malay political forces re-emerged to challenge the old order in Malaya, driven by the same social and ideological imperatives behind the destruction of the Indonesian old order.

Malay reactions to the revolution

Despite the exertions of proponents of unification with Indonesia, Malayans' nationalism by and large lagged behind that of their Indonesian kin.[60] Though Indonesian nationalism was very much centred in Java in the pre-war years, by the end of the war it had spread throughout the entire archipelago. Further, while there still remained a lingering concern within the Indonesian nationalist movement towards Javanese domination, there nevertheless evolved a sufficiently strong, broad-based commitment to a staunch anti-colonial, national, and egalitarian political ideology that emphasized national unity and territorial integrity to sustain the movement. In stark contrast, nationalism in the Malay Peninsula remained a relatively quiescent force even after the war, and never experienced the consensus towards anti-colonialism resembling that of Indonesia's civic nationalism. Aside from the radical nationalist elements led by Burhanuddin (Ibrahim Yaacob had escaped to Indonesia before the British return), who remained in the minority, the vast majority of those in social and political leadership positions in Malaya (with the possible exception of the predominantly ethnic-Chinese communist movement) were restrained in their response to the re-imposition of British rule. Part of the reason for this seemed to lie in the nature of the colonial experience itself. While colonialism under the Dutch was a particularly harsh experience for Indonesia, British rule was comparatively benign, as the British made efforts to ensure that the greater part of the Malay social-political structure, namely the sultans, *kerajaan*, and aristocratic feudal class, remained intact.[61] In retrospect, while Dutch colonialism effectively alienated the Indonesian masses through such harsh and exploitative policies as the Cultural System, British colonial initiatives, which included the introduction of popular economic policies, pre-empted the emergence of strong anti-British sentiments. In adopting prudent policies that kept various ethnic groups at a distance, and courting the traditional Malay leadership by preserving their ceremonial status and position in Malay society, the British managed to create a political environment of relative equanimity and also to foment a general nonchalance towards, if not acceptance of, colonialism among the vast majority of the Malayan population.[62] The full effect of Malay feudalism's embrace of colonialism on their perceptions of nationalism became clear in the manner in which the traditional Malay elite were wary of and guarded in their response to the Indonesia-inspired socialist Malay politics of the KMM.[63] If not unabashed Anglophiles, many among the aristocratic class were at least admirers of things British, and their outlook certainly resembled that of the West more than that of Indonesia. The fact that the traditional elite's version of nationalism was articulated as '*Hidup Melayu*' (Survival of the Malays) and 'Malaya for the Malays' within (as opposed to against) the context of loyalty to the British inspired an opinion that 'another common feature of all the [political] associations was the definite note of loyalty to the British Government and Rulers'.[64]

Unlike the Malay radical movement, whose ethos was being built around Islamic reformist journals as well as the *Kaum Muda* movement, and echoed the egalitarian, nationalist character of its Indonesian counterparts, the brand of Malay politics espoused by traditional elements continued to revolve around parochial state identities; and it was also becoming increasingly ethnic in its disposition. The political preoccupations of the traditional elite were geared more towards the protection of the Malay *bangsa* (race) from the increasing number of people belonging to minority populations such as the Chinese, Indian, and *Peranakan* (indigenous Chinese) than towards the excesses of British colonialism.[65] As a result, the *kerajaan* never challenged the status quo in the manner that the radical nationalists were doing.[66] As for the Malay masses themselves, the slight degree of social dislocation brought about by British colonialism ensured that they remained less politicized than their Indonesian kin, and less susceptible to the social revolution that engulfed every stratum of Indonesian society in the wake of the national revolution.

Contested identities

Despite the peripheral impact of radical anti-colonialism in the unfolding of Malayan history, it did contribute to the discourse and development of Malay nationalism. Hence, careful consideration of the ideology behind this movement is critical in order to appreciate the various facets of the perceptions of Indonesia on the part of the Malay leadership, for it is in the ideological cleavage of pre-independence Malay politics between the radical nationalists and traditional elite that one finds the discourse on kinship with Indonesia most fascinating.[67]

As suggested earlier, a motivation for the divergent perspectives and outcomes of anti-colonialism lay in the colonial experience itself. By portraying theirs as a common struggle against foreign imperialism, the pan-nationalists in effect papered over substantial differences that existed as a result of fundamental divergences between the Dutch and the British colonial projects. Simply put, the excesses of Dutch colonialism created a local mindset that differed strikingly from that of the peninsular Malays, who in many ways had their pre-colonial way of life preserved, and who did not undergo nearly the same kind of dislocation as their Indonesian counterparts did. This fact certainly contributed to the kinds of responses colonialism elicited from the colonized populations, and to the fact that there was no 'Malay revolution' in the peninsula. Reflecting upon these different colonial experiences, Soenarno noted that on the eve of the Pacific War, the idea of political unity with Indonesia 'was still strange to most Malays in Malaya', and this continued to hold true after the occupation.[68] It was not so much that such views were unacceptable, but that the abstraction of such notions to a Malay society still wedged between traditional world of the sultans, aristocracy, and the *kerajaan* prevented its translation into a mass movement.[69] As Soenarno goes on to suggest, mass politics 'went too far against the established Malay tradition of respect and loyalty towards the instituted government'.[70]

For the Malay elites, the civic and egalitarian ideology behind the

Indonesian revolution was antithetical to their political objectives, while the very social-political institutions that the Indonesian masses were so bent on dismantling were elevated to the status of unifying symbols of Malay nationalism.[71] While the issue of post-colonial boundaries served as the point of reference for Indonesian nationalism, in Malaya it revolved around consociation, competition, and consensus between the dominant Malay community and ethnic minorities over the manner to which the former could impose its presence upon, while at the same time accommodate, the interests of the latter.[72] In so far as the traditionalists were concerned, nationalism was a Malay, as opposed to a 'Malay-an', phenomenon, and the challenge was the creation of an identity as a nation rather than an entity as a state. The cornerstone of the post-colonial political structure was likewise envisaged to be Malay ethnic dominance. This was represented by the centrality of Malay symbols such as the sultanate and *kerajaan*, Islam, the Malay language, and Malay primacy in Malayan society.[73] The critical importance of the sultanate and *kerajaan* in Malay culture has been described as such:

> The Malay states had long been in existence ... they had developed their own socio-cultural, economic and political norms. Loyalty and patriotism within these states had become ingrained characteristics of the public life of their people. Many of the Rulers by 1946 were descended from long lines of ancestry which imposed upon them a duty to be true to the traditions set by their forebears; above all they had always to uphold the safety, integrity and sovereignty of their states. Granted that they were largely feudal aristocrats; but there is not a shadow of doubt that the Malay rulers of 1946 understood deeply that in their persons rested the ultimate responsibility for the survival and well-being of their states ... the existence of well-established nationalist concepts of loyalty and patriotism within the nine states was thrown into bold relief when the Malays in general and from different strata of their society rallied and united to oppose the British proposals and defend the sovereignty of their rulers and states.[74]

Milner further articulated: '[L]oyalty and service to the race were described in precisely the same terms as had been used for centuries to convey devotion to a sultan';[75] while Cheah noted that 'royal power is crucial to an understanding of the Malay political mind'.[76] Invented or otherwise, the centrality of Malay identity remains synonymous to the modern Malaysian state, and its ebb and flow continue to dictate the course of Malaysian politics. Within this cultural milieu, the immediate post-war period witnessed the increasing dominance of traditional and mainstream elements and the simultaneous diminution in influence of the radical Malay movement in the evolving nationalist discourse.

While the issue of Malay supremacy was central to the Malay political psyche, it was the Malayan Union scheme, proposed by the British in October 1946 as a potential political framework for the subsequent transfer of sovereignty, that provided the catalyst for the consolidation and institutionalization of Malays' defence of their political rights and privileges as 'sons of the soil'.[77] Two implications of the Malayan Union stood out in so far as the status of the Malays was concerned. First, under the scheme the status and sovereignty of the sultan were to be circumscribed, and authority on all matters, including religion, was to be subjected to British control. Second, the Malayan Union scheme sought to enact flexible citizenship laws to allow easier access to citizenship for minorities.[78] Because the terms of the Malayan Union undermined the position of the sultans, the traditional foci of Malay loyalty and identity, and at the same time threatened Malay primacy, it was perceived as an immediate threat to Malay identity and became the impetus for the formation of UMNO (the United Malays National Organization). What was most significant about the impact of the Malayan Union scheme on the overall constellation of Malayan politics was the fact that it galvanized the traditional elite. Once they had been comfortable with their position of privilege and protection under British colonialism, but the Malayan Union proposal quickened among this traditional elite the realization that the era of colonialism was coming to its conclusion.[79]

Elements from traditional centres of power were also wary of the pan-nationalists and their socialist ideals. The latter had made no secret of their support for the Indonesian model of civic and egalitarian nationalism, and had identified with and latched onto it as a premise to politicize kinship with their revolutionary Indonesian counterparts.[80] Yet in so far as pan-national objectives of the Malay radicals were concerned, to the traditional Malay elite the concepts of *Melayu Raya* and *Indonesia Raya* were not based on equality of status for Malaya and Indonesia. Rather, they were viewed as the subservience of Malay interests to those of a proclaimed egalitarian Indonesia-inspired nationalism, which they felt was a cover for Javanese hegemony.[81] On this matter, Prime Minister Tunku Abdul Rahman once noted: 'if they [Indonesians] stuck to the present system of centralized rule by the Javanese, there could be no future peace or stability and this presented considerable dangers for Malaysia'.[82] In view of the repercussions of the Indonesian revolution for traditional structures of authority, members of this section of the Malay elite understood unification with Indonesia to mean the inevitable marginalization of the Malay community in the peninsula and a loss of the privileged status accorded them by the British. The situation was aggravated by the fact that in championing the Indonesian conception of egalitarian nationalism, their radical opponents had directly challenged Malay tradition and protocol.

The underlying difference between radical and traditional politics within the domestic arena in Malaya lay in how their respective adherents envisaged that the emancipation of Malay society was to be achieved. It has already been discussed how the radical group conceptualized emancipation through absorption into *Indonesia Raya*. The nationalist ideology (in so far as they had one) of the English-educated middle and upper class that constituted the traditional elite, however, was grounded on different premises:

> Concepts of 'the nation' ... were in fact enunciated only in the most limited and hesitant way.... What preoccupied the ideologues was the contest between several social ideals, particularly that between the monarchical vision and two other concepts of community, the first based upon the community of Allah and the other upon Malay ethnicity.[83]

For them, the preservation (albeit with some adjustments) and not eradication of the traditional Malay state structure remained the priority. This made them diametrically opposed not only to the Malay radicals, but to the spirit of Indonesian nationalism as well. This point was not lost on the Indonesian nationalists, who would have greater sympathy for the cause of the Malay radicals now grouped into the MNP (Malayan Nationalist Party, consisting mainly of members from the defunct KMM movement, formed on 17 October 1945) and to which the baton of agitation for Malayan independence under the auspices of *Indonesia Raya* was passed.[84] These different conceptions over the character of post-colonial Malaya would later play an important role in inspiring Indonesian accusations against the mainstream Malay political elite of complicity with British neo-colonialism.

In the thinking of conservative quarters in Malaya, then, the Indonesian experience had no place in Malay nationalism, and after the war the traditional Malay elite would distance themselves from the violence of the Indonesian national revolution even as the radical Malay nationalists embraced and sought inspiration from it. In truth, the suspicion among the Malay traditional elite that Dutch colonialism was merely supplanted through revolution by Javanese cultural and political imperialism appeared to be corroborated by the post-revolution politics that was taking shape in Indonesia in the 1950s, where a disconcerting increase in Javanese dominance of the Indonesian political process was taking place. Consequent professions of impartiality by the central government cut no ice with discontented elements in the regions, and separatist movements throughout the archipelago. The key grievances these anti-republican regional movements harboured included the domination of central government by the Javanese and a lack of attention to the economic and political development of outer provinces.[85] It was also becoming evident to the Malayan political elite that not all the ills of the new Republic of

Indonesia were attributable to the cumulative effects of three centuries of colonialism; some were directly attributable to the disruptive forces unleashed in the name of revolution.[86] Chief among their concerns was the possibility of a spill-over of Indonesia's revolutionary fervour into their comparatively tranquil political domain. This was a particularly disturbing prospect given the fates of their kith and kin from the Sumatran aristocracy and *kerajaan* caught against the tide of Indonesian nationalist fervour. In so far as the traditional elite in Malaya were concerned, their opponents from the MNP were tainted with the brush of Indonesian radicalism. Two incidents in the early 1950s sharpened Malayan sensitivities. The first pertained to the Indonesian government's pursuit of the perpetrator of the Westerling rebellion into Malaya.

In January 1950, Captain 'Turk' Westerling, an officer in the Dutch armed forces, attempted a violent takeover of Bandung in the hope of triggering an Indonesia-wide uprising against the new Indonesian republican government. Though the rebellion was swiftly quashed by the Indonesian military, Westerling escaped. Because Westerling was thought to have operated out of Singapore and Penang, the Indonesian government subjected the British and local authorities in Singapore and Malaya to a barrage of accusations of connivance in the rebellion.[87] A second incident surrounded what has come to be known as the Hertogh affair. This incident revolved around the fight for custody over Maria Hertogh, a Dutch Catholic girl who was placed by her mother in the care of a Malay nursemaid during the Japanese occupation. When the battle for custody between the foster and biological mothers was resolved in favour of the latter after prolonged litigation, Singapore and Malayan Malays of Indonesian origin were suspected of having been actively involved in instigating the racial riots in Singapore and Malaya that followed the unpopular court decision.[88] Indeed, British intelligence reported the detention of some 700 pro-MNP Indonesians and people 'of Indonesian race' in Malaya under emergency regulations.[89] Both these incidents alerted the conservative elements within the Malayan leadership to the spectre of unwelcome violence threatened by the interest of over-enthusiastic, politicized Indonesians in Malayan affairs.

The concern among Malaya's conservative elite and the sultans towards the influence that Indonesia could have on elements of the radical Malay political movement was also shared by the British.[90] Poulgrain intimated British anxieties in the following manner:

> The imposed colonial boundary along the Malacca Straits did not alter the traverse of local culture or the exchange of people and ideas, nor was it an impediment to the flow of revolutionary idealism from Indonesia to Malaya. In ethnic terms, many of the people who live on either side of the Malacca Straits are Malay. The proximity of Malaya and Sumatra created a historical conduit, not only longitudinal – up

and down the famous Malacca Straits – but also transverse. Had Indonesian colonialism, harboured for centuries, crossed the narrow watery division between archipelago and peninsula and taken hold, then Britain's tenuous post-war position in Malay would have been jeopardized.[91]

In response to the establishment of the API (*Angkatan Pemuda Insaf*, Cohort of Conscious Youths) youth movement under the auspices of the MNP to encourage the Malay community to support the party's call for immediate independence within an Indonesian federation, British intelligence reports warned: 'One need only remember the close kinship between Malays of Malaya and the Malayan peoples of the rest of Indonesia. What the latter can do, can be done equally well by the Malays of this Peninsula.'[92] Ultimately, it was their close alliance with the British colonial administration that saw the conservatives prevail in this contest of identities with the radical Malay nationalists. In the search for 'ideological consensus', left-wing parties and ideologies that espoused pan-nationalism were quickly labelled subversive and deviant, and eliminated by colonial repression and, after independence in 1957, by coercive instruments of control deployed to justify the preservation of internal security and stability.

The situation was exacerbated by the persistence of the issue of political unification with Indonesia, which continued to be a key political objective of radical Malay movements into the early 1950s. While UMNO and the British colonial administration were focused on ironing out the terms of independence, elements from the MNP were expressing through their party manifesto their unremitting desire to draw Malaya closer to Indonesia. Three points in the manifesto stood out to that effect. These were the desire, first, to unite the Malay nation (*bangsa Melayu*) and to inculcate national feelings in the hearts of the Malay people (*orang-orang Melayu*) with the ultimate aim of making Malaya unite with the big family, namely, the Republic of Greater Indonesia (*Republik Indonesia Raya*); second, to foster friendly relations with other domiciled races in the country to create a united and prosperous Malaya as a component member of *Republik Indonesia Raya*; and third, to support the Indonesian nationalist movement for the achievement of independence.[93] As with its predecessors, the MNP's brand of Malayan nationalism that sought to win independence via unity with Indonesia stemmed from the need of the Malays to compensate for the fact that they were fast becoming a minority in their own homeland in the wake of the encroachment into their politics and economics by Chinese and Indian minorities. In return, Indonesian youths sympathetic to the cause of the MNP subsequently moved to form the *Perikatan Pemuda Malaya – diluar Tanah Air* (Overseas Malayan National Youth Movement) in Jakarta to propagate the MNP cause of Malayan independence. When the MNP was later banned in 1953, it resurfaced in Indonesia as *Kesatuan Malaya Merdeka* (the Independence of Malaya Movement).

Popular pressures

Notwithstanding the obvious concern among the vast majority of the political leadership in Malaya towards the impact the Indonesian revolution and its legacy for the future of Malaya, the question of how to relate to Indonesia in light of the two countries' historical links as well as more recent experiences remained a complex issue. The primary reason for this lay in the observation that the concern Malay leaders had about identifying themselves closely with Indonesia at the political level was still clouded by the fact that even these aristocrats and conservative elites in the peninsula (let alone the Malay population in general, who continued to have family ties across the Melaka Straits) were to some extent constrained by the historical legacy of kinship the Malay population at large shared with their Indonesian cousins. Nowhere was this dichotomy starker than in the impact of the Indonesian revolution on Malay popular opinion. Anecdotal evidence exists, for example, of how many peninsular Malays had, in the wake of Indonesia's struggle against colonialism, erected photographs and portraits of Indonesian heroes such as Sukarno and Mohammad Hatta, and named streets after Indonesian heroes of the past and present.[94]

The intensity of popular support for Indonesia was not lost on the Malay elite. During his battle against the Malayan Union project, Onn bin Jaafar explicitly appealed to Indonesian migrants to 'safeguard the positions of the Malays'.[95] After independence, the Tunku himself was aware that 'a large proportion of the Malays had other loyalties – to Indonesia'.[96] It has also been noted earlier that many Malays from the peninsula actively participated in the Indonesian revolution. Throughout the 1950s, 17 August independence celebrations at the Indonesian Embassy in Malaya were a matter of festivity for Malays, and the event was celebrated in a 'village atmosphere' akin to traditional festivals in Malay–Indonesian culture.[97] Even the Malayan authorities have conceded the fact that to most Malays, Sukarno and Hatta were champions not merely of Indonesia, but of the Malays in the peninsula as well.[98] Such popular sentiments forced the Malay elite to temper public expressions of their reservations towards Indonesia, and this was reflected in the public statements of even the most wary of Malay leaders. UMNO founder-president Onn bin Jaafar once mentioned the possibility of Malaya integrating itself into a United States of Indonesia along with British Borneo.[99] Onn had apparently expressed the opinion that a pan-Malay union consisting of Malaya, Indonesia, and Borneo should be a political objective of the leaders of the Malay world.[100] Later, even Tunku Abdul Rahman, though incredulous at the idea of any kind of union, felt obliged to express similar sentiments when he opined that Malaya 'want[s] to unite with Indonesia, but as an independent country'.[101]

Concluding remarks

The ease with which kinship appeared to be socially and culturally constructed in anti-colonial discourse in the Indo-Malay world creates a difficult puzzle that this and the previous chapter have attempted to
illuminate. If, in fact, similar language and religion are prerequisites for
nationalism, why indeed did two separate states emerge out of what
appears to be one *Ethnie*? In attempting to disentangle the convolutions of
kinship politics in nationalist discourse during this complex period of the
region's history, it emerges that the unfolding of the kinship factor was
indelibly linked to the highly contested discursive terrain of identity, and
in particular Malay identity, as well as to the emergence of distinct brands
of nationalism not only in response to these contested notions of identity,
but also through political expediency as a result of the sudden termination
of the Pacific War.

By the end of the war, two nationalist assemblages had evolved in colonial Malaya, with distinct ideologies and positions on affiliation with
Indonesia. Where nationalist discourse in Malaya had been the sole prerogative of the socialist radicals of the KMM before the war, the post-war
Malayan Union saw to it that a galvanized traditional elite would emerge
to stake their political claims, rejecting the notion of political union with
Indonesia in the process. Uppermost in the minds of this elite, particularly
those in the upper echelon of UMNO, the inheritors of the colonial state,
was the impact of the Indonesian revolution itself, which served as a disin-
centive to union. Whatever empathy the Malay political elite of UMNO
felt towards the Indonesian nationalist struggle was blighted by the
debacle of the social revolution in Sumatra, which witnessed the decima-
tion of traditional Malay structures that were still widely respected in the
peninsula. Consequently, perceptions of kinship on the part of these mainstream Malay political leaders were clouded by the victimization of their
cousins in Sumatra in the wake of Indonesian nationalism. The matter of
the nascent Indonesian central government's inability or reluctance to
stem the tide of the social revolution left a mark on the minds of the mainstream Malayan nationalists, who ironically had by then embarked on
their own nationalism, defined paradoxically by the preservation of traditional political structures and symbols. In time, the negative perception of
Indonesia as a Javanese-dominated state that made little attempt to
accommodate the Malay–Sumatran *kerajaan* in the newly formed republic
would be further exacerbated by the left-leaning posture of the Sukarno
administration and its proscription of the influential Sumatran-based
Islamic party *Masyumi*, which enjoyed close ties with Malayan leaders.

The matter of social origins and political socialization of the respective
nationalist leaders would serve to further aggravate already-pronounced
differences. On the peninsula, anti-colonial activity was by and large insti-
gated and led by Indonesia-inspired radical nationalists, most of whom

were from humble backgrounds. In contrast, it was a pro-British, Western-educated traditional elite who stood at the forefront of mainstream Malay nationalism. In many ways, the English-educated Malay bureaucratic elite were socially and culturally alienated from the masses. Aristocratic elites, by virtue of their feudal nature, were even more so. This contrasted with the Indonesian experience, where members of lower- and middle-class Dutch-educated elites from Java and Sumatra such as Sukarno, Moham-mad Hatta, Sutan Sjahrir, Agus Salim, Muhammad Yamin, and others formed the backbone of the anti-colonial movement and identified with the social, political, and economic alienation of the masses, and subse-quently rose to prominence through the trials and tribulations of detention and subsequently revolution.[102] Because of their alienation, the Malay conservative elite still had to come to terms with a society that, though respectful of traditional structures of authority, regarded the Indonesian nationalists as 'Malay heroes'.

From the Indonesian perspective, the aristocratic and conservative advo-cates of mainstream Malayan nationalism were trapped in their world of feudalism and moderation, and hence were illegitimate representatives of national struggle.[103] Clearly, the egalitarian Indonesian nationalism that was emanating from Java and driving the re-stratification of society, destruction of tradition, and eradication of the feudal and aristocratic class was the very antithesis of the Malay-based nationalism many on the peninsula hoped to pursue. It was evident from the consequences suffered by the traditional Sumatran elite, who agitated for the protection of their privileged status, that the new Indonesian state would not entertain such political demands.[104] Not surprisingly, the alacrity with which political conservatism was dis-pensed with as a result of their clash of conceptions with the revolutionaries over the social-political basis of the new state (or rather, the position of Sumatra and other outer island territories within the Javanese-dominated Indonesian state and societal structures) was viewed as a disturbing devel-opment, and tempered traditional Malay elite support for Indonesian de-colonization.[105] Representing the apprehensions of the ruling elite, the following thoughts of Tunku Abdul Rahman reveal the sober sense of vul-nerability they felt in the wake of the appeal of Indonesian nationalism:

> The Rulers who had enjoyed sovereignty and prestige under the British rule were equally concerned. After independence they had seen how many thrones in India, Pakistan and Indonesia had toppled. What would be their fate if the British left? Would the people accept them? They felt that they would be at the mercy of the Malay extrem-ists. The general pre-*Merdeka* feeling was that this country would go the way of our neighbours, from prosperity to poverty, from happiness to sadness and from peace to violence. Even Datuk Onn, the founder of UMNO and a great Malay leader, had shared the views of the Rulers and others against complete independence.[106]

The Tunku's musings spoke much of the contradictions confronting the traditional Malay elite as they viewed developments in Indonesia. First, it was clear that, unlike the Indonesian nationalists' opinion of Dutch colonialism, the Malay elite were of the view that colonialism under the British was a time of 'sovereignty', 'prestige', 'happiness', 'prosperity', and 'peace'.[107] Moreover, many among the Malay elite were also of the opinion that total independence, which Indonesians were spilling blood for, was antithetical to the security of Malaya in view of the problem of communalism and communism, which required British assistance to subdue. Finally, many mainstream nationalists shared at the time an opinion that the kind of unification their opponents in the radical MNP proposed with Indonesia would have relegated Malays to the peripheries of *Indonesia Raya*. In view of this, it was portentous that Sutan Sjahrir, a former Sumatran Prime Minister of Indonesia and one of the more moderate of the Indonesian revolutionaries, had exhorted Onn bin Jaafar to 'remain in friendship with the British and to build up his own show'.[108]

This final point, however, revealed a fundamental cleavage in perceptions of kin-based pan-identity between its Malay and Indonesian proponents that not many have recognized. To Ibrahim Yaacob, Burhanuddin, and their compatriots, unification with Indonesia was based on a subscription to what they perceived in their minds to be the preponderance of Malay identity in the region.[109] Hence, unity within *Indonesia Raya* was assumed to be based on equal status for all Malay-dominant populations, which to them centred on Malaya, Indonesia, and the Philippines. Correspondingly, a brand of nationalism could be constructed across these territories along ethnic lines of *bangsa Melayu* ('Malay nationhood').[110] In effect, the Malay radical nationalists' train of thought echoed Muhammad Yamin's vision of an 'Austronesian Confederation' of Indonesia, Malaya, and the Philippines.[111] For them, co-identification with Indonesia was to be premised on the dominance of *bangsa Melayu*, of which Indonesia was a part.

From the Indonesian perspective, however, *Indonesia Raya* was primarily grounded neither in racial-ethnic affinity nor in the preponderance of Malay identity, even though this did lie at the surface of pan-Indonesian ideology. According to Indonesian interpretations of the ethno-historical record, the Malay Peninsula was part of the great Javanese Majapahit Empire, and political unification with Malaya in contemporary times was coterminous with its reconstruction.[112] Its foremost ideologue, Muhammad Yamin, articulated this legacy in the following manner:

> To separate Malaya from the rest of Indonesia amounts to deliberately weakening from the outset the position of the People's State of Indonesia in her international relations. On the other hand, to unite Malaya to Indonesia will mean strengthening our position and completing our entity to accord with our national aspiration and consistent with the interest of geopolitics of air, land and sea.[113]

Knowingly or otherwise, on the part of these Indonesians, underwriting their conception of pan-identity was a notion of Javanese dominance;[114] and because *Indonesia Raya* was a geopolitical rather than a racial or ethnic concept, this allowed them to discard the visions of pan-nationalism more easily when the complexities of the post-war political environment truncated any possible usurpation of British Malaya on this pretext.[115] In a profound demonstration of the different terms of reference, the term *Melayu Raya*, popularized by Malay radicals, was hardly used among the Indonesian nationalists to describe what they saw more aptly as *Indonesia Raya*, a greater Indonesian nation whose boundaries spanned what they believed to be the extent of the ancient kingdom of Majapahit.

The politicization of kinship in the Indo-Malay world was hence clearly riddled with ambiguities. It generated both binding and divisive dynamics, and the manner in which it played out depended in particular on how the various streams of nationalist thought on the peninsula conceptualized their affiliation with Indonesia, on which of these streams eventually inherited the post-colonial order, and on the shape of Indonesian and Malayan nationalism and national identity as they evolved. Ultimately, it was all these dynamics that played the crucial role in influencing how Indonesian and Malaysian leaders came to understand the terms of reference of their relations as post-colonial kin states. Left unresolved as they were, these convolutions would eventually have repercussions for the fulfilment of expectations and obligations of kinship in the post-colonial years.

Part II

Diplomatic history of Indonesia–Malaysia relations

4 Ties that divide, 1949–1965

The previous chapter discussed in detail the politicization of kinship in the nationalist projects in the Malay world. While solidarity was no doubt magnified in the common struggle against colonialism, underneath this lay substantial differences in terms of how the kinship factor was conceived to be a basis for affinity among various political quarters in Indonesia and Malaysia. Concomitantly, these contested conceptions of kinship resulting from alternative interpretations of history and historical experience played a significant role in influencing the shape and direction of post-colonial relations. As the process of state consolidation and post-colonial identity creation was put into motion, so too did the different worldviews that emerged out of respective historical experiences work to further transform conceptions of kinship in the era of post-colonial boundaries. It was also in the post-colonial era that the functional aspect of relatedness took on greater prominence in political relations, when the translation of affinity into policies was seen as a necessary expression and outcome of kin solidarity.

The shaping of foreign policy outlooks

An accomplished scholar of Indonesian foreign policy has described the post-colonial Javanese-dominated Indonesian worldview in the following manner:

> The struggle for independence exposed the weakness and vulnerability of the Indonesian state arising from its fragmented social and physical condition. In addition, an awareness of the attraction of Indonesia's bountiful natural resources and the importance of its strategic location between the Indian and Pacific Oceans reinforced an apprehension of external powers. By contrast, that common international outlook encompassed also a proprietary attitude towards the regional environment.[1]

The 'proprietary attitude' alluded to stemmed from the fact that Indonesian independence was won through revolution and the central Indonesian state created through a conspicuous act of nationalist will. This informed the outlook of the political elite in Jakarta towards newly formed states within Indonesia's geographic locale. Malaya in particular was singled out as a state requiring 'revolutionizing' as a result of its 'counterfeit independence'.[2]

The belief prevalent among the political and military elite in Jakarta at the time was that independence could never be granted by imperialists or won in collaboration with them, but had to be fought for if it were to be considered authentic. By this token, it was not surprising that the Indonesian leadership was highly critical of the nationalist credentials of the Malay ruling elite on the peninsula. This was corroborated by Weinstein's survey of the attitude of Indonesian leaders towards Malaysia: he found that 'as for Malaysia, there was more to admire, but there were still grave doubts about the authenticity of its independence'.[3] Symptomatic of this was a quip directed at the Malayan Prime Minister, Tunku Abdul Rahman, by Sukarno. On the occasion of the former's visit to Jakarta in 1955 as Chief Minister of British Malaya, Sukarno reportedly turned to him during a public rally and proclaimed, 'Here is a man I am trying to persuade to fight.'[4] Indeed, the condescension in Indonesian attitudes to Malayan leaders set in train subsequent perceptions of expectations in relation to bilateral relations. Because of the nature of their respective independence struggles, many among the Indonesian leadership viewed Malaya's standing as one of deference. Yet under the Tunku, as was soon to become clear, Malaya was unwilling to dance to this tune.

It needs to be said that the revolutionary diatribes of the Jakarta leadership during this period were hardly an issue of mere political rhetoric. Indonesian foreign policy, described in official discourse as *bebas dan aktif* (independent and active), strove to provide substance to flamboyant policy statements. Very early on, this was manifested in the Hatta government's rejection of a Philippine suggestion for the formation of an anti-communist Pacific Pact in May 1950. This trend was followed by subsequent governments from Mohammad Natsir, who succeeded Hatta in August 1950, through to 1959. Later, foreign policy-making during the period of Guided Democracy (1959–1965) became auxiliary to the domestic purpose of sustaining the revolutionary culture of Indonesian politics. The nationalistic character of Indonesia's foreign policy during this period was registered most conspicuously in Jakarta's demand for West Irian, an unresolved issue carried over from the 1949 Round Table Conference at which the Dutch reluctantly recognized Indonesian independence, and which was a symbol of national fulfilment no Indonesian administration could afford to compromise. By the mid-1950s, the non-aligned impetus to foreign policy began taking on more concrete form in Indonesia's founding role at the 1955 Bandung Afro-Asian Conference. As further evidence of Indonesian attempts to project a non-aligned foreign policy, Jakarta also roundly condemned Washington's sponsorship in September 1954 of a Collective Security Defence Treaty for Southeast Asia and took a decidedly anti-Western position in response to the British and French invasion of Egypt in 1956.

By mid-1957, however, it was becoming clear that the Sukarno administration's 'independent and active' policies were becoming more aligned with those of the Soviet Union and China. This was particularly noticeable after the President's visits to the two communist powers the year before. The advent of Guided Democracy saw diplomatic belligerence raised to a level where much resource and attention was given to the prescription of an alternative regional and international order. Jakarta's radical foreign policy was taken to the extreme as much out of a need to divert domestic attention from the increasingly precarious political and economic situation in Indonesia as to an intensified assertion of the revolutionary legacy of Indonesia's international outlook. Indeed, many of Indonesia's trademark policies during this period were targeted at challenging the prevailing regional and international order. It is from this perspective that the Jakarta's relationship with Malaya should be viewed.

Of interest during this time was Jakarta's inordinate interest in the evolution of independent Malaya, the international outlook of Malaya's political leadership, and its position on international affairs. Setting this tune at the Malayan independence celebration, the Indonesian Foreign Minister, Subandrio, had expressed to the Australian High Commissioner the sentiment that Malaya was 'particularly important' to Indonesia.[5] This active interest in Malaya's affairs would be magnified by Indonesia's proprietary attitude to regional entitlement on affairs concerning archipelagic Southeast Asia. It was from this vantage point that Jakarta questioned the 'neutrality' of early Malayan foreign relations. Robert Tilman, a close observer of Malayan foreign policy, has described Kuala Lumpur's position on international affairs as that of a 'committed neutral'.[6] This characterization of Malayan foreign policy, particularly in the early years of independence, has been erroneous. Many of those in Kuala Lumpur policy circles were avowed anti-communists. Most notable was Tunku Abdul Rahman, who himself claimed that

> It is sheer hypocrisy to suggest that when democracy is attacked we should remain silent and consider ourselves at peace with the world. Small as we are, we are not cowards and we are not hypocrites. In fact, today neutralism is no guarantee of one's safety. India was neutral before she was attacked. Many other countries will soon find themselves in the same predicament.[7]

Because of Malaya's underlying concern over communism, it was difficult for the newly independent Malayan government to convince Indonesia (or indeed its own domestic opposition) of its neutrality. Its strong foreign policy inclinations towards the West were epitomized by the priority placed on relations with Britain and the Commonwealth.[8] Furthermore, it was the ANZAM (Australia, New Zealand, and Malaya) agreement of 1949 and subsequently the Anglo-Malayan Defence Agreement (AMDA) signed with Britain in October 1957 that underwrote Malayan security.[9] While one could suggest that Malayan commitment to neutrality and non-alignment was exemplified by Kuala Lumpur's absence from SEATO (the South-East Asia Treaty Organization), the fact that the Malayan government remained firmly committed to the AMDA and was part of ASA (the Association of Southeast Asia), an organization that included two countries (Thailand and the Philippines) which were signatories of security arrangements with the United States, was in itself indicative of Malaya's inclinations on questions of alignment.[10] The ambiguity surrounding Malaya's position on SEATO in particular evoked the ire of an Indonesian government strongly convinced of the organization's futility and suspicious of its intentions. The Tunku had noted in private that while he and his cabinet 'fully understood that the ultimate defence of Malaya lay in SEATO, politically the word "SEATO" could not be safely used in connection with anything Malayan without provoking hysteria'.[11] It is probable that on his mind was the pressure being exerted by pro-Indonesian forces within the Malayan parliament for Kuala Lumpur to dissociate itself from Britain. While the Malayan leadership saw the need for rhetorical compromise, it was also keenly aware of London's warnings 'not to give handle to Indonesian propaganda ... to the effect that British forces are here primarily for [our] own purposes rather than to defend Malaysia and that defence agreement is a neo-colonial imposition on Malaysia'.[12] In fact, the Tunku had tacitly supported the security function of SEATO. This was transcribed in the Commonwealth Secretary's report to the British Prime Minister, Harold Macmillan, of his meeting with the Malayan Prime Minister:

> If it were a question of active operations in support of SEATO, no difficulties would be placed in our [Britain's] way. So long as his [the Tunku's] government was in power, we [Britain] could safely plan on the assumption that British forces could move by road or any other means direct from Malaya into Siam.[13]

On another occasion, the Tunku had gone to the extent of claiming that 'the Federation of Malaya, by signing a mutual defence treaty with Britain is indirectly in the SEATO'.[14] This association between Malaya's commitment to AMDA and Britain's obligation to SEATO was clear from Article VI of the so-called Singapore Proviso in the Malaysia Agreement of 1963. The provision, which was essentially an extension of the AMDA agreement of 1957 to cover the additional territories of Malaysia in 1963, gave Britain the right 'to make such use of these [Malayan] facilities as the [British] Government may consider necessary for the purpose of assisting in the defence of Malaysia, and for Commonwealth defence and the preservation of peace in Southeast Asia'. It is clear from the final sentence of Article VI that these provisions were designed to secure maximum cooperation of Malaya in a SEATO contingency, when the 'peace in Southeast Asia' was threatened. Interpreted in this manner, this agreement certainly lent credence to Indonesian suspicions that AMDA was a neocolonial imposition with Malayan contrivance.

Given Malaya's tacit backing of SEATO, it is also interesting to note that the Tunku's administration still refrained from official commitment to the organization. As often as he espoused the value of SEATO to Malaya, he was also fervent in publicly rejecting any prospect of Malaya's official participation, arguing that Malaya did not believe in alliances.[15] On the issue of SEATO membership, it has come to light that his administration refrained from participating in SEATO for purely domestic reasons, for fear that sentiments in Malaya were strongly against Malayan involvement in any military alliance.[16] The vagaries behind the Malayan government's policy proclivities towards SEATO surfaced in public debates over Malaya's involvement in Laos in the late 1950s, in which Malaya only barely managed to convince Britain that evoking the AMDA agreement would put Kuala Lumpur in a tenuous position on the domestic political front.[17] Explaining this, the British High Commissioner noted:

Even the Malays are divided on issues of the greatest importance to the Government. This division arises from the fact that a large proportion of them ... are of Indonesian origin and sympathizers, and that most of the Malay vernacular press is under Indonesian influence. This group has shown signs of regarding the Tunku as too much committed to the West. ... As a whole they seem to incline towards socialism and neutralism on the Bandung model. These trends have been discernible in UMNO itself, particularly in its youth sections.[18]

As for Indonesia's response to Malaya's commitment to the West, any hopes that Jakarta harboured of weaning Malaya away from the West and SEATO influence were effectively laid to rest when, during his visit to Jakarta in November 1958, the Malayan Deputy Prime Minister, Tun Abdul Razak, expressed the opinion that while Malaya was not part of SEATO, it did not and would not oppose it.[19]

Not only was Malayan foreign policy during this period effectively pro-West in substance if not in form, it was also marked by attempts to manage regional security issues. Malaya was the progenitor of the regional cooperation initiative SEAFET (the South-East Asia Friendship and Economic Treaty) in February 1959, which would eventually evolve through an arduous process into ASA (the Association of Southeast Asia) by July 1961. As it happened, Malayan interest in regional leadership coincided with heightened Indonesian activism in Indonesia's own regional locale, and the latter's response to Malayan prescriptions for regional order clearly illustrated the extent of the clash that seemed inevitable under these circumstances. Indonesia frowned upon Malaya's SEAFET and ASA proposals, arguing that they ran counter to the Bandung spirit and weakened Afro-Asian solidarity.[20] Compounding matters was the Tunku's public disregard for the Non-Aligned Movement. In January 1958, the Tunku criticized non-aligned countries for not taking a definite stand against communism. Later, in a veiled challenge to Indonesia, he contested the viability and effectiveness of Bandung, the jewel in the crown of Indonesia's international activism, by querying mockingly: 'Where is this conference? Where is its permanent organization which the Bandung conference proposed? To whom do we apply to become members?'[21] In a further affront to the Sukarno regime, the Tunku jested that guided democracy meant 'you don't know which way you're going to be guided'.[22]

Bilateral tensions as a result of divergent conceptions of regional order were aggravated, paradoxically enough, by the fact that Malaya's opposition and challenge to Indonesian regional primacy did not actually preclude the possibility of Indonesian membership and participation in the regional organs envisaged by Kuala Lumpur. Nevertheless, Indonesia's participation in any of Malaya's regional initiatives was clearly an issue involving prestige. Bearing this in mind, participating in and contributing to the realization of any regional initiative that originated from outside of Jakarta was viewed as a capitulation of its regional leadership role, a surrendering of its prestige in Southeast Asia and the Third World, and an undermining of its revolutionary legacy. Indeed, these differences in perceptions of each other's regional role would prove to be a major stumbling block for attempts to premise their relations as sovereign nation-states on kinship terms.

The Indonesia–Malaya Treaty of Friendship, 17 April 1959

Even before contending regional perspectives came to the fore, tension between Indonesia and Malaya had already been brewing with the latter's independence. Indonesian suspicions of the benign circumstances surrounding Malayan independence in August 1957 was certainly portentous of the potential problems that would confront relations between these kin states. Likewise, the fact that the Malayan political elite viewed Indonesia as a possible security threat was evident early in Malayan independence when Kuala Lumpur expressed reservations that Britain's contemplated arms supply to Jakarta would add to Indonesia's offensive potential.[23] On the other hand, Malayan leaders were also acutely aware of the special consideration that relations with Indonesia demanded. In assessing the popular pressures he faced, the Tunku's belief was reported by High Commissioner Critchley to the following effect:

There was now a very strong feeling amongst many Malays who looked to Indonesia as a 'big brother' which his government could not ignore. He pointed out that two-thirds of the Malays in Johore, most of the Malays in Kuala Lumpur, and one cabinet minister (Sardon) were Indonesian. He also said that most of the Malay press was controlled by Indonesian-trained journalists.[24]

Domestic pressures dictated attempts to premise relations with their larger kin neighbours on the kinship factor of shared language, religion, and cultural practice.[25] In an attempt to place relations on such a footing, Tunku Abdul Rahman had earlier paid a goodwill visit to Indonesia in his capacity as Chief Minister of Malaya in 1955. Subsequently, in early 1957, Malaya opened a diplomatic mission in Jakarta. When the mission was converted to an embassy after Malayan independence, the Tunku chose as his ambassador a trusted political ally, Senu bin Abdul Rahman. The following observations on Senu's arrival in Jakarta were telling of the terms of Indonesian expectations at that juncture:

> In accordance with a pleasant local custom, all other commonwealth Heads of Mission joined ... to offer an informal welcome to Malaya's first Ambassador.... These occasions are normally small and quite unofficial, with no Indonesians present other than a representative of the protocol division of the Ministry of Foreign Affairs. Yesterday's arrival ... attracted considerable attention. The airport was thronged with press reporters and photographers; the proceedings were broadcast by Radio Republik Indonesia; and the airport building was decorated with an enormous welcoming poster.[26]

During an official visit to Jakarta in November 1958, however, the Deputy Prime Minister, Razak, for reasons never made clear, was apparently confronted abruptly with a cultural agreement in a final form and his signature promptly solicited. Needless to say, Razak was taken aback by the forcefulness of this Indonesian gesture. He explained that the Federation government could not conclude treaties in this fashion, and that a draft would have to be examined in Kuala Lumpur and agreed by the cabinet before any commitment was made. It would have been clear to Malayan policy-makers that these early events were hints that bilateral relations would entail subservience to an enthusiastic Indonesia seeking to exert influence upon Malayan policy. For Malaya, a thin, easily transgressed line lay between cordial bilateral relations on the one hand, and what could be conceived as Malayan acquiescence to Indonesian tutorship and directives on the other.

Notwithstanding the problems that simmered beneath the surface in those formative years, both states were receptive enough to the potential for collaboration as kin states to have entered into a friendship treaty.

From a Malayan perspective, the signing of the treaty itself is significant in that it remains the only Treaty of Friendship ever signed by Kuala Lumpur.[27] Signed on 17 April 1959 on the occasion of the goodwill visit to Malaya by the Indonesian Prime Minister, Djuanda, the treaty was supposed to 'restore blood and racial relations' and help the two countries 're-discover common heritage', building on precisely the historical ties of kinship that were felt to have existed and that functioned as a rallying point for anti-colonial struggle. The main clauses of the treaty, focusing as they did on language standardization and enhanced cultural and educational exchanges, attested to attempts at emphasizing avenues of kinship as a basis for bilateral relations.

Djuanda's visit, however, did not pass without controversy, even if tensions were masked by forced displays of camaraderie. It was notable, for example, that the Indonesian delegation did not appreciate the inordinate amount of time spent on formal calls to feudal rulers.[28] Also, Indonesia's cool reception of Tunku Abdul Rahman's scheme for the establishment of SEAFET did not pass unnoticed. On his part, the Tunku was reluctant to express overt support for the five principles of Bandung, choosing instead to make reference to the UN Charter. It was clear from this that Malaya was still anxious not to be drawn too far into the Afro-Asian fold with which Indonesia was closely identified. Malaya's emphasis on SEAFET over Bandung was viewed as an affront in Indonesian circles. Two years later, in a commentary comparing ASA, the successor to SEAFET, and Bandung, the Malayan media reported provocatively: 'the one remains what it was at Bandung, the expression of nationalist fervour among ex-colonial territories; the other is an association looking to economic, social and cultural advance'.[29] The Indonesian press retorted by arguing that the association was doomed to failure without Indonesian participation.[30] Central to Jakarta's reaction to Kuala Lumpur's foreign policy initiatives was its dislike of what it saw as a newcomer taking the initiative in an area where it considered itself to be the rightful leader. Jakarta resented how the Malayan leaders could declare themselves to be 'neutral' while in effect showing benevolence to the West. In the words of an Australian observer, '[the] Tunku has been showing too much initiative and independence for the liking of a people who promoted and staged the Bandung Conference and who confidently expected to have the new independent Malaya in their pocket'.[31] This acrimonious exchange culminated in the cancellation of Prime Minister Djuanda's visit to Kuala Lumpur in 1961.[32]

Contending perspectives on regional security were not the only focus for discord between the two kin states. Other indirect diplomatic fracas included Indonesia's criticism of Malaya's condemnation of China in the wake of the latter's annexation of Tibet, which Indonesia saw as a matter of China's 'domestic affairs', as well as Jakarta's withdrawal of its UN contingent from the Belgian Congo, apparently from a change of policy position, but one that tellingly coincided with the arrival of the Malayan contingent.

It was quite evident, then, that Malaya's foreign policy prerogatives were emerging as diametrically opposed to those of Indonesia. With hindsight, it is not surprising that in spite of the promptings of the opposition Pan-Malayan Islamic Party, consisting of residual elements from the pro-Indonesia MNP, the Friendship Treaty was not followed up with further plans to strengthen cooperation.[33] Similarly, while a measure of cultural cooperation persisted, particularly in the realms of language policy and religious exchange, politics remained at a level separate from everyday affairs. In fact, events of the day indicated that the leaderships of these two kin states were instead heading towards confrontation. It would be three issues pertaining directly to Indonesia's sense of national and territorial vulnerability that would become the definitive markers of the undercurrents of bilateral ties, and of how leaders of both Indonesia and Malaya perceived and interpreted their relations as kin states in this period.

The PRRI/Permesta rebellion

A major crisis that had long-standing repercussions for relations pertained to Malaya's policy towards a renegade regional movement that sought to challenge the Indonesian central government in Java.

By the late 1950s, regional dissent against the central Indonesian government was fast transforming itself into a political movement to challenge the authority of Jakarta. In December 1956, the West Sumatra military command revolted and took over civil administration. In March 1957, a similar military-based regional political movement was formed in Sulawesi. Named Permesta (an acronym for *Piagam Perjuangan Semesta Alam*, Universal Struggle Charter), this movement was formed in retaliation against the Jakarta government's clampdown on smuggling activity undertaken by the military commanders and units in Sulawesi to supplement the meagre funding given by the central government.[34] Later, on 15 February 1958, a group of dissident politicians and military officers in Sumatra formed the PRRI (*Pemerintah Revolusioner Republik Indonesia*, Revolutionary Government of the Republic of Indonesia) in Padang and Bukittinggi, West Sumatra. What was noticeable about the PRRI/Permesta movement was that it consisted of essentially non-Javanese, Muslim, and generally pro-Western elements in Indonesian politics. By virtue of this, the PRRI rebels had propensities similar to the newly independent administration in Malaya. Apart from their similar political outlook, the kin affiliation felt by the Malays in Malaya towards Sumatra was much more resilient than their feelings towards the Javanese, and this would subsequently define both Malaya's response to the rebellion and the Javanese-dominated Indonesian central government's interpretation of Malayan intentions.

One of the immediate factors that precipitated the regional rebellion was the rapid decline of non-Javanese influence in the upper echelons of the central government. This was significant, because until then Sumatra had enjoyed a strong presence in the highest levels of leadership in Indonesia through Masyumi and PSI (*Partai Sosialis Indonesia*, Indonesian Socialist Party), both regional parties with close links to Malayan political organizations (UMNO in the case of the former, and elements of the MNP in the case of the latter). By the mid-1950s, however, Javanese elements started to assert themselves in government, taking over key positions with the help of Sukarno. Symbolic of this was the resignation of the most prominent Sumatran nationalist, the respected Vice-President and Prime Minister Mohammad Hatta, in July 1956 out of a sense both of disillusionment at Indonesian developments and of helplessness regarding the country's slide into political and economic chaos.

Alongside the decline in regional (and especially Sumatran) influence in the central government was the heightened tendency of the Sukarno administration towards authoritarianism and communism. A shift in the administration's ideological propensities had begun to take shape by 1955–1956. Indicative of this was the decline in essentially pro-Western regional elements in the central government and the President's increasingly active flirtation with the left. By that time, Sukarno, duly impressed during his visits to the Soviet Union and China, had begun seriously contemplating establishing a form of leftist authoritarian rule in the wake of Indonesia's apparently incurable political and economic problems.

When the Sumatran rebellion broke out, Malaya declared a policy of non-interference. At an official level, Kuala Lumpur also denounced foreign aid to the rebels and condemned external interference in Indonesian affairs. While ostensibly a public commitment to abstain from supporting the rebellion, the Malayan government's condemnation of foreign interference was also a veiled attack on Soviet support for the central government in the latter's clampdown on the rebels. On the other hand, the rebels were receiving support – psychological as well as material – from Britain and the United States.[35] To London and Washington, the emergence of this alternative power centre was a good check on the reactionary potential of the forces of Indonesian nationalism represented by Sukarno and his supporters.[36] Further to that, the rebel government in Indonesia was also looking for SEATO assistance to overthrow Sukarno.[37] These developments created a predicament for a Malayan government closely allied to these Western powers.

The situation was exacerbated by the fact that the rebels shared a deep affinity with Malaya. By virtue of the fact that most of the rebels were Sumatran, there was a strong kinship bond between them and the Malays of the peninsula, with whom they shared much by way of indigenous culture, and in some respects even ethnicity. Moreover, the rebels were also staunch anti-communists, further availing an ideological avenue of sympathy. This made it difficult for the Malays to view with equanimity the suppression of their Sumatran cousins by an overwhelmingly Javanese Indonesian military.[38] There is also evidence that at a conference of dissident leaders in Sumatra in January 1958 the desirability of federation between Malaya and Sumatra was discussed, and prominent rebels such as Colonels Hussein and Barlian were in favour of the idea in principle.[39] On another occasion, the rebel leaders in Sumatra were alleged to have informed the Dutch that if Java fell into communist hands, Sumatra would declare independence.[40]

Despite Malayan proclamations of non-involvement, Jakarta was well aware of the fact that the rebels had easy access to arms purchased via Singapore and the Thai–Malayan border. The rebels were also able to obtain foreign exchange by engaging in trading activity through Singapore and Penang.[41] Most galling was the fact that PRRI rebels and sympathizers were permitted to visit the Federation regularly to publicize their cause.[42] In the face of accusations of complicity, Kuala Lumpur maintained that these rebels held valid visas that the government was 'bound to honour'.[43] Bilateral tensions reached new heights in the aftermath of the collapse of the regional rebellion, when, despite protestations by Jakarta, rebels continued receiving asylum in Malaya on 'humanitarian grounds'.[44] It has also been suggested in certain quarters that some Malayans of Sumatran origin actively facilitated these rebels' flight to Malaya.[45] Using juridical arguments, the Malayan government had maintained that there was no extradition treaty in place with Indonesia, and hence no basis for repatriation. Nevertheless, to placate the Indonesian government's feelings, Kuala Lumpur legislated that visas would be issued to Indonesians only after they signed an undertaking not to engage in politics while in the Federation. Kuala Lumpur also requested from Jakarta a list of names of offenders along with their invalidated travel documents so that the Malayan government could take legitimate measures to prevent their entry. By then, however, a substantial number of these dissident rebels had already arrived in Malaya, knowing that they need not worry about repatriation.

In sum, Jakarta resented the Federation's harbouring of Sumatran rebels, as well as what it perceived to be Malaya's reluctance to curb their activities in Malaya. Indonesian expectations were for Malaya to take an active position to condemn the rebellion and provide support for the central government in Java. In the perception of the central government, diplomatic support from Malaya would have been significant, given the knowledge in Jakarta that Britain, the United States, and Australia were actively supporting the rebels.[46] Moreover, any declared support on the part of Malaya for the central government would have assuaged Jakarta's enduring suspicion that Malayan foreign policy was in fact voluntarily skewed towards the West. Needless to say, this support was not forthcoming from Kuala Lumpur, and the failure, or rather unwillingness, of

Malaya to 'fulfil' such expectations was viewed with disdain in Jakarta. Indonesian disappointment at Kuala Lumpur's position on the rebellions would be publicly expressed several years later in a government report.[47] Evidently, President Sukarno was by that time already highly suspicious of Malaya's sincerity and intentions, and he was quoted as opining at a public meeting on 8 April 1958 that an attempt was being made by Malaya to create a new Islamic bloc in Southeast Asia, including an independent Sumatra.[48]

On Malaya's part, its official position was that blood brotherhood, in so far as it existed with Indonesia, should not impede the application of international law, which Kuala Lumpur intended to abide by with regard to the repatriation of asylum seekers. Beneath this, however, lay a concern for the manner in which Jakarta's demands of the Malayan government clearly betrayed the former's expectations of deference on the part of the 'younger brother' to its wishes. The Malayan government also found it difficult to condemn the Sumatran rebels for another reason: many among the Malay political elite considered Sumatra the cradle of the Malay race, whereas Java was seen as more distant (both geographically and culturally) and also the stronghold of communists.[49] The Tunku himself was known to have harboured strong sympathies towards the rebels.[50] The slant of the kinship factor in this instance is particularly interesting, for, as suggested earlier, it was the close affinity between the Malays of the peninsula and Sumatra that impeded close cooperation between Malaya and the Javanese-dominated central government. Attesting to the potential political utility of this affinity, the opinion of Ghazali Shafie, expressed during a later visit to Washington, is worthy of note:

> Regional feelings were strong in the country [Indonesia], and especially so in Sumatra and Sulawesi. He [Ghazali] could cite no current dissidence in Sumatra but said he was in very close touch with the situation and with many responsible Sumatran leaders and was convinced that Sumatra is 'on the move'.... Ghazali said that Malaysia was quite capable of taking advantage of this situation, but insisted that his country is not taking action to do so just yet. He felt that when the time came the mistakes of 1958 should be avoided, that the United States and the West should stay out of the picture, and that Malaysia should be the power to stimulate action, using Indonesians with whom it is in contact.[51]

With fewer words but no less authority, Tunku Abdul Rahman was known to have expressed his opinion that if he had so much as stretched out his hand at that time, Sumatra would have been his.[52] Indonesia's concern for the lack of support on the part of Malaya for its territorial integrity was further aggravated by Kuala Lumpur's position on the former's claim over the Dutch territory of West Irian.

West Irian

Indonesia's claim to West Irian was carried over from the inconclusive terms of the 1949 Round Table Agreement, when sovereignty over the Dutch East Indies was transferred to Indonesia.[53] The Agreement provided that the political status of West Irian was to be determined by negotiations between the signatories within a year of its signing. Negotiations took place at various times from 1952 to 1956, but proved inconclusive, as the Dutch refused to rescind their claim. Jakarta, on the other hand, claimed that *de jure* sovereignty rested with it. Diplomatic support for Indonesia's cause was provided by the Soviet Union and the Afro-Asian bloc. As sabre-rattling over West Irian intensified, the Dutch dispatched military reinforcements to West Irian in mid-1960.[54] Indonesia retaliated by stigmatizing this action as 'provocative', and launched an intense propaganda campaign within the Afro-Asian bloc against the Dutch. The fiery and abrasive rhetoric of Indonesian leaders fed the nationalistic fervour that the West Irian issue was inspiring in Indonesia. Matters came to a head when Jakarta declared a policy of 'Confrontation' against the Netherlands over West Irian on 21 July 1960; diplomatic ties were broken on 17 August 1960, Indonesia's independence anniversary.

West Irian not only remained a thorn in relations between Indonesia and the Netherlands, but also emerged as an increasingly precarious security issue in Southeast Asia. Indeed, it was precisely the destabilizing potential of a military conflict over West Irian that drew Malaya into the fray as a possible mediator. More specifically, it was the expressed fear of the Malayan government at the time that an Indonesian confrontation with the Dutch over West Irian would play into the hands of the PKI (*Partai Komunis Indonesia*, Indonesian Communist Party) and give the communists a foothold in the largest country in Southeast Asia, thereby threatening the security of Malaya itself. The fact that communist countries were Jakarta's major source of political support and Moscow their main source of material assistance further aggravated Malayan concerns.[55] The situation was made even more precarious by the fact that in pursuit of the nationalistic, propagandistic objectives in his West Irian campaign, Sukarno had brought the Indonesian economy to the brink of collapse in order to make a political point.[56] It was these concerns that drove Tunku Abdul Rahman to offer himself as a mediator on the West Irian issue.[57]

The notion of Malaya playing the role of mediator in this dispute was from the very beginning questioned by the Indonesian government. Given that Malaya had abstained from voting on the West Irian question at the Twelfth UN General Assembly in September 1957, and in so doing drawn a negative response from Indonesia, it was hardly surprising that elements within the Indonesian government had misgivings towards Malayan intentions.[58] The perceptual and diplomatic repercussions of this lack of support from Kuala Lumpur were aggravated by the fact that after a trip to Kuala

Lumpur, the Indonesian Foreign Minister, Subandrio, had ostensibly returned with 'assurance' of Malayan support.[59] Subsequently, Malaya's reluctance to throw its lot behind Indonesia's claims at the United Nations drew criticisms not only from Indonesia, but from pro-Indonesia Malay circles in Malaya as well. Indeed, the domestic repercussions caught the Malayan government by surprise, and prompted a change in policy towards the Indonesian claim when the matter arose again at the United Nations in November that same year.

After November 1957, Malaya intensified its interest in West Irian and began pressing for the peaceful departure of the Dutch.[60] Malaya's Ambassador to Jakarta, Senu Abdul Rahman, was dispatched with a personal letter from the Tunku to President Sukarno to ascertain Indonesia's willingness to accept Malayan mediation. In Sukarno's absence, the Malayan offer was accepted by the Prime Minister, Djuanda.[61] The Indonesian government's positive response was further reiterated by Armed Forces General Nasution during his visit to Malaya in 13 October 1960.[62] Nevertheless, other parties expressed doubts as to the efficacy of Malayan mediation. To that effect, the British High Commissioner noted somewhat prophetically in October 1960: 'It is questionable whether he [Tunku Abdul Rahman] has appreciated the delicacies and difficulties of the issue or realized that his activities in his self-appointed role as mediator may do little more than annoy both parties.'[63]

With Indonesia's apparent blessing, expressed through Djuanda and Nasution, the Tunku proposed for West Irian to be placed under UN trusteeship (monitored by Malaya, India, and Ceylon), after which sovereignty was to be transferred to Indonesia. To gain support for his proposal, the Tunku embarked on an international tour that took him to the capitals of the major Western powers.[64] Despite the expressed reservations of those consulted, by the close of his diplomatic tour the Tunku and Dutch Prime Minister Jan de Quay signed a communiqué stating *inter alia* that 'the Netherlands Government was willing to subject their [*sic*] policies in Netherlands New Guinea to the scrutiny and judgment of the United Nations'.[65] While seemingly clear, the communiqué in fact suffered from fundamental misinterpretations on the Tunku's part that led to the unravelling of his diplomatic effort as well as the generation of negative sentiments in both the Indonesian government and the Indonesian public towards him. In the main, the Tunku had misread Dutch intentions. The Dutch, as de Quay made clear to the Tunku *after* the signing of the communiqué and the press conference that followed, had agreed to his proposal to transfer West Irian administration to UN trusteeship *with the sole objective of self-determination for the West Irian population.*

Despite the Tunku's public claims that 'it would not be in keeping with my own nationality to side with somebody who has got no blood connection with us whereas, on the other hand, the Malays and Indonesians are, what we might call, blood brothers', the signing of the communiqué amounted to a diplomatic *faux pas* that cast doubts in Indonesian minds over Malayan intentions.[66] The situation was further aggravated by the Tunku's delay in presenting the terms of the communiqué to Jakarta officials, who first came to know of it only via the media. The Foreign Minister, Subandrio, criticized the Tunku in public for acting without prior consultation with Jakarta, and declared that the only UN intervention acceptable to Jakarta was its supervision of the transfer of West Irian from the Netherlands direct to Indonesia.[67] A scathing Indonesian press campaign against the Malayan Prime Minister followed.[68] Kuala Lumpur protested against Subandrio's criticisms and the press attacks by highlighting the Jakarta government's previous support for the Tunku's initiative. In a move to vindicate himself, but one that would also undoubtedly have humiliated Jakarta, the Tunku threatened to divulge a letter from Djuanda, which they both had earlier agreed to commit to secrecy, explicitly approving Malayan mediation.[69] Subandrio subsequently issued a measured apology through an official from the Indonesian Foreign Ministry, Suska, expressing gratitude for the Tunku's efforts and goodwill, but also making clear Indonesia's inability to accept the latter's UN Trusteeship scheme.

Even though bilateral relations were prevented from deteriorating further with Subandrio's apology, events surrounding the Tunku's mediation attempt touched raw nerves in Jakarta and revealed Indonesian perceptions of and attitudes towards Malaya. First, it was clear that beneath Jakarta's apparent approval of the mediation efforts, suspicions of Malaya's intentions persisted. This was evident in the fact that several members of the Indonesian government, such as Subandrio and Nasution (before he was made aware of Indonesia's 'official' position), were less than enthusiastic over the Tunku's proposal. Sukarno's position on Malayan mediation was also questionable, though it should be noted that in the aftermath of the Tunku's failed attempt at mediation, he did send a personal letter to the latter acknowledging his efforts. Nevertheless, still implicit within his appreciative words was Sukarno's dissatisfaction at the outcome of the Tunku's mediation:

> Although the Indonesian Government did not expect that a Joint-Communiqué would be issued by your Excellency and the Dutch Government, yet we did not make any announcement at that time, despite the fact that the Joint-Communiqué had already created doubts among the Indonesian populace. . . .
>
> I am sure Your Excellency would have understood that the Joint-Communiqué with all the accompanying explanation would set a strong reaction in Indonesia against the Government of the Indonesian Republic and Your Excellency, if there was [*sic*] no firm objections from yourself or your side. Due to this, Minister of Foreign Affairs, Subandrio, considered it necessary to issue a statement opposing the statement made by Mr. Luns. . . .

As Your Excellency knows, whether it was in my explanation or
from the letter of Dr. Djuanda from the President's office, the people
of Indonesia regard West Irian as an Indonesian territory.... Based
on this consideration, the Indonesian people regard the additional
statements on the Joint-Communiqué as an attempt to force Indonesia
to acknowledge Dutch sovereignty over West Irian.[70]

The veiled import of the letter is evident upon close reading. In it,
Sukarno essentially approved of Subandrio's actions and indicated that the
Tunku made a mistake in signing the joint communiqué, and that Indone-
sia would not recognize the document.

Second, the fact that throughout the entire West Irian episode (including the period of the Tunku's mediation) the Malayan government never
once declared official support for Indonesia's position on West Irian was
not lost on the Jakarta government. As one scholar observed:

It is an indication of the mental gulf that separated their [Malayan]
thinking from that of the Indonesians that Tunku Abdul Rahman
should have offered, on his own initiative, to mediate the Indonesian–Dutch dispute. The substance of his proposals was in itself highly
offensive to the Indonesians, who considered that Irian should have
been surrendered together with the rest of the Netherlands East
Indies at the time of the transfer of sovereignty. The very proposition
of such terms implied that the Malayans were more concerned with a
bloodless compromise between the two parties than with any genuine
conviction of the rightness of Indonesia's case. That Tunku Abdul
Rahman, as a fellow Malay and Asian, should have made such proposals at all, 'arbitrating' or mediating between the colonial power and
its former victim added insult to injury.[71]

If anything, this entire episode hardened Indonesian views of Malaya as a
colonial stooge that still danced to the tune of imperialism.

Finally, it can be ascertained with hindsight that evidence existed to
corroborate Indonesian suspicions of the Tunku's intentions. Records of
the Tunku's private conversations with the British Prime Minister, Harold
Macmillan, revealed that he, the Tunku, in fact sympathized with and supported the Netherlands' position that West Irian should only be relin-
quished via referendum.[72] When Macmillan expressed doubts over his
proposal to hand West Irian over to Indonesia after a year of UN trusteeship, the Tunku replied that

the trustees need not hand over to anyone. The UN should decide....
The Indonesians could not afford to spend any money on West New
Guinea which would be an expensive trusteeship for anyone to take
on. The Indonesians would no doubt hope that the inhabitants of

West New Guinea would eventually opt for union with Indonesia, but as they were still cannibals it would take some time before they were able to decide anything at all for themselves.[73]

On another occasion, he had admitted to the Commonwealth Secretary that 'Indonesia has no claim on legal or racial grounds to this territory [West Irian]'.[74] As late as 1963, the Tunku and his Foreign Secretary, Ghazali Shafie, were still meeting leaders of the Freedom Movement of West Papua and expressing sympathy for their cause against the Indonesian government.[75]

Jakarta's apprehensions mirrored the fact that in Indonesian opinion, Malaya's attempt to fashion a neutral mediatory role belied a policy of 'fence-sitting'. In this light, the gesture of mediation in effect flew in the face of Indonesia, which had expected unwavering support from its Malayan kin. Instead, mediation was interpreted as the audacious act of a government that had never struggled for its national independence, but that presumptuously deemed itself 'qualified' to mediate over an issue that was clearly a vestige of Indonesia's anti-colonial struggle. Bearing this in mind, it was indeed ironical that the final solution that Jakarta accepted for the resolution of the West Irian crisis in 1962 bore striking similarity to the initial Malayan proposal for UN trusteeship of West Irian.

Bilateral tensions notwithstanding, the fact that there was marked support among Malays for Indonesia's cause during this entire episode should not be overlooked. When Malaya voted positively in support of a UN resolution on Irian in November 1957, the Malay press lauded it as 'the right move in support of Indonesia, which is closely linked with Malaya'.[76] UMNO Youth members even sought permission from the Malayan government to volunteer for Indonesia's cause against the Dutch, should conflict break out.[77] The pro-Indonesia daily *Utusan Melayu* also emphasized:

> It is with such a feeling of brotherhood that the people of Malaya are careful about any deed or word which might hurt the feelings of the Indonesian people and government. In fact, a similarly close feeling could not be shown towards Malaya's other neighbours although Malaya desires good relations based on mutual understanding and aid.[78]

Correspondingly, the Indonesian Ambassador noted that these responses 'proved that Indonesia's expectations about the Federation's foreign policy, particularly on colonial issues, was [*sic*] well justified'.[79] The Tunku himself was aware of the constraints of popular sentiments of affinity on his policy choices, as he had on occasion noted to his British counterpart (almost apologetically, it seemed) that in the event that hostilities broke out between Indonesia and the Dutch over West Irian, 'Malaya ...

because of her affinity with Indonesia, might have to declare openly her support of Indonesia'.[80] British officials had also noted prophetically in 1957 that 'racial affinity with Indonesia and closeness of it [*sic*] make it politically difficult for [the] Tunku to advocate policies unsympathetic to Indonesia and this will be one of his main political dilemmas'.[81] Following this, London expressed reservation for what it saw as Malaya's deference to Indonesia represented in its support for the tabling of Indonesia's claims at the UN.[82]

Notwithstanding popular support, the events that took place immediately after the Tunku's failed attempt at mediation did have a considerable impact on Malayan perceptions of Indonesia. At an individual level, Indonesia's rejection of his initiative after first endorsing it was clearly a personal affront to Tunku Abdul Rahman.[83] The Tunku observed that 'the Malays had in the past tended to look up to Indonesia as a big brother but they were now angry over the attack that had been made on him'.[84] The Tunku also opined to the Dutch Ambassador, van Gulik, that he regarded the Indonesian mission to Moscow to secure material and diplomatic support and Subandrio's public rebuff as 'having slammed the door in my face and in these circumstances, any further attempt to mediate would be regarded as a sign of weakness'.[85] Clearly from this statement, the Tunku was determined not to permit Indonesia to undermine his and Malaya's international stature established in the process of mediation.

The two events of the PRRI/Permesta Rebellion and West Irian crisis generated mutually reinforcing dynamics that influenced the leaders of Indonesia and Malaya. The Indonesian leadership were highly suspicious of Malayan complicity during the regional rebellion. Instead of backing a fellow kin state, Indonesian leaders perceived Malaya to have contributed to moves to undermine it. Subandrio reportedly opined, for instance, that the Tunku was 'seeking to annex Sumatra because he needs Indonesia badly to face Chinese equality with the Malays inside Malaya'.[86] More importantly, while choosing a declaratory policy of distance, the Malayan government expressed sympathy for, and even provided indirect assistance to, the rebels in private.

Similarly, over the West Irian issue the Malayan Prime Minister's attempt to mediate implied again that Kuala Lumpur adopted a position of neutrality on an issue that involved Indonesian unity. This was unacceptable to Jakarta, which once again expected Malayan support in the spirit of kinship. In signing the communiqué with the Dutch, the Malayan government was seen to have taken a position without prior consultation with Jakarta, and one that was directly opposed to Jakarta's interests. Not surprisingly, the Malayan government was subjected to severe criticism in the Indonesian press, which clearly reflected a sense of betrayal on the part of Indonesia. For instance, one newspaper reported that Indonesia 'should have refrained from too much enthusiasm when Malaya received her independence'.[87] Another claimed in response to Malaya's lack of support for Indonesia's struggle to preserve national unity and territorial integrity that Indonesia 'was surprised that her neighbour, a nation of the same blood and stock as Indonesians, did not follow the attitude of other newly-born nations such as Ghana, Tunisia and Morocco'.[88]

From the Malayan perspective, these two episodes also left bilateral ties with much to be desired. Malayan hands were tied over the issue of Sumatra, when the government clearly was unable to meet the expectations of Jakarta. Not only was the cause of their Sumatran cousins uppermost in the minds of the Malayan political leaders, but also the fact that the rebellion in effect worked to Malaya's own interest in seeing the tide of communism in the region stemmed. Matters were no less complicated over West Irian. For Malaya, West Irian presented an opportunity for active engagement in international diplomacy. This was important not only for reasons of security, but also for the newly independent state to establish itself as an actor of some consequence in the international political arena. In that vein, it was important for Malaya not only to assert its sovereignty, but to do so independently of Indonesian influence. This of course did not go down well in Jakarta. The Indonesians disliked the idea of a newcomer taking the initiative in an area where they considered themselves the rightful leaders by virtue of their size and legacy of national struggle. The Tunku's apparently 'easy' assumption of a leadership role in Southeast Asia was seen as upstaging Sukarno, and Indonesia was incensed with his 'insolence' in thinking that Malaya should become a model for all newly independent nations.[89] Even more difficult for Jakarta to swallow was the fact that several of Malaya's activist foreign policies involved Indonesia's own political predicaments, such as West Irian. In so far as Malaya's own security was concerned, the Indonesian leadership's persistence in making West Irian a highly charged nationalist affair and its constant reiteration of race- and ethnic-based irredentism as the basis of its claims were unsettling for a Malayan political leadership still uncertain of Indonesian intentions towards Malaya. These concerns were further aggravated by the militaristic cloak with which Jakarta asserted its claims. Indeed, the underlying concern of Malayan leaders, that such tactics might well be applied at a later time against Malaya itself, was soon to become a reality.

Konfrontasi

On 27 May 1961, Tunku Abdul Rahman mooted the idea for the confederation of Singapore, Sarawak, North Borneo, and Brunei with Malaya into a single political entity to be called the Federation of Malaysia.[90] To this proposal Indonesia initially raised no objections. In fact, in Sukarno's own words, the Malaysia project was welcomed in Jakarta as long as it was advanced as a de-colonization project.[91] By January 1963, however, matters had turned around. Indonesia officially rejected the Malaysia plan and launched a policy of *Konfrontasi* (Confrontation) against the new federation. The impetus behind Jakarta's aggression has been the subject of much scholarly debate. Mackie viewed it essentially as a result of Indonesia's convoluted domestic politics playing out between the triumvirate of Sukarno, the PKI, and the military.[92] Others have chosen to locate *Konfrontasi* against the broader picture of the Cold War, and they explore the event in that context.[93] Some have even suggested Western-inspired intelligence conspiracy as a possible cause.[94] Aside from Mackie's work, most of these theories interpreted *Konfrontasi* as a diplomatic quandary inspired by external factors. While this view is not disputed, one should also consider the internal political dynamics within the Malay world and its influence on events. By this token, *Konfrontasi* can also be viewed as the climax of antagonistic diplomacy between two kin states whose understanding of the basis of their relations as sovereign nation-states was evolving along diametrically opposite planes. Prior to expanding on this argument, however, it would be worthwhile to recall the key events of *Konfrontasi* in brief.

Not long after its initial reaction to the Tunku's proposal in 1961, Jakarta soon became convinced that the Malaysia project was not an act of de-colonization but rather a manifestation of neo-colonialism in its back yard.[95] This confirmed suspicions the Jakarta elite had held towards Kuala Lumpur since 1957, that because of the close cooperation the latter maintained with Britain, it was susceptible to colonial influence. These suspicions should be viewed in the context of the international politics of the day, when anti-colonialism was at its peak and de-colonization projects were often marked by bloody revolution. Malaysian camaraderie with Britain was indeed a peculiar phenomenon in this light. Further fanning the flames of suspicion was Kuala Lumpur's apparent support, manifested in its position on the PRRI/Permesta rebellion, West Irian, and the AMDA treaty, for the seemingly provocative postures of certain Western states towards Indonesia. This view crystallized among the Jakarta elite in the wake of the Brunei revolt of 8 December 1962 in opposition to the Malaysia plan.[96] The Brunei revolt was led by A.M. Azahari, who was highly regarded in Indonesian nationalist circles for his anti-colonial activities in the Sultanate as opposed to the reticence of Malaya's architects of independence.[97] The Indonesian leadership viewed the Brunei revolt as evidence that the Malaysia plan was being pushed forward against the will of the population in the Borneo territories, and this fanned their suspicions of the relationship between the Malaysian elite and the West. Other centres of power in Indonesia shared similar reservations. The military viewed Malaysia as a potential Chinese fifth column at Indonesia's doorstep that would threaten the security of the archipelago, while the PKI saw Malaysia as a legacy of imperialism in Southeast Asia.[98]

In so far as the Indonesians were concerned, *Konfrontasi* was a statement against the neo-imperialism that Malaysia was seen to represent.

This was encapsulated in Sukarno's radio address on the eve of the launch of *Konfrontasi*, in which he declared:

> We were born in fire. We were not born in the rays of the full moon like other nations. There are nations whose independence was presented to them. There are nations who, without any effort on their part, were given independence by the imperialists as a present. Not us, we fought for our independence at the cost of great sacrifice. We gained our independence through a tremendous struggle which has no comparison in this world.[99]

Indonesian suspicion and distrust of the motivations behind the Malaysia plan were later articulated by Michael Leifer in the following manner:

> Certainly evident was a resentment of a revision of political boundaries in the vicinity of Indonesia which reconfirmed the legacy of colonialism in determining the territorial basis of state succession. Indonesia, in terms of population and scale as well as experience, had adopted a role of regional leadership which was not acknowledged in Kuala Lumpur. Its government, under Sukarno, held a strong presumption that it was entitled to be a party to territorial changes, especially where defence arrangements gave a former colonial power the right to use proximate bases as it deemed necessary for the preservation of peace in South-East Asia.[100]

The early stages of *Konfrontasi* were marked by regular diatribes emanating from all sections of the Jakarta government against Malaysia. Coercive diplomacy was synchronized with limited military action that began with the intrusion of Indonesian guerrillas into Sarawak in support of a 'national liberation movement', an act that subsequently led to clashes with British forces.[101] Warnings were also issued to the effect that Malayan fishing vessels caught 'poaching' in Indonesian waters would be 'burnt on sight'.[102] Confrontation was subsequently intensified with troop landings on the peninsula.[103] Policy-makers in Kuala Lumpur interpreted these incursions as acts of reprisal for Malayan aid to the regional rebels from Sumatra and Sulawesi.[104]

Despite Sukarno's vitriolic rhetoric and the periodic military incursions undertaken by Indonesian paramilitary forces, it is important to note that active diplomacy was being undertaken on a separate track as Indonesia sought to extricate itself from a crisis that was fast growing out of proportion for an Indonesian state increasingly destabilized by economic failure. From the outset of *Konfrontasi*, active diplomacy had been undertaken by the governments of Japan, the United States, Thailand, and the Philippines, together with the United Nations. Feelers were also being sent out by various factions within the Indonesian government in an attempt to pursue the path of diplomacy beneath the aggressive veneer of Indonesian rhetoric, while Sukarno and Tunku Abdul Rahman also met for a summit in Tokyo in June 1963 in an ultimately failed attempt to iron out their differences.

Because Jakarta viewed Malaysia as an illegitimate neo-colonial creation supported by an Anglophile leadership, initial opinions were that termination of their *Konfrontasi* policy could only be brought about by secret Anglo-Indonesian talks, without the involvement of Kuala Lumpur.[105] This position was maintained for a substantial period, and the Indonesian government only began to re-assess its position on this when its own internal structure of power shifted away from Sukarno and Subandrio, whom the British considered 'the real nigger in the woodpile'.[106] Even then, Sukarno was reluctant to meet the Tunku in the latter's capacity as 'Prime Minister of Malaysia'.[107] On his part, the Tunku was aware that if Anglo-Indonesian talks proceeded, this could be construed by Jakarta as evidence that the British were indeed the 'puppet masters' behind the formation of Malaysia.[108] Attesting further to Malaysian suspicions over Indonesian gestures, the Tunku refused to entertain Sukarno's suggestion, made in September 1964, that a plebiscite be conducted to determine the will of the Borneo people towards absorption into Malaysia, or to commit himself to abide by its result.[109] To the Tunku, such an act was tantamount to affirmation of Indonesia's right to a voice in Malaysian affairs.[110]

Following Kuala Lumpur's refusal to submit to Anglo-Indonesian negotiations, moves were taken to bring both the Indonesian and the Malaysian governments to the negotiation table. Of the many diplomatic overtures undertaken during this period, it was an attempt to build a sub-regional organization on the basis of race and ethnicity, termed Maphilindo, that was most intriguing.

Maphilindo: illusion or reality?

Maphilindo was essentially a proposed confederation of the states of Indonesia, the Philippines, and Malaysia, which found endorsement through the Manila Agreement of July–August 1963. The brainchild of Philippine President Diosdado Macapagal and an acronym coined with the diplomatic contrivance of Subandrio, Maphilindo was envisaged to bring the three states into close association on the basis of Malay regional unity.[111] Maphilindo was to build on the Tokyo meeting between Sukarno and the Tunku in early June 1963, where Sukarno apparently announced the termination of his policy of *Konfrontasi* and both leaders reaffirmed their commitment to the 1959 Friendship Treaty.[112] It was at the Manila summit that Sukarno, Tunku Abdul Rahman, and Macapagal devised a mechanism for regular consultation in order to achieve consensus on the matter of regional order.[113] On its part, Indonesia agreed to cease its confrontation with Malaysia, and the latter acceded to a UN survey to determine the wishes of the Borneo populations towards Malaysia. Beneath these concessions lay a further logic: Maphilindo also had as a sub-text a coordinated and implicit expression of concern at an increasing Chinese presence, in the internal political environment in the three countries as well as the broader regional context.[114] This was reflected in Subandrio's comment that 'the Malayans, who could not handle the Chinese alone, might do so in a wider concept of Malay confederation'.[115]

The Manila Agreement was set up as a 'face-saving' device to enable Indonesia to withdraw from *Konfrontasi*. But this was contravened when Malaysia announced the new date for its formation before the UN survey team could announce their findings, as should rightfully have been the procedure.[116] Predictably, this announcement elicited a negative response from Indonesia, with Sukarno claiming that it violated the Manila Agreement and, as a consequence, Indonesia was not bound by the results of the UN mission. Following this, Sukarno called for the reinstatement of the policy of aggression. Even though Maphilindo witnessed a revival with the Tokyo Summit of 20 June 1964, again involving Indonesia, Malaysia, and the Philippines, it suffered a similar fate, as both Indonesia and Malaysia refused to surrender any ground.

It is clear from hindsight that the two Maphilindo summits were nothing more than an exercise in grandiose public relations. They suffered from a host of shortcomings that all but destroyed any chance of re-organizing bilateral relations. Not least among these was the lack of sincerity on the part of the two main players, Malaysia and Indonesia. Evidence made available recently draws attention to the highly questionable sincerity of Sukarno and Subandrio towards rapprochement on the principles of blood brotherhood encapsulated in the Maphilindo spirit. On their part, it has also become clear that in private, the likes of Tunku Abdul Rahman and Ghazali Shafie, the main policy-makers at the Malaysian end, remained suspicious of Indonesian intentions. It was noted that at the Maphilindo summits the Malaysian delegation was subjected to much patronizing cant by Indonesia for being 'our Malay brothers'. The Malaysians were evidently unimpressed by this, and their tough negotiation at the second round of tripartite talks in February 1964 exemplified their disdain:

> Listening to them [the Malaysians] talk, one had the fear not that the Malaysians would not be tough in dealing with the Indonesians ... but that they might be so aggressive as not to see good opportunity for calming things down if one arose.[117]

Added to that was the fact that Maphilindo was itself subject to different interpretations among its proponents. Kuala Lumpur saw Maphilindo as Indonesian acceptance of 'Malaysia'; Jakarta viewed it as sounding its death-knell. This ambiguity was encapsulated in a singular clause of the Manila Agreement, that the formation of the Malaysian Federation would be approved 'provided the support of the people of the Borneo territories is ascertained by an independent and impartial authority, the Secretary-General of the United Nations or his representatives'. In fact, this ambiguity led to a perception in some quarters that Maphilindo was expressed as a Southeast Asian Munich, tantamount to Malaysian capitulation.

Quite clearly, suspicion and apprehension dominated each party's perception of the other during this period. While it is certainly true that Indonesia's internal political dynamics played an important role in dictating the course of Jakarta's policy towards Malaysia during this time, it would be a gross over-simplification to attribute *Konfrontasi* solely to this. It should be noted that even when the initiative passed from Sukarno to the new administration of Suharto and Adam Malik (as Foreign Minister), military incursions persisted, and the policy of confrontation remained intact for another year. Within the broader context of the evolution of relations, it was obvious that historical undercurrents and circumstances had an equally important role in fomenting *Konfrontasi*.[118]

Several factors account for Indonesian hostility towards the Malayan government in this regard. First, Malayan foreign policy during this period was construed by the predominantly Javanese elite in Jakarta as a move to challenge Indonesia's rightful leading role. Indonesia, it appeared, could not stomach the fact that 'a country peopled by the same race of people, speaking a common language, and yet smaller and with fewer resources, was making a success of things whereas Indonesia was getting nowhere'.[119] Added to that was the belief that London and Kuala Lumpur had bulldozed the Borneo territories into Malaysia, in Indonesian eyes clearly an act of imperialist intent in their own back yard.[120] That neo-colonial collaboration between Britain and the UMNO-led government in Malaysia was a primary concern was corroborated by the following confession of a Sukarno confidant in the wake of clandestine negotiations for a solution to the conflict: 'If the British Government were now to announce a date, however remote ... for the withdrawal of British bases in Malaysia, such action would make more credible Britain's claims that Malaysia was not a threat to Indonesia.'[121] More important than Malaysia being a neo-colonial creation was the fact that Indonesia was clearly irked that Malaysia was created without proper consultation with Jakarta. This was evident in the fact that although it accused Malaysia of being a neo-colonial creation (thus implying a re-imposition of British imperialism), Indonesian vitriol was always targeted at Malaya, not Britain. Corroborating this were the various early Indonesian attempts to negotiate a settlement with Britain as well as Sukarno's many urgings for London to pressure Tunku Abdul Rahman to return to the terms of the Manila Agreement.[122] The Malaysian affront was further repeated when, contrary to what was apparently agreed upon, Kuala Lumpur proceeded with the pronouncement of Malaysia Day in advance of the publication of the report of the UN commission to determine the wishes of the Borneo peoples. Second, the emergence of regional groupings such as the Malaya-inspired SEAFET and ASA threatened to weaken the Afro-Asian spirit that Indonesian foreign policy was so closely identified with.[123] Third, there was residual resentment in Jakarta over the Malayan government's lack of support during the regional rebellions and over West Irian. While some might argue that these factors were merely rhetorical cover for Indonesia's real purpose of *Konfrontasi*, namely, to divert domestic attention from a failing regime, recently released documents on private negotiations between Indonesian and Malaysian leaders show that many of these were genuine concerns being felt by the Indonesian government at the time.[124]

Beyond this lay broader strategic concerns. Malaysia was also viewed as a potential challenge to Indonesia's own territorial integrity.[125] Harking back to the regional crises in Sumatra and Sulawesi and the suspicions of Malayan involvement, there was a genuine fear in Jakarta that a successful Malaysia could inspire dissident groups in Sumatra to rise again and agitate to join in the federation.[126] Leifer summarized Jakarta's concerns as follows: 'Malaysia was perceived and depicted as an unrepresentative alien-inspired polity designed to perpetuate colonial economic and military interests in Southeast Asia which, by their nature, posed a threat to the viability and regional role of Indonesia'.[127] To that effect, concerns over the strategic implications of 'Malaysia' were an extension of an already apprehensive attitude in Jakarta towards Kuala Lumpur's foreign relations proclivities and commitments manifested in ASA and SEAFET. Jakarta's distaste for Kuala Lumpur's increasing assertiveness in the international arena, which it interpreted as being undertaken at Indonesia's expense, was mirrored in the deterioration of the personal relationship between Sukarno and the Tunku.

For the conservative Malaysian government the implications of *Konfrontasi* were unequivocal. However Jakarta attempted to rationalize it, it was simply an encroachment upon Malaysian sovereignty and territorial integrity. In this sense, it was the climax of an increasing Indonesian reluctance to disengage its interest in Malaysia's domestic affairs that had been brewing even before Malayan independence in 1957. The persistence of Indonesian interest and involvement in Malaysian politics was expressed, for example, in the activities of General Djatikusuma, Indonesian Ambassador in Malaysia at the genesis of *Konfrontasi*, who was suspected of stirring up anti-Chinese feelings in Malaya.[128]

Concluding remarks

Indonesia's confrontation policy towards Malaysia officially lasted until 12 August 1966, when the two parties reached an accord in Bangkok to cease hostilities and pledged to move towards the restoration of diplomatic relations. On its part, Indonesia was finally able to abandon its policy of confrontation after the purge of the PKI (after the latter's abortive 30

September 1965 coup), and the transfer of power to Suharto's New Order administration in July 1966. This begs the question as to how the political dynamics of kinship found expression during this period.

If indeed the proposition expressed earlier – that relations between kin states need not always be defined by amity – is viable, then clearly it is possible to conceptualize *Konfrontasi* as a manifestation of problems between kin states, rather than a problem for the concept of kinship itself. In this event, it is important to register that even as *Konfrontasi* reached its height, Indonesian and Malaysian leaders repeatedly expressed their despondency at the deterioration of relations in the language of kinship. For instance, it was noted that one of the main reasons why Indonesia did not oppose Malaysia when the idea was mooted in the beginning was because 'they feared this would alienate Sumatran Malays still further from Jakarta'.[129] A Malaysian government publication later testified:

> There has always been a strong desire on the part of the Malayan people for a very close and friendly relations with the people of Indonesia not only because of the sentimental and blood ties which bind a major part of the population of the Federation of Malaya with that of Indonesia but also because, apart from Thailand, Indonesia is the nearest neighbour of the Federation with which close cultural and economic relations existed.[130]

Likewise, *Konfrontasi* was viewed in some Malay circles as an Indonesian 'sell-out of peninsular Malays'.[131]

Of course, rhetoric could not conceal the fact that by 1963 the familiar pattern of political rivalry between these two kin states was repeating itself again. Nevertheless, it was with the termination of *Konfrontasi* that the notion of blood brotherhood was revived in Indo-Malay diplomacy. The first indication of this was evident in the warm greetings offered by Malay ministers and officials to the Indonesian military mission from KOGAM (*Komando Ganjung Malaysia*, the Crush Malaysia Command) upon the latter's arrival in Kuala Lumpur on 27 May 1966 in preparation for the Bangkok meeting (1 June 1966). It was noted by Leifer that upon the party's arrival at the Tunku's house for discussions, they were confronted by a banner in Malay above the door, which proclaimed: 'Welcome to our blood-brothers on this goodwill visit.'[132]

Aside from the rhetoric of kinship emanating from political circles surrounding the termination of *Konfrontasi*, what was less well known was the fact that, however small, there was still some measure of support and sympathy among the Malays in the peninsula for the spirit, if not the means, of Indonesian policy. At the popular level, sentiments were far less abrasive as people questioned the logic of 'blood brothers' going to battle against each other. It was suggested by a prominent Malay journalist, for instance, that 'on the surface, it appeared that the Confrontation was directed at the new nation of Malaysia, but in fact, it was meant to confront Western powers that had masterminded the creation of Malaysia'.[133] In Indonesia too, certain quarters questioned the logic of confrontation between kindred populations.[134]

Equally significant, the termination of *Konfrontasi* was an important event in relation to Indo-Malay concerns over the ascendancy of the Chinese communities in their midst:

> At the root of much of the Malaysian jubilation over the ending of Confrontation is the feeling that the Chinese in the Borneo territories, and particularly in Malaya and Singapore, will be securely boxed in by more than 100 million people of the Malay race. It was precisely this feeling which led a Malaysian minister to say of Singapore that it was now a nut in a nutcracker.[135]

This commentary echoed the private concerns of Singapore's Prime Minister, Lee Kuan Yew, that rapprochement might be directed at Singapore.[136] Indeed, the spectre of the Chinese 'issue' had already been lurking in the shadows of *Konfrontasi* at its outbreak, when Ambassador Djatikusomo saw its utility as a propaganda tool and admitted that his work in Malaya 'was to save Malays from being swallowed up by Chinese.... Only Indonesians would bathe in blood to help Malaya.'[137] Again, shorn of rhetoric, the insinuations and implications behind this statement are telling.

It is worth noting also that despite the fact that their numbers were curtailed and ideology wounded by government repression, proponents of pan-unity with Indonesia persisted in pressuring the UMNO-led government to adopt more conciliatory approaches towards Indonesia.[138] The likes of Ahmad Boestamam, former KMM and MNP member and at the time chairman of the PRM (*Partai Rakyat Malaysia*, the Malaysian People's Party), and Ishak Mohamed, chairman of the MPSF (the Malayan People's Socialist Front) worked together in the formation of *Gerakan Pemuda Melayu Raya* (Greater Malaysia Youth Movement) to further the cause of pan-unity. Their endeavour was supported by the Labour Party of Malaya, the PMIP (Pan-Malayan Islamic Party) under the leadership of Burhanuddin Al-Helmy, and the former government minister Abdul Aziz Ishak, chairman of 'the United Opposition Parties'.[139]

Indonesia even found quiet sympathy in the corridors of the Malayan parliament. While the Indonesian neo-colonial critique did not weaken Malaysian resolve to resist Indonesia, 'it was nevertheless seen by many Malaysians, including moderates, as humiliatingly true'.[140] UMNO Youth persistently pushed for closer relations with Indonesia, and its leader Syed Jaafar Albar, Deputy Prime Minister Abdul Razak, and parliamentarian Mahathir Mohammad were all known to have sympathized with the spirit behind the Indonesian campaign. Without the Tunku's knowledge,

Mahathir led a Malaysian delegation to the May 1965 Afro-Asian People's Solidarity Organization (AAPSO) meeting in Ghana. There he supported a negotiated settlement between Indonesia and Malaysia, thinking that that would facilitate British withdrawal from the country.[141] Evidently, opposed as they were to Indonesia's military incursions, these Malaysian leaders nevertheless identified with the subtext of Indonesia's policy in so far as continuing the fight against Western imperialism was concerned.

Noticeably, it was the kinship factor that was advocated as the basis for a new phase of Indonesia–Malaysia relations. The following exposition captures the essence of this:

> A significant number of politically minded Malay, particularly of the younger and more educated generation, seem to be attracted by an anti-imperialist Indonesia free of international Communist associations. And these people offer a point of entry for the Indonesians to exploit such attitudes to their advantage. Indeed, many Malays would feel little alarm at Indonesian hegemony; such an arrangement would relegate the economically dominant and numerically important Chinese community to the similar minority position which they occupy in Indonesia.
>
> The Malaysian Government has no desire to sacrifice its independent existence on the altar of Malay blood-brotherhood, yet the Bangkok Accord and the related agreement in Jakarta may have opened up a Pandora's box of racial affinity which could be a more serious threat than military confrontation.[142]

Indeed, the above commentary on the implications and subtext to the rhetoric of blood brotherhood was telling in light of the sympathy felt among many Malays towards the spirit of Indonesia's *Konfrontasi* policy. Moreover, the comments also highlighted an increasingly pertinent dimension to the kinship factor that was taking shape in this relationship: the need to reinforce Indo-Malay solidarity and identity in the face of the increasing political weight of their respective domestic Chinese constituencies.

5 Re-building the 'special relationship', 1966–1980

Konfrontasi, as it emerged, signalled the apex of bilateral tension that had been building up since Malayan independence, as well as the crystallization of the negative perceptions of each other by the two countries' elites. For Jakarta, the Malaysia plan was a manifestation of the neo-colonial influences against which Indonesian foreign policy was staunchly opposed. For Kuala Lumpur, Indonesia's response to the formation of Malaysia should have been predictable in view of the Sukarno government's bellicose and aggressive postures towards Malaya and regional rebels. While this Java-centric, 'big brother' attitude did garner some measure of support from certain quarters in Malaysia, it was not appreciated in government circles. As Ghazali Shafie highlighted to the British High Commissioner, Gilchrist:

> It remained extremely difficult [to get rid of Sukarno] if only because so many Javanese, probably not excluding Suharto himself, identified themselves with Sukarno. He was in some semi-mystic way an embodiment of the Javanese people and personality, and there was a deep grained feeling that by condemning him they would condemn themselves.[1]

Beyond this, *Konfrontasi* also had a fundamental impact on kinship discourse. Notwithstanding the measure of popular support from within Malaysia for the Indonesian anti-colonial project, there was a sense among the Malay population in the peninsula that Indonesia had stepped out of line by encroaching upon Malaysian soil. This fact severely dented the political objectives of the pan-unionist Malays in the peninsula. It was hence not surprising that the PAS (*Partai Islam Se-Malaysia*), successors to the MNP, turned away from the political objective of pan-unification in the aftermath of *Konfrontasi*.

Yet paradoxically, it was in the wake of *Konfrontasi* that the politics of kinship seemed to find new impetus in bilateral relations. Talk among Malaysian and Indonesian leaders of blood brotherhood as a basis for post-*Konfrontasi* reconciliation gained increased prominence and publicity. Reconciliation based on blood brotherhood was portrayed as an attempt to repair a bilateral relationship scarred not so much by unwarranted Indonesian aggression as by foreign policy lapses during the Sukarno–Tunku era. This sparked a re-assessment of *Konfrontasi*, with some reflecting that 'referring to Indonesia the Tunku never wavered in his belief that there was a permanent bond of brotherly relationship between the people of Indonesia and those of the peninsula'.[2] Correspondingly, Indo-Malay rapprochement was portrayed as a return to the pre-*Konfrontasi* kinship relationship,[3] and immediately became a policy 'popular with the Malays'.[4]

Such was the extent of Indonesia–Malaysia goodwill that rumours circulated of the Malaysian government's preparation for a mass migration of Indonesians to offset the shift in Malaysia's communal balance towards the Chinese.[5] Echoing the discourse surrounding Maphilindo, the end of *Konfrontasi* witnessed a resurgence of attention given to the idea of 'Malay regionalism'. This time, however, it appeared that Malaysia was more prepared to accept Indonesia's 'political paramountcy'.[6] Central to the resurgence of Malay regionalism during this period was the solidarity built upon the shared concern for the Chinese factor in domestic and regional politics. As an Australian intelligence report suggested:

> There is undoubtedly an element of encircling Singapore in their [Malaysian] current thinking and ... the attractions of a deal with Indonesia that will keep the Chinese in their place and permanently ensure Malay hegemony in this area must loom larger than in the past.[7]

This view was reaffirmed when Toh Chin Chye, Deputy Prime Minister of the Chinese-dominated city-state of Singapore, expressed the view that 'Singapore had to watch that it was not squeezed between brother Malays'.[8] Given the acrimonious separation of Singapore from Malaysia in 1965, such sentiments were hardly surprising.

To be certain, events immediately following *Konfrontasi* bore compelling evidence of these attempts to re-cast bilateral relations on the basis of kin fraternity. In a symbolic gesture of sincerity on the part of both parties to re-establish relations on firmer grounds, a commission to unify language and spelling was set up immediately.[9] More striking were joint efforts to root out remnant communist elements in Borneo. Insurgency remained a problem for post-*Konfrontasi* Indonesia and Malaysia as a result of lingering PKI activities along the border areas in Sabah and Sarawak. In response, the Indonesian and Malaysian governments cooperated to an extent and in a manner few would have thought possible only months earlier. Following a mutual security arrangement in March 1967, joint counter-insurgency operations, which included intelligence sharing and joint military patrols, were carried out on a regular basis.[10] Supplies for Indonesian regiments were also permitted to be channelled through Sarawak (Malaysian territory) instead of Kalimantan's inadequate roads and difficult rivers, and a General Border Committee (GBC) was established to coordinate Indonesian and Malaysian military activities along this border. Such was the extent of military cooperation that one observer noted that it assumed the quality of a *de facto* alliance.[11]

Transformation in foreign policy outlook

It has already been suggested that *Konfrontasi* terminated with domestic political change in Indonesia. This is an important point to register, for the change did more than just end three years of hostility and open the door for rapprochement. From a broader perspective, it also facilitated the re-establishment of bilateral relations on more stable foundations. With the consolidation of Suharto's New Order administration, Indonesian foreign policy made a firm shift away from revolutionary symbolism and expression. Foreign policy was re-directed to fervent anti-communism (demonstrated in the suspension of diplomatic ties with the People's Republic of China in October 1967 and a significant improvement in relations with the United States) and an emphasis on trade and economics. The logic behind this shift was simple. The New Order government felt that Indonesia's claim to be a nation of consequence in the regional and international political arena had to be backed by political stability and economic vibrancy if it was to be recognized. This pragmatism was encapsulated in the pronouncement of *Ketahanan Nasional* (National Resilience) as the basis for Indonesia's subsequent conduct of international affairs. An active foreign economic policy was subsequently emphasized by the foreign ministry as Jakarta quickly resumed trade relations with major Western powers and Japan. In order to attain its political goal of stability, the principles of Sukarno's *Pancasila* were resurrected to form the cornerstone of Indonesian society after the domestic turmoil of the later Sukarno years.[12]

The advent of change, however, was noticeably balanced by streams of continuity as well, in particular the Java-centric view of the regional standing and vulnerability of archipelagic Indonesia that was formed during the struggle for independence.[13] Continuity also persisted because of the nationalistic character of Indonesia's new-found anti-communism.[14] Indeed, as the Foreign Minister, Adam Malik, said, Indonesia's declaratory foreign policy at this time was still targeted at 'the elimination of colonialism and all its manifestations'.[15] This was illustrated in the new regime's continued abidance by two tenets of earlier foreign policy practice: a continued opposition to membership of military alliances, and aspirations to pre-eminence in the management of regional order.[16] This view was corroborated by Suharto when he visited Washington in 1966:

Indonesians see themselves as potentially the dominant power of the Malay world – and possibly of all Southeast Asia. They have learned, however, that the aggressive policies of Sukarno did more to damage than to promote the kind of leadership that Indonesia seeks. Thus, the Suharto government has chosen to follow the path of regional cooperation instead of conflict.[17]

It was also reflected in the recognition by the Indonesian military's Commander-in-Chief, General Panggabean, that 'Indonesia has a very great role to play in safeguarding Southeast Asia.... This heavy task resting upon our shoulders, as a consequence, also brings very great responsibilities.'[18]

The confluence of continuity and change was profoundly evident in Indonesia's post-Sukarno policy towards regional cooperation. As previously registered, one vehicle of contention for Indonesia–Malaysia relations during the Sukarno years centred on the matter of regional cooperation. Many of these differences surfaced again as the theme of regional cooperation emerged as a key agenda of the Adam Malik–Tun Razak talks in Bangkok in May–June 1966 aimed at terminating *Konfrontasi*. As mediators for the Bangkok Accords, Thailand was actively pushing for the inclusion of Indonesia within a regional framework. Jakarta itself seemed increasingly amiable towards this prospect. Malaysian response, however, was markedly subdued. Still largely the prerogative of Tunku Abdul Rahman at the time, Malaysian policy towards Indonesia remained cautious. The Tunku was adamant that an Indonesia dominated by Javanese politicians and military commanders was not to be embraced with open arms so soon after they had challenged a nation that they declared was kin. In his view, 'if [Indonesia] stuck to the present system of centralized rule by the Javanese, there could be no future peace or stability and this presented considerable dangers for Malaysia'.[19] Discussions in Bangkok also uncovered the Malaysian position that 'the Bangkok Accord was reached in order to help Indonesia overcome its problems, and not as a settlement between two equal nations agreeing to end a dispute on parity'.[20] By this token, Malaysia was in fact not interested in 'grand schemes' of regionalism, especially those proposed by Indonesians. To Kuala Lumpur, Indonesia's inclusion into the ASA was seen as the only acceptable gesture of their sincerity.[21]

Clearly, threads of continuity amid the change wrought by *Konfrontasi* also had a significant impact on how Malaysia viewed post-1965 Indonesia, tempering any immediate exuberance Kuala Lumpur might have felt in reaction to the change in government in Jakarta. The experience of *Konfrontasi* had resulted in a marked transformation in Malaysian foreign policy outlook. What had surprised the Tunku and his conservative government most about that experience was not so much Indonesian audacity in landing troops in the peninsula, or even Jakarta's willingness to engage Kuala Lumpur's British and Australian allies militarily in what was clearly a mismatch; rather, it was the amount of sympathy Indonesia managed to elicit from Third World states for the spirit of its confrontation with Malaysia.[22] Correspondingly, this alerted Kuala Lumpur to the need for a re-think of the Malaysian approach to international affairs.[23] This was intimated by the Foreign Minister, Ghazali Shafie, who noted that 'Confrontation by a big neighbour in 1963 provided a stimulus to foreign policy. For example, several new diplomatic missions in Africa and Asia have been established and foreign service recruitment accelerated.'[24] Another scholar noted more specifically that the event was 'the turning point for Malaysian relations with the Muslim World'.[25] This change in international outlook set in motion a move to enhance Malaysia's presence in international affairs.

Sensing a more reticent administration in Jakarta, the Tunku moved cautiously to set a new tone for bilateral relations. During his visit to Indonesia in March 1968, the Tunku could not resist airing misgivings, and proceeded to lecture his Indonesian audience about the need for 'wise leadership' in managing a multi-racial society, suggesting that Indonesia could learn from Malaysia's experience.[26] Needless to say, his Indonesian counterparts were unimpressed.[27] Malaysia's triumphant attitude, however, masked lingering concerns over Indonesia. In so far as dealing with a post-Sukarno Indonesia was concerned, Tunku Abdul Rahman remained convinced that Indonesian arrogance and aggression had not subsided with the end of *Konfrontasi*. His train of thought could be easily distilled from the fact that he frequently made plain in private that he did not fully trust the Indonesian government, even as he made reconciliatory remarks in public.[28] This view was shared by his advisers, some of whom were still concerned that there were lingering anti-Malaysian elements among some of the leading generals in Jakarta as well as 'relics of the Subandrio era' in the Indonesian Foreign Ministry.[29] To them, this suspicion alone warranted caution in negotiating a resumption of bilateral relations.[30] To that effect, Indonesia's reluctance to make concessions in the prelude to the resumption of diplomatic ties served only to heighten suspicions further. In its Note of Intent, Indonesia reiterated its position that diplomatic recognition was to be extended to the Malaysian government on the understanding that the people of Sabah and Sarawak be given an opportunity at an early date to re-affirm their wish to be part of Malaysia.[31] Indonesia's special envoy to Malaysia, Sunarso, commented to his Malaysian counterpart in private that while Suharto and Adam Malik were supportive of the restoration of ties even before elections, such a move would be unpopular with significant groups in the Indonesian parliament.[32] The Tunku took exception to this and refused to agree to any linkage of recognition with elections. He felt that Malaysia had already provided sufficient guarantees and that Indonesia's decision to establish diplomatic relations should not be made conditional in such a manner.[33] Malaysia's position was articulated as follows:

> Although the Malaysians remained relaxed at the prospect of not having diplomatic relations with the Indonesians for another year they are

rather irritated at the way the Indonesians have chopped and changed in their recent public statements. Their feeling is that little attention has been paid to Malaysia's position or prestige in these statements.[34]

Indeed, such was the Tunku's ire towards Indonesia's terms that he had contemplated at the time a postponement of the re-establishment of relations.[35] That the Indonesian government eventually relented was telling of Jakarta's desire to prove its sincerity, if not contrition. Together with a concerted push for the establishment of ASEAN, Jakarta's acceptance of the Malaysian interpretation of the Bangkok Accords inspired confidence in the latter that relations could finally be based on firmer ground.

ASEAN

The change in Jakarta's attitude towards the terms for the normalization of ties with Malaysia paved the way for the formation of ASEAN (the Association of South East Asian Nations). By abandoning initial demands that normalization be contingent upon elections, the Suharto government evinced a measure of humility and compunction that was crucial in dispelling at least some of the lingering concerns that Kuala Lumpur had about its intentions. In return, the Malaysian government saw that there was an urgent need to cultivate the new Suharto administration and keep it afloat in what at the time were extremely rough Indonesian political waters. Certainly for Malaysians, for all their misgivings towards Indonesians in general and the Javanese in particular, and with the memories of *Konfrontasi* still fresh, it was clear that the evidently staunchly anti-communist Suharto government was their best hope for closer ties with their larger kin state.[36] It was against this backdrop that the matter of Indonesian participation in a regional organization was resurrected. This time, the Tunku left it to his deputy, Tun Abdul Razak, to negotiate.

The formation of ASEAN in August 1967 is widely accepted among scholars as one of the clearest expressions of Indonesia–Malaysia rapprochement.[37] Some policy-makers have been amenable to this suggestion as well, noting, for example, that ASEAN was 'conceived out of the pangs of *Konfrontasi*, an idea to obviate all future *Konfrontasis* in the region'.[38] What is important to note about the formation of ASEAN for present purposes is the central role Indonesia and Malaysia played in the build-up to its formation. Attempts to locate rapprochement within the framework provided by a regional institutional structure had previously been thwarted by contending conceptions as to the terms of this new regionalism. As noted earlier, the Malaysian government was of the view that a regional structure was already in place in the form of ASA. On its part, Indonesia desired a 'clean slate' in the form of a new organization. This was of particular importance to Jakarta for two reasons. First, it allowed Indonesia to avoid giving the impression that it was capitulating. Second, it would have been a humiliation for the Suharto regime if Indonesia were forced into membership of regional organizations whose principal values were directly opposed to the fundamental and unchanging tenets of Indonesian foreign policy. It was these prerogatives that prompted the Indonesian Foreign Minister, Adam Malik, to suggest in a secret letter to Razak in June 1967 the establishment of a bigger ASA grouping.[39] Malaysian accession to Indonesia's initiative was contingent on Jakarta's recognition of Malaysian sovereignty over Sabah and Sarawak as determined in the 1966 Bangkok Accords. In turn, Malaysia reciprocated by supporting Indonesia's proposal for the formation of this new organization, which in effect satisfied Jakarta's lingering desire to play a managerial role in regional affairs.[40] During initial negotiations on the preamble to the ASEAN Declaration, Indonesia and Malaysia reached a watershed that foretold of the subsequent shape of relations over the next decade, when both shared the similar position that foreign bases should be removed from ASEAN member states.[41]

Symptomatic of the measure of Malaysian and regional deference to benign Indonesian primacy within ASEAN was the decision to hold the first ASEAN ministerial meeting and house the ASEAN Standing Committee in Jakarta. What is important to note regarding events surrounding the formation of ASEAN is the fact that Kuala Lumpur made a deliberate decision to accept and defer to Jakarta's leadership of this new organization, even if this managerial role was deliberately downplayed.[42]

Malaysia's Indonesia policy in transition

For Malaysia, the formation of ASEAN marked a turning point in its relations with Indonesia. In essence, it locked Indonesia into a regional framework that functioned as a symbolic non-aggression pact. This transformation in Malaysians' attitudes towards their larger kin state was further manifested in the Tunku's visit to Indonesia in March 1968, which opened with his portentous invocation of blood brotherhood:

> Malaysians are blood brothers of the Indonesians. We are few in number. I sometimes wonder whether the Malays would have come into being if it had not been for the Indonesians. Thanks to Allah, Confrontation is over. It was not Indonesians confronting Malays, but communists opposing non-communists.[43]

While the 1968 visit did achieve much in terms of cultural and economic cooperation as well as a Malaysian declaration that Malaysia would extend the country's territorial waters in synchrony with a corresponding Indomerican declaration (a matter to be discussed at greater length later), it was 'a significance which goes beyond the letter of the published Communiqué'.[44] The visit marked an important intimation on Malaysia's part that Kuala

Lumpur was ready to make efforts to rebuild bilateral ties on more sub-stantial grounds. It was also of great consequence that during his visit the Tunku made a clarion call to all ASEAN members to render assistance to the Suharto government as it sought to bring growth and stability to a ravaged country.[45] Also notable were attempts during this visit to institu-tionalize a joint effort to unify the Malay and Indonesian languages, as well as suggestions that the 1959 Friendship Treaty be revived. Yet notwith-standing the symbolic value of the meeting between the Tunku and Suharto, there were still residual differences. Of particular interest was the Tunku's attempt to engage Suharto in discussions over the possibility of framing the friendship treaty as the cornerstone of an ASEAN defence agreement.[46] This had in fact been an option the Malaysian government had been contemplating in view of Britain's decision to withdraw its forces.[47] To this, Suharto was not disposed, politely opining that 'it was not desirable at this time'.[48] Interpreting the impetus behind the Tunku's pro-posal as a Malaysian desire to 'neutralize' the Indonesian 'threat', Indone-sia's rejection was itself driven by its leaders' belief that Jakarta's accession to the Malaysian suggestion would have been tantamount to an acceptance of Malaysia's historical suspicions of Indonesia. Clearly, the Indonesian and Malaysian delegations both carried their own suspicions to the meeting, and while it was indeed a watershed event that did much to alleviate many of their private concerns, it did not entirely remove these suspicions.[49]

Nevertheless, residual mistrust did not dampen further attempts by either side to rebuild bilateral ties on firmer grounds. This was expressed when the Tunku lent his voice to Suharto's supplications for clemency from the Singapore government for two Indonesian marines sentenced to death for their role in sabotage activities.[50] Tunku Abdul Rahman's visit in 1968 was reciprocated by an equally monumental visit in March 1970, when President Suharto became the first Indonesian head of state to set foot on Malaysian soil. Again the language of brotherhood was employed to underscore the event: 'There are many things in common between Indonesia and Malaysia and therefore we want to foster our brother rela-tions with the Malaysians.'[51] The Malaysian press went to great lengths to portray Suharto as the 'antithesis in personality of Sukarno – modest, gentle, hard-working, reticent'.[52] These efforts to rebuild ties were re-affirmed with the signing of a Treaty of Friendship, reviving a similar agreement signed in 1959 but rendered void by *Konfrontasi*.

By the end of Tunku Abdul Rahman's tenure as Prime Minister, the tone of relations with Indonesia had begun to shift. The aristocratic leader, whose term was marked by deep suspicions of the Javanese-centred mind-sets of the Indonesian leadership, was himself beginning to re-orientate his attitudes towards Jakarta. His homage to former President Sukarno on the occasion of the latter's death, when the Tunku publicly acknowledged his former nemesis as a leader who 'bravely fought the forces of colonialism and stirred up a strong wave of nationalism in Malaya', was especially poignant.[53] This eulogy was followed by tributes from Abdul Razak and the Home Affairs Minister, Ismail Abdul Rahman. Yet if the final years of the Tunku's administration set in train the transformation of Malaysia's policy towards Indonesia, it was the transfer of leadership to Tun Abdul Razak that in effect codified this volte-face in the tone of Indonesia–Malaysia relations, a change that would have seemed impossible only a few years earlier. Malaysia's relations with Indonesia during this period of transition experienced a noticeable shift when significant events taking place in the Malaysian domestic political arena transformed attitudes and ultimately the complexion of policy towards Jakarta.[54] Most notable of these events was the rupture to Malaysia's domestic political tranquillity that was wrought by the race riots of 13 May 1969.

The events of 13 May and the resurgence of the Chinese 'issue'

Since 1957, the multi-racial Alliance coalition had managed to hold together a potentially disparate polity in Malaysia through a mixture of sound economic policies and political accommodation. This political formula unravelled, however, when Malays and Chinese clashed in the wake of Malay reaction to the Chinese opposition's exuberance on their success at the 1969 national election.[55] In the aftermath of the racial riots, issues surrounding national identity leaped to the forefront of national discourse, and have remained there ever since.

Though primarily a domestic crisis, the racial riots of 13 May 1969 had three international dimensions. First, because they involved the brittle relations between the Malay and Chinese communities, they drew attention to the issue of relations with China and Chinese-dominated Singapore, and the potential influence that close ties with Indonesia might have in relation to these concerns. To that effect, a Malaysian political affairs report had hypothesized that 'Good relations with Indonesia have overriding significance because, to the Malays, Indonesia represents their ultimate source of strength in a region under the heavy shadow of communist China and with large overseas Chinese populations of unpredictable loyalty.'[56]

Even prior to the riots, this racial dimension had already been an underlying influence on the triangular relations between Indonesia, Malaysia, and Singapore. In the wake of Indo-Malaysian rapprochement, Benny Moerdani had noted that 'it seemed inevitable ... that one day Malaysia and Indonesia would come together' and 'Singapore would need to adjust its relations with Malaysia and Indonesia in order to fit in with the circumstances of the region'.[57] Singapore's leaders themselves were always uneasy about the pace of this rapprochement.[58] It has also been suggested that it was Indo-Malay rapprochement that motivated Singapore's decision to significantly expand its military capabilities in 1966.[59]

Second, 13 May also encouraged interest on the part of Indonesians in the repercussions the riots had for their Malay cousins as well as their own indigenous population, who themselves were harbouring deep-seated distrust towards the ethnic Chinese community in Indonesia. This phenomenon was aggravated by the fact that the 1965 anti-communist coup in Indonesia had provided greater stimulus for Malay communal feelings throughout the region. Commenting on this influence on Malaysia, an Australian intelligence source reported portentously:

> The moderates [in Malaysia] see in a new relationship with Jakarta some element of insurance against the Chinese.... More radical Malay feeling may move the government in Kuala Lumpur further in an anti-Chinese direction, and towards greater concerting of Malaysian and Indonesian policies.[60]

In fact, many among the Malay community, particularly the radicals, believed that in the event of a clash with the Chinese, Indonesia would come to their assistance.[61] The negative implications of such a state of affairs for the fragile multi-racial Malaysian national identity was that 'backed by Indonesia, and stimulated by Indonesia's attitudes towards the Chinese ... the radical Malays could increasingly campaign to use Malay predominance in Government and administration for anti-Chinese measures'.[62] Hence, it was in this context that the 13 May riots were followed closely in Indonesian circles. Although Jakarta was careful not to get involved, it was concerned enough to convene meetings at the highest levels to determine the course of action to be undertaken should the Malaysian situation deteriorate. General Tjokropranolo, a close aide to Suharto, believed that 'the Indonesian people as a whole felt they had an obligation to help the Malays in their "struggle" with the Chinese'.[63] Evidently, Malaysian students even visited Indonesia to study tactics used during the Indonesian student riots of 1965–1966, and the PMIP allegedly worked closely with Indonesian Muslim parties and organizations to stir up Malay sentiments against the Chinese.[64]

Finally, the riots all but brought an end to the administration of Tunku Abdul Rahman and confirmed the transfer of power to Abdul Razak.[65] Changes at the helm of Malaysian politics were not merely cosmetic, for they signalled the emergence of a new national discourse that preached Malay supremacy in the construction of Malaysian national identity.[66] Closely associated with this discourse, but yet to receive much scholarly attention, was the manner in which it related to and impacted upon the shape of Malaysian foreign policy. While perhaps the change was not as fundamental as its impact in the domestic political sphere, Malaysian foreign policy did experience a discernible shift under Razak, and it was in policy towards Indonesia that this was evident. Razak was far more accommodating towards Indonesian desires to assume an active leadership role in regional affairs than his predecessor.[67] For example, as Deputy

Prime Minister, Razak eagerly kept Jakarta informed of developments in the Five-Power Talks – discussions that led to the formation of the FPDA (Five-Power Defence Arrangement), and which were sparked by Britain's impending withdrawal from the region.[68] While there were clearly strategic reasons for him to adopt a more obliging position towards Malaysia's much larger neighbour, there was also a strong sense that the Buginese Razak was a keen believer in building a strong foundation for bilateral relations on the basis of the kinship factor. As a senior Malay diplomat intimated to the author, it was Razak who 'did have visions of *Rumpun*'.[69]

Razak's influence on Indonesia policy effectively took shape in the years during confrontation with Jakarta. Conspicuously less open with outright condemnations of Sukarno's '*Ganjang Malaysia*' ('Crush Malaysia') campaign than his predecessor, Razak's role in fact focused on behind-the-scenes negotiations with elements of the Indonesian military and government less averse to Malaysia's existence. Unlike his predecessor, Razak had also long supported Indonesia's nationalist cause, and ironically enough, maintained a close friendship with the Indonesian Foreign Minister, Subandrio (who along with Sukarno was considered an instigator of *Konfrontasi*).[70] During *Konfrontasi*, it was Razak who urged that 'Malaysia wanted to live in peace with Indonesia' and said that he hoped strained relations would be a 'passing phase'. Later, in a statement revealing the future basis of bilateral relations during his tenure, Razak commented during a motion in parliament to welcome agreement with Jakarta on the termination of *Konfrontasi* that 'we [Malaysia and Indonesia] must totally reject outside elements which aim at destroying peace, stability and progress of our region. It is in this context that Malaysia ... regard[s] the role of Indonesia ... as of utmost importance.'[71] More to the point, it was Razak, not Tunku Abdul Rahman, with whom Indonesia chose to negotiate the termination of *Konfrontasi*. It was also Razak who convinced the Tunku of the need to create a new regional organization (ASEAN) in order to capitalize on Jakarta's new-found humility and willingness to work in unison with Malaysia to secure regional order.[72]

Subsequently, when he replaced Tunku Abdul Rahman as Malaysian Prime Minister in the aftermath of the May 1969 racial riots, Razak moved to cement relations with Indonesia at a level never before experienced between these two states, much to the chagrin of Malaysia's feudal leaders.[73] The subtext to Razak's policy towards Indonesia appeared to be deference for what his administration viewed as a larger kin state. In an attempt to consolidate national identity in the aftermath of May 1969, the Razak administration introduced the concept of *Rukun Negara* (Articles of Faith of the State) on 31 August 1970. As a blueprint for national solidarity and the re-establishment of national identity, the *Rukun Negara* echoed the *Pancasila* of Indonesia, itself a concept rejuvenated during Suharto's New Order administration. Again echoing Indonesia's security policy imperatives, Malaysia's priorities after the May 1969 racial riots were also orientated towards internal economic and social development.[74] The Razak administration also actively sought to re-frame Malaysia's posture on international affairs away from its traditional identification with the West, and plot out a more independent outlook on foreign affairs which he termed 'free and neutral'.[75] This transformation in Malaysia's international outlook brought it closer in strategic vision to Indonesia.

Evidence emerged early in Razak's tenure that under him Malaysia would pay close attention to improving relations with Indonesia. When Indonesia experienced a severe rice shortage in the early 1970s, Suharto's personal appeal to Malaysia for assistance was promptly met with a dispatch of a substantial amount of food aid.[76] Zainal Sulong, the Malaysian Ambassador to Jakarta during this period, recounted that upon relaying an emergency Indonesian request for 20,000 tons of rice to Razak, the latter's immediate offer of 5,000 tons was quickly increased by 15,000 when Sulong convinced him that their 'Indonesian brothers' needed help urgently, and that Malaysia 'had to do more'.[77] This act elicited an appreciative response on the part of President Suharto, who declared that 'this was how brothers should act'.[78] This episode in effect set the tone for an extended period of close rapport between Indonesia and Malaysia. Such was this camaraderie that on the occasion of his visit to Malaysia in July 1971, the Indonesian Foreign Minister, Adam Malik, was personally invited by Razak to stay in the latter's private house for the duration of his visit.[79] This close rapport subsequently led to convergence in strategic perceptions as well, of which one of the earliest manifestations was the joint Indonesia–Malaysia position on the Melaka and Singapore Straits, and Kuala Lumpur's attendant support of Indonesia's archipelagic principle.[80]

Indonesia's archipelago doctrine

On 13 December 1957, the Indonesian government made a unilateral declaration that:

> All waters surrounding, between and connecting the islands constituting the Indonesian state, regardless of their extension of breadth, are integral parts of the territory of the Indonesian state and, therefore, parts of the internal or national waters which are under the exclusive sovereignty of the Indonesian state.

Following this statement, the Jakarta government further declared an extension of the breadth of its territorial sea from the customary 3 miles to 12 nautical miles. The government also adopted the concept of straight baselines, in effect drawing a boundary connecting the outermost points of its outermost islands to demarcate what Indonesia argued were its internal seas, which consequently lay outside the purview of international maritime law. Foreign ships travelling through these waters were no longer considered to enjoy the 'right' of innocent passage as they would in international waters. Instead, their innocent passage through sovereign Indonesian waters would be 'granted' pending Indonesian approval. These statutes have come to be known as the Djuanda Declaration or 'Archipelagic Principle'.[81] In so far as the impetus behind the enunciation of the Archipelagic Principle is concerned, it is likely that it was formulated and passed as a direct result of Jakarta's concern for the potential of its waterways being used by external powers to threaten Indonesian security, as was the case during the 1945–1949 revolution.[82] The implications of this declaration were significant; notwithstanding practical capabilities for policing its waters, the Indonesian government could conceivably deny naval passage to any maritime power anywhere within its 'legal regime' of internal waters. This same implication would later hold for the Indonesia–Malaysia agreement of November 1971 to deny the customary legal status of the Melaka and Singapore Straits.

Running alongside the Archipelagic Principle was the Act of Innocent Passage of 1962, which regulated the 'innocent passage' of foreign ships across Indonesia's waterways, and the doctrine of *Wawasan Nusantara* (Archipelagic Outlook). An initiative of the Indonesian military to revive and revise the archipelagic principle in the wake of the transfer of government from the Sukarno to the Suharto administration, *Wawasan Nusantara* not only reiterated the statutes of the Djuanda Doctrine, but 'also had the effect of formalizing the notion that this area was a strategic area [where] ... the whole entity of land and water becomes a single strategic defence system'.[83] Explaining the relationship between the Archipelagic Principle and the doctrine of *Wawasan Nusantara*, the former Foreign Minister and architect of the concept, Mochtar Kusumaatmadja, clarified:

> Whereas the archipelagic state principle is a concept of national territory, the *Nusantara* concept is a way of looking at the political unity of a nation and people that subsumes the national geographic reality of an archipelagic state. It can also be said that the concept of the unity of land and seas contained in the concept of the archipelagic state constitutes the physical forum for the archipelago's development.[84]

It is evident that the rationale behind Indonesia's promulgation of the archipelago principle was twofold. First, it reflected Jakarta's acute sense of political and strategic vulnerability. To that effect, it has been opined by the Indonesian government that:

> the *Wawasan Nusantara* must become a reality. Our stand has been quite clear for a long time past. Just as in our national anthem we speak of land and water, there is no other country that makes similar mention. The *Wawasan Nusantara* concept is life or death for us.[85]

Indeed, Indonesian politics since 1945 has witnessed much undesired external intervention, and this gave credence to the Indonesian perception that freedom of navigation in the waters surrounding the country actually constituted a threat to both the sovereignty and the territorial integrity of the Indonesian state.[86] To the power brokers in Jakarta, the waterways cordoning and intersecting the archipelago were clearly within Indonesia's strategic milieu, and hence had to be secured.

A second justification for the Archipelago Principle lay in its nationalist imperative. Because the post-colonial political boundary of the Dutch East Indies had always been the point of reference for Indonesian nationalism, drawing borders around the archipelago by adjoining outermost points of furthermost islands was a logical foreclosure of *Indonesia Raya* (*sans* Malaya). Hence, this cartographic exercise demonstrated Indonesia's assertion of total sovereignty over its motherland or '*Tanah Air*' (literally 'land and waters'), and represented the apex of the political aspirations of Indonesian nationalists who envisaged the territory of Indonesia united as one nationality, one language, and one homeland. Noticeably also, Indonesia's position on its waterways had strong historical coincidence to the pre-modern Sumatran kingdom of Srivijaya and its control of the surrounding waters. This prompted one scholar to opine that what the post-colonial Jakarta government was articulating was in fact the 'outlook of Palembang'.[87] It would hence be interesting to note in this context the omission of the Malay Peninsula, for, as an earlier chapter has already discussed, the latter historically fell into the sphere of influence of Srivijaya.

Although a unilateral policy undertaking based on Indonesia's domestic political and security concerns, the postulation of Jakarta's archipelagic principle had implications beyond Indonesian borders. Most striking was its impact on relations with Malaysia, Jakarta's closest neighbour, *vis-à-vis* the shared waterways of the Melaka and Singapore Straits.[88] Indonesia's claim to application of the straight baseline system as well as the extension of territorial waters from 3 to 12 miles challenged the international status of the Melaka Straits guaranteed in the Anglo-Dutch Treaty of 1824, and posed legal and juridical problems for the international community. In the first instance, adoption of the straight baseline system was argued by Jakarta to be in accordance with precedence set by the Anglo-Norwegian Fisheries Case decided at the International Court of Justice in 1951, even though:

> in the case of the Indonesian claim ... there does not appear the special conditions and factors given by the Court to justify its exceptional approval of the application of the special method. *The Indonesian case is totally different from the Norwegian case; there is no similarity at all* [emphasis added].[89]

Further to that, the extension of territorial waters from 3 to 12 miles was valid only if other states sharing similar waters (in this case Malaysia) adopted similar measuring standards. On its part, Malaysia was at that time signatory to the Geneva Conferences on the Law of the Sea of 1958 and 1960, which abided by the 3-mile rule.

In order to bring the vision of *Wawasan Nusantara* to fruition, Indonesia embarked on a massive diplomatic initiative to rally support for its cause among Third World states. This diplomatic initiative began with a delegation to the UNCLOS (United Nations Conference on the Law of the Sea) meeting in Geneva in February 1958, where the Indonesian government presented its case to the international community. Following that, Indonesia's claim to the archipelago principle was raised with the Afro-Asian Legal Consultative Committee, the Sea-Bed Committee of the United Nations General Assembly and at all subsequent UNCLOS meetings. Beyond pursuing its case through multilateral institutional means, Indonesia also cultivated like-minded states at a bilateral level.[90] Nevertheless, the one state apart from Indonesia that had the greatest stake in the archipelago doctrine, and whose support was critical to the Indonesian cause, was Malaysia. Indonesia's realization of *Wawasan Nusantara* hinged on Malaysia's backing because part of what Jakarta claimed as Indonesia's 'territorial waters' actually lay between the peninsula and East Malaysia.

Differences had emerged in the initial years of Indonesia–Malaysia dialogue on the legal status of the Straits. These differences were traced back to the Anglo-Dutch Treaty of 1824, which guaranteed the international juridical status of the Melaka Straits and subsequently served as the measure of Malaysian and Indonesian responsibilities as inheritors of British and Dutch colonies to treaty obligations. Upon being granted independence, the Malayan government was prepared to abide by all treaties signed by the British colonial government. Reflecting this commitment, it was noted in the devolution clause signed by these two governments that:

> All obligations and responsibilities of the Government of the United Kingdom which arise from any valid international instrument are, from August 31, 1957, assumed by the Government of the Federation of Malaya, in so far as such instruments may be held to have application to or in respect of the Federation of Malaya. The rights and benefits heretofore enjoyed by the Government of the United Kingdom in virtue of the application of any such international instrument to or in respect of the Federation of Malay are from 31st August, 1957, enjoyed by the Government of the Federation of Malaya.[91]

In Indonesia's case, however, Dutch treaties signed with regard to their East Indies possessions were accorded no such commitment. Instead, it was declared at the Round Table Conference at The Hague in 1949:

> The Kingdom of the Netherlands and the Republic of the United States of Indonesia understand that . . . the rights and obligations of the

Kingdom arising out of treaties and other international agreements concluded by the Kingdom shall be considered as the rights and obligations of the Republic of the United States of Indonesia only where and inasmuch as such treaties and agreements are applicable to the jurisdiction of the Republic of the United States of Indonesia and with the exception of rights and duties arising out of treaties and agreements to which the Republic of the United States of Indonesia cannot become a party on the ground of the provisions of such treaties and agreements.[92]

It is clear from these two statements that the countries accorded a different measure of consideration towards the treaty obligations committed to by their colonial masters. Once again, the divergence in approach can no doubt be attributable to their different anti-colonial experiences.

Problems also arose as a result of the different perspectives held in Jakarta and Kuala Lumpur over the definition of territorial seas. Indonesia, because of its indented coastline, claimed the application of the straight baseline system to define its territorial seas. Malaysia, on the other hand, because of its straight coast, insisted on the application of the prevailing coastline system. The problems with these contending definitions have been elaborated on by K.E. Shaw:

An adoption of the system claimed by Indonesia is *ipso facto* a further extension of Indonesian territorial sea towards the coast of the Malay Peninsula, as the base-line for measuring the outer-limit of territorial sea would under this system start at the line linking all the islands within the archipelago and thus part of the free High Seas would become internal sea of Indonesia. This system together with the claim for extension of territorial sea from 3 to 12 miles would make up a double-extension putting a large part of the Strait-waters under Indonesian jurisdiction. This certainly compromises Malaysia's interests, and a struggle starts accordingly.[93]

This divergence in views was no doubt exacerbated by the Malayan government's concern over the potential for Indonesian hegemony, which by the early 1960s had heightened as a result of Indonesia's belligerent claim to West Irian and, later, its policy of confrontation with Malaysia.[94]

Nevertheless, in a reflection of a gradual change of Malaysian attitudes towards Indonesia, the Malaysian government eventually acceded to the abandonment of the 3-mile limit in favour of the extension of territorial waters to 12 miles in accordance to Indonesian measurements and codified in Jakarta's declaration of the Archipelagic Principle. The Malaysian government also adopted the system of straight baselines that the Indonesians employed. This was a marked shift from the original position of the Malaysian government, which until then had adhered to London's stipulation of the boundaries of British Malaya as the colonial power.[95] Needless to say, Kuala Lumpur's move to align Malaysian boundary claims to Indonesian standards was not welcomed in Britain. Nevertheless, the Bill to extend Malaysia's territorial waters was submitted to the Malaysian parliament in 1967. Notably, the two-year hiatus between the submission of the bill and its eventual passing (in 1969) has been explained by some analysts as an abeyance in lieu of a perceived need in Kuala Lumpur to consult with Indonesia.[96] The agreement between Malaysia and Indonesia to delimit the continental shelves was eventually signed on 18 March 1970 on the occasion of President Suharto's watershed visit to Malaysia.[97]

Indo-Malaysian conformity in demarcating territorial waters, however, shifted attention to the question of the status of the Melaka Straits, which fell into the sphere of both parties if the 12-mile delimitation mark was observed. This raised the further issue of the terms of navigation through the Straits. The foregoing discussion has already highlighted the international status of the Melaka Straits, protected under the Anglo-Dutch Treaty of 1824. By way of the Indo-Malaysian agreement of 1970, both Jakarta and Kuala Lumpur sought to exercise the right to regulate traffic along the Melaka Straits, in so doing denying the customary legal status of the Straits. Indeed, it has been noted that the 'adamant' and 'emotional' nature of the Indonesian and Malaysian push to revoke the international status of the Straits heightened Singapore's sensitivity to the threat that the congruent positions of Jakarta and Kuala Lumpur posed in the form of an Indo-Malay attempt to corner the Chinese-dominated city-state.[98] Singapore's concerns certainly seemed justified in certain respects. It has been noted, for example, that during negotiations, officials from the Malaysian and Indonesian delegations both felt that 'little progress was possible in a tripartite forum in which Singapore is present'.[99] A US intelligence report also noted that Indonesia and Malaysia had deliberately omitted Singapore from negotiations over the legal status of the Melaka Straits.[100]

Of greater concern in terms of bilateral relations, however, was the issue of Indonesia's archipelago principle and its implications for Malaysia's management of the waterways linking East Malaysia to the peninsula. To that effect, Kuala Lumpur's initial response is best described as cautious. After it had expressed rhetorical support, a Memorandum of Understanding was finally signed in 1974 between the two parties prior to the UNCLOS meeting at Caracas in July that year. In it, Malaysia expressed conditional support for Jakarta's Archipelagic Principle and its propagation. In return, Indonesia was to take into account the legitimate interests of Malaysia, defined as the right for free and unimpeded communication flow between the Malay Peninsula and East Malaysia, as well as the establishment of a special corridor of passage. In spite of these commitments, the Malaysians continued to press their case concerning the need for Indonesian recognition of their rights and interests further at Caracas and also the Geneva UNCLOS meeting in May 1975. This persistence did not go down well in some Indonesian circles. Certain quarters in

Jakarta were of the opinion that Malaysia was attempting to 'negate and diminish' Indonesia's archipelago principle.[101] On Malaysia's part, there were some concerns within domestic circles that Kuala Lumpur might be bending too far backwards in synchronizing its position with Jakarta's. As Leifer articulated:

> Within the Malaysian foreign ministry, a sense of reserve has existed about its maritime policy in as far as it has been believed that Malaysia moved somewhat precipitately in serving Indonesian interests more than its own, especially in as far as initiatives over the Straits of Malacca and Singapore seemed to have strengthened Indonesia's archipelago claim, which did not accord fully with Malaysian interests.[102]

The stalemate was broken when Suharto and Razak met in Prapat, North Sumatra, on November 1975. It was at this meeting that Malaysia made a commitment to 'fully support' Indonesia's declaration of the Archipelagic Principle. This agreement took the form of another memorandum signed in September 1976. The 1976 document set basic terms covering the recognition by Malaysia of archipelagic state principles and Indonesian sovereignty over its territorial sea and archipelagic waters, and the recognition by Indonesia of Malaysia's existing rights and legitimate interests, which it had traditionally exercised in the Indonesian territorial sea and archipelagic waters between West Malaysia and Sabah and Sarawak. It is important to note, however, that despite Razak's personal enthusiasm in pushing forward Malaysia's recognition of Indonesia's archipelago doctrine, the rank and file at the foreign ministry continued to harbour reservations regarding their Prime Minister's eagerness to appease Jakarta.[103] Consequently, Kuala Lumpur's position *vis-à-vis* the archipelagic principle remains to be ratified by the Malaysian parliament.

Neutralization and ZOPFAN

Attendant to bilateral accommodation around the issue of the Melaka Straits and Indonesia's Archipelagic Principle was Indo-Malaysian cooperation over the neutralization of Southeast Asia as part of the management of order in the region. The idea of creating a zone of peace, freedom, and neutrality (ZOPFAN) in Southeast Asia was the brainchild of former Malaysian Home Minister Tun Ismail, and was primarily a reaction to the changing regional security circumstances brought about by British military withdrawal. The ZOPFAN initiative can be traced back to the 'Ismail Peace Plan' based on Ismail's suggestion made in parliament in January 1968 that 'the time is ... ripe for the countries in the region to declare collectively the neutralization of South-East Asia'.[104] Tun Ismail's proposal for the neutralization of Southeast Asia contained three core tenets: first, the neutralization of the region had to be guaranteed by the Great Powers (the

United States, the Soviet Union, and China); second, it would be based on non-aggression pacts among regional states; and finally, it would also stand on a policy of peaceful coexistence among the countries of the region.[105] Following Ismail's presentation of his proposal, the push for the neutralization of Southeast Asia gained greater urgency with the enunciation of the Guam doctrine, signalling the pulling out of US troops from Southeast Asia. Whereas neutralization was brushed aside by Tunku Abdul Rahman,[106] it found support from his deputy, Abdul Razak.[107] Predictably, it was during the Razak administration that the neutralization proposal was pushed to the fore of ASEAN's regional security agenda, and became an international initiative that first surfaced at the Lusaka Non-Aligned Movement Conference in 1970, when Razak presented Malaysia's plan to create a 'zone of peace, freedom, and neutrality'.[108] Again, this prescription for regional order was to be premised on respect for sovereignty and territorial integrity among the ASEAN states, and the undertaking by the key external powers to exclude the region from power struggles as well as to play a supervisory role in guaranteeing the neutrality of the region.[109]

Indonesia's initial response to Malaysia's proposal was carefully calibrated. In reaction to Razak's presentation of the scheme at Lusaka, Adam Malik opined that while it was something worth looking into, Jakarta's bone of contention with the Malaysian proposal revolved around the understanding that in order to create a neutral Southeast Asia, 'the understanding and the help of the big states was needed'.[110] This clause was unacceptable to Indonesia. Jakarta's initial response was followed by scepticism as to whether states like Malaysia that maintained security arrangements with foreign powers could realistically abide by such tenets of the neutralization scheme. In a veiled criticism, an Indonesian editorial argued that 'the real neutralization of Southeast Asia will have many consequences for several member countries that have so far fostered historical relations with powers outside Southeast Asia. Agreements on defence, special political relations, and the rest must be released'.[111]

At the heart of Jakarta's unwillingness to endorse the Malaysian proposal for neutralization wholeheartedly was the issue of Great Power guarantees, which in effect granted external players virtual policing rights in the region. Indonesian concern was articulated by Adam Malik, who noted that 'neutralization that is the product of "one-way" benevolence on the part of the big powers, at this stage, would perhaps prove as brittle and unstable as the interrelationship between the major powers themselves'.[112] The notion that the neutrality of the region required the guarantee of external powers stood in direct contradiction to Jakarta's own prescription for regional order – that the latter had to be grounded on regional resilience.[113] The Indonesian military in particular were wary of the fact that China was to be included in the regional formula as a guarantor.[114] Consequently, Jakarta officials warned their Malaysian counterparts to be 'realistic' in their pursuit of non-alignment, and not to depend on others.[115]

The issue of the neutralization of Southeast Asia featured prominently in the Razak–Suharto talks of December 1970, and at Razak's impromptu meeting with Adam Malik in July 1971.[116] What comes across clearly from this series of bilateral meetings was that Kuala Lumpur was moving proactively and unilaterally to consult with Jakarta on a matter relating to their regional initiatives. As a result of these consultations, by the time the neutralization proposal was tabled and jointly agreed upon at the ASEAN Foreign Ministers' meeting in November 1971, its complexion had fundamentally changed. Taking Indonesian reservations into consideration, ZOPFAN was expressed in what has become known as the Kuala Lumpur Declaration as 'a desirable objective' in line with Indonesia's position that the neutralization of Southeast Asia was likely to be a long-term prospect.[117] Razak himself was to offer a further concession to Indonesia. In a marked shift away from the original Malaysian proposal, which stipulated a requirement of external power guarantees, Razak instead announced at the Kuala Lumpur ministerial meeting that 'the premise of the neutralization proposal is regional and national resilience'.[118] Indeed, such was Malaysia's willingness to take Indonesian concerns and sensitivities into account that, despite its eventual imprecise form, 'neutralization of Southeast Asia as had been proposed by Malaysia is mentioned neither in the operative part of the Declaration nor in the Joint Communiqué which goes with it'.[119] By the time the 'desirable objective' of ZOPFAN had evolved into a more concrete formula for regional order in 1976, its determining character had transformed from the external power guarantee and non-aggression pacts of the original Malaysian proposal to the notion of regional resilience, which was identified and accepted as Indonesia's prescription for regional order. To that effect, an Indonesian analyst made the prescient observation that 'Indonesian leaders, in fact, claimed that the ZOPFAN idea was basically theirs since Indonesia was the country that had consistently stressed the concept of an indigenous Southeast Asian regional order from the beginning of ASEAN'.[120] This was further manifested when Indonesia subsequently moved to tie its proposal for the establishment of a nuclear weapons-free zone (SEANWFZ, the South-East Asian Nuclear Weapons Force Zone) to the concept of ZOPFAN.[121] Likewise, Malaysia's willingness to allow the dilution of its original proposal in order to accommodate Indonesian perspectives was telling of its willingness to defer to Indonesian proclivities.

Malaysia's abidance by Indonesia's Archipelagic Principle, as well as its attendant position on the Melaka Straits, and Indonesia's accommodation of Malaysia's neutralization proposal, albeit with some adjustment to its terms, represented a quid pro quo that served once again to illuminate the extent to which international outlooks had converged over a short period of time, and further reinforced the perception that the Indonesia–Malaysia relationship formed the core of ASEAN.[122] While these events were revealing of the level of Indonesia–Malaysia fraternity during Razak's administration, they were by no means the only examples of the extent to which bilateral ties had recovered from *Konfrontasi*. The Razak administration visibly threw its support behind Jakarta when the latter moved to annex Portuguese Timor in 1975.[123] In defence of Indonesian actions that were increasingly subjected to harsh international criticisms, Razak argued that 'the obvious future for Portuguese Timor is for the territory to become part of Indonesia'.[124] Central to Malaysia's concern, which it shared with Jakarta, was the spectre of the revival of communist insurgency in the event of Timorese independence. This concern was drawn from the fact that the Portuguese and Macau governments were at the time under communist control, and the latent fear in Malaysia and Indonesia was that Portugal and China would facilitate the dispatch of communist elements from Macau to support the Fretilin government in an independent Timor, a move that would have repercussions for Kuala Lumpur and Jakarta in their own fights against local communist insurgents.[125] Correspondingly, Ghazali Shafie was dispatched to Bali in 1976 to mediate between the Apogethi Party and the Jakarta government in order for an agreement to be reached for the absorption of Portuguese Timor into the Indonesian Republic. Malaysia's position on this matter stood in noticeably stark contrast to that taken during the 1950s on Sumatra and Sulawesi, where Malaysian sympathy lay with the anti-Jakarta camp. Further cooperation was evidenced in Malaysia and Indonesia jointly sponsoring UN resolutions, such as the de-colonization of Brunei.[126]

Relations with China

Events surrounding Malaysia's normalization of ties with China in 1974, in particular, marked how the potential for diplomatic tension arising from contradictory policy positions was extinguished by kinship diplomacy between these two kin states.

The fact that both post-Sukarno Indonesia and Malaysia viewed China as a security threat stemmed from China's reluctance to disavow support for the predominantly ethnic Chinese communist movements in both countries. Be that as it may, drastic changes in the strategic environment (most notably President Nixon's visit to Peking) alerted Kuala Lumpur to the need for a re-assessment of its policy towards the People's Republic of China.[127] This re-assessment began with Kuala Lumpur's support for China's membership of the United Nations and peaked with Razak's landmark visit to Peking in May 1974 to establish diplomatic ties. These developments were of further significance for the fact that not only did Malaysia become the first ASEAN state to establish ties with China, but its policy seemed to run against the grain of strategic thinking *vis-à-vis* China in the region at the time. In particular, it seemed to contradict Indonesia's own policy towards China, which was still very much defined by suspicion concerning the latter's intentions.

While it does appear on the surface that a fundamental contradiction existed with regard to the Indonesian and Malaysian positions on China, several issues are worth noting. First, it must be acknowledged that Malaysia's move to normalize ties with the People's Republic of China was defined more by a reaction to changing geopolitical circumstances than by a removal of suspicion of Peking.[128] In this, Indo-Malaysian perspectives of China did not essentially differ. Second, and perhaps of greater significance, was the fact that since 1971 the Malaysian government had consistently consulted Jakarta on its intention to review policy towards China. This was done in order to mollify anticipated concerns from Indonesia.[129] In fact, Razak had consulted personally with Suharto prior to Malaysia's landmark vote at the 1971 United Nations General Assembly to support the admission of the People's Republic of China into the United Nations.[130] Razak had further dispatched Ghazali Shafie on several private and unpublicized visits to Jakarta to consult the Indonesians on the matter of China policy.[131] As a result, while the authorities in Jakarta may have initially felt slighted by Malaysian gestures towards China undertaken without prior consultation with them, after active consultation the Indonesian government declared publicly that Indonesia recognized Malaysia's right to establish relations with China.[132] Consequently, the normalization of ties between Malaysia and China in May 1974 passed without much furore in Jakarta, owing to the fact that Indonesia was satisfied with the logic behind Malaysia's decision, and, more importantly, that Kuala Lumpur had kept Jakarta well informed at every stage of its negotiations with China.[133] In a move that once again reflected the convergence of strategic perspective between Indonesia and Malaysia as well as Malaysia's own lingering concerns over Chinese objectives, the Kuala Lumpur government continued to publicly support Jakarta's position of suspicion towards Peking's intentions, notwithstanding its own normalization of ties with China.[134]

From Razak to Hussein Onn

Thus, the change in Malaysian attitudes towards Indonesia owed much to Tun Abduk Razak and his approach to relations with Jakarta. Because he was less suspicious of Indonesian, and especially Javanese, intentions than Tunku Abdul Rahman, Razak and key Indonesia policy-makers in his administration felt able to embrace the New Order government in Indonesia. After Razak's untimely death in January 1976, the baton was passed to Tun Hussein Onn, who immediately proclaimed that Malaysian foreign policy would continue along the lines set by his predecessor.[135] Malaysia's Indonesia policy under the Hussein Onn government certainly held true to this proclamation. As a manifestation of the continued priority given to ties with Indonesia, Hussein Onn made Jakarta the first foreign port of call of his premiership, on 28 January 1976.[136] It was at this visit that Indo-

Malaysian 'brotherliness' was re-affirmed by Suharto and Hussein Onn.[137] Subsequently, this tête-à-tête would become an annual event during the Hussein Onn administration, just as it was during Razak's. It was also during Hussein Onn's administration that Indonesia–Malaysia relations reached a new stage of amity with the expansion of military cooperation. Not only did GBC meetings and anti-communist offensives in Borneo continue unabated, but military exercises between the navies, air forces and armies of Indonesia and Malaysia became regular events on the diplomatic calendar. *Malindo Samatha* (search and rescue exercises), *Malindo Jaya* and *Malindo Mini* (naval exercises), *Elang Malindo* (air force exercises), and *Keris Kartika* (army exercises) were either instituted or continued with admirable regularity. *Keris Kartika* in particular was a milestone, for it marked the first incidence where the Indonesian army engaged in joint military exercises. Additionally, the Malaysian military was granted permission to train in Indonesia.[138] When Malaysia declared its 200-mile economic zone in July 1977 after the G-77 and UNCLOS meetings, it enjoyed strident Indonesian support.[139] Both Hussein Onn and Suharto also made combined efforts to mediate between the Moro Liberation Front Islamic separatists and the Philippine government.[140] The Indonesian and Malaysian governments also shared similar positions in condemning the Soviet occupation of Afghanistan and Israeli attacks against Iraq and Lebanon.[141] Collaboration also included the establishment of a joint arms-production industry and satellite technology exchange.[142]

Strategic convergence: the Kuantan Principle

Shared strategic perspectives born of heightened sensitivities to kinship affiliation between Jakarta and Kuala Lumpur found further expression alongside events in Indo-China. As early as 1970, Indonesia and Malaysia already shared perspectives over the Indo-China crisis when Kuala Lumpur expressed enthusiasm over an initial Indonesian move to mediate the regional crisis under the auspices of the Jakarta Conference on Cambodia. Indeed, it has been observed that of all the ASEAN states, it was only Malaysia that 'appeared to respond with any real enthusiasm to Indonesia's initiative'.[143] Subsequently, the uncertain regional environment created after US withdrawal, the fall of Saigon, and the unification of Vietnam in 1976 in effect produced a security problem on the doorstep of ASEAN. The urgency that this event created among the ASEAN states resulted in the convening of the first ASEAN summit, held in Bali in February 1976. It was at the Bali summit that the blueprint for the realization of ZOPFAN, which had been under discussion since the Kuala Lumpur Declaration of 1971, was endorsed by the ASEAN heads of government in the form of the TAC (Treaty of Amity and Cooperation). ASEAN solidarity wrought of the TAC was to function as a basis through which dialogue with the Indo-Chinese states, especially Vietnam, could be initiated.

While attempts at engaging Vietnam intensified within ASEAN, so too did the difference in strategic perspectives among its members towards developments in Indo-China. Of especial significance was the direction in which Indonesia and Malaysia were moving on the issue.

Apprehension towards communism notwithstanding, Jakarta also took the view that Vietnam could be considered a potential regional partner and bulwark against creeping Chinese influence. This coincidence in strategic perspectives could be further built on through the fact that both states also shared strongly nationalistic values that underpinned their respective foreign policies.[144] Largely as a result of this perception, Jakarta's response to Vietnamese aggression against Cambodia was visibly muted. In fact, Jakarta policy-makers construed that Vietnam's seemingly aggressive policies were essentially 'a reaction away from Peking'.[145] This certainly was a reflection of Indonesian attitudes towards China, which was viewed in many circles in Jakarta as Indonesia's main security threat. In a telling comparison of Vietnamese and Chinese attitudes, the Indonesian Foreign Minister, Mochtar Kusumaatmadja, intimated that 'Indonesia should be continuously vigilant with regard to People's China because ... it would not make such a statement like Vietnamese Prime Minister Pham Van Dong, that his country would not support subversive movements in other countries.'[146] What was of equal import was the position that Malaysia was taking on this issue. Indo-China topped the agenda at the Suharto–Hussein Onn summit meeting in March 1979, at which Indonesia appeared to sway Malaysian opinion on the crisis.[147] Given the lingering suspicions that both Indonesia and Malaysia had concerning Chinese expansion into the region (in the latter's case, despite the normalization of ties in 1974), the Indo-Malaysian position that eventuated was centred on the logic that the Vietnamese invasion of Kampuchea was in effect motivated by Hanoi's antipathy towards China, an antipathy that was partially justified in the light of China's subsequent military reprisal.[148] What was of further significance in the Indo-Malaysian position on Indo-China was that it contradicted the stance taken by the two countries' ASEAN neighbours, which sought to take a stronger position against Vietnam.

In a bilateral meeting at Kuantan in May 1980 between Suharto and Hussein Onn, the Indonesian and Malaysian governments issued a statement in the spirit of ZOPFAN, declaring that for Southeast Asia to be a region of peace, Vietnam must be freed from Soviet and Chinese influence. The Kuantan Principle, as the statement came to be known, was a result of Indo-Malaysian diplomacy extended to Hanoi earlier in the year, and was motivated by four factors.[149] First, Vietnam's struggle against the United States and subsequently China was perceived in Jakarta and Kuala Lumpur as an essentially nationalist struggle. This coincided with Indonesia's long-standing conviction that such struggles ought to be supported. Indeed, this remained a key thread of continuity between the Sukarno and Suharto regimes. Even for Malaysia, the shifting shade of foreign policy after 1970 meant that more sympathy was accorded to nationalist struggles of such nature as well. Second, both (but in particular Indonesia) saw the value of Vietnam as a potential regional partner, if not strategic ally. This was important in view of their shared concerns over the creeping influence of China. Third, it seemed that the leadership in Indonesia and Malaysia saw the Kuantan Principle as an opportunity to lay a solid foundation for what ASEAN had sought to achieve since 1976: the eventual acceptance of Vietnam and the Indo-Chinese states into the organization. Finally, the Kuantan Principle also provided an opportunity for both to re-assert the concept of ZOPFAN by making the call for the Soviet Union and China to exit Indo-China.[150]

Concluding remarks

Although the Kuantan Principle ultimately failed to prove a viable solution to the regional crisis as a result of Vietnam's ensuing aggression against Thailand (itself an ASEAN opponent of the Principle), it was nevertheless a significant manifestation of converging perspectives driven by an awareness and politicization of kinship ties traceable to the Razak administration. This alignment of Malaysian policy with Jakarta's, which covered the gamut of issues discussed earlier in the chapter, began when Malaysia followed the Indonesian lead in walking out of the August 1971 Non-Aligned Movement conference in Guyana to protest that the principle of consensus had been violated when the conference admitted the Vietcong and Sihanouk delegations to full membership. This move was poignantly described by one observer as 'self-induced subordination' of Malaysian interests to Indonesia.[151] Justifying this observation, Zainal Sulong reportedly opined that it 'would not be in Malaysia's interest ... by not showing [*sic*] some deference to the prestige of their [Indonesians'] government'.[152] In a resounding declaration pregnant with significance, Ghazali Shafie publicly announced at a GBC meeting in Jakarta:

> It is a fact that whatever serves as a threat to any of the two countries [Indonesia and Malaysia] will also be regarded as so by the other.... Let the understanding and cooperation now closely binding the two countries serve as a warning to any power that has ill intentions towards us. We will act together to oppose this threat completely and we shall never tolerate any nonsense from anywhere.... Let this joint stand of ours be understood by all, particularly by those who have designs on us.[153]

It was also Ghazali Shafie who later related a specific instruction issued by Suharto and Razak to the Indonesian Security Minister, Ali Moertopo, and himself to take all necessary steps to ensure that '*pisang jangan berbuah dua kali*' (never again should there be confrontation between the two people of the same stock).[154]

6   The Indonesia–Malaysia 'prestige dilemma', 1981–2000

The Kuantan Principle of 1980 was formulated on the basis of shared strategic perception of regional developments and their impact on Indonesian and Malaysian security. While the case could no doubt be made that the Principle was issued in reaction to strategic developments in Indo-China, the fact that prior to Kuantan, Indonesia and Malaysia had already shared a decade of harmony and stability in bilateral relations certainly facilitated the building of consensus. In turn, the convergence of interest seems to have been underlined by the rejuvenation of relations on the basis of blood brotherhood that had been liberally espoused by both the Indonesian and the Malaysian leaderships since the termination of *Konfrontasi*.

As hinted in the previous chapter, relations during the 1970s were premised on Malaysia's acceptance of Indonesian primacy in this relationship, resulting in a noticeable congruence between kinship rhetoric and Malaysian foreign policy. It can be discerned from the politics of policy-making over the previous decade that both the Razak and Hussein Onn administrations were ready, first, to ensure that Jakarta was consulted on matters of foreign policy, and second, to align Malaysian foreign policy as closely as possible to Jakarta's. The most poignant expressions of this can be found in the two major policy initiatives in the 1970s: the formulation of ZOPFAN and the normalization of ties towards China. The latter case was particularly telling. While the May 1974 normalization of ties with Peking could conceivably have been a source of tension for the two kin states given Indonesia's acute suspicions of China, the Razak government ensured that Jakarta was consulted and sufficiently satisfied with Malaysian reasons for a policy shift prior to Razak's landmark visit to Peking to effect the change. In a move signifying Jakarta's interest in cementing the upturn in relations of that decade, the Indonesian government made clear its preference for Ghazali Shafie as Hussein Onn's successor for the sake of policy continuity on matters relating to bilateral ties.[1] Indonesian preference for Ghazali was premised on his role as the prime Malaysian interlocutor in relations with Indonesia during the years since *Konfrontasi*; he would represent a welcomed continuity in bilateral ties. Furthermore, the fact that Ghazali was himself of Sumatran

(Mandaeling) origin and related to the former Indonesian Foreign Minister Adam Malik probably endeared him further to the Indonesians.[2] The eventual choice of the outspoken Malay nationalist Mahathir Mohamad, however, elicited a different response from Jakarta. While the Indonesian leaders took easily to Razak and Ghazali, they greeted Mahathir's ascension with caution and reservation.[3] Indeed, their initial consternation would prove portentous of the future of relations.

With the advent of the Mahathir administration in Malaysia in 1981, observers were quick to suggest that a 'new dimension' to bilateral relations was required.[4] What was significant about this period of bilateral ties was how the transformation of foreign policy dispositions that resulted from internal reconstruction of their respective national identities further impacted on perceptions and interpretations of the kinship factor in Indonesia–Malaysia relations on the part of the political elite in Jakarta and Kuala Lumpur. The Mahathir administration heralded a period in Malaysian history when Malaysian conceptions of identity experienced a transformation that was manifested noticeably in foreign policy. Likewise, the late 1980s witnessed a renewal of Indonesian interest in international affairs as part of a political effort to regain a sense of national pride 'lost' amid the debacle of *Konfrontasi* and the failed communist coup of the mid-1960s. These developments had a direct impact on Indonesian and Malaysian perceptions of their respective role and status in international society, and how both saw their position in the Indo-Malay world. In so far as bilateral relations were concerned, the pressing question that arose was whether the momentum gathered during the Razak and Hussein Onn periods would be sustained during the Mahathir administration.

Bilateral relations in the 1980s appeared to be a continuation of earlier traditions, with kinship-speak emphasized in the language of diplomacy. Commenting on Indonesian reports of a visit made by Mahathir to Indonesia in 1988, Yang Razali Kassim observed:

> There is a particular line which the Indonesian media reserves for no visiting dignitary except a Malaysian – cultural affinity.... As the Indonesian press portrayed it, the encounter was like one between two members of the same family, embracing each other in mutual back-patting.[5]

The manner in which Suharto received Mahathir, Yang Razali further noticed, was pregnant with significance. Suharto had insisted that the meeting be held in Jogjakarta, near to his birthplace and the site where he fought during the Indonesian revolution, and on his 67th birthday. Furthermore, he had arranged for Sultan Hamengku Buwono IX, the most respected of the remaining sultans in Indonesia and governor of Jogjakarta, to receive Mahathir at the airport and join in their deliberations.[6] No doubt these observations were telling of the persistent imprint of the kinship factor in Indonesia–Malaysia relations. Ironically, however, these comments were made at a time when the underlying rivalry in Indonesia–Malaysia *Rumpun* brotherhood was re-emerging with great intensity.

The advent of a 'new stage' in relations

It is a fact that the study of international politics needs to account for change and transformation. Illustrative of this, as colonial states evolve into sovereign political entities, more often than not foreign policy perspectives shift as a consequence. That is the case with Indonesia and Malaysia, two states that by the advent of the 1980s had consolidated into politically stable and economically dynamic political entities. This in turn was reflected in foreign policy outlooks that saw Jakarta and Kuala Lumpur engage each other as diplomatic rivals in a contest for political primacy in the region.

The impact of Mahathir himself on Malaysian foreign policy was a crucial factor behind the shift in Malaysian dispositions towards Indonesia from the calculated deference of the Razak and Hussein Onn years to a diplomatic nonchalance that was creeping into his administration's policy towards Jakarta. Indeed, such is the pervasiveness of Mahathir Mohamad's imprint in the conduct of Malaysian foreign policy that studies on the latter subject cannot but focus on the impact of his role.[7] One overriding characteristic that defines Malaysian foreign policy under Mahathir is diplomatic adventurism underscored by an enviable record of political stability and economic growth. Clive Kessler has explained the association between Malaysian nationalism, state-building, and the Mahathir factor in this manner:

> Having ensured, by assuring Malay ascendancy, that completing the unfinished agenda of preindependence Malay nationalism would remain the core objective of postindependence Malaysia as a Malay-based 'but-more-than-just-Malay' multiethnic nation, Dr. Mahathir then allied his domination of the state to consolidate Malay corporate economic power, enabling it ... to play a significant, even strategic, international role; to be players of consequence not only throughout Southeast Asia but also the Pacific, Southern and West Africa, Central Asia, Latin America and even Europe. This, for him, was part of a larger world-historical agenda, one that was essential if the nationalist aspirations of countries such as Malaysia were to achieve adequate modern realization.[8]

Diplomatic adventurism found expression in policies such as Buy British Last and Look East, which carried significant symbolic weight in so far as Malaysia's emergence as a champion of Third World interests was concerned. Even if the policies failed to achieve any substantive results, their impact lay in the fact that Malaysia's standing in international affairs soared. This recognition, along with the increasing primacy given to Malaysia's role and example among states and governments in the developing world, initiated and contributed to a kind of ideological awakening within Malaysia. Mahathir's adoption and propagation of the ideology of developing world unity against what he portrayed as the oppressive and predatory Western developed world brought about a substantial normative change in the belief system of Malaysians and a reconstruction of Malaysian identity, resulting in widespread support for Mahathir's nationalist slogan of '*Malaysia Boleh*' ('Malaysia is able').

Mahathir Mohamad paid especial attention to the Islamic dimension of Malaysia's foreign policy, a move that inadvertently slighted Indonesia, the world's largest Muslim nation. Partly as a result of the legacy of Tunku Abdul Rahman's era (when Mahathir was a staunch and vocal critic of the Tunku's overtly pro-West foreign policy), and partly in response to the heightened Islamic consciousness in Malaysian society at the time, Mahathir made a point of publicizing Malaysia's foreign policy towards its Muslim brethren.[9] Because of this, one could be forgiven for expecting relations with Indonesia, perceived as brethren in religion, to benefit from this Islamization of foreign policy. Yet the substance of Mahathir's activism did not go down well in Jakarta. Malaysian attempts to project the country as a member of consequence in international society clashed with Indonesia's own ambitions, and were viewed as a direct challenge to Indonesian primacy.

Indonesia, it may be recalled, had during the early years of the Suharto presidency shunned strident international political advocacy for the more pragmatic objective of national resilience, of which economic development and internal political stability were primary pillars. Consequently, Jakarta deliberately adopted a much lower international profile. This move, however, appeared to have been lamented in certain quarters within the Indonesian establishment. Indeed, many among the Indonesian political leadership felt that the success of the national resilience programme, which brought about vibrant economic development and stable internal politics, granted Indonesia 'the right to assert a higher profile'.[10] To that effect, the observations of Dewi Fortuna Anwar are worth quoting in full:

> There was a discernible sense of national grandeur amongst some sections of the Indonesian political elite. Indonesian political elite members were very conscious of the fact that Indonesia is the largest country in Southeast Asia and the world's fifth most populous state and that it has the potential to become a middle power. Many still cherished the memory of Indonesia's heavy concentration on foreign policy under Sukarno, which had resulted in rapidly increasing international interest in the country. A significant element within the Indonesian political elite, therefore, believed that Indonesian foreign

policy should have a higher profile, and be more active and more focused on the common interests of the Third World or the South, than it hitherto had under the New Order government.[11]

To what extent this view was representative of key policy-makers in Indonesia will no doubt be difficult to discern. Be that as it may, it is true that these activist ideals never strayed far from the surface of Indonesians' perceptions of their own identity and position in international society, and 'although tempered by current realities, they remain potent among Indonesia's contemporary intellectual establishment'.[12] Echoing these impressions, another scholar has intimated: 'A Java-centric view of the regional standing and vulnerability of archipelagic Indonesia which was formed during the struggle for independence has been sustained since its attainment.'[13] Certainly, in so far as the 'rightful' identity of Indonesia was concerned, domestic politicians were in consensus that Indonesia was a regional power.

This pressure for Indonesia to break out of its diplomatic dormancy subsequently led to a shift in international outlook among the political elite in Jakarta that was discernible in Indonesian foreign policy ventures during the mid to late 1980s. For example, some scholars view Jakarta's decision to commemorate the 1955 Bandung Afro-Asian Conference in 1985 as a watershed in Indonesian foreign policy.[14] This led to various calls for Indonesia to take on a more proactive role in regional affairs.[15] Others have cited Indonesia's active interest in resolving the Indo-China crisis as evidence of an awakening of Jakarta's once dormant foreign policy.[16] During the watershed visit of the Armed Forces chief, Benny Moerdani, to Vietnam in July 1984, Jusuf Wanandi observed: 'We're [Indonesia] emerging from a long period of dormancy in foreign affairs. . . . The world is going to be hearing a lot more from Indonesia now.'[17]

There have been suggestions that the rationale behind Indonesia's diplomatic resurgence could be attributed to the emergence of a 'second generation' in Indonesian nationalism.[18] While the nationalist spirit inherent in the Indonesian political psyche certainly accounted in some measure for this renewed impetus to activism, this rationale only reflected the fact that there probably has always been a latent belief among the political elite in Indonesia that Jakarta is an international player of consequence, and hence should re-assert its role to that effect. This drive for greater international prominence brought Indonesia into direct diplomatic conflict with Malaysia, which, as discussed above, was itself embarking on international activism driven by a rejuvenated Malaysian nationalism.

Malaysia's move towards increasing its international profile saw Mahathir fashion for himself a role as the unofficial spokesperson of the Third World. Under his watch, Malaysia's track record in international diplomacy was impressive. Contradicting Indonesian preferences for enhanced North–South dialogue, Mahathir was instrumental in pushing

South–South cooperation.[19] Malaysian leadership also extended to the political front, and has been manifested most strikingly in Mahathir's active politicking at the United Nations. Greater international prominence has seen Malaysia voted in as a member of the UN Security Council for two terms, in 1988–1990 and 1998–1999. Further to that, Malaysia has held the rotational position of President of the UN General Assembly (51st Session), along with the chairs of the G-77 and the Commission on Sustainable Development. Malaysian leadership has also been exemplified in the country's participation in UN peacekeeping, which has been unrivalled by any other Third World state (and, for that matter, by few developed states). Mahathir has continued Malaysia's tradition of active support for and participation in UN peacekeeping operations, overseeing Malaysia's involvement in Namibia, Cambodia, Somalia, Kuwait, the Iran–Iraq border, and, more recently, Bosnia and East Timor, and has made Malaysia a centre for peacekeeping training.

Mahathir was also among the first Third World leaders to call for the Non-Aligned Movement to take on a new, more active role in the post-Cold War world order. This activism was evident at the 1992 Non-Aligned Movement conference in Jakarta, where he purportedly 'stole the thunder' and 'virtually became, as a *Far Eastern Economic Review* cover story described it, the "new voice for the Third World" or even a "little Sukarno", as some of the Indonesian media opined'.[20] This reference to an Indonesian legacy was profoundly ironic, for it codified opinions already being formulated in Jakarta that the Mahathir administration was out to undermine Indonesia's traditional role of regional primacy as the 'first among equals', as well as its international political ambitions.[21] The context of Mahathir's implicit challenge to Indonesia's diplomatic position in regional and international affairs during the 1992 Non-Aligned Movement summit in Jakarta takes on further significance for another reason: the 1992 summit was supposed to mark the 'return' to prominence of an Indonesian government that had for a long period subdued its natural propensity to leadership.[22] Not surprisingly, the Indonesian media were highly critical of what they perceived as Mahathir's attempt to upstage Suharto at an event seen in Jakarta circles as a landmark occasion for Indonesian foreign policy. Rumours later emerged that the Indonesian press was instructed to edit and blot out key elements of Mahathir's speeches to prevent him from outshining Suharto.[23] Tension was further exacerbated with the substantial and obvious distance between Indonesian and Malaysian positions on international affairs that came to the fore at the Non-Aligned Movement summit in Jakarta, where diplomatic manoeuvrings by both parties generated speculation that Indonesia–Malaysia relations were heading for another tailspin.[24] Whereas Suharto spoke, as chairman of the Non-Aligned Movement, of the need for non-aligned states to take on a more cooperative tone in relations with the developed world, Mahathir chose a confrontational approach, unleashing his characteristic spleen against the West. This indeed was frowned upon by Indonesia not only because it was clearly an implicit and disrespectful challenge to the chair, but also because Jakarta was aware that in actual practice, Malaysia was a close economic and military ally of the West.[25] Moreover, Indonesia did not take too kindly to Malaysia's excessively strong pro-Islamic stance in support of Bosnia, which it saw as a further affront to the state with the world's largest Muslim population.[26] Predictably, the fact that it appeared as if it was Mahathir, not Suharto, who was completing in the late twentieth century 'the victory of what President Sukarno used to refer as the "newly emerging forces" over the "old established forces"' further fuelled the flames of acrimony between the two leaders and the two governments.[27] This, in turn, was aggravated by the fact that many Indonesians privately welcomed Mahathir as the new champion of the Third World, a fact that further galled Suharto.[28]

Differences in policy orientations between Jakarta and Kuala Lumpur have also surfaced at Track-Two conferences. In general, Malaysia has given little regard to Indonesian efforts at mediation over the contending claims for the South China Sea islands through the Workshops on Managing Potential Conflicts in the South China Sea run by Indonesia.[29] One such example was Malaysia's open rejection of Indonesia's proposed solutions to contending South China Sea territorial claims involving Kuala Lumpur and several other regional states.[30] In fact, Malaysia has challenged Indonesia's neutrality in the South China Sea dispute in light of Jakarta's own dispute with one of the South China Sea claimants, Vietnam, over the continental shelf of the Natuna Islands.[31]

The creeping resurgence of diplomatic tension notwithstanding, it was an awareness that historical and political circumstances were changing that brought leaders from both countries to launch a series of dialogues in the late 1980s and early 1990s in an attempt to relocate their historical affinity in a contemporary political context. These dialogues included the *Dialog Pemuda Indonesia–Malaysia* (Indonesia–Malaysia Youth Dialogue) and the Malaysia–Indonesia Conference series. The impetus for these exchanges was a concern that both kin states still held expectations of each other that neither appeared ready or willing to fulfil. This dichotomy was impressed upon in the following comments by the then Malaysian Ambassador to Jakarta, Abdullah Zawawi:

> The question to ask ourselves is to what extent do we invoke the sentiments or [sic] our common heritage in the conduct of our bilateral relations. The dilemma is that so much is expected from it – each harbouring hopes that the other could be sympathetic because of the common heritage – more than we expect from others, including our immediate neighbours and friends. Unfortunately, while we understand if a favourable consideration is not forthcoming from these others, we do not feel the same way in a similar situation between us.[32]

What emerged from these exchanges is worthy of note. First, it is curious that while the main emphasis of these dialogue sessions was declared to be Indonesia–Malaysia relations, the vast majority of the panels and papers presented focused not on the aspects of this relationship, but on issues roundly classifiable as 'ASEAN in the post-Cold War era', signifying perhaps an inability or reluctance to discuss the profoundly complex yet fundamental causes of Indonesia–Malaysia problems. Second, in the panels and papers that did dwell on the Indonesia–Malaysia relationship, different perspectives and interpretations clearly emerged. Firdaus Abdullah observed for instance that at the Youth Dialogue meetings the Malaysian representatives 'made no effort to hide their enthusiasm or attachment to the *Serumpun* concept', while the Indonesian delegation had conspicuously lacked empathy towards the cause.[33] Indeed, in a noticeable change from earlier attitudes, Indonesian representatives challenged the very notion that Malays and Indonesian emerged from a shared stock, arguing the point highlighted previously that 'Malays' remained a small ethnic enclave in Eastern Sumatra and Riau. Similarly, while Malaysian delegates indicated their willingness to overlook the mistakes of *Konfrontasi*, calling it an 'aberration', Indonesian attitudes were much more sober, and were represented by Benny Moerdani's warning that 'confrontation and hostility in those years is living proof that relations between the two countries cannot be taken for granted'.[34]

Lingering differences also impeded attempts at greater defence cooperation. While military exchanges sanctioned during the 'golden age' of the Razak and Hussein Onn administrations continued, little further progress was made. In 1990, however, the Indonesian Justice Minister, Mochtar Kusumaatmadja, proposed the formation of a defence pact between Indonesia, Malaysia, and Singapore.[35] This proposal was presented to Malaysia as a possible replacement for the FPDA, which Jakarta had always suspected to betray a lingering distrust of Indonesia. With *Konfrontasi* long since forgotten (or so it seemed), Jakarta perceived that the time was ripe for ties with Malaysia to move beyond the mistrust of earlier years. This sentiment, however, was not shared in Kuala Lumpur circles, and the proposal was roundly dismissed for the following reason: 'A trilateral security arrangement is counter-productive for ASEAN security in the long run. It could ... cause unnecessary alarm and it would therefore be wise for ASEAN to stay with the existing bilateral security arrangements.'[36]

Reflecting upon this proposal, one scholar has inferred that Mochtar's suggestion for the formation of a trilateral defence pact was in fact just another manifestation of Indonesia's latent desire to play a leadership role in regional affairs.[37] If this is so, the response from Kuala Lumpur is understandable. Yet the events surrounding the proposal are also telling of the lingering suspicions harboured in Kuala Lumpur over Jakarta's intentions towards its immediate locale. Paradoxically, the Malaysian authorities had also earlier expressed reservations about Indonesia's heightened military cooperation with Singapore, to which Malaysian media reports responded: '[A]lthough Indonesia had the right to establish relations with another country, it should take into account the special ties between Kuala Lumpur and Jakarta which encompassed all aspects of life'.[38]

While there was undoubtedly continuity in traditional apprehension towards Indonesian intentions during this period, there was also a notable change in the terms of relations. The transformation of the respective Indonesian and Malaysian foreign policy outlooks in accordance with national priorities has already been noted. It was this transformation in foreign policy orientations and outlooks that locked Indonesia and Malaysia in a game of diplomatic brinkmanship which, though driven by different impulses, was profoundly ironic for its uncanny similarity to events leading up to *Konfrontasi*. What this amounted to was a perceptible shift in strategic outlook which in fact contravened a declaratory position that 'we [Indonesia and Malaysia] may say that between our two countries there is a common perception on the way we put ourselves in the international plane whether regional or globally'.[39]

Predictably, divergent strategic outlooks eventually led Jakarta and Kuala Lumpur to cross diplomatic swords on several issues in the 1990s. Three, in particular, captured the mood of this period of bilateral ties and manifested lucidly this contest for political primacy within the Indo-Malay Archipelago. The first of these issues revolved around Malaysian proposals for the establishment of a new regional trade and economic body; second was the diplomatic dispute that arose from the revival of territorial claims that had been held in abeyance since the 1970s; the final, and perhaps the most complicated issue of all, was the problem of illegal immigration.[40] These differences, while more symbolic than substantial, nevertheless exposed the frailties that continued to plague the bilateral relationship between two kin states gradually drifting apart.

The East Asian Economic Caucus

On the occasion of Chinese premier Li Peng's visit in December 1990, Mahathir announced that 'the countries of the region should strengthen further their economic and market ties so that eventually an economic bloc would be formed to countervail the other economic blocs'.[41] Subsequently, it was reported in the media that Malaysia would 'take the lead' in establishing this 'trade bloc'.[42] This grouping was envisioned to include the members of ASEAN along with the major East Asian economies of China, Japan, and South Korea, with the United States and Australia conspicuously omitted.[43] As an institution, it was to be modelled along the lines of the EEC (European Economic Community), where the free flow of goods underpinned and augmented collective power and shared interest. From a Malaysian perspective, the EAEG (East Asian Economic

Grouping) proposal was rationalized as a necessary response to the failure of the GATT (General Agreement on Tariffs and Trade) talks in November and December 1990 (which entrenched Malaysian perceptions that global trade was being dictated by Western interests), as well as disappointment with ASEAN's inability to register any substantial advancement in trade and economic cooperation.

Mahathir's EAEG formula was a characteristically audacious diplomatic move in several ways. First, it was a direct challenge to US interests in the region, one of sufficient potential severity that the US Secretary of State, James Baker, apparently responded with a specific memorandum to Japan urging the latter not to take part in the grouping.[44] More to the point was the fact that the EAEG proposal was seen in Jakarta circles as a deliberate affront to Indonesia. In the face of criticisms from numerous quarters (Japan, South Korea, and several ASEAN members were cautious in their response to the proposal), the Malaysian authorities moved to avert a diplomatic imbroglio by elaborating that the original EAEG proposal was not meant to be a trade bloc, but merely a 'consultative forum' to foster free trade.[45] Yet even when Kuala Lumpur moved to refine its proposition, Indonesia remained unwavering in opposition. Indonesia–Malaysia differences on this issue came to the fore at an ASEAN Senior Economic Officials' Meeting in February 1991 when, despite earlier Malaysian assertions that ASEAN had endorsed its proposal, a Malaysian attempt to include the EAEG proposal on the agenda was blocked by the Indonesian delegation.[46] While the Malaysian delegation hoped to institute EAEG as an independent body outside the framework of existing organizations and institutions, the Indonesians were of the opinion that any East Asian economic grouping had to be linked to APEC (Asia Pacific Economic Cooperation), which Jakarta stridently supported. As a result of concerns associated with the original proposal, the EAEG was recast as a caucus (the East Asia Economic Caucus, EAEC) at the ASEAN Foreign Ministers' Meeting in Kuala Lumpur in October 1991. The change in nomenclature that fronted the Malaysian proposal was noteworthy in one respect. As the word 'caucus' indicates, the EAEC would now have to be defined as a smaller grouping within a larger body or organization. In that sense, the EAEC was now taking a form more akin to Jakarta's counter-proposal of having the grouping operate within the larger APEC, rather than the original Malaysian vision. Beyond this significance, however, this change in name did little to alter the shape of the Malaysian proposal, or its ultimate goal of creating a regional trade bloc. Indeed, Mahathir himself was of the opinion that the name change would have little impact on his expectation of the region evolving into a trade bloc; nor did it transform Jakarta's reading of and opposition to Malaysian objectives in any substantial way.[47]

Indonesian responses to the EAEG proposal reflected fundamental opposition to it. In a veiled critique of the Malaysian proposal, former

President Suharto opined that ASEAN needed to enhance intra-organizational cooperation as well as cooperation with its dialogue partners, but this should not entail the formation of a trading bloc.[48] Symbolically, the Indonesian position was reiterated by Suharto and his Foreign Minister, Ali Alatas, at the same regional conference at which Mahathir expressed his opinion that the EAEG was something of a stepping-stone to a regional trade bloc.[49] Instead, as mentioned earlier, Indonesia sought to alter the complexion to suit what Jakarta considered the appropriate purpose for such an organization. This the Indonesians did by insisting that if the grouping was to come into being, it could function only within the rubric of APEC.[50] The outcome of these contested versions of the purpose and character of the EAEC reached a climax at the ASEAN summit meeting in Singapore in January 1992. The endorsement Kuala Lumpur sought at the summit was not forthcoming as Jakarta once again proved to be a stumbling block, urging caution in implementing the EAEC and calling for 'further refinements' to the concept.[51] The extent to which Indonesian opinions prevailed was made plain when the EAEC was placed beneath the AFTA (ASEAN Free Trade Agreement) and CEPT (Common Effective Preferential Tariffs) proposals on the summit agenda in terms of priority. The final straw came when the summit declaration gave only token mention to the EAEC, specifying that it was an adjunct to APEC, and that it was only a forum that would meet 'as and when the need arises'.[52] Indeed, Indonesia's success in relegating the status of the EAEC to that of a caucus within APEC took on greater consequence in view of the fact that one of Malaysia's rationales for proposing the grouping in the first place was to have it challenge APEC as the primary trade and economic vehicle for the countries of East Asia.[53] In accomplishing what it did, Jakarta effectively pulled off a diplomatic counter-coup that bore a superficial resemblance to Indonesian instigation of Malaysia's capitulation to Indonesia's original proposal on neutralization two decades before.[54]

No doubt several factors explain Indonesia's rejection of the Malaysian plan. First, the fact that the United States was Indonesia's largest trading partner and the second largest market for Indonesian products meant that any move to marginalize US interests in the region would not have been beneficial to Jakarta.[55] Second, the logic behind the original Malaysian proposal (that since the rest of the world was forming trade blocs, East Asia should also do so) was viewed in some quarters in Indonesia as unnecessarily hostile towards international trade.[56] Beneath this economic logic, however, lay more deep-seated reasons. Like the diplomacy of the Tunku before him, Mahathir's proposal of the EAEG was made without prior consultation with Jakarta. Furthermore, Indonesians took issue with Mahathir's aggressive style in pushing diplomatic initiatives, which was antithetical to how Indonesian leaders believed foreign policy should be conducted. Ultimately, the fact of the matter was that Jakarta held the opinion that in so far as the issue of hierarchy was concerned, it was

Indonesia that should rightfully be at the forefront of international affairs and pushing international initiatives.[57] Correspondingly, in a response pregnant with implications, the Malaysian media retaliated by questioning whether Indonesia's staunch opposition to the EAEC was not in fact a manifestation of a deeper desire to dominate ASEAN, or even Malaysia.[58]

Re-emergence of territorial disputes

Territorial disputes have never been a prominent feature of bilateral friction between Indonesia and Malaysia. It is important to recognize that even at the height of *Konfrontasi*, Jakarta never made any territorial claims on Malaysian soil. While the issues surrounding *Konfrontasi* involved conceptions of sovereignty, these did not amount to a challenge to the territorial limits of the newly envisioned state of Malaysia. It is in this respect that the territorial dispute between Jakarta and Kuala Lumpur over the islands of Sipadan and Ligitan takes on prominence, not only because this was the first bilateral impasse centred on territorial counter-claims, but also because of the timing behind the two parties' enunciation of their respective claims. While this territorial dispute has already been resolved in favour of Malaysia, of interest to this study is the tension that had arisen from previous claims and counter-claims. The potential severity of this dispute was insinuated by then Indonesian Ambassador to Malaysia, Soenarso Djajusman, who warned that 'border problems have always been the most sensitive issue in a relationship between two neighbouring countries'.[59] Given that it was only since the late 1980s that both parties had sought to assert their respective claims to the islands, this draws further attention to changes in the complexion of the relationship during this most recent phase in bilateral ties.

Sipadan and Ligitan are located off the northeastern coast of the island of Borneo, in the Celebes Sea. Historical ownership of these two islands is not clearly documented. Indeed, it is this cartographical vagueness that has permitted both Indonesia and Malaysia to press their claims. During the colonial period of the region's history, the islands of Sipadan and Ligitan were administered as part of the Tirun district of islands and riverine states, and were the subject of competing Spanish and Dutch claims by the advent of the nineteenth century.[60] Sovereignty over the two islands was later claimed by the British when the North Borneo Trading Company took over jurisdiction of the territory of North Borneo in 1877. Subsequently, as a result of Dutch interests and pressure, Britain and the Netherlands signed a convention in 1891 that delimited the seas off the coast of North Borneo into separate British and Dutch spheres. This effectively placed Sipadan under Dutch jurisdiction and Ligitan within both Dutch and British spheres of influence.[61]

Indonesian independence in 1945 saw Indonesia inherit the entire territorial expanse of the Dutch East Indies (sans West Irian). To the

Indonesian leadership, this included both the islands of Sipadan and Ligitan.[62] Indonesia's claims were later underscored by the December 1957 declaration of the archipelago doctrine delineating Indonesian territory. To Kuala Lumpur, however, the two islands were critical to the extension of its own continental shelf claims.[63] The drawing of territorial basepoints on the basis of Malaysian sovereignty over Sipadan and Ligitan allows the Malaysian government to, among other things, lay claim to petroleum resources that might fall within this ambit,[64] not to mention offer up further maritime buffer space *vis-à-vis* Indonesia and the Philippines.[65] The extent to which legalistic maritime problems have arisen from Malaysian claims to these islands was articulated by Mark Valencia as follows:

> Malaysia's inferred baseline, which links Malaysian territory on Sebatik Island with Pulau Sipadan does not connect islands fringing her coast nor does it enclose a coast which is deeply indented, and it deviates appreciably from the general direction of the coast. With respect to Indonesia, Malaysia has unilaterally drawn the common territorial sea boundary as a line which bisects the angle formed by Indonesia's archipelagic baseline and Malaysia's inferred baseline. . . . Even assuming that Malaysia owns Sipadan and Ligitan, Malaysia has claimed territorial seas and a section of the continental shelf which extends beyond a line of equidistance with these two neighbours.[66]

Given the potential for legal wrangling and diplomatic conflict as a result of these respective assertions of ownership over the two islands, it is interesting to note that prior to 1991, little was made of these contending claims. Sovereignty over the islands was omitted from the agenda of maritime matters discussed in a host of bilateral meetings that began in 1969.[67] Furthermore, the then Malaysian Deputy Prime Minister, Tun Razak, had allegedly expressed to Indonesian President Suharto during a tête-à-tête that Malaysia would not assert any claim to the islands of Sipadan and Ligitan.[68] Whether or not such an undertaking was in fact given by Razak, it is clear that maintaining the status quo for the most part defined the attitude of both parties to the contested claims.[69] Problems surfaced soon after the transfer of power in Malaysia from Hussein Onn to Mahathir. Tensions mounted in 1982 when rumours circulated in Indonesian circles that Malaysia had stationed troops on Sipadan, resulting in the mobilization of the Indonesian military.[70] These rumours later proved unfounded.[71] In a move to forestall the escalation of tensions, the Indonesian Law Minister, Mochtar Kusumaatmadja, declared that the islands 'belonged to both states'.[72] The issue was then transferred to the jurisdiction of the GBC, which had already been put in place to delineate the land borders in Borneo, and an accord signed to preserve the status quo.

The issue of the contested claims over the two islands re-emerged in

June 1991, when Indonesia issued a 'reminder' in response to heightened Malaysian tourism development activities on the islands.[73] While it was declared by both parties that the problem could be solved on the basis of 'the spirit of ASEAN and brotherliness of the two countries', this 'reminder' also marked the beginning of deteriorating relations.[74] It was Indonesia's case that by proceeding with development projects on the islands, Malaysia was deliberately violating the 1982 accord that maintained the status quo over ownership of the islands.[75] In response to these accusations, Kuala Lumpur dispatched a government team to visit the islands, and officials retorted that 'for all intents and purposes, they are Malaysian islands'.[76] Tensions subsequently mounted with the appearance of Indonesian military forces around the islands, not only demonstrating the Indonesian claim, but also conveying the message that the use of force was being considered as an option in Jakarta.[77]

In a provocative act that further amplified tensions, the Indonesian navy detained a Sabah fishing boat for violating the Indonesian EEZ (exclusive economic zone) within the vicinity of the contested islands.[78] Although the fishing vessel was fined and released two days later, a private meeting initiated by the then Malaysian Deputy Prime Minister, Ghafar Baba, with President Suharto to discuss the issue further aggravated the situation, when the Indonesian President emerged from that meeting apparently irritated and annoyed by Ghafar's presumptuous attitude.[79] The swift deterioration of relations drove home the point that existing levels of interaction and exchange were insufficient for the respective claimants to 'agree to disagree'. Malaysia, in particular, was deeply concerned that Indonesian military activities around the island were resurrecting the ghost of *Konfrontasi*. This was evidenced in the repeated admonition, especially on the part of the Malaysian leadership, not to permit relations to revert back to the days of *Konfrontasi*. Correspondingly, Kuala Lumpur mooted the creation of a joint commission both to facilitate ministerial talks and, more specifically, to look into resolving the Sipadan and Ligitan dispute. In an indictment of the vaunted 'ASEAN way' of dealing with conflicts, the Malaysian Foreign Minister, Abdullah Badawi, openly expressed the view that 'traditional methods of solving problems were no longer sufficient'.[80] Consequently, the Malaysia–Indonesia Joint Commission held its inaugural meeting in Kuala Lumpur from 7 to 11 October 1991, with both parties declaring their commitment to 'intensify discussions' to resolve the dispute.[81] Although driven by the need to avert further deterioration in relations as a result of counter-claims, the Joint Commission was to present a forum for the comprehensive management of bilateral disputes, and its inauguration was publicized as the dawning of a new era in Indonesia–Malaysia cooperation.[82]

Public proclamations notwithstanding, problems did not abate. For example, the Indonesian military made a point of engaging in exercises of gunboat diplomacy during periods when official negotiations were taking place. Illustrating the Indonesian military's initiation of this game of brinkmanship, it was reported that 'Indonesian air force planes usually make low passes over the island whenever senior Malaysian officials visit the islands'.[83] Similarly, Indonesian and Malaysian naval vessels routinely circled the islands on the occasion of Joint Committee Meetings (JCMs) while Malaysia also carried out its own military manoeuvres in the vicinity.[84] Indonesian intelligence officials have also divulged instances when Malaysian forces stationed on the islands fired at Indonesian military personnel.[85] In 1994, the Indonesian government publicly voiced concern over a military exercise staged by a Malaysian rapid deployment force in nearby Langkawi to 'capture' an island.[86]

While tensions were permitted to gradually blow over, the inability of six subsequent JCMs to find some sort of resolution to their differences demonstrated not only the severity of the problem, but also the extent to which relations had deteriorated as compared with the 1970s.[87] In February 1993, the Indonesian Foreign Minister, Ali Alatas, intimated that both states could eventually submit their respective claims to the International Court of Justice (ICJ), 'but this would be the last resort if bilateral ties between Indonesia and Malaysia broke down'.[88] His assessment was indeed prescient, for after much resistance to third-party mediation, ironically enough particularly on the part of Jakarta, both parties finally agreed via a memorandum of understanding to take the dispute to the ICJ in October 1996.[89] On 17 December 2002, the ICJ ruled in favour of Malaysia.

While the contest for jurisdiction over Sipadan and Ligitan was undoubtedly the most prominent of territorial disputes between the two avowedly fraternal states, it was by no means the only incident of boundary contestation.[90] Potential border problems persist, such as claims over Sebatik Island and over the Semantipal and Sinapad rivers, which flow through Borneo.[91] Problems over the delineation of the Indonesia–Malaysia border, particularly in Borneo, came to light recently when members of the Indonesian armed forces seized five Malaysian employees of a logging company for crossing over into Indonesian territory, and allegedly demanded a ransom for their release.[92] Malaysia responded by accusing Indonesian security forces of having moved a Malaysian boundary marker. Third-party diplomatic sources confirmed that at the time, both militaries were put on alert along the Borneo border.[93] Border problems between Jakarta and Kuala Lumpur also created another quandary for bilateral ties: illegal Indonesian migration into Malaysia.

Immigration issues

As we have seen, migration within the Indo-Malay Archipelago has long been a feature of the interaction and exchange that defined the identity of the region, especially in the pre-colonial era. In the more recent colonial past, British and Malay authorities in the peninsula also encouraged the migration of workers from Indonesia. Because of perceived shared racial and cultural traits, Indonesian immigrants were viewed by the Malay aristocracy and royalty in the nineteenth century as demographic buffers against the British-sanctioned influx of Chinese and Indian labour. Later in the 1950s and early 1960s, Indonesian migration into Malaya was encouraged by Kuala Lumpur for political reasons, as it allowed 'Malays' to maintain a numerical superiority over the Chinese and Indian communities.

While Indonesians have historically migrated into the peninsula and played a critical role in shaping the culture that has evolved there, in more recent times Indonesian migration has been viewed in a markedly negative light, and migrants have been blamed for a host of social problems that have plagued Malaysia. While the issue has yet to boil over into open diplomatic and military conflict, this relatively new character of Indonesian migration has been a thorn in the flesh, as it were, of recent bilateral relations. The inability to find a satisfactory solution has also been something of an embarrassment to both governments, culminating in the mass expulsion of Indonesian illegal immigrants in July 2002.

The contemporary phenomenon of Indonesian economic migration into the peninsula is not new.[94] It began in the early 1970s, when the expansion of the Malaysian economy as a result of an industrialization programme, undertaken on the back of the New Economic Policy, that demanded more labour than the local market could supply. In particular, the urban migration of Malay youths opened the door for Indonesian labour in the agricultural sector. Push factors included unemployment problems and over-population in Java, while the relatively higher wages found in the peninsula were a major pull factor. Added to that was the fact that the easy assimilation of Indonesian migrants into Malay society sometimes also allowed the 'guests' to benefit from affirmative action programmes of the NEP as well.[95] Even without such inducement, the fact that Malaysia was not only a location of close proximity but also a nation whose majority population shared much with the Indonesians in terms of language, culture, and even ethnicity meant that the peninsula would be the obvious choice for Indonesian workers looking to relocate to greener pastures.

By the late 1980s, Indonesian labour had moved from agriculture to the construction and service sectors in tandem with the urbanization of Malaysia. Numbers also rose substantially to meet increased demand. This increase in numbers has raised alarm over its potential rupturing effect on the fabric of Malaysian society, because the influx of foreign, largely Indonesian, labour in Malaysia has evidently coincided with an increase in crime rates. Indeed, Indonesian labourers have been implicated in and indicted for crimes ranging from petty theft to high-profile robberies and murders.[96] Matters were further aggravated by the fact that a large proportion of Indonesian workers in Malaysia had entered the country illegally.

In 1981, for example, it was estimated that there were 100,000 illegal Indonesian immigrants in Malaysia.[97] By 1987, this figure was estimated by the Malaysian Trade Union Congress to have surpassed 1 million. It was further estimated in 1987 that 36 per cent of prison inmates throughout Malaysia were illegal Indonesian immigrants.[98] Clearly, the phenomenon of Indonesian illegal immigrants was fast becoming a security problem for Malaysia. It was not surprising that this was accompanied by a perceptible shift in Malaysian attitudes towards Indonesian immigrants, which also provided a telling insight into the changing nature of relations. An observer of this phenomenon had written that in the early years these immigrants were 'silently welcomed' by the Malays, for:

> [t]he immigrants were then perceived as *Bangsa Serumpun* who would eventually assimilate with the local *Bumiputra*. Thus, in the long run the Indonesian immigrants were regarded to have strengthened the Malays' electoral power vis-à-vis the non-Malays because it was assumed that they will be assimilated with the local Malays.[99]

However, the increase in the number of these *bangsa serumpun* was leading to more intense competition for jobs, and especially those traditionally the preserve of Malay commerce. In more recent times, it became apparent to the Malaysian authorities that many of the Indonesian immigrants (illegal or otherwise) were in fact Christians who had begun using shared language and ethnicity as an avenue to proselytize among the Malay community.[100] Such was the severity of this problem that a Malaysian cabinet minister had considered the spreading of Christianity among the Malay population by their Indonesian cousins to be the 'biggest threat facing Muslims in Malaysia today'.[101]

Several measures were undertaken at a bilateral level to stem the swelling tide of illegal immigration. For instance, an agreement was signed in 1984 in Medan, Sumatra, which stipulated that Indonesia would supply six specific categories of workers for two-year contracts whenever requested to do so by Malaysia.[102] In 1988, Jakarta announced that Indonesians working illegally in Malaysia would be issued passports to provide them with 'protection' and 'help them earn better pay'.[103] Correspondingly, Malaysia announced new laws in 1991 that stipulated stricter penalties for employers of illegal immigrant workers as well as a minimum wage and other terms to improve working conditions. Under this scheme, Indonesian illegals, when caught, would still be permitted to work provided they registered with the Malaysian immigration department and obtained valid travel documents from the Indonesian embassy. While these efforts may be applauded, they have done little to stem the flow of illegals from Indonesia; nor has this cooperation been without its own obstacles and problems. The bureaucratic nature of the solutions meant a long and arduous, sometimes even expensive, process that was a burden for immigration departments and too complex for the potential Indonesian illegal migrant to comprehend. More importantly, there has been, in the minds of each party, the perception that the other has not been doing its part in the joint attempt to eradicate this problem of illegal immigrants. The Malaysian authorities, for example, have drawn attention to Jakarta's apparent unwillingness to render maximum cooperation in repatriating Indonesian illegals caught or imprisoned for crimes. This lack of cooperation has led to overcrowding and deteriorating detention conditions, in turn resulting in problems such as the hostage siege in Kuantan Prison on 9 January 1987. On their part, certain quarters in Indonesia have criticized Malaysia for dramatizing the issue and portraying Indonesians in a 'degrading and disparaging' manner.[104]

By early 2002, Malaysia's policy on Indonesian labour seemed primed for a shift when, in response to another all-too-familiar incident of rioting by Indonesian immigrant workers in Negri Sembilan, the Law Minister, Rais Yatim, noted:

> Besides defying authority, they [Indonesian immigrant workers] had the cheek to wave the Indonesian flag. They are not in Jakarta. They are in Malaysia.... Indonesia's Ambassador here need not say sorry anymore. We are going to take stern action. Malaysians in general cannot tolerate the violent behaviour of the Indonesians who are being too extreme and ungrateful.[105]

Following this, Prime Minister Mahathir expressed the opinion that it was time for Indonesian workers in Malaysia to be 'replaced' by workers of other nationalities.[106] Not long after, in response to outbreaks of criminal incidents involving Indonesian workers, the Malaysian government embarked on a total shift from the traditional policy of welcoming the 'cousins' from the archipelago to a large-scale repatriation of Indonesian illegals, the stipulation of severe penalties for those who continued to stay, and the closing of Malaysia's doors to Indonesian labour via the implementation of a 'Hire Indonesians Last' policy.[107] The Indonesian illegal immigrant problem was heavily 'securitized' by a Malaysian press that repeatedly blamed immigrants for a host of security problems involving riots and robberies.[108] These moves elicited a heated response from the Indonesian media. In an article bearing the provocative title 'Remember *Konfrontasi*', the *Jakarta Post* launched a stinging attack against Malaysia's actions, arguing that the new policies were far too extreme, and that 'there was a time, not so long ago, when Indonesia would not take such a belligerent act from a neighbouring country lying down'.[109]

A side note to the illegal immigration problem has been the issue of Acehnese immigrants and political refugees, which inadvertently involved a reluctant Malaysian government in the internal affairs of a Jakarta administration struggling to contain a politically motivated separatist revolt in the northern tip of the island of Sumatra.

The problem of Aceh

Despite widespread speculation, the extent of Malaysia's historical involvement in the Aceh conundrum remains unclear. Prime Minister Mahathir often reiterated the Malaysian government's non-involvement in what he claimed is an Indonesian domestic affair. Likewise, Indonesian President Suharto never publicly questioned Malaysian declarations of non-involvement, though on several occasions he did allude to 'external sources' of interference. In point of fact, there remains little by way of concrete evidence to implicate government-sanctioned involvement on the part of Malaysia, apart from knowledge that Acehnese rebels are making their way to the peninsula either as asylum seekers or as illegal immigrants.[110] To such effect, the Aceh situation is an extension of the broader problem of illegal Indonesian immigration into Malaysia. This has created some problems for the Malaysian authorities, who have had to choose between repatriation (which would probably lead to further prosecution) or asylum (which could potentially dampen ties with Indonesia). Such a dilemma was demonstrated in 1991, when 112 Acehnese asylum seekers who landed in Penang and Kedah were initially classified as illegal immigrants, and hence to be repatriated, but were eventually given the choice by the Malaysian government to stay on in Malaysia.[111] To further complicate matters, some of these Acehnese refugees in fact possessed dual nationality.

Despite constant pledges by Malaysian government authorities that Malaysia did not support the cause of the GAM (*Gerakan Aceh Merdeka*, the Aceh Independence Movement), the fact that among certain pockets of the Malay population in the peninsula there was more than passing interest in the Aceh situation has meant that relations between Indonesia and Malaysia have remained testy over Aceh. As was hinted in an earlier chapter, in a number of ways Aceh is closer geographically and spiritually to Malaysia than it is to Jakarta. The economic and political interaction between Aceh and the Malay sultanates through the centuries has resulted in many Acehnese settling in the peninsula, particularly in Kedah and Penang. Several top Malaysian government officials have Acehnese roots as well.[112] In more recent times, the potential complexity of these historical ties has seen Malaysian consular officials in the Northern Sumatran capital of Medan being kept at a distance by their Indonesian counterparts, suspicious of their ties with Acehnese separatists.[113]

While the Indonesian government has refrained from direct criticism of Kuala Lumpur for not curbing Malaysian public interest in the Acehnese struggle, some in the military have suspected that the Acehnese were permitted to 'live freely in Malaysia despite being guilty of violent actions against the Indonesian military'. These comments were made by General Pramono, commander of the North Sumatra garrison, who further intimated (without providing details) that 'certain quarters in Indonesia had accused specific groups and individuals in Malaysia of aiding the rebels directly'.[114] Suggestions have regularly been made by the Jakarta authorities that armed Acehnese civilians were able to travel between Aceh and Malaysia without any problem.[115] Evidence in the form of pro-GAM material that quotes Acehnese sources in Malaysia and refers to rebels who have fled to Kuala Lumpur has apparently surfaced to justify the Jakarta government's suspicions.[116] It has also come to light that the GAM leadership has on occasion operated out of Malaysia.[117] Indeed, the assassination of an Acehnese rebel leader (on 2 June 2000, allegedly due to an internal struggle) in Kuala Lumpur demonstrated, much to the Malaysian government's embarrassment, that Acehnese separatists were in fact present and moving freely in Malaysia. GAM military commanders have also publicly revealed that their militia have on occasion received training in Malaysia.[118] Concomitantly, in the light of the most recent Acehnese exodus, brought about by the Jakarta government's crackdown on GAM forces since May 2003, Indonesian lawmakers have warned Kuala Lumpur to exercise caution before granting political asylum, particularly to Acehnese with affiliations to GAM.[119]

The Aceh conundrum in Indonesia–Malaysia relations has brought to light once again the Islamic dimension to the kinship factor in the politics of the Malay world.[120] Hundreds of Malaysian students still travel to religious schools in Aceh for their education. Religious co-identification was further strengthened during the Suharto years, when the Acehnese rejected the former president's *Pancasila* democracy (which they viewed as un-Islamic) and sympathized with the staunch adherence to Islamic principles found in the state administrations of Kelantan and Kedah in Malaysia.[121] Indeed, religious undercurrents to the Aceh issue in Indonesia–Malaysia problems provide an arresting sign of how politicized religion and kinship politics intertwine at a popular level.

Political Islam

Despite the status of Indonesia and Malaysia as co-religionists, in their post-independence histories Islam has never been utilized as a channel for bilateral cooperation or policy coherence in Indonesia–Malaysia relations, at least in so far as governmental interactions are concerned. Yet while Islam has consistently been downplayed by the governments of Indonesia and Malaysia during the post-colonial era, it has never drifted far from the surface of popular politics.[122] Consequently, it is the recent resurgence of political Islam in both countries that draws attention to the instrumentality of religion as a cohesive factor for bilateral relations in future.

It will be recalled that the Islamic links between the peninsula and archipelago in the context of Islamic resurgence and anti-colonial struggle were particularly strong, built on the back of shared experiences in the Middle East and South Asia among sojourning Indo-Malay religious students. Co-religious identification with Indonesia among Malay anti-colonialists, however, did not stem only from their Arab connections. Here, it is important to note that the politicization of Islam in the Indonesian anti-colonial struggle played a crucial role in grafting Islam onto the political scene in colonial Malaya. The first Islamic political organizations and structures to be found in the archipelago were located in Indonesia, and they had a profound influence on the subsequent emergence of similar movements in Malaya.[123] A brief survey of the birth of political Islam in Malaysia will illustrate this point.

It was through the political struggle of the Islamic *Masjumi* Party (*Majlis Masyuarat Muslim Indonesia*) in Indonesia after the Pacific War that an overtly Islamic quality was injected into Malay politics in the peninsula. *Masjumi* leaders were present as special guests at a Malay nationalist and religious leaders' conference (*Persidangan Ekonomi-Agama Sa-Malaysia*) held on March 1947 at Gunung Semanggol in Perak to discuss the role of Islam in Malayan politics. It was during this conference that the *Masjumi* representatives shared their conception of the Islamic struggle for sovereign nationhood with their counterparts in Malaya. Further to that, the Indonesian representatives, in their public address, suggestively articulated that 'the greater Indonesian Empire will consist of equal autonomous states which will be free members of the Indonesian Commonwealth'.[124] The Gunung Semanggol event was to have a significant influence on the worldview of future Malay Islamic political leaders.[125] It was also via the experiences garnered from these meetings that Malay nationalists envisaged the formation of the *Lembaga Islam Se Malaya* (All-Malaya Islamic Council), later renamed MATA (*Majlis Agama Tertinggi Malaya*, Malayan Supreme Religious Council).[126] This religious organization was modelled on *Majlis Islam Al Indonesia* (the Council of Muslim Parties of Indonesia) in Indonesia, the predecessor of *Masjumi*.[127] MATA itself was to undergo metamorphosis into 'the first institutionalization of the Islamic reformist stream in Malay nationalism'.[128]

In its response to Britain's Malayan Union plan of 1946, MATA moved to call for a Malay Congress in March 1948 to discuss issues such as the formation of an Islamic political party as well as the establishment of an economic bureau and an Islamic university.[129] Aside from representatives from all quarters of Malay society (including UMNO and Malay elements of the Communist Party), the Congress also had in attendance three prominent Sumatran *ulama* (religious teachers): Kiai Masyhur from West Sumatra, Tengku Osman from Medan, and Haji Shamsuddin Mustaffa from Siak. Notably, the Congress opened with the singing of the *Masjumi* song '*Selamat Masjumi*'.[130] It was at the Congress that the *Hizbul Muslimin* ('Muslim Party') was formed. Needless to say, the party was inspired by *Masjumi*, and its leaders such as Abu Bakar al Bakri and Mohammad Asri soon developed close relations with Indonesian *ulama* and nationalists.

Because of the close association between its members and those of the nationalist party MNP, *Hizbul Muslimin* has been considered the 'Islamic wing' of Malay nationalism.[131] Not only did the *Hizbul Muslimin* take on the organizational structure of *Masjumi*, it also subscribed to a similar political and religious philosophy. In the spirit of the Indonesian revolution, and more specifically the Islamic revolts in Java and Sumatra that were taking place at the time, party leaders unanimously called for active revolt against the forces of colonialism. This was reflected in the following excerpt from a speech of one of the party's leaders: 'Indonesia had achieved her independence by the sacrifice of many lives ... Malays would not obtain their independence by just asking for it. Independence ... could only be obtained by bloodshed.'[132] The basis established during this period for religious and political collaboration between politicized Muslim elements in Indonesia and Malaya was amplified by the formation of religious schools known as *sekolah rakyat* (people's schools) throughout the peninsula. Again, these schools, established after a decision taken at a MATA meeting in September 1947 which witnessed the formation of LEPIR (*Lembaga Pendidikan Rakyat*, People's Education Board), were to be modelled after the *Muhammadiyah* schools in Indonesia.[133] This was a significant development, because at that time *Muhammadiyah* was actively engaged in preaching and practising radical nationalism in Sumatra. For the first time too, religious students from the peninsula were sent not only to Aligarh, Medina, or Al-Azhar, but also to Indonesia to further their education.[134]

What is significant in the preceding discussion is that the coalescing of the political ideologies of *Hizbul Muslimin*, *Muhammadiyah*, and *Masjumi* would prove to have an incisive influence on the ideologies of later representations of Islamic reformism and nationalism in the MNP, PMIP, and PAS.[135] These early linkages also formed a firm basis for Islamic groups from Indonesia and Malaysia to maintain close relations despite the decline of Islam as a political factor in the post-colonial domestic politics of both countries. These links have also endured through the various stages and changing shape of relations at the government level, particularly during periods of tension. Indeed, it has been suggested that the *Dakwah* (Islamic revival) that took place in Malaysia in the 1970s had benefited from precisely these long-standing relations with Indonesian religious organizations, for the Indonesians were the movement's 'first influential international contact' and thus 'provided an important stimulus to Islamic revivalism in Malaysia'.[136] In recent times, both countries have witnessed a revival of Islamic discourse in their respective political arenas, and in contrast to earlier trends, it has been Indonesian Islam that has been looking to the Malaysian model of Islamic resurgence.[137] During the final years of the Suharto administration, Islam was resurrected as the President sought to balance the increasing influence of the military. Likewise in Malaysia, the resurgence of the PAS has led to increasing Islamic consciousness within the dominant UMNO party as well, exemplified by the exertions of former Deputy Prime Minister, Anwar Ibrahim, to shore up the party's Islamic identity. Ties between Islamic groups were given greater impetus via the exchanges between the IKD (*Institut Kajian Dasar*, Institute of Policy Studies), a think-tank established by Anwar Ibrahim, and ICMI (*Ikatan Cendekiawan Muslim Indonesia*, Indonesian Muslim Intellectuals' Association), established by B.J. Habibie.[138] In its prime, the government-linked IKD and ICMI network was instrumental in fostering bilateral harmony through its regular organization of joint seminars and conferences on *serumpun*, exploring ways and means to encourage closer relations and greater exchange on this basis.[139] It is also well known that Anwar cut a popular figure among Indonesian Muslim circles, and had close links with several other Indonesian Muslim groups.

Radicalizing affinity: Islamic militancy in the Indo-Malay world

While transnational Islamic links between the peninsula and archipelago appear to have taken on renewed prominence in recent times, the porous cultural-religious borders in the Indo-Malay world have also given up more radical forms of Islamic co-affiliation. In the midst of the current war against Muslim militancy, evidence has emerged that the Islamic linkages between the Indonesian and Malaysian *Ummah* have extended to radical and militant Islam as well. Cooperation between regional security and intelligence agencies has uncovered the existence of a regional terrorist organization, JI (*Jemaah Islamiyah*, Islamic Organization), 'directed' by an Indonesian leadership. Gradually, information has surfaced that the JI enjoys a regional influence among the Muslim communities in the Indo-Malay world, and, as an organization, was built around a regional network of study-groups spawned out of the teachings of JI spiritual leader Abu Bakar Bashir.[140] While these militant elements thus far remain peripheral players (in terms of their membership numbers), their stated objectives of forming a *Daulah Islamiyah* (Islamic state) comprising Indonesia and Malaysia, along with the southern Philippines and southern Thailand, raises the spectre of previous attempts, such as *Indonesia Raya–Melayu Raya* and Maphilindo, to unify the Indo-Malay world on the basis of common identity. The plan for establishment of a *Daulah Islamiyah* itself was an intriguing and elaborate long-term strategy. Though it involved terrorist activities, it was essentially built around the socialization of young Muslims through religious training in Indonesia, who would later be integrated into state administrations and mainstream politics in order to transform Indonesia and Malaysia into part of a broader Islamic state via legitimate electoral processes.[141] Though the current scope of JI influence, which operates outside the control of the state, remains a matter of debate among both scholars and policy-makers, it is clear that under the banner of Islam a form of Indo-Malay consociation has been revived, highlighting one aspect of contiguity across the cultural-territorial identity of the Indo-Malay world.

Concluding remarks

Considering its relatively recent content, this chapter has had to rely on secondary resource material with which to sketch recent permutations of the Indonesia–Malaysia relationship, given the unavailability of primary sources. Even so, a comprehensive picture has emerged of how the kinship factor has undergone further transformation as relations have evolved.

Under the Mahathir administration, Malaysia attempted to restructure the terms of relations with Indonesia that were established during the tenures of Tun Razak and Tun Hussein Onn. Mahathir seems to have departed from his predecessors' policy of 'self-induced subordination' to Jakarta. The proactive and nationalistic foreign policy that the Mahathir administration embarked upon, particularly since the late 1980s, coincided with resurgence in Jakarta's own interest in assuming a role as a key mover of Third World politics. This has resulted in a clash of policy perspectives that threatens to unravel the efforts of an earlier generation of leaders who had sought to establish relations on a firmer footing provided by the conscious fulfilment of expectations and obligations as kin states.

In some ways, competition between Indonesia and Malaysia is understandable. Both had made quick strides in economic development by the 1990s. Furthermore, national identity-building in both states has also advanced substantially. This has had an impact not only on the personal and cultural identities of the populations, but on their loyalties as well, as far as kinship sentiments are concerned. This transformation has witnessed foreign policy play a major role in the national identity-building project in both Indonesia and Malaysia. During the 1980s and 1990s, not only were Indonesian and Malaysian foreign policies focused on regional and international activism, but they were also distinctly nationalistic. The fallout of this phenomenon for bilateral relations, however, stems from the fact that both have appealed to their respective audiences on similar issues, with the same objectives in mind, but have nevertheless approached these issues from different and antagonistic angles. Consequently, nationalistic imperatives of these two kin states wrought foreign policies that in the end provoked each other.

Given the significance of the 'Chinese factor' in framing kin relations during the Razak–Hussein Onn era of Malaysian relations with Indonesia, it is also notable that the weakening premises of kinship during the 1990s have further coincided with a marked reduction in Indo-Malay concerns for relations with Beijing, as well as with their own domestic ethnic Chinese communities. Indonesia normalized ties with China in 1990, and domestic factors were identified as drivers behind this policy shift.[142] In Malaysia's case, relations with China in fact improved substantially in the

1990s, as did inter-communal relations within the country.[143] Consequently, while lingering concerns for the 'Chinese factor' may have anchored Indo-Malay co-identification in the 1970s, the diminution of these concerns as a result of transformations of Indo-Malay national identities to accommodate ethnic Chinese within a national framework at the domestic level, and improved relations with China at the international level, has led to the decline of this 'anti-Chinese' impetus to kinship affiliations.

Whether the sense was that Malaysia suffered from a 'small brother' syndrome in relation to Indonesia which compelled the Mahathir administration to overcompensate, as certain Indonesian political players are wont to believe,[144] or whether Indonesia was peeved because the Mahathir government simply did not abide by the unwritten rule of deference set in place by Tun Razak for the conduct of Malaysia's relations with Indonesia, as some Malaysians maintain,[145] the fact of the matter is that during the 1980s and especially the 1990s, kinship amity, which was established during the Razak–Ghazali Shafie and Suharto–Adam Malik era as a foundation for bilateral relations, was put aside as the two states engaged in a contest for primacy, originating from divergent assumptions as to the fundamental basis of their relations.

At another level, there was a further sense that on the part of Indonesia in particular, the construction of kinship identity along ethnic (i.e. Malay) lines, already a clearly tenuous exercise from an anthropological point of view, without adhering to the functional aspects to such relatedness, was becoming increasingly irrelevant. This opinion was expressed by Jusuf Wanandi, who noted that 'generally both Malaysia and Indonesia may be Malay nations ... but they should not expect too much from Indonesia based on the "Malay stock" factor. ... The vast majority of Indonesians are Javanese, who do not regard themselves as Malay.'[146] Given this opinion, and Indonesia's frustration at the Mahathir administration's disregard for the tradition set by previous administrations of regular consultation with and deference to Jakarta on foreign and security policy matters, it was clear that in Indonesian eyes, *rumpun*-based fraternity was premised on the functional aspects of kinship expectations defined as Malaysian consultation with and deference to Jakarta on policy matters relating to the latter's interests, rather than vague notions of ethno-racial affiliation. This, it seemed, was being increasingly contravened by Malaysia's perceived lack of regard for these functional terms of kinship.

Conclusion

The evocation of Indo-Malay kin fraternity has been a distinctive feature of the sociology and politics of Indonesia–Malaysia relations. Riding on the legacy of intermarriage, social-cultural exchange, and migration, the pull of kinship has always been strong, and, going by its regular evocation in diplomatic and cultural discourse, continues to be a source of intelligibility for those keen on emphasizing camaraderie between Indonesia and Malaysia. Indeed, the impact of intermarriage and migration that has given rise to a shared linguistic and cultural legacy continues to define much of the cross-border interchange in the Indo-Malay world today. Artistic and literary traditions of the peninsula continue to be traced back to Indonesia. In the early years of Malayan independence, the Malay education system was built around Indonesian teachers, and these educational exchanges remain a feature of relations today. The Indonesian revolution was celebrated in many Malayan quarters in the early post-colonial years, and Indonesian anti-colonialists continue to be lauded as Malay heroes.[1] Given the emergence of terminology such as *'Berkampung'* (to come together as in a village or tribe), *'Diplomasi Serumpun'* (racial diplomacy), and *'Musyawarah dan Muafakat'* (consultation and consensus) over the years, a language of kinship appears to have emerged in the lexicon of political relations, one that harks back to pre-colonial notions of community and identity. The resilience of such ideas, along with the continued existence of avenues through which closer relations can be plotted, indicates that the phenomenon of kinship remains of some import in the affairs and identity of the Indo-Malay world.

However, even during the early years of anti-colonial struggle, a period that was arguably the height of Indo-Malay fraternity, there was a sense that ethno-historical distinctions, which also formed a significant facet of the pre-colonial Indo-Malay world, assumed little significance in the minds of Western-educated proponents of kinship more conscious of opposition to colonial forces than of distinctions among themselves. These differences, simmering beneath the veneer of solidarity, quickly re-emerged during the post-colonial attempts to organize relations on the premises of kinship. Despite ideal depictions, association between kin was shot through with contradictions. On one level, the spirit of anti-colonial struggle, augmented by legends and genealogies of the glorious past, bound Indonesia and Malaysia against a common antagonist and around the shared political objective of emancipation; yet on another, the historical and contemporary narrative also documents wars, intrigue, diplomatic brinkmanship, and disillusionment that define bilateral relations. To some extent, these contradictions have begun to spark a re-assessment of the Indo-Malaysian relationship. Certainly, while the historical legacy of social-cultural exchange has continued into contemporary times, there is a sense within some quarters that the relationship has not been conducted on an equal basis. This is so at least in Malaysian eyes, which continue to view cultural exchange as a one-sided phenomenon:

> In cultural exchanges ... more Indonesian songs are aired in Malaysia, more films shown, more books and magazines available, to the Malaysian public than are Malaysian items available to the Indonesians. Similarly close to a thousand Malaysians are studying in Indonesia and very few Indonesia students are in Malaysia, whereas many Indonesian students do study abroad, including Singapore. Is the teaching in Bahasa Malaysia a problem? Are there no suitable institutions? Will Indonesian students not feel comfortable in Malaysia?[2]

In the light of this, the issue was raised when the Malaysian Ambassador, Abdullah Zawawi, shared his candid impression that 'in the equation of our two countries' present relations, Malaysia and Indonesia have not been equally committed in our efforts to give meaning to the *"Rumpun"* factor'.[3] Yet given the propensity in Malay popular opinion to view Indonesians as ethnic kin and Indonesia's reluctance to be associated as such, this imbalance is hardly surprising. Not too long ago, Indonesians too sought to construct kinship along ethno-cultural lines, suggesting that

> Except for some minor differences wrought by history ... the two nations could well be one. In the first place, Malaysia in the minds of Indonesians, is Malay – Brothers of the Malay race. This impression is hard to change, although Indonesians know that according to the statistics Malays actually make up only slightly more than half of the population of Malaysia. On their television sets, Indonesians watch Malaysian artistes perform dances or play music that can hardly be distinguished from those of Indonesia's own regions. Indonesians can communicate with Malaysians as easily as Englishmen with Americans.[4]

In more recent Indonesian thinking, however, such potentialities have been overshadowed by the reality of political rivalry between Indonesia and Malaysia which, in so far as Jakarta has been concerned, has been a result of what Indonesians perceived to be Malaysian disregard of and challenge to Indonesian primacy in the Indo-Malay world. From these observations, then, it is clear that while there is conceptual room to speak about kinship between Indonesia and Malaysia, at the level of politics and relations between these two states, harmonious relations expressed as a consequence of the kinship factor remain elusive. This state of affairs, the present study has argued, has essentially been a consequence of contested interpretations of history and the terms of kin affinity that underscored the language and discourse of kinship, as well as the perceived failure of Indonesia and Malaysia to fulfil the expectations and obligations entailed in a relationship expressed as that between kin. In turn, both problems have been born of fundamental differences in their respective historical experiences of national self-determination. The manner in which conceptions of affinity have shaped and been shaped in the course of Indo-Malay political history in fact highlight the fact that kinship cannot be divorced from issues of identity and nationalism, which are precisely the avenues through which kinship is given political expression. Thus, in the study of Indonesia–Malaysia relations, it appears that tensions have as much to do with conflicts of identity as they do with conflicts of interests.

Race, ethnicity, and hegemony

It is clear from much of the diplomatic language that Indo-Malay leaders frame kinship in terms of shared racial and cultural characteristics. In so doing, they echo conceptually the social-anthropological literature discussed earlier, which discuss broader 'pseudo' and 'fictive' permutations of social relations categorized as kin. Despite substantial common social-political ground between Indonesia and Malaysia, this study has also shown that some of the historical and ethno-cultural reference points alluded to by those who evoke Indo-Malay affinity are themselves contestable, and because of this they actually amplify differences when attempts are made to transcribe such romanticism unto the political sphere.

The politics of blood brotherhood can be traced to the anti-colonial struggle, when kinship was expressed as *pribumi* identity constructed against the common adversary, Western imperialism.[5] Yet this portrayal of affinity concealed a fundamental difference between respective conceptions of pan-identity held by the various political actors that diluted the psychological and nationalistic appeal of the singular Indo-Malay nation-state. These discrepancies were exposed in the motivations behind *Indonesia Raya* and *Melayu Raya*.

Indonesia Raya was the most profound Indonesian expression of the politics of kin solidarity. Pan-nationalists such as Muhammad Yamin and Sukarno, motivated by the legacy of the Javanese kingdom of Majapahit, claimed to be heirs of this ancient polity whose extent was interpreted, by their reading of history, as having included the Malay Peninsula. Such a conceptualization dictated the pre-independence Indonesian anti-colonial vision of the territorial boundaries of the post-colonial state. *Melayu Raya* was also conceptualized along the lines of the re-awakening of a historical identity based on another ancient kingdom, Srivijaya. In the same way that Muhammad Yamin, the key ideologue behind *Indonesia Raya*, interpreted Indonesian history, Burhanuddin al-Helmy's exposition of *Melayu Raya* read from Malay history the extension of the great kingdom of Srivijaya into contemporary geopolitics. Unlike Yamin, however, who in the main conceptualized his pan-identity on the basis of historical territorial claims, the authenticity of *Melayu Raya* derived primarily from ethnic and cultural bases. These different frames of reference made it clear very early on in the history of the politics of kinship in the Indo-Malay world that fundamental problems would follow the conceptualization of pan-identity. Most Indonesians *are not* ethnic Malay, and attempts by pan-Malay nationalists at recasting history to suggest that they were proved to be cavalier at best, counter-productive at worst. Hence, in order to understand the construction of relatedness in this region it is critical, among other things, that one appreciates the distinction between Indonesian and Malay understandings of ethnicity and 'Malayness', for this distinction lies at the heart of the identity of the Indo-Malay world, and was never convincingly reconciled by the proponents of pan-unity.

Nor did the champions of pan-unity on either side of the Melaka Straits give heed to the empirical record of tension between the Malay and Javanese kingdoms that defined much of the pre-colonial narrative of Indo-Malay geopolitics. A fundamental problem that was recognized even among prominent Indonesian nationalists plotting the territorial boundaries of the post-colonial state was the danger that a pan-Malay state could be construed as a mask for Javanese hegemony and territorial ambition, particularly if the kingdom of Majapahit were used as a model. Such a perception was aggravated by the inevitably Javanese-orientated character of nationalism (owing to the concentration of educated Indonesians in Java and the limited extension of Western notions of modernity to the outer islands), and in many ways echoed the pre-colonial regional order of the Indo-Malay world that was defined by discord between kingdoms centred on Java and the surrounding proximate regions, including the Malay Peninsula. The fact that proponents of pan-Malayism attempted to make a historical argument for the existence of a 'Malay nation' out of a common race or ethnicity and encompassing the territorial expanse of the Indo-Malay Archipelago without taking into consideration the ethnographic, political, and strategic realities of the time certainly lends further credence to the belief that kinship was constructed without due regard to historiographical complexities and antagonisms.

While the roots of the geographical partition of the Indo-Malay world can be traced to colonialism, it was with the advent of nationalism that differences that transcended kin solidarity intensified. Despite initial common objectives, the growth and intensification of nationalism in the Indo-Malay world ultimately pulled the two nationalist movements apart as a consequence of different premises of Indonesian and Malayan ideologies of national self-determination. The Indonesian quest for modern statehood was advanced along civic and egalitarian, not ethnic or racial, lines. The 1928 Youth Pledge taken at Bandung, when leaders of the anti-Dutch movement from throughout the archipelago gathered and proclaimed their loyalty to one nation, language, and flag, epitomized this. The making of Indonesia, then, was presented as a Batavia-centric, and not Java-centric, phenomenon.[6] Consequently, despite Yamin's romanticism, it would eventually be Dutch colonial boundaries that served as the point of reference for Indonesian nationalism.

In contrast to Indonesia's egalitarian nationalist ideology, the transition from communal to national identity in Malaya was characterized by the peaceful imposition of a system of governance that preserved the rights of a dominant ethnic community, the Malays. Led eventually by the conservative elite bent on retaining their status, rather than pan-Malay socialists or Islamic reformists, nationalism in Malaya stood as antithetical to the civic and egalitarian character of the Indonesian experience of self-determination, in which the aristocracy and traditional elite were viewed as obstacles as opposed to facilitators of independence. Within this ethnic framework, it was Malay nationalism (as opposed to Malayan nationalism), which had as its epicentre the competition between the traditional aristocratic ruling elite and the Indonesian-influenced radical Malay nationalists, that dominated. The benign character of Malayan independence also contrasted profoundly with the Indonesian revolution, and it should be no surprise that this dichotomy informed the Malay leadership's perception of relations with Indonesia and their leaders. The conservative Malay elite harboured discomfort at the nature and manifestation of anti-colonial agitation in Indonesia even as they applauded its spirit. What compounded matters was the fact that during the course of the Indonesian revolution the traditional Malay elite, highly protective and conscious of their identities and social status as the privileged indigenous people, witnessed a wholesale restructuring of society in Indonesia via a bloodbath against traditional forces in Sumatra. This experience had a profound impact on the conservative Malay leaders from the peninsula, and it was hardly surprising that these perceptions were carried into the era of post-colonial relations when they eventually inherited the colonial state.

Differences stemming from events of the revolution were compounded by the close relationship between British Malaya and Sumatra. Sumatra was the bastion of feudal society in Indonesia and shared much closer affinity with the state and societal structures in peninsular Malaya than did Java or any other East Indies territory. Consequently, as it was the Sumatran feudal structure that was demolished by what appeared to be a

Java-centred republican revolution, Malay suspicion of Javanese designs behind the Indonesian Republic was not surprising. In the same vein, suspicions of Malay–Sumatran complicity in retaliation were never far from the minds of Indonesia's Javanese leaders. Many of the complications surrounding kinship politics in early Indonesia–Malaysia relations were related to questions of Sumatran loyalty to the Indonesian nation-state as opposed to narrow ethno-cultural identity, and Malaya's role in instigating or encouraging separatist tendencies. In turn, it is evident that these cross-currents were associated with the fact that Malays from the peninsula share personal and cultural identity with Sumatrans to a much greater degree than they do with other Indonesian communities, not to mention a shared and unremitting aversion to Javanese regional dominance. It was on this basis that the subsequent formation of Malaysia was viewed as potentially divisive from an Indonesian perspective in terms of the possibility that it might encourage Sumatran separatism.[7] The fact that the Malay political elite had close relations with the then-influential Sumatra-based *Masjumi* Party further heightened Javanese concerns. It is also telling, for instance, how during the early years of relations Jakarta politicians were wary of Malay diplomats who cultivated Sumatran contacts.[8]

What the anti-colonial advocates of Indo-Malay kinship failed to realize was that framing fraternity in ethno-cultural terms would undoubtedly privilege Malay–Sumatran relations to an extent greater than what a Javanese-led government would be comfortable with. Consequently, some Indonesians have registered their disapproval to the conceptualization of kinship explicitly on ethnic grounds. Indeed, it was in response to such attempts that Moerdani warned:

> Communities in both countries have strong reasons to believe that they have similarities in various aspects of life. However, we must also be wise enough to say that there are a number of differences in both communities' socio-cultural and economic life.... These differences should not be overlooked as they can be the source of a split in perception.[9]

Some have made the observation that certain Indonesians see '*rumpun*' as holding much more appeal to Malays precisely because of the continued emphasis on racial and ethnic identity in contemporary Malaysian politics.[10]

Much of this tension was also reflected in the personal dynamics between the leaders of Indonesia and Malaysia, and surfaced in the course of the conduct of statecraft and diplomacy. Of the first four Prime Ministers in Malaysian history, for instance, only the Buginese Razak could claim pure Indonesian descent.[11] This could perhaps partially account for the 'archipelagic orientation' of his worldview, although such a parallel is ultimately difficult to quantify. In like manner, Presidents Sukarno and

Suharto came from a Javanese tradition that has often perceived itself as culturally superior in the Indo-Malay world. Further, Indonesia–Malaya relations in the immediate post-colonial period were defined as much by the lack of rapport between Sukarno and Tunku Abdul Rahman as by other issues. Gullick summarizes the tenuous relationship as follows:

> President Sukarno and Tunku Abdul Rahman cordially dislike each other. The Indonesian President had climbed to power from humble origins by way of Dutch prisons and armed revolution. He despises the Malay prince as being ... in the camp of the colonial power. The Tunku, disconcerted and displeased by the flamboyant demagoguery of Sukarno, distrusts his domestic alliance with Indonesian communism and despises his regime for the economic chaos which it has allowed to engulf a once prosperous country.[12]

A key element of the hostility between the two leaders, as records perused in the course of this study have suggested, stems from ethnic and ideological differences. In contrast, the blood ties between Adam Malik and Ghazali Shafie (the two were distant cousins), as chief advisers to Suharto and Razak respectively during the 1970s, led to the perception among Indonesian and Malay leaders of that era that the kinship factor could and should provide a viable basis for the organizing of relations. Likewise, Suharto's relationship with Mahathir has been subjected to much scrutiny, and anecdotal evidence abounds that attests to the distance between them. It is known that Suharto's relationship with Mahathir lacked the cordiality and affinity that characterized his rapport with Razak. In fact, Mahathir's outlook towards Indonesia was antithetical to Razak's willingness to align Malaysian policy positions with Jakarta through active consultation and deference on policy matters that impinged on Indonesian interests. Indeed, the prevailing opinion in Javanese-dominated Indonesian political circles was that Mahathir lacked respect for Suharto.[13] In private, Mahathir had on several occasions expressed sentiments that were critical of Suharto, while the latter, when considering Malaysia's 'lack of regard' for Indonesian sensitivities, had implicated Mahathir's non-Malay roots.[14]

Returning to the conceptual difficulties in politicizing kinship, it is clear from the permutations Indo-Malay nationalisms were undergoing that while both adhered to broad historical premises in their initial attempts to construct post-colonial identities, thus identifying them as kin states, these identities in fact were shaping up to be fundamentally different. One shunned ethnic logic to statehood while the other embraced it; one destroyed the feudal elements in society while the other glorified their status. These fundamental differences set up a clash of identities that would compound the problems surrounding the expectations and obligations both sides read into their post-colonial relationship. Moreover, as a historical discourse, conceptualizations of Indo-Malay kinship cannot get away from the fact that the pre-colonial Indo-Malay world which was looked back upon was one defined by a regional network of intermarriage and migration that was characterized by affinity but also discord. Indeed, while the populations of Indonesia and Malaysia have much in common in terms of race and culture, there were also significant differences in their respective understandings of social and subsequently national identity that could not simply be bracketed out.

Nationalism and the basis of expectations and obligations

Notwithstanding the contested nature of the concept, kinship took on further prominence in the period of post-colonial relations when Indonesian and Malay leaders sought to premise political ties on the basis that Indonesia and Malaysia shared a 'special relationship'. At a conceptual level, this 'special relationship', as the study has suggested, necessarily implied a functional dimension to relatedness in the form of expectations and obligations. It is when kinship is conceived of as a functional principle with attendant norms that the correlation between the kinship factor and the process of national self-determination and identity-building comes into even greater relief. It has been argued that in the case of Indonesia and Malaysia, contested nationalisms have not merely framed dissonance in how Indonesian and Malaysian leaders understood the historical, cultural, and functional basis to their political relationship; the fact that these divergent experiences and motivations of nationhood continue to be sustained and nurtured in the post-colonial era in the worldviews and international outlooks of the political elite, and have subsequently been manifested in nationalistic foreign policies, has also meant that these historical differences have endured.

Long-time observers of Indonesian foreign policy such as Michael Leifer and Franklin Weinstein have contended that an 'aspiration to greatness' and 'regional sense of entitlement', born of Indonesia's revolutionary experience during its anti-colonial struggle, lies at the heart of the Indonesian political psyche. This was certainly characteristic of the Indonesian worldview during the excesses of Sukarnoism, but also held true during the Suharto administration. No doubt under Suharto, Indonesian foreign policy turned away from the grandiloquence of his predecessor. Yet this shift of focus from politics to economics was underlined by Suharto's belief that powerful states had powerful economies, while Indonesia's push for international recognition of its archipelagic regime during Suharto's presidency was fashioned to give substance to aspirations to greatness. Moreover, ASEAN's principle of regional resilience was grafted from Indonesian domestic political lexicon to provide the subtext to regional security, thereby further institutionalizing Jakarta's sense of entitlement. Within ASEAN, Indonesia was widely recognized as *primus inter pares* and the prime manager of regional order.[15] As for relations with

Malaysia, conceptions of kinship could not be divorced from Indonesian primacy. This was evident from comments such as the following, taken from an Indonesian Armed Forces daily in the aftermath of *Konfrontasi*:

> There is much we can note to prove that Malaysia and Indonesia are in fact brothers – eggs of the same nest. . . . It is not only in the cultural field that Malaysia feels itself our younger brother, but in other fields as well. We should respond to this, not arrogantly but as an elder brother.[16]

From Jakarta's perspective, the fact that Malayan de-colonization took place in cooperation with the colonial power contravened the ideologies of the Indonesian leaders, who had come to develop a worldview and culture of politics that based legitimacy of states primarily on the nature of their independence struggle. By this token, the fact that Malayan independence was born out of a collaborative effort between the Western-educated aristocratic and feudal elite and the British colonialists made it a travesty in Indonesian eyes. To them, a kindred relationship expressed in equality of separate statehood and adhered to without revolution was something they found difficult to accept.

It is evident from records explored in this study that the Indonesian leaders had expected Malayan recognition of Indonesian primacy, and for Kuala Lumpur to assume a subsidiary, if not deferential, role towards its more established kin state. This was manifest, among other things, in the expectation to be consulted on foreign policy matters. Instead, independent Malaya was regularly seen to have given little consideration for Jakarta in the course of its leaders' policy initiatives. This was apparent from the very outset when, to Jakarta, the kinship rhetoric preached by Malayan leaders did not synchronize with the policies they practised. Tunku Abdul Rahman's pro-West inclinations were viewed suspiciously within Jakarta circles, as were his attempts to manage regional affairs through his SEAFET and ASA projects, initiated without consultation with Jakarta. Not only did Malaya not acknowledge Indonesia's leadership, its sympathies for rebels who perpetrated the rebellion of 1957–1958 and ambivalence on Indonesia's West Irian claims further sharpened Indonesian impressions that far from declaring unequivocal support for a kin state, Malaya had sought to undermine the sovereignty and integrity of Indonesia, not to mention challenge Indonesia's conceptions of regional order and its 'right' to dictate the pattern of regional security developments.

Returning to a point established earlier, there is certainly a distinct cultural dimension in terms of kinship hierarchy in the Javanese mindset that, though difficult to grasp, should not be overlooked. Ricklefs has written that Javanese political culture emphasizes a strict observance of hierarchy.[17] Considering that since the mid-1950s, and particularly during

Suharto's New Order regime, a disproportionate number of Javanese have occupied the seats of Indonesian power, it is clear that in some respects the Javanese outlook and worldview has been a particularly salient influence on how the Indonesian government perceives and interprets its relations with Malaysia. Jakarta certainly viewed early Malayan policy during the Tunku's administration as lacking the deference to Jakarta that should have underscored the 'special relationship'. Instead, Malayan policy in the early post-colonial period engendered a belief in Indonesia that, far from acting as kin, Malaya was 'an unrepresentative alien-inspired polity designed to perpetuate colonial economic and military interests in Southeast Asia which, by their nature, posed a threat to the viability and regional role of Indonesia'.[18] In Indonesian eyes, Malaya, while declaring its desire to associate with Indonesia on the basis of kinship, had in fact undermined Indonesia's national unity, territorial integrity, and claim to political primacy in the region. Subsequently, whatever its eventual domestic political rationale, the outbreak of *Konfrontasi* reinforces a perception that Indonesian aggression was rooted in the Indonesians' misgivings towards a perceived lack of respect on the part of Malaya.[19]

Relations during the Razak administration in Malaysia, however, stood in striking contrast to the enmity that marked the Tunku's milieu. It is during this time that one finds the 'golden age' of bilateral ties – when perspectives, outlooks, and policies converged to an extent never before (and never since) experienced, as the key protagonists of the Razak administration (Razak himself, along with his lieutenants Ghazali Shafie and Zainal Sulong) unilaterally built relations on a policy of 'self-induced subordination'. A popular explanation for Malaysia's volte-face has been the observed need to facilitate the re-integration of post-*Konfrontasi* Indonesia into regional affairs, and to foster a new Indonesian government that was aware of the responsibilities that came with regional preponderance, which, unlike the Tunku before him and Mahathir after, Razak was apparently ready to accept. It was also clear from the complexion of Malaysia's positions on issues such as the neutralization of Southeast Asia, the status of the Melaka Straits, Indonesia's Archipelago Doctrine, and even China policy that Malaysia pro-actively sought to re-orientate its relations with Indonesia on the basis of deference expressed in regular consultation and policy alignment with Jakarta. Malaysia in effect surrendered the neutralization initiative to Indonesia when consideration for the latter's sensitivities towards its original proposal led to the final adoption of the Indonesian, as opposed to the Malaysian, draft; while ZOPFAN was Malaysian in name, it was clearly Indonesian in principle. Likewise, Razak's willingness to recognize Indonesia's Archipelagic Doctrine without initial confirmation of Malaysian rights to free communication between East and West Malaysia further evinced this attitude of deference, becoming a matter of frustration for his own foreign ministry officials.

During the administration of Mahathir Mohamad, however, Indonesia–Malaysia relations seemed to revert to earlier patterns of rivalry. In a profoundly ironic twist, Mahathir's Malaysia posed a challenge to Indonesian regional leadership on the back of the same anti-Western crusade that is identifiable with Sukarnoism. To be sure, Mahathir came into office with an explicit pro-Malay and nationalist agenda. Nevertheless, his version of Malay nationalism paid little regard to affinity with Indonesia, certainly not with the Javanese who dominated the upper echelons of the Jakarta government. Furthermore, his explicit focus on foreign policy as an avenue through which to assert resurgent Malay nationalism brought Malaysia into direct conflict with Indonesia, for which foreign policy has always been a matter of prestige. With the re-orientation of Malaysian foreign policy towards activism and vocalism, Mahathir sought to project Malaysia to the forefront of Third World international affairs. This locked Malaysia and Indonesia in a prestige dilemma defined by a contest for international prominence and regional primacy, while diplomatic norms of kinship established earlier were increasingly breached as the policy of consultation and alignment with Jakarta that characterized the Razak and Hussein Onn administrations was jettisoned.

This tension was most acute in the 1990s, when Malaysian assertiveness in international affairs clashed with Indonesia's own renewed interest in foreign policy as an expression of national identity and consciousness. The incident at the 1992 Non-Aligned Movement summit, when Mahathir was referred to as a 'Little Sukarno', particularly incensed Indonesian leaders.[20] Throughout the 1990s, several events further illustrated Malaysia's challenge to Indonesian conceptions of regional order and primacy. This included the controversy surrounding Mahathir's EAEG proposal, Malaysia's rejection of Indonesian attempts to facilitate the management of the South China Sea territorial claims, and the divergent positions taken by Kuala Lumpur and Jakarta as to the recognition of the coup by Hun Sen against Prince Ranariddh in Cambodia in 1997 in the build-up to ASEAN expansion. In relation to Indonesia policy, Mahathir's brand of nationalism was not only a deliberate attempt not to toe the Indonesian line, but in many ways an attempt to enhance Malaysian prestige in regional and international affairs by assuming the role of Asian and Third World 'leader', without much regard for the sensitivities of the Indonesian government, which views itself as the traditional proprietor of this role. This state of affairs elicited the following response from a former senior Indonesian foreign ministry official: 'Malaysia suffers from a "little brother" complex and compensates by diplomatic activities to break out of Indonesian shadow. This has been an undercurrent to relations in the 80s and 90s.'[21]

Cross-currents associated with kin affinity have taken on various forms that have posed problems for the Indonesian and Malaysian governments in recent times. While the Malaysian government has publicly disavowed any support for GAM, many segments of the Malay population in the peninsula have long been sympathetic to the cause of Acehnese separatism. In addition, there seems to be evidence that some measure of material support and even military training had been given to the Aceh independence movement from sources in peninsular Malaysia. This has understandably created problems for the Malaysian diplomatic establishment. Paradoxically, the fact that Kuala Lumpur has seen the need to reiterate its non-support and non-recognition of the *Aceh Merdeka* cause is indicative of how complex and potentially divisive the problem of Aceh remains for Indonesia–Malaysia relations. Malaysia's recent lack of understanding and indulgence on the matter of illegal Indonesian migration, manifested in its demand for the immediate repatriation of Indonesian illegal workers and the provision of less-than-respectable holding accommodation for Indonesians awaiting repatriation, has not been taken well by a Jakarta government conscious of the historical role Indonesian migrants have played in Malaysian political and economic development. In Indonesian eyes, Malaysia's 'legalistic' pursuit of such policies was being undertaken with no consideration for the special relationship that Kuala Lumpur claims to exist between the two kin states.

The nature of bilateral disputes during this period further draws attention to the close relation between kinship and national identity. In a marked shift from questions of identity and sovereignty that defined earlier periods of post-colonial relations, recent Indonesia–Malaysia contestations have centred on territorial disputes and a contest for primacy in the Indo-Malay world, in so doing exposing the widening gulf between the two kin states. In essence, this suggests that the extent to which the kinship factor can give intelligibility to international relations cannot be divorced from the state- and nation-building context defined by the transition from kinship to national loyalties.[22]

It is quite evident, then, that though leaders of Indonesia and Malaysia regularly evoke the history and language of kinship in an attempt to give meaning and intelligibility to bilateral ties, these conceptions of kinship have by and large not been able to generate harmony in political relations. This state of affairs brings to light the contested perceptions and interpretations each has had towards the terms of kinship, the divergent and ultimately antagonistic paths along which their national identities have evolved, and the consequent failure of one or the other to meet the 'functional aspects of relatedness' that flowed from their contested understandings of their shared histories and the terms of their fraternal relations. Certainly, these problems are further suggestive of the tensions within the building of post-colonial identities, in particular the issue of how to re-conceptualize loyalties and re-frame post-colonial relations in the context of historical legacies.

The enduring relevance of *pribumi* identity?

Given the problems associated with transplanting kinship ties into the political sphere in the period of post-colonial relations, and the fact that the politicization of kinship in the form of nationalism has seen it foster greater dissonance than congruence between Indonesia and Malaysia, it is certainly tempting to be dismissive of the potential for Indo-Malay fraternity. As this book has made apparent, however, Indonesia–Malaysia relations have also enjoyed episodes of harmony when kinship-speak coincided with policy congruence. In this respect, it is worth noting that kinship has played a persuasive and politically expedient role when the need to assert Indo-Malay *pribumi* identity has been most imperative. Such was the case in relation to shared Indo-Malay concerns over Chinese political influence in the region.

Beneath the rhetoric of ethnic Malay blood brotherhood employed to justify reconciliation after *Konfrontasi* was an anti-Chinese agenda, which subsequently underpinned relations during the ensuing decade. This agenda came into greater prominence in the 1970s, when Indonesian and Malay interpretations of national identity premised on the primacy of indigenous interests were perceived to be under threat from Chinese encroachment onto *pribumi* political 'space'. Domestically, the riots of 13 May 1969 and the ethnic Chinese challenge to Malay primacy re-ignited ethno-nationalist fervour among the Malay population in Malaysia and re-kindled suspicion of the Chinese community. On the international front, despite the normalization of ties with Peking, Malaysia still harboured suspicions of China. Malaysian concerns on these fronts were shared by Jakarta, which under Suharto harboured concerns regarding Peking and its own ethnic Chinese communities in Indonesia in the wake of the 1965 communist coup attempt. It was in this manner that the Chinese represented a 'problem' for both Indonesian and Malaysian security and identity. Hence, it is not surprising that developments in Malaysia after 13 May were followed with great interest in Jakarta, just as many in the Malaysian government looked to Indonesia for assurance and justification. The loyalties of the Chinese communities have been regularly questioned in both states, and their control of economic resources has caused anti-Chinese sentiments to fester. By the late 1960s, both Indonesia and Malaysia shared the same concerns towards the threat from Peking-inspired communist activities along the shared border in Borneo. In this regard, it is suggested that dealing with the 'Chinese problem' overshadowed all else as a policy prerogative for both states during this period. Consequently, the need for policy convergence in relation to this problem was given expression in the creation of the General Border Committee, close consultation on the matter of policy towards Peking, and finally in the 1980 Kuantan statement.

Hence, while there was certainly a measure of belief among policy-makers in both governments during the late 1960s and the 1970s that

Indo-Malay kinship could provide an avenue for the strengthening of ties, kinship was also framed in terms of shared concerns towards communist China and the challenge to *pribumi* primacy from domestic ethnic Chinese communities. In this respect, it should not be surprising that Malaysia's improvement of relations with Indonesia in the 1970s occurred in tandem with the re-assertion of Malay dominance. To the Malay leadership, this could be conveniently accomplished by reinvigorating affinity with Indonesia along racial and ethnic lines. Put differently, Indonesia became an ally of Malaysia as it sought, after May 1969, to accentuate Malay primacy over the Chinese. In the same way that the complexities of ethno-cultural affinity were brushed aside in the early years of the anti-colonial movement, many Malays, including those in seats of power, looked to Indonesia at this time as a bastion of 'Malay' identity in order to broaden their socio-political base. Such was the extent of these attempts at reviving affiliation that the Malaysian Chinese, as well as the leadership of Chinese-dominated Singapore, were keenly aware of the threatening possibility of an Indo-Malay confederation taking shape with an anti-Chinese subtext.

Given its geopolitical circumstances, Singapore has been especially sensitive to Indo-Malay fraternity. There was mention, for example, that in the build-up to the formation of ASEAN, ethno-religious kinship groupings sought initially to exclude Singapore from membership.[23] Similarly, when Suharto appealed for clemency for two Indonesian marines scheduled to be hanged in Singapore, he was supported by Tunku Abdul Rahman.[24] Malaysia's alignment with Indonesia on the issue of the status of the Melaka Straits, which resulted in attempts to block the internationalization of the Straits, can also be construed as a move to strategically corner Singapore.[25] Indonesia shared Malaysian reservations over a remark made in 1987 by Singapore minister Lee Hsien Loong questioning the loyalty of Singapore's minority Malay population in a time of crisis with its neighbours, as well as over the visit of Israeli President Chaim Herzog to the city-state.[26]

In sum, the 'Chinese' and 'Singapore' issues have featured not only as a viable domestic political bogey for both Indonesia and Malaysia, but in some respects also as a motivation for policy congruence between the kin states. All this indicates that while the inclusiveness of kinship, in terms of the translation of cultural and ethnic affinities into political reality, or even the interpretation and fulfilment of expectations and obligations, continues to be a matter of contestation, kinship exclusivity defined as unity against a common threat to Indonesian and Malay national identity and security appears to generate more persuasive logic for Indo-Malay fraternity.

The kinship factor could also potentially take on greater political consequence in the event of a resurgence of political Islam in both countries. This study has indicated that while Islam stood at the sidelines of political discourse in both Indonesia and Malaysia for long periods, a recent resurgence in Islamic politics can be noticed in the domestic sphere in both countries (more so in Malaysia, it must be added). Of course, the extent to which the abstract notion of Islamic brotherhood can provide a basis upon which state-to-state relations can be built will depend on how deep the roots of political Islam lie in the two societies. It does appear that its current prospects are dim, owing to the largely secular nature of the Malaysian and Indonesian governments. Nevertheless, the emergence and increasing popularity of radical Islamic ideologies that are creeping into mainstream political discourse, not to mention the sudden re-emergence of Islam as a key factor in international politics, highlights the possibility that Islam might have the potential to succeed in giving deeper meaning to kinship discourse in the Indo-Malay world.

In sum, this study has aimed at contributing to the study of Indonesia–Malaysia relations by introducing kinship and the attendant factor of nationalism as frames of reference with which to understand the Indonesia–Malaysia relationship and by placing them in a historical-narrative framework that identifies continuities and change. This approach has illuminated the variance in perceptions and interpretations of kinship, the interaction of the kinship factor with prerogatives of identity, nation, and state construction, and the manner in which leaders have or have not employed the kinship factor in their understanding of how relations should be framed. There is no doubt that there is much common social-cultural ground between Indonesia and Malaysia in terms of the historical linkages enjoyed by the peoples of these two states, and these linkages continue to feed the quest for greater meaning and intelligibility in the construction of the Indo-Malay 'special relationship'. In the main, however, it is also evident that Indonesia–Malaysia relations have been characterized more by diplomatic discord than by harmony. This has resulted from clashes of national histories and identities.

Without doubt, the shape of the kinship factor has been transformed over time as Indonesia–Malaysia relations have evolved. Kinship evidently featured more prominently in the early history of relations with the introduction of pan-Malayism, yet because the notion of kinship was premised on ethno-cultural grounds, the concept itself was a contestable one, and remains so, in academic circles.[27] Subsequently, attempts at organizing relations on the basis of kinship have met with varied success. Three observations can be gleaned from this study that explain this. First, the genealogical and anthropological logic and evidence of kinship ties remains a matter of contested interpretation that has impeded open embrace of kinship. Second, notwithstanding the above observation, the successful mobilization of the kinship factor has hinged on the fulfilment of perceived obligations and expectations, and Malaysian deference to Indonesia appears to be integral to this dynamic. Yet as this study has shown, Malaysia in particular has rarely chosen the path of deference. Rather, Kuala Lumpur has often challenged Indonesian primacy in this relationship. This has in turn given rise to much bilateral acrimony. Third, while the kinship factor took on political form most trenchantly in Indo-Malay nationalism, the fact that the manner through which Indonesia and Malaysia constructed post-colonial identity and arrived at sovereign statehood diverged substantially further emphasized the distinctions, rather than affinity, that kinship has generated in Indonesia–Malaysia political relations. Unless Islam emerges as the predominant social-political force in the Indo-Malay world in the near future, or Indo-Malay *pribumi* primacy and identity in the region are perceived to again be under threat from alien influence, it is difficult to envisage Indo-Malay fraternity assuming more than a rhetorical role in the politics of this 'special relationship'. Certainly, as national identities continue to take shape, Indonesia and Malaysia will also find additional terms of reference, beyond the kinship factor, through which to articulate bilateral ties. It seems, then, that the essence of this relationship, in so far as kinship is concerned, is best captured in the Malay–Indonesian metaphor that warns of the potential, if not inevitable, friction between two entities as close as '*gigi dan lidah*' (teeth and tongue) – they will remain close, and it is precisely for that reason that there will invariably be problems between Indonesia and Malaysia, their kinship notwithstanding.

Glossary

adat   customary law
Arkib Negara   National Archives of Malaysia
Bangsa   nation; sometimes used interchangeably with race
berkampung   to come together as in a village community
daerah   region
Daulah Islamiyah   regional Islamic state
Dunia Melayu   Malay world
elang malindo   air force exercises
Ganjang Malaysia   Crush Malaysia
hikayat   story, tale
Indonesia Raya   Greater Indonesia
Kaum Muda   Reformists
Kaum Tua   Conservatives
kerajaan   royal government; kingdom
keris kartika   army exercises
Ketahanan Nasional   National Resilience
Konfrontasi   Confrontation
Lembaga Islam Se Malaya   All-Malaya Islamic Council
madrasah   modernist Islamic school
malindo jaya   naval exercises
malindo mini   naval exercises
Masuk Melayu   to become a Malay
Melayu Raya   Great Malay nation
Melayu Sungguh   authentic Malay
musyawarah dan muafakat   consultation and consensus
Naluri Rumpun Melayu   Malay family or stock instinct
negara   the State
Nusantara   the Malay Archipelago
orang asli   native
pangreh praja   administrative elite
Pemuda   Youth
pesantren   Javanese Islamic institution
pribumi   indigene

Priyayi   upper-class Abangan Javanese
Rabitatul Mujahidin   League of Warriors
Rukun Negara   Articles of Faith of the State
rumpun   race, stock
Sejarah Melayu   Malay Annals
sekolah rakyat   people's schools
Semenanjung Melayu   Malay Peninsula
serumpun   similar stock or race; blood brotherhood
Suku Melayu   Malay ethnic community
tanah air   land and waters
Tumpah-dara Indonesia   the Indonesian fatherland
ulama   Muslim religious teacher
Wawasan Nusantara   archipelagic outlook

Notes

Introduction

1 D. Emmerson, 'Indonesia, Malaysia, Singapore: A Regional Security Core?' in R. Ellings and S. Simon (eds), *Southeast Asian Security in the New Millennium*, Armonk, NY: M.E. Sharpe, 1996.

2 There have been several book-length studies of the Indonesia–Malaysia Confrontation, the most illuminating of which are J.A.C. Mackie, *Konfrontasi: The Indonesia–Malaysia Dispute, 1963–1966*, Kuala Lumpur: Oxford University Press, 1974; G. Poulgrain, *The Genesis of Konfrontasi: Malaysia, Brunei, Indonesia, 1945–1965*, Bathurst, NSW: Crawford House Publishing, 1998; J. Subritzky, *Confronting Sukarno: British, American, Australian and New Zealand Diplomacy in the Malaysian–Indonesian Confrontation, 1961–65*, New York: St Martin's Press, 1999; and M. Jones, *Conflict and Confrontation in Southeast Asia, 1961–1965: Britain, the United States, and the Creation of Malaysia*, Cambridge: Cambridge University Press, 2001. It needs to be said, however, that of these four studies, only Mackie provided an indigenous account of the dynamics behind Confrontation. Poulgrain, Subritzky, and Jones focused on the role of external players. Nevertheless, owing to its time of publication, Mackie's work relied largely on secondary and newspaper sources for its empirical evidence.

3 For example, N. Ganesan, *Bilateral Tensions in Post-Cold War ASEAN*, Singapore: Institute of Southeast Asian Studies, 1999; A. Tan, *Intra-ASEAN Tensions*, London: Royal Institute of International Affairs, 2000.

4 N. Woods, 'The Uses of Theory in Studying International Relations' in N. Woods (ed.), *Explaining International Relations since 1945*, Oxford: Oxford University Press, 1996, p. 11.

5 For a study of the history-identity nexus, see G. Gong (ed.), *Memory and History in East and Southeast Asia: Issues of Identity in International Relations*, Washington, DC: CSIS Press, 2001. For a broader discussion, see C. Cruz, 'Identity and Persuasion: How Nations Remember Their Past and Make Their Futures', *World Politics*, 52(3), April 2000.

6 See R. Jackson, 'The Political Theory of International Society' in K. Booth and S. Smith (eds), *International Relations Theory Today*, Oxford: Polity Press, 1995, pp. 124–126.

7 B. Buzan, 'The English School as a Research Program', paper presented at the BISA Conference, Manchester, December 1999 [online] Available HTTP: http://www.ukc.ac.uk/politics/englishschool/buzan99.htm (accessed 12 November 2001).

1 Kinship and nationalism in international relations

1 By 'mainstream', this study refers primarily to realism and liberalism.
2 In a sense, this is not unlike Martin Wight's conception of the cultural basis to international society in that common culture forms the base upon which to build common identity and shared norms. See M. Wight, *Systems of States*, London: Leicester University Press, 1977. Nevertheless, as will be suggested later, the 'special relationship' between kin states is premised on much more than shared culture.
3 The case for a social anthropological approach to studying international relations is presented in C.A.W. Manning, *The Nature of International Society*, London: Macmillan, 1975; see also H. Suganami, 'C.A.W. Manning and the Study of International Relations', *Review of International Studies*, 27, 2001; P. Mandaville, 'Reading the State from Elsewhere: Towards an Anthropology of the Postnational', *Review of International Studies*, 28, 2002; J. Snyder, 'Anarchy and Culture: Insights from the Anthropology of War', *International Organization*, 56(1), 2002.
4 See T. Huxley, 'Southeast Asia in the Study of International Relations: The Rise and Decline of a Region', *Pacific Review*, 9(2), 1996; S.S. Tan, 'Rescuing Realism from Realists' in S. Simon (ed.), *The Many Faces of Asian Security*, Lanham, MD: Rowman & Littlefield, 2001.
5 The implicit application of this paradigm comes out in Firdaus Abdullah, 'The Rumpun Concept in Malaysia–Indonesia Relations', *Indonesian Quarterly*, 21(2), 1993; A. Baroto, 'Similarities and Differences in Malaysia–Indonesia Relations: Some Perspectives', *Indonesian Quarterly*, 21(2), 1993, 156–157; Dewi Fortuna Anwar, *Indonesia in ASEAN: Foreign Policy and Regionalism*, New York: St Martin's Press, 1994, pp. 228–229; Leo Suryadinata, *Indonesia's Foreign Policy Under Suharto*, Singapore: Times Academic Press, 1996, pp. 69–74; N. Ganesan, *Bilateral Tensions in Post-Cold War ASEAN*, Singapore: Institute of Southeast Asian Studies, 1999, p. 30. While Lee Kam Hing's broad survey of 'milestones' of Indonesia–Malaysia relations from 1957 to 1990 provides what until now has been the most detailed study of contemporary Indonesia–Malaysia relations, the articles offer little by way of theoretical frameworks. See K.H. Lee, 'From Confrontation to Cooperation: Malaysia–Indonesia Relations, 1957–1990', *Sarjana*, Special Issue, 1994. Furthermore, his study, like Firdaus Abdullah's, makes no mention of the importance of co-affinity in opposition to the increasing prominence of ethnic Chinese in both countries. This phenomenon, as this study will argue, is vital to an understanding of the underlying dynamics of Indonesia–Malaysia relations.
6 This distinction lies at the heart of the defensive–offensive realism debate. See J. Taliaferro, 'Seeking Security under Anarchy: Defensive Realism Revisited', *International Security*, 25(3), 2000/2001.
7 See, for example, M. Leifer, *Conflict and Regional Order*, London: International Institute of Strategic Studies, 1980; T. Huxley, 'Singapore and Malaysia: A Precarious Balance?', *Pacific Review*, 4(3), 1990.
8 For instance, there is a difference in international relations theory between realists and theorists from the English School tradition over the consequences of anarchy. Realists see anarchy as the cause of suspicion and the struggle for power and survival among states. English School theorists, on the other hand, see that it is precisely the uncertain international environment epitomized by anarchy that compels 'rational' states to cooperate. The archetypal articulation of this position has been H. Bull, *The Anarchical Society*, New York: Columbia University Press, 1977.
9 For example, J. Nye, 'The Changing Nature of World Power', *Political Science*

Quarterly, 105(2), 1990; S. Guzzini, 'Structural Power: The Limits of Neorealist Power Analysis', *International Organization*, 47(3), 1993.

10 Even realist scholars themselves have begun considering more cognitive aspects of power. See, for example, S. Walt, *Origins of Alliance*, Ithaca, NY: Cornell University Press, 1987.

11 See C. Geertz, 'Centers, Kings, and Charisma: Reflections on the Symbolics of Power' in C. Geertz (ed.), *Local Knowledge: Further Essays in Interpretive Anthropology*, New York: Basic Books, 1983, pp. 121–146; also B. Anderson, 'The Idea of Power in Javanese Culture' in C. Holt, B. Anderson, and J.T. Siegel (eds), *Culture and Politics in Indonesia*, London: Verso, 1972, pp. 1–69; A.C. Milner, *Kerajaan: Malay Political Culture on the Eve of Colonial Rule*, Tucson: University of Arizona Press, 1982.

12 For an illuminating theoretical study of the problems inherent in current understanding of the concept of national interests, see M. Finnemore, *National Interests in International Society*, Ithaca, NY: Cornell University Press, 1996, pp. 1–33.

13 B. Frankel, *National Interest*, London: Pall Mall, 1970, p. 17.

14 There is an increasing pool of scholars from the Southeast Asia international relations community who are exploring non-material bases to the international politics of the region. See A. Acharya, *The Quest for Identity: International Relations of Southeast Asia*, Singapore: Oxford University Press, 2001; J. Haacke, *ASEAN's Diplomatic and Security Culture: Origins, Development, and Prospects*, London: RoutledgeCurzon, 2002.

15 For example, D. Lake and D. Rothchild (eds), *The International Spread of Ethnic Conflict*, Princeton, NJ: Princeton University Press, 1998; V. Volkan, *Bloodlines: From Ethnic Pride to Ethnic Terrorism*, Boulder, CO: Westview Press, 1998; T. Ambrosio, *Irredentism: Ethnic Conflict and International Politics*, London: Praeger, 2001.

16 These issues lie at the junction of the so-called 'structure–agency debate'. See Y. Lapid and F. Kratochwil (eds), *The Return of Culture and Identity in IR Theory*, London: Lynne Rienner, 1996; S. Hobden and J. Hobson (eds), *Historical Sociology in International Relations*, Cambridge: Cambridge University Press, 2002.

17 Some examples include A. Johnston, *Cultural Realism*, Princeton, NJ: Princeton University Press, 1995; P. Katzenstein (ed.), *The Culture of National Security*, New York: Columbia University Press, 1996; M. Barnett, *Dialogues in Arab Politics*, New York: Columbia University Press, 1998; D. Jacquin-Berdal, A. Oros, and M. Verweij (eds), *Culture in World Politics*, London: Macmillan, 1998; C. Reus-Smit, *The Moral Purpose of the State: Culture, Social Identity, and Institutional Rationality in International Relations*, Princeton, NJ: Princeton University Press, 1999; B. Jahn, *The Cultural Construction of International Relations*, New York: Palgrave, 2000; C. Brown, 'Cultural Diversity and International Political Theory', *Review of International Studies*, 26(2), April 2000. For a general discussion on the role of culture in social theory, see M. Archer, *Culture and Agency: The Place of Culture in Social Theory*, Cambridge: Cambridge University Press, 1999.

18 See R. Hall, 'Moral Authority as a Power Resource', *International Organization*, 51(4), Autumn 1997; T. Risse, S. Ropp, and K. Sikkink (eds), *The Power of Human Rights*, Cambridge: Cambridge University Press, 1999; A. Wenger, 'The Internet and the Changing Face of International Security', *Information and Security*, 7, 2001; J. Nye Jr, *The Paradox of American Power*, New York: Oxford University Press, 2002.

19 A. Wendt, 'Anarchy Is What States Make of It: The Social Construction of Power Politics', *International Organization*, 88(2), 1994, 397.

20 In Wendt's words, 'interests are dependent on identities'. See ibid., 385. A sample of the international relations literature of identity will include D. Campbell, *Writing Security: United States Foreign Policy and the Politics of Identity*, Manchester: Manchester University Press, 1992; O. Weaver, *Insecurity and Identity Unlimited*, Copenhagen: Centre for Peace and Conflict Research, 1994; T. Biersteker and C. Weber (eds), *State Sovereignty as Social Construct*, Cambridge: Cambridge University Press, 1996; A. Wendt, *Social Theory of International Politics*, Cambridge: Cambridge University Press, 1999; B. McSweeney, *Security, Identity and Interests: A Sociology of International Relations*, Cambridge: Cambridge University Press, 1999; R.B. Hall, *National Collective Identity: Social Constructs and International Systems*, New York: Columbia University Press, 1999.
21 See, for example, J. Vasquez, *The Power in Power Politics*, Cambridge: Cambridge University Press, 1999; A. Moravcsik and J. Legro, 'Is Anybody Still a Realist?', *International Security*, 24(2), Fall 1999.
22 G. Hellman, 'Correspondence: Brother Can You Spare a Paradigm?', *International Security*, 25(1), Summer 2001, 170.
23 B. Buzan, 'The Timeless Wisdom of Realism?' in S. Smith, K. Booth, and M. Zalewski (eds), *International Theory: Positivism and Beyond*, Cambridge: Cambridge University Press, 1996, p. 63. Jack Snyder has also suggested the marrying of 'material' and 'symbolic' factors in explaining war and international relations. See Snyder, 'Anarchy and Culture'.
24 D. Sills (ed.), *International Encyclopaedia of the Social Sciences,* vol. 8, New York: Macmillan and the Free Press, 1968, pp. 309–413.
25 M. Fortes, *Kinship and the Social Order*, London: Routledge & Kegan Paul, 1969, p. 52.
26 Ibid., p. 53.
27 This was Schneider's seminal treatise published as D. Schneider, *A Critique of the Study of Kinship*, Ann Arbor: University of Michigan Press, 1984.
28 See P. Schweitzer, 'Concluding Remarks' in P. Schweitzer (ed.), *Dividends of Kinship*, London: Routledge, 2000, p. 207.
29 M. Nuttall, 'Choosing Kin: Sharing and Subsistence in a Greenlandic Hunting Community' in Schweitzer (ed.), *Dividends of Kinship*, p. 34.
30 W. Connor, *Ethno-nationalism: The Quest for Understanding*, Princeton, NJ: Princeton University Press, 1994, pp. 197–212.
31 For a recent exploration of this debate in anthropology, see J. Carsten (ed.), *Cultures of Relatedness: New Approaches to the Study of Kinship*, Cambridge: Cambridge University Press, 2000.
32 J.B. White, 'Kinship, Reciprocity and the World Market' in Schweitzer (ed.), *Dividends of Kinship*, p. 124.
33 See C. Geertz, *The Interpretation of Cultures*, New York: Basic Books, 1973, pp. 255–310.
34 J. Gould and W.L Kolb (eds), *A Dictionary of the Social Sciences*, New York: The Free Press, 1964, p. 58.
35 Nuttall, 'Choosing Kin', p. 34.
36 Carsten, *Cultures of Relatedness*, p. 4.
37 Ibid., pp. 4–5.
38 This idea is expanded in the chapters by Hutchinson, Edwards, and Strathern in Carsten, *Cultures of Relatedness*.
39 M. Strathern, *After Nature: English Kinship in the Late Twentieth Century*, Cambridge: Cambridge University Press, 1992, p. 87.
40 Carsten, *Cultures of Relatedness*, p. 26.
41 Schneider, *A Critique*, p. 75, emphasis in the original.
42 R. Wagner, *The Curse of Souw: Principles of Daribi Clan Definition and Alliance in New Guinea*, Chicago: University of Chicago Press, p. 66.

43 See R. Astuti, *People of the Sea*, Cambridge: Cambridge University Press, 1995.
44 See C. Stafford, 'Chinese Patriliny and the Cycles of Yang and Laiwang' in Carsten, *Cultures of Relatedness*.
45 See B. Bodenhorn, '"He Used to Be my Relative": Exploring the Bases of Relatedness among Inupiat of Northern Alaska' in Carsten, *Cultures of Relatedness*.'
46 M. Weber, *Economy and Society: An Outline of Interpretive Sociology*, vol. 1, New York: Bedminster Press, 1968, pp. 385–398.
47 O. Patterson, 'Context and Choice in Ethnic Allegiance' in N. Glazer and D. Moynihan (eds), *Ethnicity: Theory and Practice*, Cambridge, MA: Harvard University Press, 1975.
48 For the role of 'values' in foreign policy-making, see J. Frankel, *The Making of Foreign Policy: An Analysis of Decision Making*, London: Oxford University Press, 1963, pp. 111–122.
49 K. Yelvington, *Producing Power: Ethnicity, Gender, and Class in a Caribbean Workplace*, Philadelphia: Temple University Press, 1995, p. 168.
50 A.D. Smith, *Ethnic Origins of Nations*, Oxford: Basil Blackwell, 1986, p. 97, and Smith, *National Identity*, London: Penguin, 1991, p. 21.
51 A.D. Smith, *Nations and Nationalism in a Global Era*, Cambridge: Polity Press, 1995, p. 56.
52 Ibid., p. 57.
53 It is notable that Anthony Smith is more sympathetic to such primordial forces than other theorists of nationalism. See E. Gellner, *Encounters with Nationalism*, Oxford: Basil Blackwell, 1994.
54 That said, it must also be emphasized that Smith's reading of primordialists such as Geertz is more nuanced and hence Smith would not consider himself a 'primordialist', even if he does share some of their assumptions.
55 A.D. Smith, 'Theories of Nationalism' in M. Leifer (ed.), *Asian Nationalism*, London: Routledge, 2000, p. 12.
56 D. Brown, *Contemporary Nationalism: Civic, Ethnocultural and Multicultural Politics*, London: Routledge, 2000, p. 42.
57 Ibid., p. 40.
58 See B. Anderson, *Imagined Communities: Reflections on the Origins and Spread of Nationalism*, 2nd edition, London: Verso, 1991. Anderson suggests that the advent of print capitalism was the crucial catalyst in the imagination of the nation, as it assisted in the spread of the national 'myth'.
59 J. Mayall, 'Nationalism and International Order: The Asian Experience' in Leifer (ed.), *Asian Nationalism*, p. 189.
60 See N. Gutierrez, 'Ethnic Revivals within Nation-States?' in H.R. Wicker (ed.), *Rethinking Nationalism and Ethnicity: The Struggle for Meaning and Order in Europe*, New York and Oxford: Berg, 1997, pp. 166–169. See also A.D. Smith, 'Ethnic Myths and Ethnic Revivals', *European Journal of Sociology*, 25, 1984, and 'Ethnic Election and Cultural Identity', *Ethnic Studies*, 10, 1993.
61 An exhaustive list of references obviously cannot be provided here. A sample of the conceptual literature, however, can include A. Heraclides, *The Self-Determination of Minorities in International Politics*, London: Frank Cass, 1991; D. Jacobson, *Rights across Borders: Immigration and the Decline of Citizenship*, Baltimore: Johns Hopkins University Press, 1996; N. van Hear, *New Diasporas: The Mass Exodus, Dispersal and Regrouping of Migrant Communities*, London: UCL Press, 1998; G. Smith, *Nation-Building in the Post-Soviet Borderlands: The Politics of National Identities*, Cambridge: Cambridge University Press, 1998; R. Ganguly and R. Tarras, *Understanding Ethnic Conflict: The International Dimension*, New York: Longman, 1998; S. Vertovec and R. Cohen (eds), *Migration, Diasporas, and Transnationalism*, Cheltenham: Edward Elgar,

1999; A. Motyl, *Revolutions, Nations, Empires: Conceptual Limits and Theoretical Possibilities*, New York: Columbia University Press, 1999; D. Conversi (ed.), *Ethnonationalism in the Contemporary World: Walker Connor and the Study of Nationalism*, London: Routledge, 2002; C. Scherrer, *Ethnicity, Nationalism and Violence: Conflict Management, Human Rights and Multilateral Regimes*, Aldershot, UK: Ashgate, 2003.

62 See J. Mayall, *Nationalism and International Society*, Cambridge: Cambridge University Press, 1993, Introduction.

63 H. Suganami, 'Narrative and Beyond', paper presented at ISA 2001 Convention, Chicago, 24 February 2001, 3. Even E.H. Carr, one of the pioneers of American realism, stressed the historical conditioning of any thought on the international system. See E.H. Carr, *The Twenty-Years Crisis, 1919–1939*, London: Macmillan, 1949, p. 65.

64 Nor did they disregard the possibilities that other forms of international order might subsequently supplant the prevailing Western-centred international society. See Bull, *The Anarchical Society*, pp. 233–317.

65 An example of this Third World 'reaction' to the Western-orientated international society Third World countries were entering was the Afro-Asian Conference. Some others include the Non-Aligned Movement, G-77, and the 1974 call for a New International Economic Order.

66 Mandaville, 'Reading the State from Elsewhere', 204.

67 That is not to say, however, that the unity derived from the Bandung spirit of non-alignment was in any way deeply entrenched. In fact, it was rather short-lived and marked by internal contradictions.

68 Mayall, 'Nationalism and the International Order', p. 190.

69 Interview with an Indonesian Islamic scholar, Singapore, 20 November 2001.

70 Some of these include T. Svensson and P. Sorensen (eds), *Indonesia and Malaysia: Scandinavian Studies in Contemporary Society*, London and Malmö: Curzon Press, 1983; Muhammad Yusoff Hasim, *Pensejarahan Melayu: Kajian Tentang Tradisi Sejarah Melayu Nusantara*, Kuala Lumpur: Dewan Bahasa dan Pustaka, 1992; M. Hitchcock and V.T. King (eds), *Images of Malay–Indonesian Identity*, Kuala Lumpur: Oxford University Press, 1997; A. Gordon (ed.), *The Propagation of Islam in the Indonesian–Malay World*, Kuala Lumpur: Malaysian Sociological Research Institute, 2001, and, for more dated studies, J. Bastin and R. Roolvink (eds), *Malayan and Indonesian Studies*, Oxford: Clarendon Press, 1964; Syed Naquib Al-Attas, *Preliminary Statement on a General Theory of the Islamization of the Malay–Indonesian Archipelago*, Kuala Lumpur: Dewan Bahasa dan Pustaka, 1963; R.M. Koentjaraningrat, *Introduction to the Peoples and Cultures of Indonesia and Malaysia*, Menlo Park, CA: Cummings, 1975.

71 For a critique, see C.G. Kwa, 'The Historical Roots of Indonesian Irredentism', *Asian Studies*, 8(1), April 1970.

72 'Why Gus Dur Is Not Happy with Singapore', *Straits Times*, 27 November 2000.

73 'KL Sends Back Shiploads of Overstayers', *Straits Times*, 20 November 2001.

74 Ghazali Shafie, *Malaysia, ASEAN and the World Order*, Bangi: Penerbit University Kebangsaan Malaysia, 2000, p. 382.

75 See Abdullah Badawi, keynote address delivered at the Second Malaysia–Indonesia Conference, Penang, 11–14 December 1990 (emphasis added).

76 J. Baylis, *Anglo-American Relations since 1939*, Manchester: Manchester University Press, 1997, pp. 8–9.

77 'Behind the Suharto, Mahathir Meeting', *Straits Times*, 25 June 1988.

78 The idea that social-political life in the Indo-Malay world derives order from a framework of hierarchy based not only on material but also on 'normative' premises has been studied at length in the field of area studies. See, for

example, H. Feith and L. Castles (eds), *Indonesian Political Thinking,*
1945–1965, Ithaca, NY: Cornell University Press, 1969, sections V and XV;
Holt, Anderson, and Siegel (eds), *Culture and Politics in Indonesia*; B. Anderson, *Language and Power*, Ithaca, NY: Cornell University Press, 1990; M.C.
Ricklefs, 'Unity and Disunity in Javanese Political and Religious Thought of
the Eighteenth Century', *Modern Asian Studies*, 26(4), 1992.
79 Abdullah Zawawi, speech entitled 'Malaysia and Indonesia Bilateral Relations'
delivered at the Second Malaysia–Indonesia Conference, Penang, 11–14
December 1990.
80 See M. Leifer, *Indonesia's Foreign Policy*, London: Allen & Unwin, 1983.
81 M.C. Ricklefs, *A History of Indonesia since c.1200*, Basingstoke, UK: Palgrave,
2001, pp. 18–24, 36–58. The Javanization of the New Order government of
Indonesia has also been dealt with in some detail in G. Gunn, 'Ideology and the
Concept of Government in the Indonesian New Order', *Asian Survey*, 19(8),
August 1979.
82 F. Bunnell, 'Guided Democracy Foreign Policy: 1960–1965', *Indonesia*, 11,
October 1966, 47.

2 Kinship and Indo-Malay historiography

1 Historians of Southeast Asia have been alert to this very early on. As a result,
they have observed that 'the greatest research need ... is the filling of innumerable and vexing gaps in our detailed knowledge ... of the histories of the
area's constituent parts and sub-parts'. See H. Benda, 'The Structure of
Southeast Asian History: Some Preliminary Observations' in H. Benda, *Continuity and Change in Southeast Asia: Collected Journal Articles of Harry J.
Benda*, Southeast Asia Studies, New Haven, CT: Yale University, 1972, p. 121.
With very few exceptions, contemporary works on the international relations
of Southeast Asia have made no attempts to study their topic from a historical
perspective.
2 See Raja Ali Haji ibn Ahmad, *The Precious Gift (Tuhfat al-Nafis)*, an annotated translation by V. Matheson and B.W. Andaya, Kuala Lumpur: Oxford
University Press, 1982.
3 Ibid., pp. 12–41.
4 C.G. Kwa, 'The Historical Roots of Indonesian Irredentism', *Asian Studies*,
8(1), April 1970, 44–45.
5 The capital of the Srivijayan Empire was subsequently moved from Palembang to Jambi on the southeastern coast of Sumatra in the latter part of the
eleventh century.
6 See O.W. Wolters, *The Fall of Srivijaya in Malay History*, London: Lund
Humphries, 1970.
7 See T.G. Pigeaud, *Java in the Fourteenth Century: A Study in Cultural History*,
The Hague: Martinus Nijhoff, 1960.
8 Z. Alisa and E. McKay, 'Tradition and Leadership in the Other Islands' in
E. McKay (ed.), *Studies in Indonesian History*, Melbourne: Pitman, 1976,
p. 255. This view challenged earlier assumptions expressed in W.F. Wertheim,
'The Sociological Approach' in Soedjatmoko (ed.), *An Introduction
to Indonesian Historiography*, Ithaca, NY: Cornell University Press, 1965,
pp. 348–350.
9 For a study of the impact of the Melakan Sultanate in defining the identity of
the Malay world, see Muhammad Yusoff Hashim, *The Malay Sultanate of
Malacca*, Kuala Lumpur: Dewan Bahasa dan Pustaka, 1992.
10 This point is emphasized in B.W. Andaya and L. Andaya, *A History of
Malaysia*, London: Macmillan, 1982, pp. 39–42.

11 R. Brissenden, 'Patterns of Trade and Maritime Society before the Coming of the Europeans' in McKay (ed.), *Studies in Indonesian History*, p. 87.

12 See the discussion in Andaya and Andaya, *A History of Malaysia*, pp. 14–114.

13 In Indonesia's case, this characterization applies mostly to the west Indonesian populations on Sumatra, Java, Borneo, Riau, and Sulawesi.

14 See D.J. Banks, *Malay Kinship*, Philadelphia: Institute for the Study of Human Issues, 1983; Ariffin Omar, *Bangsa Melayu: Malay Concepts of Democracy and Community*, Kuala Lumpur: Oxford University Press, 1993; A. Iwabuchi, *The People of the Alas Valley: A Study of an Ethnic Group of Northern Sumatra*, Oxford: Clarendon Press, 1994. For example, references to Mount Meru can be found in both the *Sejarah Melayu* and the *Negarakertagama*, dating from the Majapahit era. For a discussion on this conception of statecraft, see R. Heine-Geldern, *Conceptions of State and Kingship in Southeast Asia*, Ithaca, NY: Cornell University Press, 1956; L. Gesick (ed.), *Centers, Symbols, and Hierarchies: Essays on the Classical States of Southeast Asia*, New Haven, CT: Yale University Press, 1983.

15 For Indonesia, see B.J.O. Schrieke, 'Ruler and Realm in Early Java' in B.J.O. Schrieke (ed.), *Indonesian Sociological Studies*, vol. 2, The Hague: W. von Hoeve, 1957; R. Mortimer, 'Class, Social Change and Indonesian Communism', *Indonesia*, 15, 1973; M.C. Ricklefs, *Jogjakarta under Sultan Mangkubumi, 1749–1792: A History of the Division of Java*, London: Oxford University Press, 1974; A.J.S. Reid, *Blood of the People*, Kuala Lumpur: Oxford University Press, 1979; H. Sutherland, *The Making of a Bureaucratic Elite: The Colonial Transformation of the Javanese Priyayi*, Singapore: Heinemann, 1979. For Malaya, see L. Andaya, *Kingdom of Johor, 1641–1728*, Kuala Lumpur: Oxford University Press, 1975; A.C. Milner, *Kerajaan: Malay Political Culture on the Eve of Colonial Rule*, Tucson, AZ: University of Arizona Press, 1982; K.K. Khoo, *Malay Society: Transformation and Democratisation*, Petaling Jaya: Pelanduk Publications, 1991. See also the chapters by Rex Mortimer (Indonesia) and Michael Stenson (Malaya) in J.W. Lewis (ed.), *Peasant Rebellion and Communist Revolution in Asia*, Stanford: Stanford, CA: University Press, 1974.

16 Distinctions can however be made between the Malay *Kerajaan* and the Javanese *Kraton*, particularly in reference to the role of Islam in statecraft. See Soemersaid Murtono, *State and Statecraft in Old Java*, revised edition, Ithaca, NY: Cornell University Modern Indonesia Project, 1981.

17 B.W. Andaya, 'The Nature of the State in Eighteenth Century Perak' in A. Reid and L. Castles (eds), *Pre-colonial State Systems in Southeast Asia*, Kuala Lumpur: Malaysian Branch of the Royal Asiatic Society, 1975, p. 24.

18 See, for example, P.E. de Josselin De Jong, *Minangkabau and Negri Sembilan*, The Hague: Martinus Nijhoff, 1952; M.B. Hooker, *Adat Laws in Modern Malaya*, Kuala Lumpur: Oxford University Press, 1972.

19 It is a matter of fact that these traditional concepts were to be the cornerstone of rapprochement after Indonesia's confrontation of Malaysia.

20 J. Nagata, 'What Is a Malay? Situational Selection of Ethnic Identity in a Plural Society', *American Ethnologist*, 1(2), 1974, 344.

21 J. Nagata, *The Reflowering of Malaysian Islam: Modern Religious Radicals and Their Roots*, Vancouver: University of British Columbia Press, 1984, p. 134.

22 Both Malay and Javanese pre-colonial societies were feudal, and the leaders were said to derive legitimacy from mystical sources of authority (known as *daulat* in the Malay kingdoms and *wahyu* in the Javanese *Kraton*). See D.J. Steinberg (ed.), *In Search of Southeast Asia*, London: Pall Mall Press, 1971, pp. 73–86.

23 This description may not have been as relevant for Majapahit, which was essentially a land-based kingdom and hence naturally reliant on territorial borders to demarcate its sphere of influence. But even then it was difficult to determine exactly where the border stopped, as the kingdom's influence was a gradual extension in concentric fashion outwards from the power centre, waning as it widened.

24 J.W. Christie, 'State Formation in Early Maritime Southeast Asia: A Consideration of the Theories and Data', *Bijdragen tot de Taal-, Land- en Volkenkunde*, 151(2), 1995, 267.

25 O.W. Wolters, *History, Culture, and Region in Southeast Asian Perspectives*, 2nd edition, Singapore: Institute of Southeast Asian Studies, 1999, p. 25.

26 For example, the *Sejarah Melayu* chronicles the marriage between Sultan Mansur Shah of Melaka and the princess from Majapahit, Radin Galah Chandra Kirana, as well as a genealogy of their family. See C.C. Brown, *Sejarah Melayu*, Kuala Lumpur: Oxford University Press, 1970, pp. 169–171.

27 J.A.C. Mackie, *Konfrontasi: The Indonesia–Malaysia Dispute, 1963–1966*, Kuala Lumpur: Oxford University Press, 1974, p. 15.

28 See A. Reid, 'Understanding *Melayu* as a Source of Diverse Modern Identities', *Journal of Southeast Asian Studies*, 32(3), October 2001, 309–310.

29 Nothofer argues that the three main languages of Java (Javanese, Sundanese and Madurese) in fact belonged to Malay and several other languages in a relatively close-knit subgroup. See B. Nothofer, *The Reconstruction of Proto-Malayo-Javanic*, The Hague: Martinus Nijhoff, 1975.

30 For a study on the importance of language in identity-building, see J.A. Fishman, *Language and Nationalism*, Rowley, MA: Harcourt Brace Jovanovisc, 1972.

31 H. Maier, 'We Are Playing Relatives' in See C. Chou and W. Derks (eds), *Riau in Transition*, The Hague: *Bijdragen Tot de Taal-, Land- en Volkenkunde*, 1997, pp. 679–680.

32 See G.M. Kahin, *Nationalism and Revolution in Indonesia*, Ithaca, NY: Cornell University Press, 1952. Shiraishi noted that before the First World War, Javanese and Dutch had been used by the educated elite as the principal languages of communication. According to Shiraishi, it was with the formation of the Islamic-based nationalist movement *Sarekat Islam* in 1912 that Malay was introduced as a mass language and subsequently appropriated by the nationalist elite. See T. Shiraishi, *An Age in Motion: Popular Radicalism in Java, 1912–1926*, Ithaca, NY: Cornell University Press, 1990.

33 D.J. Steinberg (ed.), *In Search of Southeast Asia*, pp. 298–299.

34 For an exposition of why Malay and not Javanese emerged as the dominant language in the region, see Asmah Haji Omar, *Language and Society in Malaysia*, Kuala Lumpur: Dewan Bahasa dan Pustaka, 1993, pp. 1–18.

35 MABBIM originally encompassed only Indonesia and Malaysia and was known as MBIM. It subsequently expanded to include the Sultanate of Brunei when the latter gained independence from Britain in 1984.

36 Syed Naguib Al-Attas, *Islam dalam Sejarah dan Kebudayaan Melayu*, Kuala Lumpur: Penerbit Universiti Kebangsaan Malaysia, 1972, p. 21.

37 One could, of course, postulate that Islam in the Indo-Malay world in fact built on the pre-Islamic Hindu–Buddhist traditions, which had already offered a modicum of cohesion, albeit not as extensive as Islamic influence.

38 See Mahayudin Haji Yahaya, *Islam di Alam Melayu*, Kuala Lumpur: Dewan Bahasa dan Pustaka, 1998; P. Riddell, *Islam and the Malay–Indonesian World*, Singapore: Horizon Books, 2001.

39 See Andaya and Andaya, *A History of Malaysia*, pp. 51–55. Melaka was also considered 'the centre of Moslem learning in the Indonesian area'. See C.K.

184   *Notes*

Nicholson, 'The Introduction of Islam into Sumatra and Java: A Study in Cultural Change', doctoral dissertation, Syracuse University, 1965, p. 51.
40 Muhammad Yusoff, *The Malay Sultanate*, pp. 167–179.
41 Noticeably, the latest and arguably most comprehensive study of the Islamization of the Indo-Malay world by Riddell does not mention Melaka at all. See Riddell, *Islam*.
42 For an academic exploration of the social and political roles and functions of these Islamic schools in both Indonesia and Malaysia, see B. Anderson, *Java in a Time of Revolution: Occupation and Resistance, 1944–46*, Ithaca, NY: Cornell University Press, 1972 and Safie Ibrahim, *The Islamic Party of Malaysia: Its Formative Stages and Ideology*, Kelantan: Nawawi bin Ismail, 1981.
43 Such links are traced in H. Federspiel, 'Muslim Intellectuals in Southeast Asia', *Studia Islamika*, 6(1), 1999.
44 This is discussed in detail in A.H. Johns, 'Islam in Southeast Asia: Reflections and New Directions', *Indonesia*, 19, April 1975. See also A.J.S. Reid, 'Nineteenth Century Pan-Islam in Indonesia and Malaysia', *Journal of Asian Studies*, 26(2), 1967, and *Southeast Asia in the Age of Commerce, 1450–1680*, vol. 2: *Expansion and Crisis*, New Haven, CT: Yale University Press, 1993, pp. 132–201.
45 This classic division of Indonesian Muslims was posited by the anthropologist Clifford Geertz. See C. Geertz, *The Religion of Java*, Glencoe, New York: The Free Press, 1964. Geertz's work has since been refined by M. Woodward, *Islam in Java: Normative Piety and Mysticism in the Sultanate of Yogjakarta*, Tucson: University of Arizona Press, 1989. This can be compared to the Islam of the Malays as discussed in Murni Djamal, 'The Origin of the Islamic Reform Movement in Minangkabau: Life and Thought of Abdul Karim Amrullah', *Studia Islamika*, 5(3), 1998.
46 C. Geertz, *Islam Observed: Religious Development in Morocco and Indonesia*, Chicago: University of Chicago Press, 1968, p. 11.
47 Koentjaraningrat, *Javanese Culture*, Singapore: Institute of Southeast Asian Studies, 1985, p. 317. In drawing these comparisons, Koentjaraningrat and Geertz draw attention to Javanese distinctiveness.
48 This case is argued in Kuntowijoyo, *Paradigma Islam: Interpretasi untuk Aksi*, Bandung: Mizan, 1991, and H. Federspiel, *Muslim Intellectuals and National Development in Indonesia*, Commack, NY: Nova Science Press, 1992.
49 Unlike the British, who essentially refrained from direct involvement in religious issues in Malaya, the Dutch actively interfered in Islamic affairs in the East Indies in an attempt to turn Indonesia away from what Hurgronje called the 'narrow confines of the Islamic system'. See H. Benda, 'Christiaan Snouck Hurgronje and the Foundations of Dutch Islamic Policy in Indonesia', *Journal of Modern History*, 30, 1958.
50 See 'Nasionalisme Melayu dan Islam'[online] http://www.geocities.com/melayuislam/165.htm (accessed 2 February 2002).
51 See J.C. van Leur, *Indonesian Trade and Society: Essays in Asian Social and Economic History*, The Hague: W. van Hoeve, 1955; C.D. Cowan, 'Continuity and Change in the International History of Maritime South East Asia', *Journal of Southeast Asian History*, 9(1), March 1968.
52 This point was extracted from the presentation text of M.C. Ricklefs, which was delivered at the Institute of Defence and Strategic Studies, Singapore, on 13 February 2003.
53 Muhammad Yusoff, *The Malay Sultanate*, pp. 263–264.
54 See for example, L. Palmer, *Indonesia and the Dutch*, London: Oxford University Press, 1962, pp. 153–159. While Feith recognizes this tension in his

study of the factors that facilitated the termination of constitutional democracy in contemporary Indonesia, he suggests that it was but one of a myriad
factors. See H. Feith, *The Decline of Constitutional Democracy in Indonesia*,
Ithaca, NY: Cornell University Press, 1962, pp. 26–32.
55 B.H.M. Vlekke, *Nusantara: A History of Indonesia*, The Hague: W. van
Hoeve, 1959, pp. 41–45.
56 For a discussion on the wars between Srivijaya and Majapahit, see Andaya
and Andaya, *A History of Malaysia*, pp. 26–31. See also Wolters, *The Fall of
Srivijaya*, pp. 64–76.
57 This has been particularly so of Western scholars, who have been less averse
to focusing on the disharmony in the Malay world. The works of Vlekke,
Wolters, van Leur, Cowan, and Palmer, among others, exemplify this vein of
scholarship.
58 Many Malaysians relate that in relations with larger neighbours (presumably
Indonesia), the wit of the mousedeer is necessary to overcome the odds
imposed against Malaysia because of its size. See P.F. McKean, 'The Mouse-
Deer in Malayo-Indonesian Folklore: Alternative Analyses and the Significance of a Trickster Figure in South-East Asia', *Asian Folklore Studies*, 30, 1971.
59 Kassim Ahmad, *Hikayat Hang Tuah*, Kuala Lumpur: Dewan Bahasa dan
Pustaka, 1975.
60 See Mohd. Taib Osman, 'Trends in Modern Malay Literature' in G. Wang
(ed.), *Malaysia: A Survey*, Singapore: Donald Moore Books, 1964, pp. 212–213;
see also R. Jones (ed.), *Hikayat Raja Pasai*, Petaling Jaya: Penerbit Fajar
Bakti, 1987.
61 See S.O. Robson, 'Java in Malay Literature' in V.J.H. Houben, H.M.J. Maier,
and W. von der Molen (eds), *Looking in Odd Mirrors: The Java Sea*, Leiden:
Vakgroep Talen en Culturen van Zuidoost-Azie en Oceanie, Rijksuniversiteit
te Leiden, 1992, p. 37.
62 Wolters, *The Fall of Srivijaya*, p. 62.
63 Kwa, 'The Historical Roots', 50.
64 The question of whether the making of Third World states was more a result
of external processes (de-colonization from the metropole) or internal agency
(anti-colonial nationalism) remains contested. Central to this debate between
the metropolitan narrative and narratives of national liberation, as Harper
notes, is 'not merely a question of perspective, but one of power'. He further
suggests that 'colonial histories share the underlying tension of constructing a
history that acknowledges the realities of European domination, without con-
stricting the possibilities of giving real agency to indigenous societies'. See
T.N. Harper, 'Power and the People: The End of Empire in History' in K.S.
Jomo (ed.), *Rethinking Malaysia*, Kuala Lumpur: Malaysian Social Science
Association, 1999, p. 206.
65 Briefly, the origins of Dutch colonialism can be traced back to the appearance
of the first Dutch ships at Banten in west Java towards the end of the sixteenth
century. In contrast, active British interest in archipelagic Southeast Asia did
not materialize until the 1770s, when the British began taking an active interest in political affairs in Borneo, and subsequently in 1786, when they took
possession of Penang.
66 Wolters, *History, Culture, and Region*, p. 33.
67 L. Andaya and B.W. Andaya, *A History of Malaysia*, 2nd edition, Basingstoke, UK: Palgrave, pp. 125–126.
68 The close interaction between Sumatran and Peninsula cultures and histories
is studied in greater detail in J. Drakard, *A Malay Frontier: Unity and Duality
in a Sumatran Kingdom*, Ithaca, NY: Cornell University Southeast Asia
Program, 1990, pp. 1–62.

69 For example, Malay and Sanskrit inscriptions found in the Palembang region in Sumatra suggest that present-day Malaysia was part of the vast trading state of Srivijaya, which existed between the eighth and thirteenth centuries and whose heart was situated in Sumatra.

70 Wolters, *History, Culture, and Region*, pp. 32–33; See also E. Loeb, *Sumatra: Its History and People*, Oxford: Oxford University Press, 1972, pp. 7–12

71 This too is a matter of contention, and some scholars have in fact identified Riau as the source of Malay identity. See Chou and Derks (eds), *Riau in Transition*.

72 Andaya and Andaya, *A History of Malaysia*, 2nd edition, p. 47.

73 Correspondence between the British High Commission, Kuala Lumpur, and the Commonwealth Relations Office, London, no. 103, 12 April 1962, CO 1030/1013, PRO.

74 Quoted in J. Mossman, *Rebels in Paradise: Indonesia's Civil War*, London: Jonathan Cape, 1961, p. 75.

75 Interview with former Malaysian ambassador, Kuala Lumpur, 14 August 2001.

76 Kassim Ahmad, *Hikayat Hang Tuah*, p. 175.

77 Correspondence between the British High Commission, Kuala Lumpur, and the Commonwealth Relations Office, London, 164/104/5, 28 November 1961, DO 169/74, PRO.

78 See, for example, B. Cohn, *Colonialism and Its Form of Knowledge*, Princeton, NJ: Princeton University Press, 1996.

79 A study of British classification and categorization of local concepts and institutions, for instance, can be found in B.K. Cheah, 'Feudalism in Pre-colonial Malaya: The Past as a Colonial Discourse', *Journal of Southeast Asian Studies*, 25(2), September 1994.

80 Farish Noor, 'The One-Dimensional Malay: The Homogenization of Malay Identity in the Revisionist Writing of History in Malaysia', paper presented at the Third Annual Malaysian Studies Conference, Universiti Kebangsaan Malaysia, Bangi, Selangor, 7–8 August 2001. See also Reid, 'Understanding *Melayu*', 302–304.

81 A. Vandenbosch, *The Dutch East Indies*, Berkeley: University of California Press, 1941, p. 1. See also B. Schrieke (ed.), *The Effect of Western Influence on Native Civilisation in the Malay Archipelago*, Batavia: G. Kolff, 1929.

82 See B. Vlekke, *Nusantara: A History of the East Indian Archipelago*, Cambridge, MA: Harvard University Press, 1944.

83 This contrasted with the case in India, where colonial thought constructed the sociological view that India was a mere collection of discrete communities. See P. Chatterjee, *The Nation and Its Fragments*, Princeton, NJ: Princeton University Press, 1993, pp. 220–239.

84 See Reid, 'Understanding *Melayu*', 302. I am aware of the tenuous and contentious nature of the notion of race, which in post-colonial discourse is viewed as a social construction rather than a biological reality. While I share this latter concern, it is in colonial and local sociological and anthropological writings that race is represented as physical categorization. Rather than challenge this assumption, which would be a worthy exercise but not realistically possible here, this study prefers to explore the implications and repercussions to this understanding of race and the racialization of Malay identity.

85 E.S. De Klerck, *History of the Netherlands East Indies,* vol. 1, Rotterdam: W.L. & J. Brusse, 1938, p. 99.

86 J. Legge, *Indonesia*, Englewoods Cliff, NJ: Prentice-Hall, 1964, p. 4.

87 See A. Wallace, *The Malay Archipelago*, London: Macmillan, 1894, pp. 1–3.

88 R.O. Winstedt, *The Malays: A Cultural History*, London: Routledge & Kegan Paul, 1947, pp. 3–4.

89 T. Raffles, 'On the Malayu Nation, with a Translation of its Maritime Institutions', *Asiatic Researches*, 12, 1818, 103, quoted in Reid, 'Understanding *Melayu*', 303.
90 A.C. Milner, *The Invention of Colonial Politics in Malaya*, Cambridge: Cambridge University Press, 1995, p. 68.
91 Ibid., p. 60.
92 B. Shafer, *Faces of Nationalism*, New York: Routledge, 1972, p. 154. For a summary on European scholarship on race during that period, see T. Gossett, *Race: The History of an Idea in America*, New York: Oxford University Press, 1997, pp. 32–175.
93 The term '*Melayu*', for example, appears in the *Sejarah Melayu* and *Hikayat Hang Tuah*.
94 J.C. Bottoms, 'Some Malay Historical Sources: A Bibliographical Note' in Soedjatmoko, Mohammad Ali, G.J. Resink, and G.M. Kahin (eds), *An Introduction to Indonesian Historiography*, Ithaca, NY: Cornell University Press, 1965, p. 157.
95 J. Bastin and R. Winks, *Malaysia: Selected Historic Readings*, Kuala Lumpur: Oxford University Press, 1966, p. xiii.
96 See Firdaus Abdullah, *Indonesia Raya di Alam Melayu: Setiakawan Serumpun di Zaman Perjuangan*, Jakarta: KITLV, 1995.
97 It is not the purpose here to 'debunk' indigenous conceptions of history. Instead, regardless of historical accuracy, these indigenous conceptions provide critical insight into the mindsets and perceptions of the political elite in Indonesia and Malaysia. For a cogent criticism of indigenous interpretations of history, see Kwa, 'The Historical Roots'.
98 R. Young, *Postcolonialism*, Oxford: Blackwell, 2001, p. 2.
99 Indonesian conceptions are covered in detail in Osman Halliby, *Documenta Historica: Sedjarah Documenter dari Pertumbuhan dan Perdjuangan Negara Republic Indonesia*, Jakarta: Bulan Bintang, 1953; *Seminar Sedjarah: Laporan lengkap Atjara I dan II tentang Konsepsi Filsafat Sedjarah Nasional dan Periodisasi Sedjarah Indonesia*, Jogjakarta: Universitas Gadjah Mada, 1958; Bambang Oetomo, 'Some Remarks on Modern Indonesian Historiography' in D.G.E. Hall (ed.), *Historians of Southeast Asia*, London: Oxford University Press, 1961; Roeslan Abdulgani, *Heroes' Day and the Indonesian Revolution*, Jakarta: Prapantja Publishing House, 1964; Nugroho Notosusanto, 'A Current Concept of Indonesian History: The Relationship between Nationalism and Historiography', address delivered at the Goethe Institut, Jakarta, 23 March 1970; A.K. Pringgodigdo, *Sedjarah Pergerakan Rakyat Indonesia*, Jakarta: Dian Rakyat, 1970, pp. 164–167.
100 See Muhammad Yamin, *6000 Tahun Sang Merah-Putih*, Jakarta: Penerbit Siguntang, 1954; Abdul Haris Nasution, *Sekitar Perang Kemerdekaan Indonesia*, Bandung: Disrajah-AD dan Penerbit Angkasa, 1977. See also Mohd Dahlan Mansoer, *Pengatar Sejarah Nusantara Awal*, Kuala Lumpur: Dewan Bahasa dan Pustaka, 1979.
101 It is likely that Yamin's conceptions were influenced by works such as N.J. Krom, *Hindoe–Javaansche Geschiedenis*, 2de druk, The Hague: Nijhoff, 1931 that corroborated his ideology, as suggested in Kwa, 'The Historical Roots', 45–48.
102 See Supomo, 'The Image of Majapahit in late Javanese and Indonesian Writing' in A. Reid and D. Marr, *Perceptions of the Past*, Singapore: Heinemann Books, 1979, p. 180.
103 For example, Sukarno, *Indonesia Menggugat: Pidato pembelaan Bung Karno dimuka hakim kolonial*, Jakarta, 1956, pp. 21–22.
104 See C. Chou, 'Orang Suku Laut Identity' in M. Hitchcock and V.T. King

(eds), *Images of Malay–Indonesian Identity, Images of Malay–Indonesian Identity*, Kuala Lumpur: Oxford University Press, p. 148.

105 Nasution, *Sekitar Perang Kemerdekaan Indonesia*, p. 52.

106 The case for this is presented in R.M. Koentjaraningrat, *Introduction to the Peoples and Cultures of Indonesia and Malaysia*, Menlo Park, CA: Cummings, 1975. In point of fact, from a purely racial perspective, the Maori of New Zealand and certain segments of the Madagascan population would also be considered 'Malay'.

107 See Shaharil Talib, 'The Asiatic Archipelago: History beyond Boundaries' in *Proceedings of the International Symposium South-East Asia: Global Area Studies for the 21st Century*, Kyoto: Kyoto International Community House, 1996. Leonard and Barbara Andaya's study of Malaysian history also provides two maps indicating that, to their understanding, the 'Malay world' included the areas covering the Indonesian Archipelago. Andaya and Andaya, *A History of Malaysia*, pp. xviii–xix.

108 See K.H. Lee, 'Indonesian and Malaysian History from Dutch Sources: Reconstructing the Straits of Malacca's Past', *Sejarah*, 4, 1996, 26.

109 For a discussion of the difference between race and ethnicity, see S. Cornell and D. Hartmann, *Ethnicity and Race: Making Identities in a Changing World*, Thousand Oaks, CA: Pine Forge Press, 1998, pp. 25–34. Suffice it to say that here, race is taken to imply physical traits, while ethnicity includes elements of culture and shared history. There is also the sense in which both race and ethnicity are social and political constructions. See R. Young, *Colonial Desire: Hybridity in Theory, Culture, and Race*, London: Routledge, 1995.

110 Quoted in Kamaruddin Jaafar, *Dr. Burhanuddin AlHelmy: Politik Melayu dan Islam*, Kuala Lumpur: Yayasan Anda, 1980, p. 32. Also cited in Ariffin, *Bangsa Melayu*, pp. 40–41.

111 This theme comes across very strongly in the indigenous literature. The radical Malay nationalist ideologue Dr Burhanuddin tried to present an argument for the primordial existence of the Malay race throughout archipelagic Southeast Asia, including the Malay Peninsula and southern Thailand. See Burhanuddin Al-Helmy, *Asas Falsafah Kebangsaaan Melayu*, Jakarta, 1963. See also Amat Johari Moain, *Sejarah Nasionalisma Maphilindo*, Kuala Lumpur: Dewan Bahasa dan Pustaka, 1960.

112 Milner, *Invention of Colonial Politics*, p. 99.

113 See Adnan Nawang, 'Zainal Abidin Ahmad', *Massa*, 29 August 1998.

114 For a study on how Malays perceive the close association between their identity, language, and religion, see Asmah, *Language and Society*, pp. 1–18; see also W. Roff, *The Origins of Malay Nationalism*, Singapore: Oxford University Press, 1994, pp. 67–68.

115 See C. Hirschman, 'The Meaning and Measurement of Ethnicity in Malaysia', *Journal of Asian Studies*, 46(3), 1985.

116 Andaya and Andaya, *A History of Malaysia*, 2nd edition, p. 99.

117 This point is emphasized in Muhammad Yusoff Hashim, *Pensejarahan Melayu: Kajian Tentang Tradisi Sejarah Melayu Nusantara*, Kuala Lumpur: Dewan Bahasa dan Pustaka, 1992, pp. 1–48; see also the essays compiled in Kementerian Pelajaran Malaysia (Ministry of Education, Malaysia), *Pertemuan Dunia Melayu '82*, Kuala Lumpur: Dewan Bahasa dan Pustaka, 1987.

118 Ibrahim Yaacob, *Melihat Tanah Air*, Kuantan: Percetakan Timur, 1975, p. 12.

119 Wan Ahmad Hamid, 'Religion and Culture' in Wang (ed.), *Malaysia*, p. 181.

120 Kassim, *Hikayat Hang Tuah*, p. 189.

121 Maier, 'We Are Playing Relatives', p. 675.

122 This point was reiterated by Taufik Abdullah in an interview in Jakarta, 22 January 2002.

123 There is also the issue of the populations of east Indonesia, which would not be considered Malay, but which nonetheless remain outside the scope of early thinkers of Malay identity.

124 Interview with an Indonesian Foreign Ministry official, Jakarta, 21 January 2002.

125 R. Curtis, 'Malaysia and Indonesia', *New Left Review*, 28, November–December 1964, 6–7.

126 An exposition of the Yamin-Hatta debate is provided by H. Feith and L. Castles (eds), *Indonesian Political Thinking, 1945–1965*, Ithaca, NY: Cornell University Press, 1970, chapters by Yamin and Hatta.

127 This was a striking move that went against the grain of nationalism in the Third World.

128 Some peninsular Malay scholars have also attempted to highlight this fact. See, for example, Ariffin Omar, *Revolusi Indonesia dan Bangsa Melayu*, Pulau Pinang: Penerbit Universiti Sains Malaysia, 1999.

129 Because the Malays could not be considered *orang asli* in the strictest sense, the Malay political elite would subsequently devise the term '*Bumiputra*' (Sons of the Soil) in order to impute to the community an indigenous identity that would eventually translate to political and economic privileges.

130 C. Robequain, *Malaysia, Indonesia Borneo, and the Philippines*, London: Longmans, Green, 1954, p. 118.

131 Unless of course they are second- or third-generation Malays descended from Javanese immigrants.

132 This is further elaborated in B.W. Andaya, *To Live as Brothers: Southeast Sumatra in the Seventeenth and Eighteenth Centuries*, Honolulu: University of Hawaii Press, 1993, pp. 70–73.

133 Syed Husin Ali, *Rakyat Melayu: Nasib dan Masa Depannya*, Jakarta: Penerbit Inti Sarana Aksana, 1985, p. 8.

134 That said, peninsular Malays on the other hand also expend much effort in emphasizing Malay exclusivity in relation to other racial and ethnic groups such as the Chinese or Indians.

135 I was informed that at a particular Indonesia–Malaysia Youth Dialogue session, a group of Indonesians from the Moluccas openly and vehemently expressed their objection as to the use of ethnic measures of affinity during the session. Interview with an Indonesian diplomat, Jakarta, 15 January 2002.

136 Syed Husin, *Rakyat Melayu*, pp. 7–8.

137 Interview with Taufik Abdullah, Jakarta, 22 January 2002.

138 Compare and contrast, for instance, the Malay definition of 'Malayness' discussed here with the essays in C. Holt (ed.), *Culture and Politics in Indonesia*, Ithaca, NY: Cornell University Press, 1972, and J.J. Fox (ed.), *Indonesia: The Making of a Culture*, Canberra: Australian National University, Research School of Pacific Studies, 1980, both of which emphasize the theme of variation and diversity within the ethno-cultural entity of Indonesia.

139 See Fishman, *Language and Nationalism*. For a study of the European origins of nationalism and its impact on the Third World, see E. Kedourie (ed.), *Nationalism in Asia and Africa*, London: Weidenfeld & Nicolson, 1971.

140 Speech by Ismail Abdul Rahman at the 81st Plenary Meeting of the 14th Session of the United Nations General Assembly, 5 October 1959.

3 A tale of two nationalisms

1 Farish Noor, 'Fine Young Calibans: Broken Dreams of Melaya-Raya', www.Malaysiakini.com, 13 January 2002 [online] http://pemantau.tripod.com/ 2001/17Jan_farish.html (accessed 18 January 2002).
2 See W. Roff, 'Indonesian and Malay Students in Cairo in the 1920s', *Indonesia*, 9, April 1970.
3 G. Kahin, *Nationalism and Revolution in Indonesia*, Ithaca, NY: Cornell University Press, 1952, p. 38.
4 See Azyumardi Azra, 'The Transmission of al-Manar's Reformism to the Malay–Indonesian World: The Cases of al-Imam and al-Munir', *Studia Islamika*, 6(3), 1999.
5 Roff, 'Indonesian and Malay Students', 73.
6 Ibid., 73.
7 Ibid., 77.
8 Kahin, *Nationalism and Revolution*, p. 46.
9 W. Roff, *The Origins of Malay Nationalism*, Kuala Lumpur: Oxford University Press, 1967, pp. 64–67.
10 Emphasizing the close links they had with anti-colonial and anti-establishment Indonesians elements, the Kaum Muda movement in Malaya provided refuge for prominent Indonesian communists such as Alimin, Musso, and Tan Melaka, all of whom had escaped across the Melaka Straits after abortive communist uprisings in Java and Sumatra in 1926–1927.
11 H. Benda, *The Crescent and the Rising Sun*, The Hague: W. van Hoeve, 1958, p. 47.
12 Ibid., pp. 47–48.
13 Taufik Abdullah, *Schools and Politics: Kaum Muda Movement in West Sumatra, 1927–1933*, Ithaca, NY: Cornell Modern Indonesia Project Monograph Series, Ithaca, NY: Cornell University Press, 1971, p. 147; see also A.J.S. Reid, 'Nineteenth Century Pan-Islam in Indonesia and Malaysia', *Journal of Asian Studies*, 26(2), February 1967, 267–283.
14 Crosby to Curzon, 14 October 1920, CO 537/900, PRO. See also Mohammad Redzuan Othman, 'Call of the Azhar: The Malay Students Sojourn in Cairo before World War II', *Sejarah*, 3, 1994–1995.
15 For a detailed study into the various faces of this socialist movement in Malaya, see K.K. Khoo, 'The Malay Left, 1945–1948: A Preliminary Discourse', *Sarjana*, 1(1), December 1981.
16 See K.K. Khoo, 'Malay Society, 1874–1920s', *Journal of Southeast Asian Studies*, 5(2), September 1974.
17 Roff, *Origins of Malay Nationalism*, pp. 142–157.
18 Awang Salleh, *Malay Secular Education and Teacher Training in British Malaya*, Kuala Lumpur: Dewan Bahasa dan Pustaka, 1979, p. 43.
19 J. Funston, *Malay Politics in Malaysia: A Study of UMNO and PAS*, Singapore: Heinemann International Books (Asia), 1980, p. 32.
20 Ibrahim Yaacob, *Nusa dan Bangsa Melayu*, Jakarta: N.V. Alma'ariff, 1951, p. 65.
21 Roff, *Origins of Malay Nationalism*, pp. 172–173.
22 Funston, *Malay Politics*, pp. 31–32.
23 Firdaus Abdullah, *The Origins and Early Development of the Radical Malay Opposition Movement in Malaysian Politics*, Kuala Lumpur: Pelanduk Publications, 1985, p. 90.
24 Ibid., pp. 90–100. The participation of Malay nationalists in the Indonesian revolution is also mentioned in the autobiographies and writings of some of these nationalists. See, for example, Keris Mas, *Memoir*, Kuala Lumpur:

Dewan Bahasa dan Pustaka, 1980, p. 18; Ishak Haji Mohammad, 'Kata Pen-
dahuluan' in Ibrahim Yaacob, *Melihat Tanah Air*, Kuantan: Percetakan
Timur, 1975, p. 8; Ibrahim, *Nusa dan Bangsa Melayu*, p. 63.
25 See Muhammad Yamin, *6000 Tahun Sang Merah-Putih*, Jakarta: Penerbit
Siguntang, 1954.
26 See Muhammad Yamin, *A Legal and Historical Review of Indonesia's Sovereignty over the Ages*, Manila: Indonesian Embassy, 1959. Yamin was one of
the staunchest supporters of Malaysia's incorporation into *Indonesia Raya*.
27 W. Elsbree, 'Japan's Role in Southeast Asian Nationalist Movements,
1940–1945', doctoral dissertation, Harvard University, 1953, p. 112.
28 Minutes from this ground-breaking meeting have been circulated as Badan
Penjelidek Usaha Persiapan Indonesia, *Territory of the Indonesian State*,
Jakarta: Badan Penjelidek Usaha Persiapan Kemerdekaan Indonesia, 31 May
1945.
29 It should be noted that the results were consequently rejected by the Japanese
military administration on the grounds that Malaya was 'not ready' for
independence. See Y. Akashi, 'Japanese Military Administration in Malaya:
Its Formation and Evolution in Reference to Sultans, the Islamic Religion and
the Moslem-Malays, 1941–1945', *Journal of Asian Studies*, 7(1), April 1969.
30 An Indonesian delegation consisting of Sukarno, Hatta, and Dr Rajiman
Wediodiningrat had flown to Dalat in southern Vietnam to meet with General
Terauchi, Commander-in-Chief of the Japanese Armed Forces in Southeast
Asia, to discuss the future of Indonesia. On their way back to Java they were
met by Ibrahim Yaacob and Burhanuddin Al-Helmy in Taiping.
31 Radin Soenarno, 'Malay Nationalism, 1869–1941', *Journal of Southeast Asian
History*, 10(2), 1969, 20–21. According to Cheah Boon Kheng, however, there
were several contradictory opinions of the events at Taiping depending on
whether one took the Malayan, Indonesian, or Japanese perspective. See B.K.
Cheah, 'The Japanese Occupation of Malaya, 1941–1945: Ibrahim Yaacob and
the Struggle for Indonesia Raya', *Indonesia*, 28, 1979, 112–114. Robert Curtis
also presents another perspective of this episode, arguing that the request for
incorporation into Indonesia was 'no doubt regretfully, turned down'. See R.
Curtis, 'Malaysia and Indonesia', *New Left Review*, 28, November–December
1964, 12.
32 There are contending accounts of the Japanese military government's rejection of the concept of *Melayu Raya* and *Indonesia Raya*. Bernhard Daim
argues that the Japanese were laconic in their rejection of the concept. See B.
Daim, *Sukarno and the Struggle for Indonesian Independence*, Ithaca, NY:
Cornell University Press, 1969, p. 109; Others, however, register Japanese
sympathy towards it. See M. Nakamura, 'General Imamura and the Early
Period of the Japanese Occupation', *Indonesia*, 10, October 1970, 5. Needless
to say, this was a Japanese account.
33 Ibrahim Yaacob, *Sekitar Malaya Merdeka*, Jakarta: Kesatuan Malaya
Merdeka, 1957, pp. 28–34.
34 The Taiping meeting was mentioned fleetingly in a footnote in Legge's biography of Sukarno. Nevertheless, Legge was of the opinion that 'it is a significant
commentary on the depth of Sukarno's "Greater Indonesia" ideas that despite
that expression of interest he gave no more thought to such an association
[with Malaya]. After his return to Jakarta his preoccupation was solely with a
proclamation relating to an Indonesia narrowly conceived in terms of the
former Dutch colony' – J.D. Legge, *Sukarno: A Political Biography*, London:
Allen Lane The Penguin Press, 1972, pp. 193–194, footnote 4.
35 Mohammad Hatta, *Indonesian Patriot: Memoirs*, edited by C.L.M. Penders,
Singapore: Gunung Agung, 1981, pp. 222–223.

36 This is discussed thoroughly in B. Anderson, *Java in a Time of Revolution: Occupation and Resistance, 1944–46*, Ithaca, NY: Cornell University Press, 1971, pp. 1–66. See also W. Frederick, *Visions and Heat: The Making of the Indonesian Revolution*, Athens, OH: Ohio University Press, 1989, pp. 182–267.
37 Tan Melaka, *From Jail to Jail*, vol. 3, translated and introduced by Helen Jarvis, Athens, OH: Ohio University Southeast Asia Series, 1991, p. 106.
38 *Kedaulatan Rakyat*, 18 March 1946; *Soeara Rakyat*, 19 March 1946; *Merdeka*, 19–20 March 1946, quoted in Tan Melaka, *From Jail to Jail*, vol. 3, p. 279, footnote 1.
39 See document no. 11, 25 May 1946, CO 537/1529, PRO.
40 Kahin, *Nationalism and Revolution*, pp. 68–69; M.C. Ricklefs, *A History of Modern Indonesia Since c.1300*, Stanford, CA: Stanford University Press, 1993, pp. 170–176.
41 *Soeloeh Merdaka*, 4 February 1946, quoted in A.J.S. Reid, *Blood of the People*, Kuala Lumpur: Oxford University Press, 1979, p. 223. According to Reid, an English translation of this statement appears in Appendix C to WIS 17, 9 February 1946, WO 172/9893, PRO.
42 The specifics of Japanese policy in Indonesia are discussed in Mohammad Abdul, *Japan's Colonialism and Indonesia*, The Hague: Martinus Nijhoff, 1955; A.J.S. Reid and A. Oki (eds), *The Japanese Experience in Indonesia: Selected Memoirs of 1942–1945*, Ohio University Monographs in International Studies, Southeast Asia Series no. 72, Athens, OH: Ohio University Press, 1986; S. Sato, *War, Nationalism and Peasants: Java under the Japanese Occupation, 1942–1945*, St Leonards, NSW: Allen & Unwin, 1994.
43 See Anderson, *Java in a Time of Revolution*, chaps 4 and 5. While Anderson's study concentrated on the *Pemuda* of Java, the phenomenon that he uncovered was also present elsewhere in the archipelago.
44 Reid, *Blood of the People*, p. 223.
45 Ideologically diverse in the sense that elements of the *Pemuda* movement could be found in all ideological camps, including both the Leninist and the Trotskyite camps of Indonesian communism.
46 Geheime MvO, Ezerman, 1993, 18–19 quoted in Reid, *Blood of the People*, pp. 52–53. The *Korte Verklaring* referred to the Declaration of Allegiance to the Netherlands Indies Government signed by indigenous Indonesian rulers.
47 Reid, *Blood of the People*, p. 5.
48 Ibid., pp. 59–73.
49 In Eastern Sumatra in particular, the ruling elite came from six Malay sultanates: Langkat, Serdang, Deli, Asahan, Kotapinang and Siak.
50 Reid, *Blood of the People*, pp. 218–251.
51 Curtis, 'Malaysia and Indonesia', 12–13.
52 Reid, *Blood of the People*, p. 226.
53 Ibid., pp. 222–225.
54 Ibid., p. 234.
55 'Netherlands East Indies: General Situation, 1947', A4355 7/1/7/9, NAA.
56 See Mohammad Said, 'What was the "Social Revolution" of 1946', *Indonesia*, 15, 1973.
57 Reid, *Blood of the People*, pp. 253–263.
58 Curtis, 'Malaysia and Indonesia', 13.
59 Curtis noted that 'if there was one area where the feudal rulers suffered a total annihilation rather than eclipse and obscurity, it was in the specifically Malay Sultanates of East Sumatra – precisely the group most closely attached by family ties to the Malayan ruling class'. Ibid., 12–13.
60 Soenarno describes this disparity at the eve of the Pacific War as such: 'It

[Malay nationalism] had not entered into the political arena, but was still in the process of preparing to do so. By then the Indonesian nationalist movement had become already a formidable challenger to the Dutch colonial government.' See Soernarno, 'Malay Nationalism', 27. That is not so say, however, that Malayan history did not witness the kind of anti-colonial rebellions that featured so prominently and regularly in the histories of Third World nationalism. The Perak and Negri Sembilan Wars of the 1870s, the Pahang rebellion of the 1890s, the Kelantan uprising of 1915 and the Terengganu uprising of 1928 are but some examples of such resistance.

61 For example, in Malaya British interests were represented by the Resident, who acted in an 'advisory capacity' to the *kerajaan*.

62 Feudalism was in fact enhanced by the regalia that the British introduced to traditional Malay court practice.

63 This came across quite clearly in the early perceptions of traditional Malay leaders such as Onn bin Jaafar and Tunku Abdul Rahman. For example, Dato Onn, who became the first president of *Pertubuhan Kebangsaan Melayu Bersatu* (United Malays National Organization, UMNO), formed in 1946 to give organizational coherence to the traditional Malay political movement, was concerned at the radical Islamic bent in the activities of these reformists. See Anwar Abdullah, *Dato Onn*, Kuala Lumpur: Pustaka Nusantara, 1971, pp. 171–173.

64 Soenarno, 'Malay Nationalism', 16. The associations that Soernarno was referring to were political associations established and run throughout the peninsula by the traditional state structure.

65 Roff, *Origins of Malay Nationalism*, pp. 197–211; Ariffin Omar, *Bangsa Melayu: Malay Concepts of Democracy and Community*, Kuala Lumpur: Oxford University Press, 1993, pp. 20–26.

66 That said, there were concerns expressed by members of the traditional elite at the inability of the aristocracy to empathize with the common people. For discussion on relations between the traditional elite and the aristocracy, see J. de V. Allen, *The Malayan Union*, New Haven, CT: Yale University Press, 1967; A. Stockwell, *British Policy and Malay Politics during the Malayan Union Experiment, 1942–1948*, Kuala Lumpur: MBRAS, 1979; T.N. Harper, *The End of Empire and the Making of Malaya*, Kuala Lumpur: Oxford University Press, 1999.

67 This point has been suggested in Rustam Sani, 'Tradisi Intelektual Melayu dan Pembentukan Bangsa Malaysia: Berberapa Persoalan Sosial' in Ahmat Adam, Kassim Ahmad and Rustam Sani, *Intelektualisme Melayu: Satu Polemik*, Bangi: Faculty of Social Sciences and Humanities, 1989, pp. 73–105; C.W. Watson, 'The Construction of the Post-colonial Subject in Malaysia' in S. Tonnesson and H. Antlov (eds), *Asian Forms of the Nation*, Richmond, UK: Curzon, 1996, pp. 306–322. Alternative interpretations are found in Kassim Ahmad, *Characterization in Hikayat Hang Tuah*, Kuala Lumpur: Dewan Bahasa dan Pustaka, 1955, and D. Nonini, *British Colonial Rule and the Resistance of the Malay Peasantry, 1900–1957*, New Haven, CT: Yale University Press, 1992.

68 Soenarno, 'Malay Nationalism', 9.

69 There is hence some resonance between the traditional elite's view of radical nationalism in Malaya and the views of their counterparts in Sumatra to Indonesian nationalism. As far as the Javanese were concerned, this 'traditional world' had long been destroyed by Dutch colonialism.

70 Soenarno, 'Malay Nationalism', 22.

71 See Mohd Aris Othman, 'The Sultanate as the Basis for Malay Political and Cultural Identity from a Historical Perspective', *Sari*, 1(2), July 1983.

72 K. von Vorys, *Democracy without Consensus: Communalism and Political Stability in Malaysia*, Kuala Lumpur: Oxford University Press, 1976, p. 15.

73 For an incisive discussion on the Malay political identity, see C. Kessler, 'Archaism and Modernity: Contemporary Malay Political Culture' in J. Kahn and F.K.W. Loh (eds), *Fragmented Vision: Culture and Politics in Contemporary Malaysia*, Honolulu: University of Hawaii Press, 1992.

74 J. Ongkili, *Nation-Building in Malaysia, 1946–1974*, Singapore: Oxford University Press, 1985, pp. 46–47.

75 A.C. Milner, 'Inventing Politics: The Case of Malaysia', *Past and Present*, 132, 1991, 109.

76 B.K. Cheah, 'The Erosion of Ideological Hegemony and Royal Power and the Rise of Postwar Malay Nationalism, 1945–46', *Journal of Southeast Asian Studies*, 19(1), March 1988, 3.

77 Detailed analysis of the Malayan Union scheme have been provided by Stockwell, *British Policy and Malay Politics*; A. Lau, *The Malayan Union Controversy, 1942–1948*, Singapore: Oxford University Press, 1990; Noordin Sopiee, *From Malayan Union to Singapore Separation: Political Unification in the Malaysia Region, 1945–1965*, Kuala Lumpur: Universiti Malaya, 1974. Stockwell provides a study of the British policy and its shortcomings, Lau discusses the theme of balance between the rights and demands of the various ethnic groups, while Noordin presents the Malay side of the argument.

78 This consideration was made specifically in response to ethnic Chinese pressure for recognition of Chinese wartime resistance against the Japanese, an effort Britain felt obliged to recognize and reward.

79 Two caveats are in order here. First, the support of the mainstream nationalists for the sultans and the concept of *kerajaan* in the wake of the Malayan Union scheme did not necessarily imply predetermined loyalty. Indeed, it must be kept in mind that UMNO's objectives were primarily the protection of the Malay race and identity, and status and interests within it; the survival of the sultanate mattered only in so far as it was an integral aspect of Malay society. This was emphasized in 'Suatu Mengenai asas Kenegaraan Melayu', *Utusan Melayu*, 16 November 1983. Second, one needs also to take stock of the fissures within UMNO itself. Here, one recognizes that UMNO was itself divided between the 'old school' conservative and aristocratic elements that assumed leadership of the party in the course of negotiations for independence, and the so-called ultras who, having thrown their weight behind UMNO, still sympathized with the philosophy of the radical Malay movement in that they were critical of the conservative leadership who in their view were not articulating the political and economic interests of the majority of the Malay population. One particular trait they shared with members of the radical Malay movement was their sentiments towards Indonesia. For example, it was known that some such as Jaafar Albar, Syed Nasir, Ghafar Baba, and Abdul Aziz Ishak, were less critical of Indonesia than the old-school aristocrats of UMNO.

80 See Leo Suryadinata, 'Indonesian Nationalism and the Pre-war Youth Movement: A Re-examination', *Journal of Southeast Asian Studies*, 9(1), March 1978.

81 A prominent Malaysian historian highlighted to the author that conservative Malay leaders such as Onn Jaafar saw the Indonesian struggle as a Javanese, not Indonesian, struggle. Interview with Cheah Boon Kheng, Penang, 17 September 2002.

82 Document H 2/1-264, FCO 24/243, PRO.

83 A.C. Milner, *The Invention of Politics in Colonial Malaya*, Cambridge: Cambridge University Press, 1995, p. 282.

84 It should be noteworthy that the first president of the MNP, Moktar U'd-din, was Javanese, and the MNP had some 60,000 members who were reportedly Indonesian.
85 See WAH-2-57, 'Challenges to Central Government in Indonesia', *American Universities Field Staff Report*, Southeast Asia Series, 5(2), 28 February 1957.
86 WAH-5-56, 'Indonesia and the New Malayan States', *American Universities Field Staff Report, Southeast Asia Series*, 4(2), 20 February 1956.
87 'Angkatan Perang Ratu Adil, 1950', A4357/265, NAA.
88 WAH-5-56, 'Indonesia and the New Malay States'.
89 Telegram 159 from Commissioner General (Southeast Asia), Singapore to British Embassy, Jakarta, 13 August 1951, FO 371/92486, PRO.
90 See CO 537/1529, no. 11, 25 May 1946, quoted in A. Stockwell, *Malaya: Part I of the Malayan Union Experiment, 1942–1948*, London: HMSO, 1995, pp. 236–239.
91 G. Poulgrain, *The Genesis of Konfrontasi: Malaysia, Brunei, Indonesia, 1945–1965*, Bathurst, NSW: Crawford House Publishing, 1998, pp. 31–32.
92 CO 537/1581, nos. 14, 15 and 16, 31 May to 22 June 1946, quoted in Poulgrain, *Genesis of Konfrontasi*, pp. 245–246.
93 UMNO file SG. 96/146, Akrib Negara Malaysia.
94 Indeed, the renowned Malay poet Usman Awang once noted that 'Sukarno was our leader as much as Indonesia's. I never missed listening to his speeches.'
95 Critchley to Tange, 29 November 1957, A1838 3006/4/7 Part 1, NAA.
96 Critchley to Tange, 22 November 1957, ibid.
97 'The Malay Dream Remains as Elusive as Ever', *Far Eastern Economic Review*, 18 April 1985.
98 Department of Information, Malaysia, *Let the World Judge: Speeches of the Malaysian Chief Delegate to the Security Council, Dato Dr. Ismail bin Abdul Rahman, on 9th and 10th September 1964*, Kuala Lumpur: Department of Information, Malaysia, 1964, p. 4.
99 *Malaya Tribune*, 11 August 1948.
100 This was related in Said Zahari, *Dark Clouds at Dawn: A Political Memoir*, Kuala Lumpur: Insan, 2001, p. 161.
101 *Utusan Melayu*, 2 June 1955.
102 See Firdaus, *The Origins and Early Development*, pp. 12–13.
103 Roeslan Abdulgani, *Indonesia dan Percaturan Politik Internasional*, Surabaya: Yayasan Keluarga Bhakti, 1993, pp. 198–199.
104 Reid, *Blood of the People*, chap. 3; M. van Langenberg, 'Class and Ethnic Conflict in Indonesia's Decolonization Process: A Study of East Sumatra', *Indonesia*, 33, April 1982. Of course, in the eyes of these traditional elites outside Java, the new Indonesian state was in fact a Javanese-conceived entity, and constructed to sustain Javanese dominance.
105 See Curtis, 'Malaysia and Indonesia', 12–14; Ariffin Omar, *Revolusi Indonesia dan Bangsa Melayu: Runtuhnya Kerajaan-Kerajaan Melayu Sumatera Timur Pada Tahun 1946*, Pulau Pinang: Penerbit Universiti Sains Malaysia, 1999. For an alternative view of how traditional Indonesian royalty 'transformed' its own shape and character, see P. Carey, 'Yogjakarta: From Sultanate to Revolutionary Capital of Indonesia – the Politics of Cultural Survival', *Indonesia Chronicle*, 39, March 1986.
106 Abdul Rahman Putra, *Political Awakening*, Petaling Jaya: Pelanduk Publication, 1986, pp. 207–208. The Tunku himself was closely related to the Sultan of Langkat.
107 These terms were used in various classified documents by the traditional Malay leadership to describe their colonial experience in comparison to Indonesia.

108 CO 537/2177, 23 January 1948, in Stockwell, *Malaya*, p. 374.
109 The contradictions that confront the Malay socialists on this front are addressed in Muhammad Ikmal Said, 'Ethnic Perspectives of the Left in Malaya' in Kahn and Loh (eds), *Fragmented Vision*, pp. 277–278.
110 See Burhanuddin Al-Helmy, *Asas Falsafah Kebangsaan Melayu*, Bukit Merta-jam: Pustaka Semenanjung, 1954; See also Ariffin, *Bangsa Melayu*, pp. 191–199. Ariffin asserts that 'although Burhanuddin claimed that his concepts of *Bangsa* and *Kebangsaan Melayu* were not racial, they were nevertheless exclusive'.
111 Yamin had argued for the formation of such a confederation of the 'Three M's' – Melaka, Mataram (an ancient Javanese kingdom), and Malolos (Philippines), nations which he viewed as originating from a common stock and possessing identical culture. See A. Brackman, *Southeast Asia's Second Front*, London: Pall Mall, 1966, p. 318.
112 This comes across clearly in the speeches of Sukarno cited earlier, as well as in the works of the Indonesian Nationalist ideologue Yamin. See Muhammad Yamin, *Naskah Persiapan Undang-Undang Dasar 1945*, Jakarta: Siguntang, 1959, pp. 127–135.
113 Statement by Muhammad Yamin at the meeting of the BPKI in Badan Pen-jelidek Usaha Persiapan Kemerdekaan Indonesia, *The Territory of the Indonesian State*, Jakarta: Badan Penjelidek Usaha Persiapan Kemerdekaan Indonesia, 31 May 1945, p. 6.
114 This is interesting for the fact that Yamin, the chief ideologue and progenitor of pan-Indonesia based on a revival of Majapahit, was a Sumatran.
115 For the relatively lesser degree of significance placed on pan-idealism on the part of Indonesian nationalists, see Abdul Rahman Ismail, 'Takkan Melayu Hilang di Dunia: Suatu Sorotan Tentang Nasionalisme Melayu' in R. Sunthar-alingam and Abdul Rahman Ismail (eds), *Nasionalisme: Satu Tinauan Sejarah*, Petaling Jaya: Fajar Bakti, 1985.

4 Ties that divide, 1949–1965

1 M. Leifer, *Indonesia's Foreign Policy*, London: Allen & Unwin, 1983, p. xiv.
2 F. Bunnell, 'Guided Democracy Foreign Policy: 1960–1965', *Indonesia*, 11, October 1966, 37–76; see also G.M. Kahin, *Nationalism and Revolution in Indonesia*, Ithaca, NY: Cornell University Press, 1952, pp. 253–270.
3 F. Weinstein, *Indonesian Foreign Policy and the Dilemma of Dependence*, Ithaca, NY: Cornell University Press, 1976, pp. 166–171; Mohammad Hatta, 'One Indonesian View of Malaysia', *Asian Survey*, 5, March 1965, 139.
4 M. Ott, 'The Sources and Content of Malaysian Foreign Policy towards Indonesia and the Philippines', doctoral dissertation, Johns Hopkins University, 1971, p. 11.
5 'Relations between Malaya and Indonesia', A1838 3006/4/7 Part 2, NAA.
6 R.O. Tilman, 'Malaysia Foreign Policy: The Dilemmas of a Committed Neutral' in J.D. Montgomery and A.D. Hirschman (eds), *Public Policy*, Cambridge, MA: Harvard University Press, 1969, pp. 115–159.
7 The Tunku's address to Parliament, 5 December 1962, 39/87/2, DO 169/74, PRO.
8 This despite former Malaysian Foreign Minister Ghazali Shafie's insistence that in emphasizing relations with Britain and the Commonwealth, Malaya was not compromising on sovereignty nor subservient to British interests. See Ghazali Shafie, address delivered at Tunku Abdul Rahman Hall, Kuala Lumpur, 26 January 1960.
9 Australia and New Zealand subsequently signed up to participate in this security agreement in April 1959.

10 Of course, the Abdul Rahman government's pro-West policy expressed through AMDA was not without its critics at home. In particular, UMNO backbenchers and the opposition parties were vocal in their criticisms that the security pact compromised Malayan sovereignty. See Malaya Legislative Council, *2nd Debates*, vol. 3, *1957–58*, Kuala Lumpur: Government Printers, 1959, pp. 67–69.

11 Draft report titled 'Participation in SEATO Activities by Commonwealth Forces based in the Federation of Malaya', 28 May 1959, DO 35/9957, PRO.

12 Telegram 1306 from British High Commission, Kuala Lumpur, to Commonwealth Relations Office, London, 2 August 1965, DO 169/397, PRO.

13 Record of conversation between the Commonwealth Secretary and the Prime Minister of Malaya in London on 18 October 1960, DO 169/170, PRO.

14 Inward Telegram 32 from British High Commission, Kuala Lumpur, to Commonwealth Relations Office, London, 21 February 1958, DO 35/9957, PRO.

15 See 'Why Malaya Does Not Intend to Join SEATO', *Straits Budget*, 14 January 1959.

16 Australia High Commission Cable 2274, 14 August 1964, A1838 2498/11 Part 2, NAA.

17 See JP(59) 66(A), 28 May 1959, DO 35/9957, PRO.

18 Report entitled 'Federation of Malaya: Review of Events since Independence', CRO Reference MAL 30/11, DO 35/9957, PRO.

19 Foreign Office, London, Southeast Asia (General) File D 10362/11, December 1958, DO 35/9951, PRO.

20 Correspondence between British Embassy, Jakarta, and Southeast Asia Department, Foreign Office, London, 22 May 1959, DO 35/9913, PRO.

21 'Malaysia's Search for Identity', *Far Eastern Economic Review*, 13 February 1964.

22 Ibid.

23 See Commonwealth Relations Office Report, 28 April 1959, DO 35/9951, PRO.

24 Critchley to Casey, 7 November 1957, A1838 3006/4/7 Part 1, NAA.

25 See Department of Information, Malaysia, *Malaya–Indonesia Relations, 31 August 1957 to 15 September 1963*, Kuala Lumpur: Department of Information, 1963, p. 1.

26 McIntyre to Tange, 2 October 1957, A1838 3006/4/7 Part 1, NAA.

27 Interview with former Malaysian Ambassador, Kuala Lumpur, 14 August 2001.

28 Critchley to Casey, 30 April 1959, A1838 3006/4/7 Part 2, NAA.

29 'Beginning at Bangkok', *Straits Times*, 4 August 1961.

30 'Malaya: The Indonesia Issue', *Far Eastern Economic Review*, 9 March 1961.

31 McIntyre to Quinn, 8 March 1959, A1838 3006/4/7 Part 2, NAA.

32 Secretary of State, Prime Minister's Office, London, to Tunku Abdul Rahman, 23 January 1961, DO 35/9951, PRO.

33 'Malaysia's Search for Identity', *Far Eastern Economic Review*, 13 February 1964.

34 Much of this smuggling, it must be noted, involved Malayans.

35 See G.M. Kahin and A. Kahin, *Subversion as Foreign Policy*, Seattle: University of Washington Press, 1995; K. Conboy and J. Morrison, *Feet to the Fire: Covert Operations in Indonesia, 1957–1958*, Annapolis, MD: Naval Institute Press, 1999; M. Jones, 'Maximum Disavowal of Aid', *English Historical Review*, 114, November 1999.

36 Memo 31/3 from the Colonial Office, 26 March 1959, DO 35/9951, PRO.

37 Inward Telegram 215 from British High Commission, Kuala Lumpur, to Commonwealth Relations Office, London, 28 May 1959, DO 35/9957, PRO.

38 Correspondence between British High Commission, Kuala Lumpur, and Commonwealth Relations Office, 28 November 1961, DO 169/74, PRO.
39 'Future Relations between Indonesia and The Federation of Malaya', Foreign Office Steering Committee Paper, Southeast Asia (General), 7 April 1959, DO 35/9951, PRO.
40 Jones, 'Maximum Disavowal of Aid', 1192.
41 Colonel Simbolon himself admitted to such activities. See Payung Bangun, *Kolonel Maludin Simbolon: Liku-liku Perjuangannya dalam Pembangunan Bangsa*, Jakarta: Sinar Harapan, 1996, p. 204.
42 See Lawrey to Tange, 21 February 1958, and Cablegram 84, Australia High Commission, Kuala Lumpur, 26 March 1958, A1838 3006/4/7 Part 1, NAA.
43 Department of Information, Malaysia, *Malaya–Indonesia Relations*, p. 5.
44 These rebels included a group of former Indonesian diplomats stationed in Europe who had defected to the PRRI during the rebellion and who requested asylum in Malaya. See ibid., pp. 5–6.
45 M. Ott, 'The Sources and Content of Malaysian Foreign Policy', p. 117.
46 By July 1958, the Indonesian government could claim that it had 'been able to learn in great detail the source and scope of outside assistance to the rebels'. 'Memorandum from Robertson to Dulles, 30 July 1958' in *Foreign Relations of the United States, 1958–1960*, vol. 17: *Indonesia*, Washington, DC: 1989, p. 252.
47 *The Problem of 'Malaysia'*, London: Embassy of the Republic of Indonesia, London, 1964, p. 1.
48 G.P.S. DINF4/58/100 (Exaffs), 15 April 1958.
49 Shanahan to Tange, 1 February 1958, A1838 3006/4/7 Part 1, NAA.
50 Critchley to Quinn, 2 April 1959, A1838 3006/4/7 Part 2, NAA. In fact, the Tunku was known to have expressed some time later the view that 'it was unfortunate that Colonel's (Simbalon) revolt against Sukarno failed' – Cablegram 465, Australia High Commission, Kuala Lumpur, 23 December 1962, A1838 3006/4/7 Part 3, NAA.
51 US National Archives, RG 59, POL 7 Malaysia, memorandum of conversation, 23 July 1964, also quoted in Jones, 'Maximum Disavowal of Aid', 1214.
52 Discussions with Michael Leifer, London, 28 September 2000.
53 Anak Agung Gde Agung, *Twenty Years Indonesian Foreign Policy, 1945–1965*, The Hague: Mouton, 1973, pp. 79–177; C. Brown, 'Indonesia's West Irian Case in the UN General Assembly', *Journal of Southeast Asian Studies*, 7(2), June 1976.
54 The most memorable example of Dutch military pressure was the dispatch of the aircraft carrier *Karel Doorman* in an exercise of gunboat diplomacy towards Indonesia.
55 For a discussion of communist support for Indonesia's West Irian cause, see WAH-14-62, 'The Irian Barat Settlement', *American Universities Field Staff Report*, Southeast Asia Series, 10(18), 15 October 1962.
56 It was after the failure of Indonesian objectives at the 1957 UN General Assembly that a series of takeovers of Dutch enterprises began. Because of the still extensive Dutch economic presence in Indonesia at the time, the policy of nationalization plunged the Indonesian economy into chaos. This point was stressed in A. Vandenbosch, 'Indonesia, the Netherlands and the New Guinea Issue', *Journal of Southeast Asian Studies*, 7(1), March 1976, 110.
57 Inward telegram, Commonwealth Relations Office, London, 20 September 1960, DO 169/70, PRO.
58 See P. Boyce, *Malaysia and Singapore in International Diplomacy*, Sydney: Sydney University Press, 1968, p. 54.
59 Document 1-1 1061/3, 28 November 1957, DO 35/9951, PRO.
60 Department of Information, Malaysia, *Malaya–Indonesia Relations*, p. 8.

61 President Sukarno was away on vacation at the time.
62 It should be noted, however, that General Nasution was initially less receptive to the Malayan government's offer to mediate. It was only after he was shown Dr Djuanda's letter of appreciation that he expressed support for the idea. Government of Malaysia, *Parliamentary Debates*, Kuala Lumpur: Dewan Rakyat, 1960–1967, p. 3419.
63 Correspondence between British High Commission, Kuala Lumpur, and Commonwealth Relations Office, London, 21 October 1960, DO 169/170, PRO.
64 Tunku's proposal was in the main rejected by Britain, Canada, Australia, and New Zealand. Inward telegram to Commonwealth Relations Office, London, from Canberra, 7 November 1960, DO 169/170, PRO.
65 'Tunku meets Dutch leaders on W. Irian', *Straits Times*, 26 November 1960.
66 Government of Malaysia, *Parliamentary Debates*, p. 3414.
67 Department of Information, Malaysia, *Malaya–Indonesia Relations*, p. 9.
68 Ibid., 9–10.
69 Correspondence between British High Commission, Kuala Lumpur, and Commonwealth Relations Office, London, 27 January 1961, DO169/171, PRO.
70 The unofficial translation of Sukarno's letter was attached to the document entitled 'A Report on the Reports of the Honourable Prime Minister in Seeking a Peaceful Solution to the Problem of Irian Barat', Ministry of External Affairs, Kuala Lumpur, 15 December 1960, DO 169/171, PRO.
71 R. Curtis, 'Malaysia and Indonesia', *New Left Review*, 28, November–December 1964, 22.
72 The Tunku had given Macmillan an assurance that he would inform Jakarta that 'trusteeship need not necessarily end in handover to Indonesia'. Abdul Rahman to Macmillan, 16 November 1960, PREM 11/4309, PRO. I found no evidence to suggest that the Tunku did in fact relay this sentiment to Jakarta.
73 Correspondence between the British High Commission, Kuala Lumpur, and Commonwealth Relations Office, London, 7 October 1960, DO 169/170, PRO.
74 Record of conversation between Commonwealth Secretary and the Prime Minister of Malaya, London, 18 October 1960, DO 169/170, PRO.
75 Telegram 2328 from British High Commission, Kuala Lumpur, to Commonwealth Relations Office, London, 19 October 1963, DO 169/159, PRO.
76 'Strengthening Mutual Understanding', *Utusan Melayu*, 4 December 1957, in A1838 3006/4/7 Part 1, NAA.
77 Critchley to Tange, 24 December 1957, ibid.
78 'Establishing Closer Relations with Indonesia', *Utusan Melayu*, 26 September 1957, ibid.
79 Horne to Tange, 13 December 1957, ibid.
80 Abdul Rahman to Macmillan, 19 October 1960, PREM 11/4309, PRO.
81 Telegram 334 from British High Commission, Kuala Lumpur, to Commonwealth Relations Office, London, 29 November 1957, FO 371/129520, PRO.
82 Telegram 42 from British Embassy, Jakarta to Foreign Office, London, 30 October 1957, ibid.
83 The fact that the Tunku took Subandrio's rebuff personally was expressed to the Secretary of State for War, John Profumo, on 12 January 1961. See correspondence between British High Commission, Kuala Lumpur, and Commonwealth Relations Office, London, 27 January 1961, DO 169/170, PRO.
84 Critchley to Menzies, 20 December 1960, A1838 3006/4/7 Part 2, NAA.
85 Correspondence between British High Commission, Kuala Lumpur, and Commonwealth Relations Office, London, 21 January 1961, DO 169/171, PRO. While the Tunku's mediation was taking place, Sukarno had dispatched

Nasution to the Soviet Union to obtain arms and equipment for the enforcement of Indonesian claims to West Irian. In response, the Malayan Federation Cabinet decided on 20 December 1960 to mobilize the defence of the Federation in the event of an outbreak of hostilities. Report of the Secretary of External Affairs, Wellington, 22 December 1960, DO 169/171, PRO.

86 Department of Information, Malaysia, *Malaysia–Indonesia Relations*, p. 15.
87 'RI Papers Blast Malaya's Silence in UN Vote', *Singapore Standard*, 25 September 1957.
88 'The Irian Issue: Why Malaya Abstained', *Straits Times*, 25 September 1957.
89 'Interview with Subandrio', *Antara News Agency*, 12 February 1963.
90 He had in fact briefly mentioned such a confederation in 1957. See 'Next Step: A Greater Federation of Malaya', *Singapore Standard*, 25 September 1957.
91 C. Adams, *Sukarno: An Autobiography*, New York: Bobbs-Merrill, 1965, p. 300.
92 See J.A.C. Mackie, *Konfrontasi: The Indonesia–Malaysia Dispute, 1963–1966*, Kuala Lumpur: Oxford University Press, 1974.
93 See A. Brackman, *Southeast Asia's Second Front: The Power Struggle in the Malay Archipelago*, Singapore: Donald Moore Press, 1966; J. Subritsky, *Confronting Sukarno; British, American, Australian, and New Zealand Diplomacy in the Malaysian–Indonesian Confrontation, 1961–1965*, New York: St Martin's Press, 1999; M. Jones, *Conflict and Confrontation in Southeast Asia, 1961–1965: Britain, the United States, and the Creation of Malaysia*, Cambridge: Cambridge University Press, 2001.
94 G. Poulgrain, *The Genesis of Konfrontasi: Malaysia, Brunei, Indonesia, 1945–1965*, Bathurst, NSW: Crawford House Publishing, 1998.
95 Indonesia's case against Malaysia was laid out in *The Problem of 'Malaysia'*.
96 For details surrounding the Brunei revolt, see Mackie, *Konfrontasi*, pp. 112–122; Poulgrain, *The Genesis*, pp. 206–230.
97 The militant nature of the rebellion, however, was directed not by Azahari but by H.M. Salleh, a former vice-president of the Party Rakyat Brunei. See Poulgrain, *The Genesis*, p. 280.
98 See correspondence between Cambridge, British Embassy, Jakarta, and White, Southeast Asia Department, Southeast Asia Department, Foreign Office, London, 30 September 1964, FCO 371/176460, PRO; See also J.D. Legge, *Sukarno: A Political Biography*, London: Allen Lane The Penguin Press, 1972, pp. 364–365.
99 These comments were expressed in a radio broadcast in December 1962, and are quoted from C. Wild and P. Carey (eds), *Born in Fire: The Indonesian Struggle for Independence*, Athens: Ohio University Press, 1986, p. xix.
100 Leifer, *Indonesia's Foreign Policy*, p. 80.
101 Interestingly, there has been speculation that it was the Philippine President, Macapagal, who first made the suggestion to Sukarno to introduce Indonesian guerrillas into Britain's Borneo possessions. See correspondence between Peters, British Embassy, Manila, and Martin, British High Commission, Kuala Lumpur, 9 December 1964, FO 371/176462, PRO.
102 Correspondence between British Embassy, Jakarta, and Southeast Asia Department, Foreign Office, 5 March 1963, DO 169/74, PRO.
103 Indonesian 'volunteer' troops landed at Pontian on 17 August, there were paratroop drops into Labis on 2 September, and there was another landing in Muar on 29 October 1964, all located in the southern peninsula. For details of Indonesian incursions, see Government of Malaysia, *Indonesian Aggression against Malaysia*, vol. 1, Kuala Lumpur: Government Press, 1965.
104 Oliver, British Embassy, Jakarta, to Cable, Foreign Office, London, 9 October 1964, FO 371/176460, PRO.

105 See C. Salleh, Jakarta Embassy telegram to Foreign Office, London, 9 October 1964; Hatta to US Embassy, Jakarta, 12 October 1964; Bottomley, British High Commission, Kuala Lumpur, to Golds, Commonwealth Relations Office, Joint Malaysia/Indonesia Department, 13 October 1964, FO 371/176460, PRO.
106 Correspondence between British Embassy, Jakarta and Foreign Office, London, 30 October 1964, FO 371/176461, PRO; Telegram 2025, British High Commission, Kuala Lumpur, to Commonwealth Relations Office, London, FO 371/176461, PRO.
107 Department of State, National Archives and Records Administration, RG-59, Central Files 1964–1966, POL 321, Indonesia–Malaysia. [online] http://www.state.gov/r/pa/ho/frus/johnsonlb/xxvi/index.cfm (accessed 17 September 2002).
108 Telegram 2646 from Foreign Office, London to British High Commission, Kuala Lumpur, 27 October 1964, FO 371/176461, PRO.
109 To the Tunku, such a plebiscite was unnecessary, as a UN team had already carried out a fact-finding poll of the leaders of the Borneo states in August 1963. Sukarno had rejected those findings on the basis that Indonesia was not given sufficient representation in the committee observing the fact-finding poll.
110 Department of External Affairs, Canberra, to Australian High Commission, Kuala Lumpur, 9 October 1964, FO 371/176460, PRO.
111 It should be worth noting that the Philippines' initial proposal for a 'greater Malayan Conference' comprising the Philippines, Malaya, Singapore, Sarawak, Brunei, and North Borneo (Sabah) was put forward by then President, Carlos Garcia, in 1959. Indonesia, tellingly, was excluded from this original conception. See 'A New Manila–Kuala Lumpur–Jakarta Axis?', *Far Eastern Economic Review*, 15 January 1959. It has also been highlighted in the previous chapter that Malaysian leaders such as Onn bin Jaafar and Tunku Abdul Rahman himself had also entertained visions of pan-Malay union at various times prior to Maphilindo.
112 Interestingly, the communiqué that arose from the Tokyo meeting had as its first paragraph a Malayan 'admission' that the Malaysia plan should have been discussed initially with Indonesia.
113 The consultation and consensus phenomenon has since entered the lexicon of the international relations of Southeast Asia as the operative principles *musyawarah* and *muafakat*. See 'Philippines: Summit Results', *Far Eastern Economic Review*, 15 August 1963.
114 See A.M. Taylor, 'Malaysia, Indonesia – and Maphilindo', *International Journal*, 19(2), Spring 1964.
115 Record of conversation between Subandrio and Shann, 2 July 1963, A1838 3006/4/7 Part 9, NAA.
116 Telegram 727 from British Embassy, Manila, to Foreign Office, London, 18 September 1963, DO 169/245, PRO.
117 Marshall, British Embassy, Bangkok, to Cable, Southeast Asia Department, Foreign Office, London, 15 February 1964, FO 371/175076, PRO.
118 Taylor, 'Malaysia, Indonesia', 160–167.
119 Jamieson to Secretary, Department of External Affairs, 2 November 1961, A1838 3006/4/7 Part 2, NAA.
120 This despite the fact that a member of the Indonesian observer team, Abdul Rahman, had publicly stated that he was 'convinced of the impartiality of the UN Team's work', *Antara News Agency*, 5 September 1963.
121 Record of conversations between General Parman and Colonel Berger, Paris, 9–13 October 1964, FO 371/176462, PRO.

122 See Bottomley to Gilchrist, 24 November 1964, FO 371/176462, PRO.
123 Correspondence between British High Commission, Kuala Lumpur, and Commonwealth Relations Office, London, 21 January 1959, DO 35/9913, PRO.
124 See Bangkok Telegram 92: Foreign Ministers Meeting in Bangkok, 7 February 1964, FO 371/175074, PRO.
125 See 'Malaysian Attitudes', *Far Eastern Economic Review*, 18 April 1963.
126 C.L.M. Penders, *The Life and Times of Sukarno*, London: Sidgwick & Jackson, 1974, pp. 176–177; J.M. Gullick, *Malaysia and Its Neighbours*, London: Routledge & Kegan Paul, 1967, p. 110.
127 Leifer, *Indonesia's Foreign Policy*, p. 75.
128 See 'Malaya Fortnightly Summary', FE 58/11/1, DO 169/74, PRO.
129 Critchley to Baswick, 9 April 1962, A1838 3006/4/7 Part 2, NAA.
130 Department of Information, Malaysia, *Malaya–Indonesia Relations*, p. 1.
131 Smithies to Jockel, 12 September 1966, A1838 3006/4/9 Part 34, NAA.
132 M. Leifer, *Indonesia and Malaysia: The Changing Face of Confrontation*, Hull: University of Hull, Centre for Southeast Asian Studies, 1966, p. 395.
133 Said Zahari, *Dark Clouds at Dawn: A Political Memoir*, Kuala Lumpur: Insan, 2001, p. 159
134 Agus Soetomo (ed.), *S. Takdir Alisjahbana, 1908–1994: Perjuangan Kebudayaan Indonesia*, Jakarta: Dian Rakyat, 1999, pp. 91–92.
135 'What Comes after Confrontation?', *Canberra Times*, 5 July 1966.
136 Critchley to Plimsoll, 2 May 1966, A2908 M120 Part 6, NAA.
137 Critchley to Jockel, 29 May 1963, A1838 3006/4/7 Part 7, NAA.
138 J. Funston, *Malay Politics in Malaysia: A Study of UMNO and PAS*, Singapore: Heinemann Educational Books, 1983, p. 54.
139 See Government of Malaysia, *A Plot Exposed*, Kuala Lumpur: Government Publishers, 1965. This published document includes the confessions of Ishak Mohamed and Raja Abu Hanifah of sedition.
140 'Quadripartite Talks: Agenda Item (B)', Department of External Affairs, Canberra, 22 June 1966, A1838 3006/4/9 Part 35, NAA.
141 See *Malay Mail*, 12 May 1965.
142 Leifer, *Indonesia and Malaysia*, pp. 404–405.

5 Re-building the 'special relationship', 1966–1980

 1 Bentley, British High Commission, Kuala Lumpur, to Reed, Commonwealth Office, London, 3 March 1967, FCO 24/243, PRO.
 2 Ghazali Shafie, *Malaysia, ASEAN and the World Order*, Bangi: Penerbit University Kebangsaan Malaysia, 2000, p. 388.
 3 And, quite conceivably, a return to pre-West Irian and PRRI/Pemesta rebellion episodes as well.
 4 Eastman to Department of External Affairs, Canberra, A1838 3006/4/9 Part 37, NAA.
 5 Bentley to Reed, 14 December 1966, DO 169/413, PRO.
 6 'KL, Jakarta Talking of Axis', *Melbourne Age*, 15 October 1966.
 7 Arawa to Hasluck, 23 May 1966, A1838 3006/4/7 Part 39, NAA.
 8 Correspondence between Australia High Commission, Kuala Lumpur and Prime Minister's Office, Canberra, 22 May 1966, A1838/4/7 Part 39, NAA.
 9 This was MABBIM, discussed in Chapter 2.
10 This arrangement built on an earlier agreement on border security signed in September 1966. See J.M. Van Der Kroef, 'The Sarawak–Indonesian Border Insurgency', *Modern Asian Studies*, 2(3), July 1968.

11 M. Leifer, *Conflict and Regional Order in South-East Asia*, London: International Institute for Strategic Studies, Adelphi Paper Series, 1980, p. 8.
12 The *Pancasila* referred to the officially sanctioned philosophical precepts upon which the Republican nationalists envisioned Indonesia to be built after independence. It enunciated five principles: nationalism, internationalism, belief in God, popular sovereignty and social justice.
13 M. Leifer, *Indonesia's Foreign Policy*, London: Allen & Unwin, 1983, p. 173.
14 Department of State, INR/EAP files: lot 90D 165, NIE 54/59-65, Washington, DC, December 16, 1965 [online] www.state.gov/r/pa/ho/frus/johnsonlb/xxvi/index.cfm (accessed 12 September 2002).
15 SWB FE/5595/A3/3, 22 August 1977, 'Malik on Indonesia's relations with Asian Countries'.
16 Leifer, *Indonesia's Foreign Policy*, pp. 111–112.
17 Department of State, INR/ERP files, lot 90 D 165, NIE55-68, Washington, DC, 31 December 1968.
18 'Indonesian Armed Services' Responsibilities in Southeast Asia', *Berita Yudha*, 23 July 1968.
19 H2/1-264, FCO 24/243, PRO.
20 Correspondence between Australian High Commission, Kuala Lumpur, and Department of External Affairs, Canberra, 7 March 1967, FCO 24/243, PRO.
21 See Cabinet Minutes, 'Discussions with the Deputy Prime Minister of Malaysia', 13 April 1967, A5840 654/FAD, NAA.
22 It was Indonesian lobbying that denied Malaysia participation at the Cairo NAM Conference and the May 1965 Afro-Asian People's Solidarity Organization Conference in Winneba, Ghana.
23 See WAH-4-64, 'The Importance of Being Afro-Asian: Malaysia Feels Pressures toward Ideology', *American Universities Field Staff Report*, Southeast Asia Series, 12(11), December 1964.
24 'Malaysia's Foreign Policy', *Siaran Akhbar*, 19 July 1966.
25 S. Nair, *Islam in Malaysia's Foreign Policy*, London: Routledge, 1997, p. 57.
26 'Tunku Gives Lecture to Indonesians', *The Times*, 9 March 1968.
27 Draft Report, A1838 3006/4/9 Part 37, NAA.
28 Murray, Commonwealth Office, London to Philips, British Embassy, Jakarta, 1 May 1968, FCO 24/243, PRO.
29 Correspondence between British High Commission, Kuala Lumpur, and Commonwealth Office, London, 26 May 1967, FCO 24/243, PRO.
30 It was particularly elements from the defence and home ministries who took this cautious approach towards Indonesia. See J.C.Y. Liow, '"Visions of *Serumpun*": Tun Abdul Razak and the Golden Years of Indo-Malay Blood Brotherhood, 1967–1975', *Southeast Asia Research*, 11(3), November 2003.
31 See 'Full Ties: A big "Yes"', *Straits Times*, 26 August 1967.
32 Correspondence between British High Commission, Kuala Lumpur, and Foreign Office, London, 15 May 1967, FCO 24/243, PRO. It was further noted at this meeting that while the Indonesian foreign ministry had looked to regard the outcome of the recently concluded Sabah elections as sufficient grounds for the restoration of ties, this was blocked by the politically powerful military.
33 Correspondence between British High Commission, Kuala Lumpur, and Commonwealth Office, London, 30 August 1967, FCO 24/243, PRO.
34 Bentley to Mason, 26 May 1967, FCO 24/243, PRO.
35 Ibid.
36 See correspondence between British Embassy, Jakarta, and Southeast Asia Department, Foreign Office, London, 30 January 1967, FCO 24/243, PRO.

37 See, for example, M. Antolik, *ASEAN and the Diplomacy of Accommodation*, London: M.E. Sharpe, 1990, p. 14.
38 Ghazali Shafie, 'Think ASEAN', *Foreign Affairs Malaysia*, 16(2), June 1983, 237.
39 See 'Malik Sends Secret Note to Razak', *Straits Times*, 5 June 1967.
40 M. Leifer, *Indonesia's Foreign Policy*, pp. 142–143.
41 Interview with former Singapore Foreign Ministry official, Singapore, 2 February 2002. The terms of the preamble were only changed when Singapore objected to this clause.
42 Interview with former Malaysian foreign ministry official, Kuala Lumpur, 7 November 2001; see also McLennan to Secretary, Department of External Affairs, Canberra, 8 March 1968, A1838 3006/4/9 Part 37, NAA.
43 Correspondence between British High Commission, Kuala Lumpur, and Commonwealth Office, London, 16 March 1968, FCO 24/243, PRO.
44 Philips, British Embassy, Jakarta, to Foreign Office, Telegram 148A, 12 March 1968, FCO 24/243, PRO. For details of this bilateral agreement, see 'Indonesia–Malaysia Joint Communiqué', 7 March 1968, FCO 24/243, PRO.
45 'Tengku's Plea to ASEAN Nations to Help Suharto', *Straits Times*, 6 March 1968.
46 See 'Rebuilding Stability in Southeast Asia', *Straits Times*, 16 March 1968.
47 Falle, British High Commission, Kuala Lumpur to Moreton, Commonwealth Office, 2 February 1968, FCO 24/243, PRO.
48 'Indonesia Reaffirms Her Defence Policy', *The Times*, 17 March 1968.
49 Sutherland, British Embassy, Jakarta, to Stewart, Foreign Office, London, 19 March 1968, FCO 24/243, PRO.
50 It is also interesting to note that Malays in Kuala Lumpur and Johor also demonstrated against the hanging of the marines. See Cable 2691, Australia High Commission, Singapore, 23 October 1968, A1838 3006/4/9 Part 38, NAA.
51 'Suharto Visit Will Set Seal on Growing Friendship', *Straits Times*, 10 March 1970.
52 'Across the Straits', *Straits Times*, 10 March 1970. The Singapore newspaper was quoting Malaysian sources.
53 '"Soek-Man Who Fought Bravely" Tribute by Tengku', *Straits Times*, 23 June 1970.
54 This has also been suggested in J. Saravanamuttu, *The Dilemma of Independence: Two Decades of Malaysia's Foreign Policy, 1957–1977*, Penang: Penerbit Universiti Sains Malaysia, 1983, pp. 126–140.
55 For background on the 13 May 1969 incident, see L. Comber, *13 May 1969: A Historical Survey of Sino-Malay Relations*, Kuala Lumpur: Heinemann Asia, 1983.
56 'Extract from KL's 1967/8 Annual Report', A1838 3006/4/9 Part 38, NAA.
57 McLennan to Secretary, Department of External Affairs, Canberra, 19 December 1968, A1838 3006/4/9 Part 38, NAA.
58 Critchley to Department of External Affairs, Canberra, 15 July 1968, A1838 3006/4/9 Part 38, NAA.
59 See Draft Paper for OPD – Proposal by Singapore Government for Major Expansion of Singapore Armed Forces, PREM 13/1833, PRO.
60 'Quadripartite Talks: Agenda Item (B)', Department of External Affairs, Canberra, 22 June 1966, A1838 3006/4/9 Part 35, NAA.
61 Cable 2493, Australian High Commission, Kuala Lumpur, 26 July 1969, A1838 3006/4/9 Part 39, NAA.
62 Jockel to Hasluck, 12 May 1966, A1838, 3006/4/7 Part 39, NAA.
63 Cable 1459, Australian High Commission, Kuala Lumpur, 31 May 1969, A1838 3006/4/9 Part 39, NAA.

64 McLennan to Secretary, Department of External Affairs, Canberra, 26 September 1969, A1838 3006/4/9 Part 39, NAA.
65 Cheah Boon Kheng suggests that Razak's assumption of power 'had all the makings of a coup'. See B.K. Cheah, *Malaysia: The Making of a Nation*, Singapore: Institute of Southeast Asian Studies, 2002, p. 130.
66 Ibid., pp. 121–150.
67 See Liow, 'Visions of *Serumpun*'.
68 'Five-Power Talks', 17 October 1967, A1838 3006/4/9 Part 37, NAA.
69 Interview with former Malaysian Ambassador, Kuala Lumpur, 14 August 2001.
70 W. Shaw, *Tun Razak: His Life and Times*, London: Longman, 1976, pp. 75–79. He was also a close friend of Des Alwi, the adopted son of the former Indonesian Prime Minister Sutan Sjahrir, and who was implicated in the PRRI rebellion.
71 'Indonesia's Major Role in Region', *Straits Times*, 27 August 1966.
72 Interview with former Malaysian government official, Kuala Lumpur, 7 November 2001; interview with former Malaysian foreign ministry official, Kuala Lumpur, 8 November 2001.
73 Interview with former Malaysian foreign ministry official, Penang, 16 September 2002.
74 SWB FE/4802/A3/9 13 January 1975, 'Malaysia's Defence Policy'.
75 Since 13 May, Razak had been under intense pressure from his domestic political constituency, and in particular the Malay ultras. In order to defray some of the pressure from this group, he looked to steer Malaysian foreign policy away from the overtly pro-Western inclination that characterized the Tunku's administration. See Dunn to Sullivan, 1 July 1970, FCO 24/817, PRO.
76 Interview with Tan Sri Zainal Sulong, Kuala Lumpur, 14 August 2001.
77 Ibid.
78 Ibid.
79 Interview with former Malaysian government official, Kuala Lumpur, 7 November 2001.
80 See 'Malacca Straits: For Malaysia and Indonesia, A Family Affair', *Far Eastern Economic Review*, 15 April 1972.
81 B.A. Hamzah suggests the possibility that the declaration might actually have been an extension of the 1945 Indonesian Constitution. See B.A. Hamzah (ed.), *Malaysia and Law of the Sea*, Kuala Lumpur: Heng Lee Stationery and Printing Co., 1983, p. 4. However, Michael Leifer contends otherwise. See M. Leifer, *Malacca, Singapore, and Indonesia*, Alphen an den Rijn, Netherlands: Sijthoff & Noordhoff, 1978, pp. 17–24.
82 Dino Djalal, *The Geopolitics of Indonesia's Maritime Territorial Policy*, Jakarta: Center for Strategic and International Studies, 1996, pp. 34–42.
83 Ibid., p. 65.
84 Mochtar Kusumaatmadja, 'The Concept of the Indonesian Archipelago', *Indonesian Quarterly*, 10(4), 1982, 23.
85 *Sinar Harapan*, 30 October 1974.
86 The particular impetus provided by Indonesia's fear of foreign involvement and aggravation of regional dissent is emphasized in Mochtar Kusumaatmadja, 'The Legal Regime of Archipelagoes: Problems and Issues' in L.M. Alexander (ed.), *The Law of the Sea: Needs and Interests of Developing Countries*, Kingston: University of Rhode Island Press, 1973.
87 Leifer, *Malacca, Singapore, and Indonesia*, p. 27. Palembang was the capital of the Srivijayan kingdom.
88 Since the signing of the Safety Navigation agreement in 1971 between

Indonesia, Malaysia, and Singapore, the Melaka and Singapore straits have
become regarded as a single strait.

89 K.E. Shaw (ed.), *The Straits of Malacca: in Relation to the Problems of the
Indian and Pacific Oceans*, Singapore: University Education Press, 1979, p. 44.

90 See Leifer, *Malacca, Singapore, and Indonesia*, chap. 1 for a background to
Indonesia's early diplomatic initiatives pertaining to their declaration of the
archipelago principle.

91 Exchange of Letter concerning Succession to Rights and Obligations arising
from International Instruments, September 12, 1957, in International Law
Association, *The Effect of Independence on Treaties: A Handbook Prepared
by the Committee on State Succession to Treaties and Other Governmental
Obligations*, London: International Law Association, 1965, appendix to chap.
9. Also quoted in K.E. Shaw, 'The Juridical Status of the Malacca Straits and
its Relation to Indonesia and Malaysia' in Shaw (ed.), *The Straits of Malacca*,
p. 34. This clause was later incorporated into Article 169 of the Constitution of
Malaysia.

92 D.P. O'Connell, *State Succession in Municipal and International Law*, vol. 2,
Cambridge: Cambridge University Press, 1967, pp. 364–365.

93 Shaw, 'The Juridical Status', pp. 2–3.

94 That said, it needs to be recognized that at no time during *Konfrontasi* did the
Indonesian government make any territorial claim against Malaysia.

95 Bennett to Elliott, 14 March 1972, FCO 24/1283, PRO.

96 Leifer, *Malacca, Singapore, and Indonesia*, p. 30. It should be noted here that
the Bill passed on 2 August 1969 through an emergency ordinance. No vote
was taken because of the suspension of parliament after the 13 May 1969 race
riots in Malaysia.

97 The full text of the document is titled 'Indonesia–Malaysia: Agreement
between the Government of the Republic of Indonesia and the Government
of Malaysia Relating to the Delimitation of the Continental Shelves between
the Two Countries', and can be found in Hamzah, *Malaysia and Law of the
Sea*, pp. 295–296.

98 See Finlayson, British High Commission, Singapore, to Foreign Commonwealth Office, London, Telegram 290, 17 March 1972, FCO 24/1283, PRO.

99 Middleton to Campbell, 12 December 1972, FCO 24/1284, PRO.

100 See 'The Malacca and Singapore Straits', Research Study, Bureau of Intelligence and Research, Department of State, USA, 11 May 1972, FCO 24/1284,
PRO.

101 See Hashim Djalal, *Perjuangan Indonesia di Bidang Hukum Laut*, Bandung:
Percetakan Ekonomi, 1979. This point was also stressed in B.A. Hamzah,
'Indonesia's Archipelagic Regime: Implications for Malaysia', *Marine Policy*,
January 1984.

102 Leifer, *Malacca, Singapore, and Indonesia*, p. 157.

103 Interview with Malaysian foreign ministry official, Kuala Lumpur, 1 November 2001.

104 Taken from C. Jeshurun, *Malaysian Defence Policy: A Study in Parliamentary
Attitudes, 1963–1973*, Kuala Lumpur: Penerbit University Malaya, 1980,
p. 120.

105 H. Hanggi, *ASEAN and the ZOPFAN Concept*, Singapore: Institute of Southeast Asian Studies, 1991, p. 13.

106 D. Wilson, *The Neutralization of Southeast Asia*, New York: Praeger, 1975,
pp. 8–9.

107 Cable 253, Australian High Commission, Kuala Lumpur, 2 February 1968,
A1838 3006/4/9 Part 37, NAA.

108 The expansion of the Ismail peace plan into a detailed prescription for

regional order is expounded in Ghazali Shafie, 'The Neutralization of Southeast Asia', *Pacific Community*, 3(1), October 1971.
109 Ibid.
110 See 'The Process of Neutralization of Southeast Asia Needs a Long Time', *Kompas*, 22 December 1970.
111 'Declaration on Neutralization', *Indonesia Raya*, 30 November 1971.
112 'Towards an Asian Asia', *Far Eastern Economic Review*, 25 September 1971.
113 Leifer, *Indonesia's Foreign Policy*, pp. 148–149.
114 China was in fact the only external power that voiced support for the ZOPFAN proposal.
115 Wilford to Tomlinson, 19 March 1971, FCO 24/1164, PRO.
116 See 'Razak–Suharto Summit Talks of Vital Significance: Indonesian Press', *Straits Times*, 18 December 1970; '"Family" Talks, Then Malik Flies Home', *Straits Times*, 18 July 1971.
117 Hanggi, *ASEAN*, pp. 19–20.
118 Malaysia, Jabatan Penerangan, *Siaran Akhbar*, 1975, quoted in J. Saravanamuttu, 'Malaysia's Foreign Policy, 1957–1980' in Zakaria Ahmad (ed.), *Government and Politics in Malaysia*, Singapore: Oxford University Press, 1987, p. 142.
119 Hanggi, *ASEAN*, p. 18.
120 Dewi Fortuna Anwar, *Indonesia in ASEAN: Foreign Policy and Regionalism*, New York: St Martin's Press, 1994, p. 177.
121 See M. Alagappa, *Towards a Nuclear Weapons-Free Zone in Southeast Asia*, Kuala Lumpur: Institute of Strategic and International Studies, 1987.
122 See WAH-7-73, 'Nationalizing the Straits of Malacca', *American Universities Field Staff Report*, Southeast Asia Series, 21(8), July 1973.
123 See 'Malaysia Accepts Indonesian Action', *Straits Times*, 14 December 1975.
124 SWB FE/5040/I, 23 October 1975, 'Malaysian Prime Minister on Future of East Timor'.
125 Interview with former Malaysian foreign ministry official, Kuala Lumpur, 8 November 2001.
126 SWB FE/5061/A3/13, 19 November 1975, 'The Razak–Suharto Talks'.
127 For a study of Malaysia–China relations during this period, see R.K. Jain, *China and Malaysia, 1949–1983*, New Delhi: Radiant Publishers, 1984.
128 See S. Leong, 'Malaysia and the People's Republic of China in the 1980s: Political Vigilance and Economic Pragmatism', *Asian Survey*, 27(10), October 1987.
129 Interview with former Malaysian foreign ministry official, Singapore, 21 August 2000.
130 Interview with former Malaysian government official, Kuala Lumpur, 8 November 2001.
131 Middleton to Slatcher, 13 November 1972, FCO 24/1445, PRO.
132 *Antara Daily News Bulletin*, 7 December 1971; See also 'Foreign Minister Adam Malik: Indonesia Has No Objections if ASEAN Members Open Relations with China', *Suara Karya*, 8 December 1972.
133 This point was reiterated by key architects of Malaysia's China policy of the time in the author's interviews with them, and was confirmed on the Indonesian side during an interview with a former Indonesian foreign ministry official, Jakarta, 21 January 2002.
134 See SWB FE5969/A3/7, 15 November 1978, 'Indonesia Regrets Teng's Remarks on Insurgents in Southeast Asia'; SWB FE/5969/A3/2, 15 November 1978, 'Malaysia's foreign policy and Teng Hsiao-ping's visit'.
135 SWB FE/5118/A3/4, 27 January 1976, 'Malaysia to continue Razak's policies'.
136 It is true that in fact Hussein Onn had visited Bangkok prior to making his trip

to Jakarta. This, however, was in fulfilment of a promise made by Razak prior to his death that he would make an official visit to Thailand. Upon Razak's death, Hussein Onn took the initiative to fulfil this promise.

137 SWB FE/5122/A3/2, 3 February 1976, 'The Malaysian Prime Minister's Visit to Indonesia'.
138 SWB FE/5816/A3/6, 18 May 1978, 'Malaysian Armed Forces to Train in Indonesia'.
139 SWB FE/5581/A3/9, 5 August 1977, 'Indonesian Support for Malaysia's Proposed 200-mile Limit'.
140 SWB FE/5821/A3/2, 34 May 1978, 'Malaysian Radio on Hussein–Suharto Talks'.
141 SWB FE/6803/A3/5 17 August 1981, 'Malaysian Prime Minister Concludes Indonesian Visit'.
142 'Arms: KL-Jakarta Decision Is to Avoid Duplication', *Straits Times*, 13 December 1976.
143 Michael Leifer, *ASEAN and the Security of Southeast Asia*, London: Routledge, 1989, p. 54.
144 Leifer, *Indonesia's Foreign Policy*, p. 161.
145 SWB FE/4878/A3/10, 15 April 1975, 'Impact of Indo-China Events in Malaysia: Indonesian views'.
146 SWB FE/5945/A3/3, 18 October 1975, 'Indonesian Foreign Minister on Relations with China'.
147 'Hussein to Meet Suharto for Talks on Indochina War', *Straits Times*, 4 March 1979.
148 In fact, Malaysian leaders had already been sharing the concerns of their Indonesian counterparts in 1978. See SWB FE/5969/A3/7, 15 November 1978, 'Malaysia's Foreign Policy and Teng Hsiao-ping's Visit'.
149 The Malaysian Foreign Minister, Tengku Ahmad Rithaudeen, and the Indonesian envoy, General Benni Murdani, were dispatched at different times earlier that year to open discussions with Hanoi.
150 'The Kuantan Principle', *Far Eastern Economic Review*, 4–10 April 1980.
151 S. Chee, 'Malaysia and Singapore: Separate Identities, Different Priorities', *Asian Survey*, 13(2), February 1973, 157.
152 Record of conversation between Eastman and Sulong, Kuala Lumpur, 23 September 1967, A1838 3006/4/9 Part 37, NAA.
153 *Utusan Melayu*, 18 September 1979. This comment was made on the occasion of the Tenth Malaysia–Indonesia General Border Committee meeting in Jakarta.
154 See Ghazali Shafie, paper presented at the Second Malindo Dialogue, Bogor, Indonesia, January 1990.

6 The Indonesia–Malaysia 'prestige dilemma', 1981–2000

1 Interview with former Malaysian foreign ministry official, Kuala Lumpur, 7 November 2001.
2 Interview with former Singapore foreign ministry official, Singapore, 2 February, 2001.
3 Interview with former Malaysian foreign ministry official, Kuala Lumpur, 7 November 2001.
4 'Hubungan Malaysia–Indonesia Perlukan Dimensi Baru', *Utusan Malaysia*, 5 September 1989.
5 'Behind the Suharto, Mahathir Meeting', *Straits Times*, 25 June 1988.
6 Ibid.
7 See, for example, M. Pathmanathan and D. Lazarus (eds), *Winds of Change:*

The Mahathir Impact on Malaysia's Foreign Policy, Kuala Lumpur: Eastview
Productions, 1984; J. Saravanamuttu, 'Malaysia's Foreign Policy in the
Mahathir Period, 1981–1995: An Iconoclast Come to Rule', *Asian Journal of
Political Science*, 4(1), June 1996; B.T. Khoo, *Paradoxes of Mahathirism*,
Kuala Lumpur: Oxford University Press, 1995, pp. 74–81.

8 C. Kessler, 'Malaysia and Mahathir: Region Builder or Barrier Builder?', *The
Asia–Australia Papers*, 1, April 1999, 24.

9 For a detailed analysis of how Malaysia's foreign policy towards the Islamic
world has been driven by domestic political exigencies, see S. Nair, *Islam in
Malaysian Foreign Policy*, London: Routledge, 1995.

10 M. Vatikiotis, 'Indonesia's Foreign Policy in the 1990s', *Contemporary Southeast Asia*, 14(4), March 1993, 357.

11 Dewi Fortuna Anwar, *Indonesia in ASEAN: Foreign Policy and Regionalism*,
New York: St Martin's Press, 1994, p. 284.

12 Vatikiotis, 'Indonesia's Foreign Policy', 357.

13 M. Leifer, *Indonesia's Foreign Policy*, London: Allen & Unwin, 1983, p. 173.

14 See, for example, H. McMichael, *Indonesia's Foreign Policy: Towards a New
Assertive Style*, Nathan, Queensland: Griffiths University, Centre for the
Study of Australia–Asia Relations, 1987.

15 'RI Urged to Take Assertive Lead in SEA', *Jakarta Post*, 31 August 1992.

16 Interview with former Indonesian foreign ministry official, Jakarta, 24 January
2002.

17 'Indonesia's New Approach to Vietnam Shows Higher Profile on Foreign
Policy', *Far Eastern Economic Review*, 3 July 1984.

18 See G. Hein, 'Suharto's Foreign Policy: Second Generation Nationalism in
Indonesia', Ph.D. dissertation, University of California-Berkeley, California,
1986.

19 J.C.Y. Liow, 'Mahathir's Foreign Policy' in J. Chin and K.L. Ho (eds), *The
Mahathir Administration: Performance and Governance*, Singapore: Times
Academic Press, 2001.

20 Saravanamuttu, 'Malaysia's Foreign Policy', 6.

21 'Jakarta–KL Relations Lukewarm under Mahathir', *Jakarta Post*, 19 March
1991.

22 Interview with former Indonesian foreign ministry official, Jakarta, 24 January
2002.

23 See 'Indonesia' in *Asia 1993: Yearbook*, Hong Kong: Far Eastern Economic
Review, 1993, p. 133.

24 'The NAM Summit: Reason and Rhetoric', *Far Eastern Economic Review*,
17 September 1992.

25 Interview with former Indonesian foreign ministry official, Jakarta, 23 January
2002.

26 There was certainly a sense that Malaysia was out to make Indonesia 'look
bad'.

27 Kessler, 'Malaysia and Mahathir', 24–25.

28 Interview with former Indonesian presidential adviser, Jakarta, 18 January
2002.

29 Dino Djalal, 'Indonesia and Preventive Diplomacy: A Study of the Workshops on Managing Potential Conflicts in the South China Sea', doctoral dissertation, London School of Economics, 2000, pp. 190–196.

30 In my capacity as a participant in some of these Track-Two Conferences, I
have on several occasions personally witnessed the public disagreement
between Malaysian and Indonesian representatives over this matter.

31 Djalal, 'Indonesia and Preventive Diplomacy', p. 191.

32 Abdullah Zawawi, speech entitled 'Malaysia and Indonesia Bilateral Relations'

delivered at Second Malaysia–Indonesia Conference, Penang, 11–14 December 1990.

33 Firdaus Abdullah, 'The Rumpun Concept in Malaysia–Indonesia Relations', *Indonesian Quarterly*, 21(2), 1993, 147.

34 Benny Moerdani, speech entitled 'Kerjasama, Masalah, dan Tantangan' delivered at Dialog Pemuda Indonesia–Malaysia II, Bogor, 17–19 January 1990.

35 See Mochtar Kusumaatmadja, 'Some Thoughts on ASEAN Security Cooperation: An Indonesian Perspective', *Contemporary Southeast Asia*, 12(3), 1990.

36 'Bilateral Defence Pact Better, Says Armed Forces Chief', *Straits Times*, 8 March 1992.

37 See B. Singh, 'Singapore, Malaysia and Indonesia Triangular Defence Pact: Potentials and Perils', *Asian Defence Journal*, December 1990.

38 See *Utusan Malaysia*, 10 February 1990.

39 Soenarno Djajoesman, speech entitled 'Malaysia and Indonesia Bilateral Relations' delivered at Second Malaysia–Indonesia Conference, Penang, 11–14 December 1990.

40 See J.C.Y. Liow, 'Malaysia's Illegal Indonesian Migrant Labour Problem: In Search of Solutions', *Contemporary Southeast Asia*, 25(1), April 2003.

41 Mahathir Mohamad, speech presented at state banquet for the visiting Chinese Prime Minister Li Peng, Kuala Lumpur, 10 December 1990.

42 'PM Calls for Asia Pacific Trade Bloc', *New Straits Times*, 11 December 1990.

43 See L. Low, 'The East Asian Economic Grouping', *Pacific Review*, 4(4), 1991.

44 This was mentioned in Saravanamuttu, 'Malaysia's Foreign Policy', 5.

45 'PM: We'll Understand if EAEG's Not Endorsed', *The Star*, 8 October 1991.

46 SWB FE/0989/A3/4, 6 February 1991, 'All ASEAN countries endorse new economic grouping'; 'ASEAN to hold more talks on KL's trade group plan', *Straits Times*, 18 March 1991.

47 See Mahathir Mohamad, speech delivered at 'ASEAN Countries and the World Economy: Challenge and Change' Conference, Bali, Indonesia, 5 March 1991.

48 'Indonesia Warns against Setting Up Asian trade bloc', *Reuters News*, 3 March 1991.

49 Both opinions were expressed at the 'ASEAN Countries and the World Economy: Challenge and Change' Conference, Bali, Indonesia, 5 March 1991.

50 'Indonesia to Present New Ideas on EAEC, Alatas says', *Japan Economic Newswire*, 22 January 1992.

51 'Crux of the Matter: Major Leaders Differ on Style, Agenda', *Far Eastern Economic Review*, 16 January 1992.

52 'ASEAN Commitment on Free Trade Area', *South China Morning Post*, 29 January 1992.

53 It is well known that Malaysia had not been supportive of APEC at the time. Kuala Lumpur viewed the organization as a manifestation of Western interests, and suspected that the interests of the smaller states of ASEAN would be compromised.

54 A fundamental difference between the two episodes, though, was that in the case of the EAEC, Malaysian concessions did not extend beyond a superficial change in nomenclature. Unlike the case of ZOPFAN, which was a clearer case of Malaysian deference, Kuala Lumpur's objectives for the EAEC remained intact.

55 See *Jakarta Post*, 5 March 1991.

56 See Hadi Soesastro, *The EAEG Proposal and East Asian Concepts of the Pacific Basin*, Jakarta: Center for Strategic and International Studies, 1991.

57 'Stormy Weather: Tension behind the Smiles at Mahathir–Suharto talks', *Far Eastern Economic Review*, 29 July 1993.

58 'Indonesia's Role as Big Brother', *The Star*, 25 January 1992; 'Indonesia Rocks the ASEAN Boat', *Business Times Malaysia*, 28 January 1992.
59 'Islands Dispute an Urgent Matter for KL, Jakarta', *Straits Times*, 2 March 1992.
60 G. Irwin, *Nineteenth Century Borneo: A Study in Diplomatic Rivalry*, Singapore: Donald Moore, 1955, pp. 153–154.
61 See 'Malaysia–Indonesia Bentuk Komite Gabungan', *Suara Karya*, 19 July 1991.
62 'Havens in doubt', *Far Eastern Economic Review*, 20 June 1990.
63 B.A. Hamzah, *Malaysia's Exclusive Economic Zone: A Study in Legal Aspects*, Petaling Jaya: Pelanduk Publications, 1988.
64 M. Valencia, *Malaysia and the Law of the Sea*, Kuala Lumpur: Institute of Strategic and International Studies, 1991, p. 81.
65 Sipadan and Ligitan were in fact used as a strategic front line by the Malaysian defence forces during *Konfrontasi*, when Malaysian troops were placed there in anticipation of Indonesian saboteurs and military expeditions passing by the islands into Sabah.
66 Valencia, *Malaysia and the Law of the SEA*, p. 83.
67 According to some media reports later, this omission was made so as not to jeopardize the improving relations between the two states. See 'Ghafar Holds Bilateral Talks with Suharto', *New Straits Times*, 27 July 1991.
68 This point was highlighted to me by the late Michael Leifer, and was alluded to in 'Isle of Contention: Tiny Sipadan Becomes an Object of Rival Claims', *Far Eastern Economic Review*, 17 March 1994.
69 While to my knowledge there is no documented evidence of Razak's commitment, it would not have been inconsistent with Razak's proclivities towards Indonesia.
70 'Sipedan: Mengapa Pihak Indonesia Dan Malaysia Tak Belajar Dari Mercu Suar', *Sinar Harapan*, 4 October 1982.
71 'Jakarta: Troops on Isle Report Not True', *Straits Times*, 8 July 1992.
72 'Status P. Sipedan Dedang Dirundingkan R.I.–Malaysia', *Sinar Harapan*, 26 October 1982.
73 'Hentikan Pembangunan di Sipadan dan Ligitan', *Kompas*, 6 June 1991; SWB FE/1101/A3/3, 18 June 1991, 'Malaysia Seeks Resolution of Dispute with Indonesia'.
74 This language was reportedly used by Indonesian officials. See 'Jakarta Asks KL to Stop Developing Disputed Island', *Straits Times*, 6 June 1991.
75 'KL–Jakarta Talks on Disputed Islands Soon', *The Star*, 6 June 1991.
76 See 'Islands Are Ours, Says Abdullah', *The Star*, 8 June 1991; 'Panel Will Discuss Jakarta's Claim to Disputed Islands, Says KL Minister', *Straits Times*, 9 June 1991.
77 'Pangab: Masalah Sipadan Jangan Merusak Hubungan', *Suara Pembaruan*, 7 June 1991.
78 'Sabah Seeks Help from Jakarta, KL for Release of Fishing Boat', *Straits Times*, 13 June 1991.
79 Interview with former Indonesian ministry official, Jakarta, 24 January 2002. Apparently the Indonesians were taken by surprise by this unscheduled meeting.
80 'Let's Clear the Air', *Far Eastern Economic Review*, 1 August 1991.
81 SWB FE/1137/A3/5, 30 July 1991, 'Malaysia Sets Up Group to Resolve Territorial Dispute with Indonesia'; 'Indonesia, Malaysia to Discuss Islands Claims', *Far Eastern Economic Review*, 24 October 1991.
82 'Four Joint Panels with Indonesians Set Up', *Straits Times*, 8 October 1991.
83 'Isle of Contention: Tiny Sipadan Becomes an Object of Rival Claims', *Far Eastern Economic Review*, 17 March 1994.

212   *Notes*

84 'Bid to Avert Clashes over Disputed Isles off Sabah', *Straits Times*, 29 January 1992.
85 'KL Played Rough with Indonesia over Islands', *Straits Times*, 29 January 2003. In response to this report, the Malaysian media accused Singapore of attempting to sow seeds of discord between Indonesia and Malaysia. See *Berita Harian*, 30 January 2003.
86 'KL Played Rough with Indonesia over Islands', *Straits Times*, 29 January 2003.
87 Indeed, such was the severity that negotiations were upgraded to the level of personal envoys of the leaders of the two claimants.
88 'Jakarta to Defend Claim to Sipadan and Ligitan Isles', *Straits Times*, 8 February 1993.
89 It was understood that Mahathir had made the suggestion to Suharto during a meeting in 1994, and it appeared that the latter had politely rejected it. See 'Mahathir Has Four-Eyes Meeting with Suharto', *Straits Times*, 17 September 1994.
90 See Ministry of Defence, Indonesia, *Defending the Country Entering the 21st Century*, Jakarta, 2003, p. 24.
91 'Indonesian MPs Fear More Border Rows with KL', *Straits Times*, 21 November 1996.
92 'Border Dispute Heats Up after Four "Abductions"', *South China Morning Post*, 3 July 2000.
93 Interview with former Singapore foreign ministry official, Kuala Lumpur, 14 November 2001.
94 See Asisah Kassim, 'The Unwelcome Guests: Indonesia Immigrants and Malaysian Public Responses', *Tonan Ajia Kenkyu* (Southeast Asian Studies), 25(2), September 1987.
95 'Migrant Workers Spark Resentment in Malaysia', *Far Eastern Economic Review*, 11 January 1990.
96 For a detailed discussion of some of these cases, see Firdaus Abdullah, 'The Phenomenon of Illegal Immigrants', *Indonesian Quarterly*, 21(2), 1993.
97 'Illegal Migrant Report for Jakarta', *Straits Times*, 15 February 1981.
98 'Malaysia Acts to Stem Tide of Illegal Immigrants', *Straits Times*, 29 January 1987.
99 Firdaus Abdullah, 'Issues in Malaysia–Indonesia Relations', paper presented at the ASEAN Fellowship Seminar, Tokyo, 20 August 1992, 45–46.
100 Non-Muslim proselytizing among the Muslim community is prohibited by Malaysian federal law.
101 'Illegals Must Go', *The Star*, 9 August, 1987.
102 'KL–Jakarta Labour Pact', *Straits Times*, 20 June 1984.
103 'Passports for Illegal Indonesians in Malaysia', *Straits Times*, 6 July 1988.
104 'Jakarta Paper Raps Malaysian Press over Illegal Immigrants', *Straits Times*, 10 March 1987.
105 'Sorry Is Not Enough', *Straits Times*, 22 January 2002.
106 'Too Many, Too Much Trouble', *Straits Times*, 23 January 2002.
107 The policy was quickly rescinded as a result of intense lobbying by the Malaysian construction industry, which relied heavily on Indonesian labour.
108 See J.C.Y. Liow, 'Desecuritizing the "Illegal Indonesian Migrant Worker" Problem in Malaysia's Relations with Indonesia', *IDSS Commentaries*, 18 September 2002.
109 'Remember "*Konfrontasi*"', *Jakarta Post*, 1 February 2002.
110 For example, Acehnese refugees fleeing the fighting between the secessionist *Gerakan Aceh Merdeka* and government forces regularly land on the penin-

sula seeking asylum. SWB FE/1106/A3/4, 24 June 1991, 'Indonesian Foreign Minister Seeks "Amicable" Solutions with Malaysia'.

111 See '112 Acehnese Who Fled to Malaysia Can Stay if They Want To, Says Envoy', *Straits Times*, 1 June 1991.

112 Former Agriculture Minister and Kedah Chief Minister Sanusi Junid, for example, was related to the late Acehnese nationalist Daud Beureueh.

113 'Aceh Unrest Leads to Mounting Death Toll', *Far Eastern Economic Review*, 24 January 1991.

114 'Aceh Rebels "May Use Malaysia as Main Hideout"', *Straits Times*, 24 July 1992.

115 FBIS-EAS-1999-1222, 23 December 1999, 'Minister Says GAM Members Plying between Aceh, Malaysia'.

116 'Aceh Unrest Leads to Mounting Death Toll', *Far Eastern Economic Review*, 24 January 1991.

117 Ibid.

118 FBIS-EAS-1999-114, 14 December 1999, 'GAM Leader Confirms Military Trainings in Libya, Malaysia'.

119 'KL Should Be Cautious on Acehnese Asylum Seekers', *Antara News Agency*, 23 August 2003. After meeting with Indonesian President Megawati, Mahathir announced that Acehnese refugees would be considered illegal migrants and deported. See 'Rejecting Claims for Asylum, Malaysia Will Deport Acehnese', *South China Morning Post*, 30 August 2003.

120 'The Aceh Conflict beyond Islamic Rhetoric', Crescent International, 1–15 November 2000 [online] http://www.muslimedia.com/archives/sea00/aceh-rhet.htm (accessed 31 October 2003).

121 'Common Practices in Aceh and Kelantan', *Malay Mail*, 29 May 2003.

122 A scholar has suggested that Islam played a crucial role in the termination of *Konfrontasi*. See Muhammad Kamal, *Muslim Intellectual Responses to 'New Order' Modernization in Indonesia*, Kuala Lumpur: Dewan Bahasa dan Pustaka, 1982, pp. 120–121.

123 See W. Roff, *The Origins of Malay Nationalism*, New York: Oxford University Press, 1967.

124 MSS/PIJ (Malay Security Service/Political Intelligence Journal), Serial no. 5, 1947, Arkib Negara.

125 J. Funston, *Malay Politics in Malaysia: A Study of UMNO and PAS*, Kuala Lumpur: Heinemann Educational Books, 1980, p. 124.

126 Nabir Haji Abdullah, *Maahad Il-Ihya Assyariff Gunung Semang-gol, 1934–1935*, Kuala Lumpur: Jabatan Sejarah, Universiti Malaya, 1976, p. 149.

127 Alias Mohamad, 'PAS Platform: Development and Change, 1951–1986', doctoral dissertation, Universiti Malaya, 1989, p. 6.

128 Funston, *Malay Politics*, p. 88.

129 MSS/PIJ, Serial no. 5, 1947.

130 Alias, 'PAS Platform', p. 18.

131 Funston, *Malay Politics*, pp. 87–88.

132 MSS/PIJ, Serial no. 5, 1947. Though this view was expressed before the formation of *Hizbul Muslimin*, it was nonetheless well known that MATA members were automatic members of the party upon its formation. Hence it can be suggested that this view represented the view of the *Hizbul Muslimin* as well.

133 Delia Noer, *The Modernist Muslim Movement in Indonesia, 1900–1942*, Oxford: Oxford University Press, 1978, p. 311.

134 There were also a substantial number of African- and Arab-trained Islamic scholars of Indonesian origin who either resided in or made frequent sojourns

to the peninsula to teach. Some of these included Sjech Thaher Djalaluddin, founder of the *Al-Imam* journal, Haji Abdul Karim Amrullah, and Sjech Muhammad Chajjath.

135 Funston, *Malay Politics*, p. 140. That said, it should also be recognized that the ideology of PAS since 1982 has been influenced by Wahabi and Deobandi traditions – conversation with Chandra Muzaffar, Singapore, 22 October 2003. This contrasts markedly with the case of Indonesia today, where Islamic ideology is largely 'home-bred' through thinkers such as Sirajuddin Abbas, Harun Nasution, Nurcholish Masjid, Azyumardi Azra, and Abdur-rahman Wahid.

136 A.B. Shamsul, 'Identity Construction, Nation Formation, and Islamic Revival-ism in Malaysia' in R. Hefner and P. Horvatich (eds), *Islam in an Era of Nation-States: Politics and Renewal in Muslim Southeast Asia*, Honolulu: Uni-versity of Hawaii Press, 1997, p. 214.

137 W. Liddle, *Leadership and Culture in Indonesian Politics*, Sydney: Allen & Unwin, 1996, pp. 273–274.

138 The Anwar–Habibie link subsequently accounted for a minor bilateral dispute when Habibie, as Indonesian President, openly expressed support for Anwar after the latter was removed from power and incarcerated for alleged corrup-tion and sexual impropriety.

139 Interview with former Indonesian government official, Jakarta, 18 January 2002.

140 'JI Bigger, More Dangerous', *The Age*, 27 August 2003.

141 See 'Malaysia Knew Terrorists Had Slipped through Security Dragnet', *Straits Times*, 17 October 2002.

142 See Rizal Sukma, *Indonesia and China: The Politics of a Troubled Relation-ship*, London: Routledge, 1999.

143 For changes in Malaysia's China policy, see J.C.Y. Liow, 'Malaysia–China Relations in the 1990s: The Maturing of a Partnership', *Asian Survey*, 40(4), July/August 2000.

144 A senior Indonesian foreign ministry official commented to me that 'while this is an unexpressed feeling [on the Malaysians' part], it was an undercurrent that manifested [itself] in attitude'. Interview with former Indonesian foreign ministry official, Jakarta, 24 January 2002.

145 Interview with former Malaysian foreign ministry official, Kuala Lumpur, 8 November 2001.

146 'Towards Stronger Neighbourly Links', *Business Times*, 2 March 1988.

Conclusion

1 The recently released Malay docudrama *Embun* portrays Ibrahim Yaacob, the pro-Indonesian architect of *Melayu Raya*, as a Malay hero and patriot.

2 Abdullah Zawawi, speech entitled 'Malaysia and Indonesia Bilateral Relations' delivered at the Second Malaysia–Indonesia Conference, Penang, 11–14 December 1990.

3 Ibid.

4 Hari Hartojo, 'Confrontation', undated, A1838 3006/4/9 Part 39, NAA. This comment was made immediately after *Konfrontasi*.

5 The role of kinship myth-making in nationalism is discussed in D. Brown, *Contemporary Nationalism: Civic, Ethnocultural and Multicultural Politics*, London: Routledge, 2000, pp. 40–42.

6 It can be considered 'Batavia-centric' in the sense that it was targeted at inher-iting in its entirety the Dutch territories known as the Dutch East Indies, which had its capital at Batavia. This brand of nationalism did not in principle privil-

ege the Javanese, though they constituted up to 60 per cent of the population of the archipelago.

7 J.M. Gullick, *Malaysia and Its Neighbours*, London: Routledge & Kegan Paul, 1967, p. 110.

8 Interview with a former Malaysian foreign ministry official, Kuala Lumpur, 14 August 2001.

9 Benny Moerdani, speech entitled 'Kerjasama, Masalah, dan Tantangan' delivered at Dialog Pemuda Indonesia–Malaysia II, Bogor, 17–19 January 1990.

10 Firdaus Abdullah, 'The Rumpun Concept in Malaysia–Indonesia Relations', *Indonesian Quarterly*, 21(2), 1993, 146.

11 Tunku Abdul Rahman and Tun Hussein Onn had Thai and English blood respectively, while Mahathir's father was of south Indian origin.

12 Gullick, *Malaysia and Its Neighbours*, p. 108.

13 Interview with former Indonesian foreign ministry official, Jakarta, 23 January 2002.

14 Interview with a former Indonesian diplomat, Jakarta, 21 January 2002.

15 In considering the 'absence' of any evidence of subtle Indonesian 'benign hegemony', one should distinguish between self-restraint on the part of Jakarta, and Indonesia's reluctance to assume a leadership role. Indeed, as this book has shown, the fact that Indonesia was not consulted on matters pertaining to the security of Southeast Asia was more often than not interpreted as presumptuous by the Indonesians. This has been in evidence in Malaysian diplomatic initiatives as well as Thailand's apparent unilateral move in shifting its stand on Indo-China in the late 1980s.

16 'Wrong Key', A1838 3006/4/9 Pt 37, NAA.

17 See M.C. Ricklefs, 'Unity and Disunity in Javanese Political and Religious Thought of the Eighteenth Century', *Modern Asian Studies*, 26(4), 1992.

18 M. Leifer, *Indonesia's Foreign Policy*, London: Allen & Unwin, 1983, p. 75.

19 G.M. Kahin, *Southeast Asia: A Testament*, London: RoutledgeCurzon, 2003, pp. 158–176.

20 This was confirmed by most, if not all, Indonesian interviewees.

21 Interview with former Indonesian foreign ministry official, Jakarta, 24 January 2002.

22 See M. Desch, 'Culture Clash: Assessing the Importance of Ideas in Security Studies', *International Security*, 23(1), Summer 1998.

23 Interview with a senior Singapore diplomat, Singapore, 2 February 2002.

24 Ibid.

25 This certainly was the prevailing opinion of the Singapore leadership at the time.

26 Dewi Fortuna Anwar, *Indonesia in ASEAN: Foreign Policy and Regionalism*, New York: St Martin's Press, 1994, p. 173.

27 See A. MacIntyre, 'The "Greater Indonesia" Idea of Nationalism in Malaya and Indonesia', *Modern Asian Studies*, 7(1), 1973, and Rustam Sani, 'Melayu Raya as a Malay "Nation of Intent"' in H.M. Dahlan (ed.), *The Nascent Malaysian Society*, Kuala Lumpur: Jabatan Antropologi dan Sosiologi, Universiti Kebangsaan Malaysia, 1976.

Select bibliography

Published sources

Books in English

Abdul Rahman Putra, *Political Awakening*, Petaling Jaya: Pelanduk Publications, 1986.

Abdulgani, Roeslan, *Heroes Day and the Indonesian Revolution*, Jakarta: Prapantja Publishing House, 1964.

Adams, C., *Sukarno: An Autobiography*, New York: Bobbs-Merrill, 1965.

Alagappa, M., *Towards a Nuclear Weapons-Free Zone in Southeast Asia*, Kuala Lumpur: Institute of Strategic and International Studies, 1987.

Anak Agung, Gde Agung, *Twenty Years Indonesian Foreign Policy, 1945–1965*, The Hague: Mouton, 1973.

Andaya, B.W., *To Live as Brothers: Southeast Sumatra in the Seventeenth and Eighteenth Centuries*, Honolulu: University of Hawaii Press, 1993.

Andaya, B.W. and Andaya, L., *A History of Malaysia*, London: Macmillan, 1984.

—— *A History of Malaysia*, 2nd edn, London: Macmillan, 2000.

Anderson, B., *Java in a Time of Revolution: Occupation and Resistance, 1944–46*, Ithaca, NY: Cornell University Press, 1972.

—— *Language and Power*, Ithaca, NY: Cornell University Press, 1990.

—— Imagined *Communities: Reflections on the Origins and Spread of Nationalism*, 2nd edn, London: Verso, 1991.

Anwar Abdullah, *Dato Onn*, Kuala Lumpur: Pusaka Nusantara, 1971.

Anwar, Dewi Fortuna, *Indonesia in ASEAN: Foreign Policy and Regionalism*, New York: St Martin's Press, 1994.

Ariffin Omar, *Bangsa Melayu: Malay Concepts of Democracy and Community*. [Kuala Lumpur: Oxford University Press, 1993].

Armstrong, J., *Nations before Nationalism*, Chapel Hill: University of North Carolina Press, 1982.

Asmah Haji Omar, *Language and Society in Malaysia*, Kuala Lumpur: Dewan Bahasa dan Pustaka, 1993.

Astuti, R., *People of the Sea*, Cambridge: Cambridge University Press, 1995.

Awang Salleh, *Malay Secular Education and Teacher Training in British Malaya*, Kuala Lumpur: Dewan Bahasa dan Pustaka, 1979.

Banks, D., *Malay Kinship*, Philadelphia: Institute for the Study of Human Issues, 1983.

Bastin, J. and Roolvink, R. (eds), *Malayan and Indonesian Studies*, Oxford: Clarendon Press, 1964.

Bastin, J. and Winks, R. (eds), *Malaysia: Selected Historical Readings*, Kuala Lumpur: Oxford University Press, 1966.

Benda, H., *The Crescent and the Rising Sun*, The Hague and Bandung: W. van Hoeve, 1958.

Boyce, P., *Malaysia and Singapore in International Diplomacy*, Sydney: Sydney University Press, 1968.

Bozeman, A., *Politics and Culture in International History*, Princeton, NJ: Princeton University Press, 1960.

Brackman, A., *Southeast Asia's Second Front*, London: Pall Mall, 1966.

Brown, D., *Contemporary Nationalism: Civic, Ethnocultural and Multicultural Politics*, London: Routledge, 2000.

Brown, G., *The Dimensions of Conflict in Southeast Asia*, Englewood Cliffs, NJ: Prentice-Hall, 1966.

Bull, H., *The Anarchical Society*, New York: Columbia University Press, 1977.

Bull, H. and Watson, A. (eds), *The Evolution of International Society*, Oxford: Clarendon Press, 1984.

Carsten, J. (ed.), *Cultures of Relatedness: New Approaches to the Study of Kinship*, Cambridge: Cambridge University Press, 2000.

Cheah, B.K., *Malaysia: The Making of a Nation*, Singapore: Institute of Southeast Asian Studies, 2001.

Chou, C. and Derks, W. (eds), *Riau in Transition*, The Hague: Bijdragen Tot de Taal-, Land- en Volkenkunde, Deel 153, KITLV Press, 1997.

Cohn, B., *Colonialism and Its Form of Knowledge*, Princeton, NJ: Princeton University Press, 1996.

Conboy, K. and Morrison, J., *Feet to the Fire: Covert Operations in Indonesia*, Annapolis, MD: Naval Institute Press, 1999.

Cornell, S. and Hartmann, D., *Ethnicity and Race: Making Identities in a Changing World*, Thousand Oaks, CA: Pine Forge Press, 1998.

Daim, B., *Sukarno and the Struggle for Indonesian Independence*, Ithaca, NY: Cornell University Press, 1969.

De Jong, P.E.J., *Minangkabau and Negri Sembilan*, The Hague: Martinus Nijhoff, 1952.

De Klerk, E.S., *History of the Netherlands East Indies*, vol. 1, Rotterdam: W.L. & J. Brusse, 1938.

De V. Allen, J., *The Malayan Union*, New Haven, CT: Yale University Press, 1967.

Djalal, Dino Patti, *The Geopolitics of Indonesia's Maritime Territorial Policy*, Jakarta: Center for Strategic and International Studies, 1996.

Drakard, J., *A Malay Frontier: Unity and Duality in a Sumatran Kingdom*, Cornell University Southeast Asia Program, Ithaca, NY: Cornell University Press, 1990.

Eriksen, T.H., *Ethnicity and Nationalism: Anthropological Perspectives*, London: Pluto Press, 1993.

Feith, H. and Castles, L. (eds), *Indonesian Political Thinking, 1945–1965*, Ithaca, NY: Cornell University Press, 1970.

Finnemore, M., *National Interests in International Society*, Ithaca, NY: Cornell University Press, 1996.

Firdaus Abdullah, *The Origins and Early Development of the Radical Malay*

Opposition Movement in Malaysian Politics, Kuala Lumpur: Pelanduk Publications, 1985.

Fishman, J.A., *Language and Nationalism*, Rowley, MA: Harcourt Brace Jovanovich, 1972.

Fortes, M., *Kinship and the Social Order*, London: Routledge & Kegan Paul, 1969.

Fox, J.J. (ed.), *Indonesia: The Making of a Culture*, Canberra: Australian National University, Research School of Pacific Studies, 1980.

Frederick, W., *Visions and Heat: The Making of the Indonesian Revolution*, Athens, OH: Ohio University Press, 1989.

Funston, J., *Malay Politics in Malaysia: A Study of UMNO and PAS*, Singapore: Heinemann International Books (Asia), 1980.

Ganesan, N., *Bilateral Tensions in Post-Cold War ASEAN*, Singapore: Institute of Southeast Asian Studies, 1999.

Ganguly, R., *Kin State Intervention in Ethnic Conflicts: Lessons from South Asia*, New Delhi and London: Sage, 1998.

Geertz, C., *The Religion of Java*, Glencoe: Free Press, 1964.

—— *The Interpretation of Cultures*, New York: Basic Books, 1973.

—— *Local Knowledge: Further Essays in Interpretive Anthropology*, New York: Basic Books, 1983.

Gellner, E., *Nations and Nationalism*, Ithaca, NY: Cornell University Press, 1983.

—— *Encounters with Nationalism*, Oxford: Basil Blackwell, 1994.

Ghazali Shafie, *Malaysia, ASEAN, and the World Order*, Bangi: Universiti Kebangsaan Malaysia, 2000.

Goertz, G., *Contexts in International Politics*, Cambridge: Cambridge University Press, 1994.

Gooding, J. (ed.), *The Character of Kinship*, Cambridge: Cambridge University Press, 1973.

Gordon, A. (ed.), *The Propagation of Islam in the Indonesian–Malay Archipelago*, Kuala Lumpur: Malaysian Sociological Research Institute, 2001.

Gossett, T., *Race: The History of an Idea in America*, New York: Oxford University Press, 1997.

Gullick, J.M., *Malaysia and Its Neighbours*, London: Routledge & Kegan Paul, 1967.

Hamzah, B.A., *Malaysia and the Law of the Sea*, Kuala Lumpur: Heng Lee Stationery and Printing Co., 1983.

Hanggi, H., *ASEAN and the ZOPFAN Concept*, Singapore: Institute of Southeast Asian Studies, 1991.

Harper, T., *The End of Empire and the Making of Malaya*, Kuala Lumpur: Oxford University Press, 1999.

Hatta, Mohammad, *Indonesian Patriot: Memoirs*, translated and edited by C.L.M. Penders, Singapore: Gunung Agung, 1981.

Hitchcock, M. and King, V.T. (eds), *Images of Malay–Indonesian Identity*, Kuala Lumpur: Oxford University Press, 1997.

Holt, C. (ed.), *Culture and Politics in Indonesia*, Ithaca, NY: Cornell University Press, 1972.

Hooker, M.B., *Adat Laws in Modern Malaya*, Kuala Lumpur: Oxford University Press, 1972.

Hooker, V.M. (ed.), *Culture and Society in New Order Indonesia*, Kuala Lumpur: Oxford University Press, 1993.

Jacquin-Berdal, D., Oros, A., and Verweij, M. (eds), *Culture in World Politics*, London: Macmillan, 1998.

James, H. and Sheil-Small, D., *The Undeclared War: The Story of the Indonesian Confrontation*, Singapore: Asia Pacific Press, 1971.

Jeshurun, C., *Malaysian Defence Policy: A Study in Parliamentary Attitudes, 1963–1973*, Kuala Lumpur: Penerbit Universiti Malaya, 1980.

Jones, M., *Conflict and Confrontation in Southeast Asia, 1961–1965: Britain, the United States, and the Creation of Malaysia*, Cambridge: Cambridge University Press, 2001.

Kahin, A. (ed.), *Regional Dynamics of the Indonesian Revolution*, Honolulu: University of Hawaii Press, 1985.

Kahin, G.M., *Nationalism and Revolution in Indonesia*, Ithaca, NY: Cornell University Press, 1952.

Kahin, G.M. and Kahin, A., *Subversion as Foreign Policy*, Seattle, Washington: University of Washington Press, 1995.

Kassim Ahmad, *Characterization in Hikayat Hang Tuah*, Kuala Lumpur: Dewan Bahasa dan Pustaka, 1955.

Khoo, B.T., *Paradoxes of Mahathirism: A Political Biography of Mahathir Mohamad*, Singapore: Oxford University Press, 1993.

Khoo, K.K., *Malay Society: Transformation and Democratisation*, Petaling Jaya: Pelanduk Publications, 1991.

Koentjaraningrat, R.M., *Introduction to the Peoples and Cultures of Indonesia and Malaysia*, Menlo Park, CA: Cummings, 1975.

—— *Javanese Culture*, Singapore: Institute of Southeast Asian Studies, 1985.

Lapid, Y. and Kratochwil, F. (eds), *The Return of Culture and Identity in IR Theory*, London: Lynne Reiner, 1996.

Lau, A., *The Malayan Union Controversy, 1942–1948*, Singapore: Oxford University Press, 1990.

Legge, J., *Indonesia*, Englewood Cliffs, NJ: Prentice-Hall, 1964.

—— *Sukarno: A Political Biography*, London: Allen Lane The Penguin Press, 1972.

Leifer, M., *Indonesia and Malaysia: The Changing Face of Confrontation*, Hull: University of Hull, Centre for Southeast Asian Studies, 1966.

—— *Malacca, Singapore, and Indonesia*, Alphen aan den Rijn, Netherlands: Sijthoff & Noordhoff, 1978.

—— *Conflict and Regional Order in Southeast Asia*, London: International Institute of Strategic Studies, 1980.

—— *Indonesia's Foreign Policy*, London: Allen & Unwin, 1983.

—— *ASEAN and the Security of Southeast Asia*, London: Routledge, 1989.

—— (ed.), *Asian Nationalism*, London: Routledge, 2000.

Liddle, R.W., *Leadership and Culture in Indonesian Politics*, Sydney: Allen & Unwin, 1996.

Lim, P.H. (ed.), *The Malay World of Southeast Asia: A Selected Cultural Bibliography*, Singapore: Institute of Southeast Asian Studies, 1987.

Loeb, E., *Sumatra: Its History and People*, Oxford: Oxford University Press, 1972.

Luard, E., *The International Regulation of Civil Wars*, London: Thames & Hudson, 1972.

Lyon, P., *War and Peace in Southeast Asia*, London: Oxford University Press, 1969.

Mack, D. and Parker, G., *The Evolution of Sibling Rivalry*, London: Oxford University Press, 1997.

McKay, E. (ed.), *Studies in Indonesian History*, Melbourne: Pitman, 1976.

Mackie, J.A.C., *Konfrontasi: The Indonesia–Malaysia Dispute, 1963–1966*, Kuala Lumpur: Oxford University Press, 1974.

McMichael, H., *Indonesia's Foreign Policy: Towards a New Assertive Style*, Nathan, Queensland: Griffiths University, Center for the Study of Australia–Asia Relations, 1987.

Mayall, J., *Nationalism and International Society*, Cambridge: Cambridge University Press, 1993.

Melaka, Tan, *From Jail to Jail*, vol. 3, translated by H. Jarvis, Southeast Asia Series, Athens: Ohio University Press, 1991.

Merle, M., *The Sociology of International Relations*, translated by D. Parkin, Leamington Spa, Hamburg, and New York: Berg, 1987.

Milner, A.C., *Kerajaan: Malay Political Culture on the Eve of Colonial Rule*, Tucson: University of Arizona Press, 1982.

—— *The Invention of Colonial Politics in Malaya*, Cambridge: Cambridge University Press, 1995.

Mossman, J., *Rebels in Paradise: Indonesia's Civil War*, London: Jonathan Cape, 1961.

Muhammad Yusoff Hashim, *The Malay Sultanate of Malacca*, Kuala Lumpur: Dewan Bahasa dan Pustaka, 1992.

Nagata, J., *The Reflowering of Malaysian Islam: Modern Religious Radicals and their Roots*, Vancouver: University of British Columbia Press, 1984.

Nair, S., *Islam in Malaysia's Foreign Policy*, London: Routledge, 1997.

Noer, Delia, *The Modernist Muslim Movement in Indonesia, 1900–1942*, Oxford: Oxford University Press, 1978.

Noordin Sopiee, *From Malayan Union to Singapore Separation: Political Unification in the Malaysia Region, 1945–1965*, Kuala Lumpur: Universiti Malaya, 1974.

Nothofer, B., *The Reconstruction of Proto-Malayo-Javanic*, The Hague: Martinus Nijhoff, 1975.

Ongkili, J., *Nation-Building in Malaysia, 1946–1974*, Singapore: Oxford University Press, 1985.

Palmer, L., *Indonesia and the Dutch*, London: Oxford University Press, 1962.

Penders, C.L.M., *The Life and Times of Sukarno*, London: Sidgwick & Jackson, 1974.

Poulgrain, G., *The Genesis of Konfrontasi: Malaysia, Brunei, Indonesia, 1945–1965*, Bathurst, NSW: Crawford House Publishing, 1998.

Raja Ali Haji ibn Ahmad, *The Precious Gift (Tuhfat al-Nafis)*, an annotated translation by V. Matheson and B.W. Andaya, Kuala Lumpur, Oxford University Press, 1982.

Reid, A.J.S., *Blood of the People*, Kuala Lumpur: Oxford University Press, 1979.

—— *Southeast Asia in the Age of Commerce, 1450–1680*, vol. 2: *Expansion and Crisis*, New Haven, CT: Yale University Press, 1993.

Ricklefs, M.C., *A History of Modern Indonesia since c.1300*, Stanford, CA: Stanford University Press, 1993.

Riddell, P., *Islam and the Malay–Indonesian World*, Singapore: Horizon Books, 2001.

Robequain, C., *Malaysia, Indonesia, Borneo, and the Philippines*, London: Longmans, Green, 1954.

Roff, W., *The Origins of Malay Nationalism*, 2nd edn, Singapore: Oxford University Press, 1994.

Rosenau, J. (ed.), *International Aspects of Civil Strife*, Princeton, NJ: Princeton University Press, 1964.

Safie Ibrahim, *The Islamic Party of Malaysia: Its Formative Stages and Ideology*, Kelantan: Nawawi bin Ismail, 1981.

Said Zahari, *Dark Clouds at Dawn: A Political Memoir*, Kuala Lumpur: Insan, 2001.

Saravanamuttu, J., *The Dilemma of Independence: Two Decades of Malaysia's Foreign Policy, 1957–1977*, Penang: Penerbit Universiti Sains Malaysia, 1983.

Schneider, D., *A Critique of the Study of Kinship*, Ann Arbor: University of Michigan Press, 1984.

Schrieke, B.J.O. (ed.), *The Effect of Western Influence on Native Civilisation in the Malay Archipelago*, Batavia: G. Kolff, 1929.

—— (ed.), *Indonesian Sociological Studies*, vol. 2, The Hague: W. van Hoeve, 1957.

Schweitzer, P. (ed.), *Dividends of Kinship*, London: Routledge, 2000.

Shafer, B., *Faces of Nationalism*, New York: Routledge, 1972.

Shaw, K.E. (ed.), *The Straits of Malacca in Relation to the Problems of the Indian and Pacific Oceans*, Singapore: University Education Press, 1979.

Shaw, W., *Tun Razak: His Life and Times*, London: Longman, 1976.

Smith, A., *Strategic Centrality: Indonesia's Changing Role in ASEAN*, Singapore: Institute of Southeast Asian Studies, 2000.

Smith, A.D., *The Ethnic Origins of Nations*, Oxford: Basil Blackwell, 1986.

—— *National Identity*, London: Penguin, 1992.

—— *Nations and Nationalism in a Global Era*, Cambridge: Polity Press, 1995.

Soedjatmoko, Mohammad Ali, Resink, G.J., and Kahin, G. (eds), *An Introduction to Indonesian Historiography*, Ithaca, NY: Cornell University Press, 1965.

Soesastro, Hadi, *The EAEG Proposal and East Asian Concepts of the Pacific Basin*, Jakarta: Center for Strategic and International Studies, 1991.

Steinberg, D.J. (ed.), *In Search of Southeast Asia*, London: Pall Mall Press, 1971.

Stockwell, A., *British Policy and Malay Politics during the Malayan Union Experiment, 1942–1948*, Kuala Lumpur: MBRAS, 1979.

—— (ed.), *Malaya: Part I of the Malayan Union Experiment, 1942–1948*, London: HMSO, 1995.

Strathern, M., *After Nature: English Kinship in the Late Twentieth Century*, Cambridge: Cambridge University Press, 1992.

Subritsky, J., *Confronting Sukarno: British, American, Australian and New Zealand Diplomacy in the Malaysian–Indonesian Confrontation, 1961–1965*, New York: St Martin's Press, 1999.

Suryadinata, Leo, *Indonesia's Foreign Policy under Suharto*, Singapore: Times Academic Press, 1996.

Svensson, T. and Sorensen, P. (eds), *Indonesia and Malaysia: Scandinavian Studies in Contemporary Society*, London and Malmö: Curzon Press, 1983.

Tarling, N., *Anglo-Dutch Rivalry in the Malay World*, Brisbane: University of Sydney Press, 1962.

Taufik Abdullah, *Schools and Politics: Kaum Muda Movement in West Sumatra, 1927–1933*, Cornell Modern Indonesia Project, Ithaca, NY: Cornell University Press, 1971.

Valencia, M., *Malaysia and the Law of the Sea*, Kuala Lumpur: Institute of Strategic and International Studies, 1991.

Van Leur, J.C., *Indonesian Trade and Society: Essays in Asian Social and Economic History*, The Hague: W. van Hoeve, 1955.

Vandenbosch, A., *The Dutch East Indies*, Berkeley: University of California Press, 1941.

Vatikiotis, M., *Indonesian Politics under Suharto*, London: Routledge, 1993.

Vlekke, B.H.M., *Nusantara: A History of the East Indian Archipelago*, Cambridge, MA: Harvard University Press, 1944.

—— *Nusantara: A History of Indonesia*, The Hague: W. van Hoeve, 1959.

Wagner, R., *The Curse of Souw: Principles of Daribi Clan Definition and Alliance in New Guinea*, Chicago: Chicago University Press, 1967.

Waever, O., *Insecurity and Identity Unlimited*, Copenhagen: Center for Peace and Conflict Research, 1994.

Wallace, A., *The Malay Archipelago*, London: Macmillan, 1894.

Watson, A., *The Evolution of International Society: A Comparative Historical Analysis*, London: Routledge, 1992.

Weinstein, F., *Indonesian Foreign Policy and the Dilemma of Dependence*, Ithaca, NY: Cornell University Press, 1976.

Westad, O.A. (ed.), *Reviewing the Cold War*, London: Frank Cass, 2000.

Wild, C. and Carey, P. (eds), *Born in Fire: The Indonesian Struggle for Independence*, Athens, OH: Ohio University Press, 1986.

Wilson, D., *The Neutralization of Southeast Asia*, New York: Praeger, 1975.

Winstedt, R.O., *The Malays: A Cultural History*, London: Routledge & Kegan Paul, 1947.

Wolters, O.W., *Early Indonesian Commerce: A Study of the Origins of Srivijaya*, Ithaca, NY: Cornell University Press, 1967.

—— *The Fall of Srivijaya in Malay History*, London: Lund Humphries, 1970.

—— *History, Culture, and Region in Southeast Asian Perspectives*, 2nd edn, Singapore: Institute of Southeast Asian Studies, 1999.

Woods, N. (ed.), *Explaining International Relations since 1945*, Oxford: Oxford University Press, 1996.

Woodward, M., *Islam in Java: Normative Piety and Mysticism in the Sultanate of Yogjakarta*, Tucson: University of Arizona Press, 1989.

Yamin, Muhammad, *A Legal and Historical View of Indonesia's Sovereignty over the Ages*, Manila: Indonesian Embassy, 1959.

Yelvington, K., *Producing Power: Ethnicity, Gender, and Class in a Caribbean Workplace*, Philadelphia: Temple University Press, 1995.

Young, R., *Postcolonialism*, Oxford: Blackwell, 2001.

Articles and book chapters

Akashi, Y., 'Japanese Military Administration in Malaya: Its Formation and Evolution in Reference to Sultans, the Islamic Religion, and the Moslem-Malays, 1941–1945', *Journal of Asian Studies*, 7(I), April 1969.

Andaya, L., 'Sea of Melayu', *Itineraria*, 1999–2000.

Anderson, B., 'The Idea of Power in Javanese Culture' in Holt, C., Anderson, B., and Siegel, J. (eds), *Culture and Politics in Indonesia*, London: Verso, 1972.

Asisah Kassim, 'The Unwelcome Guests: Indonesia Immigrants and Malaysian Public Responses', *Tonan Ajia Kenkyu* (Southeast Asian Studies), 25(2), September 1987.

Azra, Azyumardi, 'The Transmission of al-Manar's Reformism to the Malay–Indonesian World: The Cases of al-Imam and al-Munir', *Studia Islamika*, 6(3), 1999.

Baroto, A., 'Similarities and Differences in Malaysia–Indonesia Relations: Some Perspectives', *Indonesian Quarterly*, 21(2), 1993.

Bodenhorn, B., '"He Used to Be My Relative": Exploring the Bases of Relatedness among Inupiat of Northern Alaska' in Carsten, J. (ed.), *Cultures of Relatedness: New Approaches to the Study of Kinship*, Cambridge: Cambridge University Press, 2000.

Bottoms, J.C., 'Some Malay Historical Sources: A Bibliographical Note' in Soedjatmoko, Mohammad Ali, Resink, G.J., and Kahin, G. (eds), *An Introduction to Indonesian Historiography*, Ithaca, NY: Cornell University Press, 1965.

Brissenden, R., 'Patterns of Trade and Maritime Society before the Coming of the Europeans' in McKay, E. (ed.), *Studies in Indonesian History*, Melbourne: Pitman, 1976.

Brown, C., 'Indonesia's West Irian Case in the U.N. General Assembly', *Journal of Southeast Asian Studies*, 7(2), June 1976.

Bull, H., 'International Theory: The Case for a Classical Approach', *World Politics*, 18(3), 1966.

—— 'The Theory of International Politics' in Porter, B. (ed.), *The Aberystwyth Papers: International Politics, 1919–1969*, London: Oxford University Press, 1972.

Bunnell, F., 'Guided Democracy Foreign Policy, 1960–1965', *Indonesia*, 11, October 1966.

Buzan, B., 'From International System to International Society: Structural Realism and Regime Theory Meet the English School', *International Organization*, 47(3), 1993.

Carey, P., 'Yogjakarta: From Sultanate to Revolutionary Capital of Indonesia – The Politics of Cultural Survival', *Indonesia Chronicle*, 39, March 1986.

Cheah, B.K., 'The Japanese Occupation of Malaya, 1941–1945: Ibrahim Yaacob and the Struggle for Indonesia Raya', *Indonesia*, 28, 1979.

—— 'The Erosion of Ideological Hegemony and Royal Power and the Rise of Postwar Malay Nationalism, 1945–1946', *Journal of Southeast Asian Studies*, 19(1), March 1988.

—— 'Feudalism in Pre-Colonial Malaya: The Past as a Colonial Discourse', *Journal of Southeast Asian Studies*, 25(2), September 1994.

Cowan, C.D., 'Continuity and Change in the International History of Maritime South East Asia', *Journal of Southeast Asian History*, 11(1), March 1968.

Curtis, R., 'Malaysia and Indonesia', *New Left Review*, 28, November–December 1964.

Desch, M., 'Culture Clashes: Assessing the Importance of Ideas in Security Studies', *International Security*, 23(1), Summer 1998.

Doty, R., 'Sovereignty and the Nation: Constructing the Boundaries of National Identity' in Biersteker, T. and Weber, C. (eds), *State Sovereignty as Social Construct*, Cambridge: Cambridge University Press, 1996.

Federspiel, H., 'Muslim Intellectuals in Southeast Asia', *Studia Islamika*, 6(1), 1999.

Firdaus Abdullah, 'The Rumpun Concept in Malaysia–Indonesia Relations', *Indonesian Quarterly*, 21(2), 1993.
—— 'The Phenomenon of Illegal Immigrants', *Indonesian Quarterly*, 21(2), 1993.
Gaddis, J.L., 'Explaining the Data Base: Historians, Political Scientists, and the Enrichment of Security Studies', *International Security*, 12(1), Summer 1987.
Ghazali Shafie, 'The Neutralization of Southeast Asia', *Pacific Community*, 3(1), October 1971.
Gutierrez, N., 'Ethnic Revivals within Nation-States?' in Wicker, H.R. (ed.), *Rethinking Nationalism and Ethnicity: The Struggle for Meaning and Order in Europe*, New York and Oxford: Berg, 1997.
Hamzah, B.A., 'Indonesia's Archipelagic Regime: Implications for Malaysia', *Marine Policy*, January 1984.
Hatta, Mohammad, 'One Indonesian View of Malaysia', *Asian Survey*, 5, March 1965.
Hellman, G., 'Correspondence: Brother Can You Spare a Paradigm?', *International Security*, 25(1), Summer 2001.
Heraclides, A., 'Secessionist Minorities and External Involvement', *International Organization*, 44(3), Summer 1990.
Hirschman, C., 'The Meaning and Measurement of Ethnicity in Malaysia', *Journal of Asian Studies*, 46(3), 1985.
Huxley, T., 'Singapore and Malaysia: A Precarious Balance?', *Pacific Review*, 4(3), 1990.
—— 'Southeast Asia in the Study of International Relations: The Rise and Decline of a Region', *Pacific Review*, 9(2), 1996.
Jackson, R., 'The Political Theory of International Society' in Booth, K. and Smith, S. (eds), *International Relations Theory Today*, Oxford: Polity Press, 1995.
—— 'Is there a classical international theory?' in Smith, S., Booth, K., and Zalewski, M. (eds), *International Theory: Positivism and Beyond*, Cambridge: Cambridge University Press, 1996.
Jones, M., 'Maximum Disavowal of Aid', *English Historical Review*, 114, November 1999.
Kessler, C., 'Archaism and Modernity: Contemporary Malay Political Culture' in Kahn, J. and Loh, F.K.W. (eds), *Fragmented Vision: Culture and Politics in Contemporary Malaysia*, Honolulu: University of Hawaii Press, 1992.
—— 'Malaysia and Mahathir: Region Builder or Barrier Builder?', *The Asia–Australia Papers*, 1, April 1999.
Khoo, K.K., 'Malay Society, 1874–1920s', *Journal of Southeast Asian Studies*, 5(2), September 1974.
—— 'The Malay Left, 1945–1948: A Preliminary Discourse', *Sarjana*, 1(1), December 1981.
Kratochwil, F. and Ruggie, J.G., 'International Organization: A State of the Art or an Art of the State', *International Organization*, 40(4), Autumn 1986.
Kusumaatmadja, Mochtar, 'The Concept of the Indonesian Archipelago', *Indonesian Quarterly*, 10(4), 1982.
—— 'Some Thoughts on ASEAN Security Cooperation: An Indonesian Perspective', *Contemporary Southeast Asia*, 13(3), 1990.
Kwa, C.G., 'The Historical Roots of Indonesian Irredentism', *Asian Studies*, 8(1), April 1970.

Lee, K.H., 'From Confrontation to Cooperation: Malaysia–Indonesia Relations, 1957–1990', *Sarjana*, Special Issue, 1994.

—— 'Indonesian and Malaysian History from Dutch Sources: Reconstructing the Straits of Malacca's Past', *Sejarah*, 4, 1996.

Liow, J.C.Y., 'Malaysia–China Relations in the 1990s: The Maturing of a Partnership', *Asian Survey*, 40(4), July/August 2000.

—— 'Mahathir's Foreign Policy' in Chin, J. and Ho, K.L. (eds), *The Mahathir Administration: Performance and Governance*, Singapore: Times Academic Press, 2001.

—— 'Desecuritising the "Illegal Indonesian Migrant Worker" Problem in Malaysia's Relations with Indonesia', *IDSS Commentaries*, 18, September 2002.

—— 'Malaysia's Illegal Indonesian Migrant Labour Problem: In Search of Solutions', *Contemporary Southeast Asia*, 25(1), April 2003.

—— '"Visions of Serumpun": Tun Abdul Razak and the Golden Years of Indo-Malay Blood Brotherhood, 1967–1975', *Southeast Asia Research*, 11(3), November 2003.

Low, L., 'The East Asian Economic Grouping', *Pacific Review*, 4(4), 1991.

McIntyre, A., 'The "Greater Indonesia" Idea of Nationalism in Malaya and Indonesia', *Modern Asian Studies*, 7(1), 1973.

McKean, P.F., 'The Mouse-Deer in Malayo-Indonesian Folklore: Alternative Analyses and the Significance of a Trickster Figure in South-East Asia', *Asian Folklore Studies*, 30, 1971.

Mandaville, P., 'Reading the State from Elsewhere: Towards an Anthropology of the Postnational', *Review of International Studies*, 28, 2002.

Milner, A.C., 'Inventing Politics: The Case of Malaysia', *Past and Present*, 132, 1991.

Mohammad Redzuan Othman, 'Call of the Azhar: The Malay Students Sojourn in Cairo before World War II', *Sejarah*, 3, 1994–1995.

Mohammad Said, 'What Was the "Social Revolution" of 1946?', *Indonesia*, 15, 1973.

Mohd. Talib Osman, 'Trends in Modern Malay Literature' in Wang Gungwu (ed.), *Malaysia: A Survey*, Singapore: Donald Moore Books, 1964.

Nagata, J., 'What Is a Malay? Situational Selection of Ethnic Identity in a Plural Society', *American Ethnologist*, 1(2), 1974.

Nuttall, M., 'Choosing Kin: Sharing and Subsistence in a Greenlandic Hunting Community' in Schweitzer, P. (ed.), *Dividends of Kinship*, London: Routledge, 2000.

Oetomo, Bambang, 'Some Remarks on Modern Indonesian Historiography' in Hall, D.G.E. (ed.), *Historians of Southeast Asia*, London: Oxford University Press, 1961.

Ott, M., 'Foreign Policy in Malaysia', *Asian Survey*, 12(2), March 1972.

Pitt-Rivers, J., 'The Kith and Kin' in Gooding, J. (ed.), *The Character of Kinship*, Cambridge: Cambridge University Press, 1973.

Reid, A.J.S., 'Nineteenth Century Pan-Islam in Indonesia and Malaysia', *Journal of Asian Studies*, 26(2), 1967.

—— 'Understanding *Melayu* as a Source of Diverse Modern Identities', *Journal of Southeast Asian Studies*, 32(3), October 2001.

Ricklefs, M.C., 'Unity and Disunity in Javanese Political and Religious Thought of the Eighteenth Century', *Modern Asian Studies*, 26(4), 1992.

Robson, S.O., 'Java in Malay Literature' in Houben, V.J.H., Maier, H.M.J., and von der Molen, W. (eds), *Looking in Odd Mirrors: The Java Sea*, Leiden: Vakgroep Talen en Culturen van Zuidoost-Azie en Oceanie, Rijksuniversiteit te Leiden, 1992.

Roff, W., 'Indonesian and Malay Students in Cairo in the 1920s', *Indonesia*, 9, 1970.

Rustam Sani, 'Melayu Raya as a Malay "Nation of Intent"' in Dahlan, H.M. (ed.), *The Nascent Malaysian Society*, Kuala Lumpur: Jabatan Antropologi dan Sosiologi, Universiti Kebangsaan Malaysia, 1976.

Saravanamuttu, J., 'Malaysia's Foreign Policy, 1975–1980' in Zakaria, H.A. (ed.), *Government and Politics in Malaysia*, Singapore: Oxford University Press, 1987.

—— 'Malaysia's Foreign Policy in the Mahathir Period, 1981–1994: An Iconoclast Come to Rule', *Asian Journal of Political Science*, 4(1), June 1996.

Schroeder, P., 'Historical Reality versus Neo-realist Theory', *International Security*, 19(1), Summer 1994.

Shaharil Talib, 'The Asiatic Archipelago: History beyond Boundaries' in *Proceedings of the International Symposium Southeast Asia: Global Area Studies for the 21st Century*, Kyoto: Kyoto International Community House, 1996.

Smith, A.D., 'Ethnic Myths and Ethnic Revivals', *European Journal of Sociology*, 25, 1984.

—— 'Ethnic Election and Cultural Identity', *Ethnic Studies*, 10, 1993.

Snyder, J., 'Anarchy and Culture: Insights from the Anthropology of War', *International Organization*, 56(1), Winter 2002.

Soenarno, Radin, 'Malay Nationalism, 1869–1941', *Journal of Southeast Asian Studies*, 10(2), 1969.

Stafford, C., 'Chinese Patriliny and the Cycles of *Yang* and *Laiwang*' in Carsten, J. (ed.), *Cultures of Relatedness: New Approaches to the Study of Kinship*, Cambridge: Cambridge University Press, 2000.

Supomo, 'The Image of Majapahit in Late Javanese and Indonesian Writing' in Reid, A. and Marr, D. (eds), *Perceptions of the Past*, Singapore: Heinemann, 1979.

Suryadinata, Leo, 'Indonesian Nationalism and the Pre-war Youth Movement: A Re-examination', *Journal of Southeast Asian Studies*, 9(1), March 1978.

Tan, S.S., 'Rescuing Realism from Realists' in Simon, S. (ed.), *The Many Faces of Asian Security*, Landham, MD: Rowman & Littlefield, 2001.

Taylor, A., 'Malaysia, Indonesia – and Maphilindo', *International Journal*, 19(2), Spring 1964.

Tilman, R.O., 'Malaysia Foreign Policy: The Dilemmas of a Committed Neutral' in Montgomery, J.D. and Hirschman, A.D. (eds), *Public Policy*, Cambridge, MA: Harvard University Press, 1969.

Van Langenberg, M., 'Class and Ethnic Conflict in Indonesia's Decolonization Process: A Study of East Sumatra', *Indonesia*, 23, April 1982.

—— 'East Sumatra: Accommodating an Indonesian Nation within a Sumatran Residency' in Kahin, A. (ed.), *Regional Dynamics of the Indonesian Revolution*, Honolulu: University of Hawaii Press, 1985.

Vandenbosch, A., 'Indonesia, the Netherlands and the New Guinea Issue', *Journal of Southeast Asian Studies*, 7(1), March 1976.

Vatikiotis, M., 'Indonesia's Foreign Policy in the 1990s', *Contemporary Southeast Asia*, 14(4), March 1993.

Wan Ahmad Hamid, 'Religion and Culture' in Wang Gungwu (ed.), *Malaysia: A Survey*, Singapore: Donald Moore Books, 1964.
Watson, C.W., 'The Construction of the Post-Colonial Subject in Malaysia' in Tonneson, S. and Antlov, H. (eds), *Asian Forms of the Nation*, Richmond, UK: Curzon, 1996.
White, J.B., 'Kinship, Reciprocity and the World Market' in Schweitzer, P. (ed.), *Dividends of Kinship*, London: Routledge, 2000.
Wight, M., 'Why Is There No International Relations Theory?' in Butterfield, H. and Wight, M. (eds), *Diplomatic Investigations: Essays in the Theory of International Politics*, Cambridge, MA: Harvard University Press, 1966.
Zalewski, M. and Enloe, C., 'Questions about Identity' in Smith, S., Booth, K. and Zalewski, M. (eds), *International Theory: Positivism and Beyond*, Cambridge: Cambridge University Press, 1996.

Government publications

Badan Penjelidek Usaha Persiapan Indonesia, *Territory of the Indonesian State*, Jakarta: Badan Penjelidek Usaha Persiapan Kemerdekaan Indonesia, 31 May 1945.
Department of Information, Malaysia, *Malaya–Indonesia Relations, 31 August 1957 to 15 September 1963*, Kuala Lumpur: Department of Information, 1963.
Department of Information, Malaysia, *Let the World Judge: Speeches of the Malaysian Chief Delegate to the Security Council, Dato Dr. Ismail bin Abdul Rahman, on 9th and 10th September 1964*, Kuala Lumpur: Department of Information, Malaysia, 1964.
Department of State, *Foreign Relations of the United States. 1958–1960*, vol. 17: *Indonesia*, Washington, 1989.
Embassy of the Republic of Indonesia, London, *The Problem of Malaysia*, London: Embassy of the Republic of Indonesia, London, 1964.
Government of Malaysia, *A Plot Exposed*, Kuala Lumpur: Government Publishers, 1965.
Government of Malaysia, *Parliamentary Debates*, Kuala Lumpur: Dewan Rakyat, 1960–1967.
Government of Malaysia, *Indonesian Aggression against Malaysia*, vol. 1, Kuala Lumpur: Government Press, 1965.
Great Britain, *Malayan Union and Singapore: Summary of Proposed Constitutional Arrangements*, London, 1946.
Kementrian Pelajaran Malaysia, *Pertemuan Dunia Melayu '82*, Kuala Lumpur: Dewan Bahasa dan Pustaka, 1987.
Malaya Legislative Council, *2nd Debates*, vol. 3: *1957–1958*, Kuala Lumpur: Government Printers, 1959.
Metcalf, K., *Near Neighbours: Records on Australia's Relations with Indonesia*, Canberra: National Archives of Australia, 2001.
Universitas Gadjah Mada, *Seminar Sedjarah: Laporan Lengkap Atjara I dan II tentang Konsepsi Filsafat Sedjarah Nasional dan Periodisasi Sedjarah Indonesia*, Jogjakarta: Universitas Gadjah Mada, 1958.

Books not in English

Abdul Rahman Ismail, 'Takkan Melayu Hilang di Dunia: Suatu Sorotan Tentang Nasionalisme Melayu' in Suntharalingam, R. and Abdul Rahman I. (eds), *Nasionalisme: Satu Tinauan Sejarah*, Petaling Jaya: Fajar Bakti, 1985.

Abdulgani, Roeslan, *Indonesia dan Percaturan Politik Internasional*, Surabaya: Yayasan Keluarga Bhakti, 1993.

Amat Johari Moain, *Sejarah Nasionalisma Maphilindo*, Kuala Lumpur: Dewan Bahasa dan Pustaka, 1960.

Ariffin Omar, *Revolusi Indonesia dan Bangsa Melayu*, Pulau Pinang: Penerbit Universiti Sains Malaysia, 1999.

Bangun, Payung, *Kolonel Maludin Simbolon: Liku-liku Perjuangannya dalam Pembangunan Bangsa*, Jakarta: Sinar Harapan, 1996.

Brown, C.C., *Sejarah Melayu*, Kuala Lumpur: Oxford University Press, 1970.

Burhanuddin Al-Helmy, *Asas Falsafah Kebangsaan Melayu*, Bukit Mertajam: Pustaka Semenanjung, 1954.

Djalal, Hashim, *Perjuangan Indonesia di Bidang Hukum Laut*, Bandung: Pencetakan Ekonomi, 1979.

Firdaus Abdullah, *Indonesia Raya di Alam Melayu: Setiakawan Serumpun di Zaman Perjuangan*, Jakarta: KITLV, 1995.

Ibrahim Yaacob, *Nusa dan Bangsa Melayu*, Jakarta: N.V. Alma'ariff, 1951.

—— *Sekitar Malaya Merdeka*, Jakarta: Kesatuan Malaya Merdeka, 1957.

—— *Melihat Tanah Air*, Kuantan: Percetakan Timur, 1975.

Ismail Hussein, *Antara Dunia Melayu dan Dunia Kebangsaan*, Bangi: Penerbit Universiti Kebangsaan Malaysia, 1990.

Jones, R. (ed.), *Hikayat Raja Pasai*, Petaling Jaya: Penerbit Fajar Bakti, 1987.

Kamaruddin Jaafar, *Dr. Burhanuddin Al-Helmy: Politik Melayu dan Islam*, Kuala Lumpur: Yayasan Anda, 1980.

Kassim Ahmad, *Hikayat Hang Tuah*, Kuala Lumpur, 1964.

Keris Mas, *Memoir*, Kuala Lumpur: Dewan Bahasa dan Pustaka, 1980.

Mohd. Dahlan Mansoer, *Pengatar Sejarah Nusantara Awal*, Kuala Lumpur: Dewan Bahasa dan Pustaka, 1979.

Muhammad Yusoff Hashim, *Pensejarahan Melayu: Kajian Tentang Tradisi Sejarah Melayu Nusantara*, Kuala Lumpur: Dewan Bahasa dan Pustaka, 1992.

Nabir Haji Abdullah, *Maahad Il-Ihya Assyariff Gunung Semanggol, 1934–1935*, Kuala Lumpur: Jabatan Sejarah, Universiti Malaya, 1976.

Nasution, Abdul Haris, *Sekitar Perang Kemerdekaan Indonesia*, Bandung: Disrajah-AD dan Penerbit Angkasa, 1977.

Osman Halliby, *Documenta Historica: Sedjarah Documenter dari Pertumbuhan dan Perdjuangan Negara Republic Indonesia*, Jakarta: Bulan Bintang, 1953.

Pringgodigdo, A.K., *Sedjarah Pergerakan Rakyat Indonesia*, Jakarta: Dian Rakyat, 1970.

Rustam Sani, 'Tradisi Intelektual Melayu dan Penbentukan Bangsa Malaysia: Berberapa Persoalan Sosial' in Ahmat Adam, Kassim Ahmad, and Rustam Sani (eds), *Intelektualisme Melayu: Satu Polemik*, Bangi: Faculty of Social Sciences and Humanities, 1989.

Shellabear, W.G., *Sejarah Melayu*, Singapore: Methodist Publishing House, 1915.

Soetomo, Agus, *S. Takdir Alisjahbana, 1908–1994: Perjuangan Kebudayaan Indonesia*, Jakarta: Dian Rakyat, 1999.

Sukarno, *Indonesia Menggugat: Pidato Pembelaan Bung Karno Dimuka Hakim Colonial*, Jakarta, 1956.

Suwannathat~Pian, Kobkua, *Asia Tenggara: Hubungan Tradisional Serantau*, Kuala Lumpur: Dewan Bahasa dan Pustaka, 1997.

Syed Husin Ali, *Rakyat Melayu: Nasib dan Depannya*, Jakarta: Penerbit Inti Sarana Aksana, 1985.

Syed Naguib Al-Attas, *Islam dalam Sejarah dan Kebudayaan Melayu*, Kuala Lumpur: Penerbit Universiti Kebangsaan Malaysia, 1972.

Thahir, Mudjahirin, *Wacana Masyarakat dan Kebudayaan Jawa Pesisiran*, Semarang: Bendera, 1999.

Yamin, Muhammad, *6000 Tahun Sang Merah-Putih*, Jakarta: Penerbit Siguntang, 1954.

—— *Naskah Persiapan Undang-Undang Dasar 1945*, Jakarta: Siguntang, 1959.

Unpublished sources

Conference papers, speeches, and dissertations

Abdullah Ahmad Badawi, keynote speech delivered at Second Malaysia–Indonesia Conference, Penang, 11–14 December 1990.

Abdullah Zawawi, 'Malaysia and Indonesia Bilateral Relations', speech delivered at Second Malaysia–Indonesia Conference, Penang, 11–14 December 1990.

Alias Mohammad, ' PAS Platform: Development and Change, 1951–1986', doctoral dissertation, Universiti Malaya, 1989.

Buzan, B., 'The English School as a Research Paradigm', paper presented at the BISA Conference, Manchester, December 1999.

Djajoesman, Soenarno, 'Malaysia and Indonesia Bilateral Relations', speech delivered at Second Malaysia–Indonesia Conference, Penang, 11–14 December 1990.

Djalal, Dino, 'Indonesia and Preventive Diplomacy: A Study of the Workshops on Managing Potential Conflicts in the South China Sea', doctoral dissertation, London School of Economics, 2000.

Farish Noor, 'The One-Dimensional Malay: The Homogenisation of Malay Identity in the Revisionist Writing of History in Malaysia', paper presented at the Third Annual Malaysian Studies Conference, Universiti Kebangsaan Malaysia, Selangor, 7–8 August 2001.

Firdaus Abdullah, 'The Origins and Early Development of the Radical Malay Opposition Movement in Malaysian Politics', doctoral dissertation, Columbia University, 1981.

—— 'Issues in Malaysia–Indonesia Relations', paper presented at ASEAN Fellowship Seminar, Tokyo, 20 August 1992.

Ghazali Shafie, speech delivered at Tunku Abdul Rahman Hall, Kuala Lumpur, 26 January 1960.

—— speech delivered at the Second Malindo Dialogue, Bogor, 17 January 1990.

Hein, G., 'Suharto's Foreign Policy: Second Generation Nationalism in Indonesia', doctoral dissertation, University of California-Berkeley, 1986.

Ismail Abdul Rahman, speech delivered at the 81st Plenary Meeting of the 14th Session of the United Nations General Assembly, New York, 5 October 1959.

Mahathir Mohamad, speech delivered at 'ASEAN Countries and the World Economy: Challenge and Change' Conference, Bali, Indonesia, 5 March 1991.

Moerdani, Benny, 'Kerjasama, Masalah, dan Tantangan', speech delivered at Diolog Pemuda Indonesia–Malaysia II, Bogor, 17–19 January 1990.

Nicholson, C.K., 'The Introduction of Islam into Sumatra and Java: A Study in Cultural Change', doctoral dissertation, Syracuse University, 1965.

Notosusanto, Nugroho, 'A Current Concept of Indonesian History: The Relationship between Nationalism and Historiography', speech delivered at the Goethe Institut, Jakarta, 23 March 1970.

Ott, M., 'The Sources and Content of Malaysian Foreign Policy towards Indonesia and the Philippines', doctoral dissertation, Johns Hopkins University, 1971.

Archival sources

School of Oriental and African Studies, London

American Universities Field Staff Reports, Southeast Asia

Public Record Office, London

COLONIAL OFFICE PAPERS

CO 1030 Far Eastern Department and successors: Registered Files (FED Series)
CO 537 Confidential General and Confidential Original Correspondence

DOMINIONS OFFICE PAPERS

DO 169 Far East and Pacific Department: Registered Files (FE Series) 1960–1967
DO 35 Original Correspondence

FOREIGN OFFICE PAPERS

FO 371 Political Departments: General Correspondence from 1906

FOREIGN AND COMMONWEALTH OFFICE PAPERS

FCO 24 South West Pacific Department: Registered Files (H and FW Series).

RECORDS OF THE PRIME MINISTER'S OFFICE

PREM 11 Correspondence Papers, 1951–1964

National Archives of Australia, Canberra

A2908 Correspondence Files, Classified Single Number Series, 1920–1968
A1838 Correspondence Files, Multiple Number Series, 1948–1989: South-East Asia, General, Political

A4355 Correspondence Files, Multiple Number Series, First System, Jakarta/ Jakarta, By 1946–1950

A4357 Correspondence Files, Multiple Number Series, Second System, Jakarta/ Jakarta, By 1948–1950

A5840 Second Holt and McEwen Ministries: Folders of Decisions of Cabinets and Cabinet Committees

Akrib Negara Malaysia, Kuala Lumpur

UMNO file SG. 96
MSS/PIJ (Malay Security Service/Political Intelligence Journal)

Newspapers and periodicals

Age, The
Antara Daily News Bulletin
Antara New Agency Reports
Asian Defence Journal
Berita Yudhya
Business Times Malaysia
Canberra Times
Far Eastern Economic Review
Foreign Affairs Malaysia
Indonesia Raya
Jakarta Post
Japan Economic Newswire
Kedaulatan Rakyat
Kompas
Malay Mail
Malaya Tribune
Massa
Melbourne Age
Merdeka
New Straits Times
Reuters News
Siaran Akhbar
Sinar Harapan
Singapore Standard
Soeara Rakyat
South China Morning Post
Star, The
Straits Budget
Straits Times
Suara Karya
Suara Penbaruan
Times, The
Utusan Melayu

Other media sources

Summary of World Broadcasts (SWB)
Foreign Broadcast Intelligence Service (FBIS)

Internet sources

Buzan, B., 'The English School as a Research Program', paper presented at the BISA Conference, Manchester, December 1999, http://www.ukc.ac.uk/politics/englishschool/buzan99.htm

Farish Noor, 'Fine Young Calibans: Broken Dreams of Melaya-Raya', www.Malaysiakini.com, 13 January 2002, also http://pemantau.tripod.com/2001/17Jan_farish.html

Nasionalisme Melayu dan Islam', http://www.geocities.com/melayuislam/165.htm

US Department of State, National Archives and Records Administration, RG-59, Central Files 1964–66, POL 321, Indonesia–Malaysia, http://www.state.gov/r/pa/ho/frus/johnsonlb/xxvi/index.cfm

US Department of State, INR/EAP files: lot 90D 165, NIE 54/59–65, Washington, DC, 16 December 1965, www.state.gov/r/pa/ho/frus/johnsonlb/xxvi/index.cfm

'The Aceh Conflict beyond Islamic Rhetoric', Crescent International, 1–15 November 2000, http://www.muslimedia.com/archives/sea00/aceh-rhet.htm

Index